Financial Survival

Going Galt In The New Normal Depression Economy

by Daxton Brown

Los Angeles MMXIV

ISBN-13: 978-1496170705

ISBN-10: 1496170709

Daxton Brown Is a writer, realtor, engineer and entrepreneur living in Las Vegas.

Contents

Preface

It is clear to anyone with eyes that we are already in a Global financial collapse as worldwide welfare states meet the brick wall of exponential deficits and aging demographics. While it is hoped the reader is a political activist, political and economic reform will not come soon enough to avert a meltdown. Thus you need to survive a Second Great Depression, but because a number of economic fundamentals have changed, your financial strategies will be tested in ways unlike the First Great Depression

The bureaucrat and entitlement classes have yoked productive citizens and future generations to a grindstone of $100s of trillions of unfunded social liabilities, environmental Gaia worship and bureaucratic strangulation. To fund the Ponzi scheme, they have found taxation through representation inconvenient and have simply allowed central banks, led by the US Federal Reserve, to monetize debt. In the United States, tax revenues only cover 57% of government expenditures, the rest being made up by various QEn Quantitative Easings.

However, unless you believe central bankers can create prosperity out of thin air (in which case they would be the first to devise a perpetual motion machine), all their actions are in effect pushing on a string. Political posturing about austerity has also been a giant farce; politicians of all stripes have continued to spend us into poverty.

But you already know this, or at least sense it, or you wouldn't have bought this book. What you want to know is how to save yourself and your family as the system creaks, groans and grinds to a halt. I know you're thinking this way because I face the same financial dilemma. No one is immune; we are all in the same lifeboat leaving a sinking economic Titanic.

Progressives will argue that big government is good for this or that social welfare - save the children, save the poor, save the racially dispossessed, save the whale. However, the absolute size of the unfunded financial liabilities to support expansive government social largesse (most of which does not realistically help the above social causes), argues that this time things are different. We cannot get out of this financial and regulatory black hole unless one of two things happens:

A. The productive class resigns itself to being tethered to a permanent millstone of egregious taxation in support of a consumption class of bureaucrats and the entitled, or
B. There is a revolt of the productive class, essentially an economic default on the obligation to support the non-productive classes, which realigns the entire system.

Truthfully, there is no need to spend a lot of time arguing about which option will be taken. That which cannot be, cannot be. The astronomical size of future entitlements cannot be overcome except through a default by the productive classes on the welfare state's overextended promises. Since option _A_, the status quo which leaves the current governmental order in place is untenable; we are left with option _B_, popular revolt as the path of necessity.

But we must be clear; this book is in no way advocating a war of freedom, an insurrection, uprisings or anything disruptive of any kind as solutions to our current dilemmas. Many good men have impaled themselves for no good purpose trying to stop the decline of civilization. The forces of disruption are already upon us and at work, so the nature of this book is entirely defensive and reactive, not proactive. This isn't a call to arms, it is a call to bolt your financial door, hide your valuables and defend yourself and family from others who are now trying to get into your home to rape, pillage and enslave you.

In other words, you can't personally change the economic devolutionary course that we are on, except at the margins; the global Leviathan state is auguring in of its own colossal weight. If you are smart though, and hunker down tightly enough, you might just get through this mess with some health and a little wealth intact. You don't stop a freight train by standing in front of it.

The inflation rate is an unsubtle form of wealth theft by the ruling elite (bankers and politicians), especially of wealth from those on fixed incomes. More subtle is that we also have deflation in many sectors (most notably housing, interest income and wages) which is just as devastating. Together these bipolar negative economic trends constitute a Biflationary Depression, a financial headwind you will face for perhaps decades (we have addressed some of these issues in a book titled *Biflationary Depression*). This requires a new look at how to structure your financial interests to preserve and expand wealth in the New Normal. You won't find strategies for protecting your assets in dual inflationary and deflationary times in classic economics textbooks. That's why you are here.

The causes of a Biflationary Depression are not generally described in the financial media, so we go to some lengths to give you a novel viewpoint based on physics and information theory that lets you cut through the haze. An ugly convergence of Federal Deficits, hyper regulation and disastrous Federal Reserve monetary policy have caused these conditions, all designed by the hubris of politicians and technocrats. The elite have left us a legacy of infinitely growing money supply and collapsing monetary velocity, a situation their obsolete Keynesian theories cannot explain. You will have to be nimble to avoid this legacy of waste.

Paradoxically, the answer to this accelerating economic morass is not to overtly resist, for example by becoming a tax protestor. The only way out is to meticulously observe every dot of financial rule and regulation the elite force on us. The government can and will destroy anyone who overtly tries to avoid their desperate engorgement on all available assets. Because these laws and regulations are so egregious, the system is a juggernaut towards collapse, which will only crush those unwary enough to stand in its way. It may be possible, however, to stand to the side and watch the juggernaut hurl itself off a cliff – an Aikido move in martial arts that uses the energy of the assailant to defeat them.

Because money and power in this global world is now so fungible due to transportation and information technology advances, the bright and industrious can now opt out and pull the legs out from under the system. You don't need to be a slave; you can and must step to the side and avoid the fall. Resistance truly is futile. However, long live the resistance!

So, this book is not revolutionary in nature, it is survivalist! This is about how you make it to the brave new world that beckons on the other side of economic collapse, not how to reform the unreformable through martyrdom. We aren't revolutionaries trying to sink the ship of state, but survivalists trying to stay out of the undertow as this Titanic goes down. It will sink without further help from any one of us.

John Galt is a fictional character in Ayn Rand's novel *Atlas Shrugged* (1957). Although absent from much of the text, he is the subject of the novel's often repeated question "Who is John Galt?" and of the driving quest to discover the answer.

Galt is a creator and inventor who symbolizes the power and glory of the human mind. He serves as an idealistic counterpoint to the social and economic structure depicted in the novel, one of oppressive central control. We now live in a similar society, based on bureaucratic functionaries and a culture that embraces stifling mediocrity and egalitarianism; in short a society of misguided socialistic idealism. In Rand's novel, the industrialists of America were a metaphorical Atlas of Greek mythology, holding up the sky, who Galt convinces to "shrug," by refusing to lend their productive genius to the regime any longer.

We are close to that same point now, where our creators, inventors and industrialists are "shrugging" and walking away from enterprise because they have been burdened with a stifling bureaucracy which taxes and regulates them from birth to death. That is, at least some of our industrialists are on strike, while others have been co-opted by the system and are now part of the problem (Government Motors, aka General Motors and the entire banking system come to mind). It is clear that those who play by the rules, trying to succeed by merit rather than by government handout, are now being suffocated and are fleeing socialist utopias like California and New York.

Hence the phrase "going John Galt" or simply "Going Galt" has been used to refer to productive members of society cutting back on work in response to the projected increases in U.S. tax rates and the use of tax revenues for causes regarded as immoral. Some people who are "going John Galt" were seen at Tea Party protests held in the United States and at banking protests in London, however this movement isn't necessarily part of any specific political agenda. In fact, it may be impossible to distinguish between those who will be dropping out of the system because of philosophical reasons, and those forced to drop out because of world encompassing economic collapse due to out-of-control Central Banks and destructive social spending by governments.

Going Galt: Financial Survival is not concerned with *why* people might want to protect themselves financially in the face of an economic collapse, it is only interested in *how* to prepare for and survive such a collapse. We are not promoting tax avoidance or protesting any government edicts – excesses of the ruling elite will take care of themselves. We simply want to prepare the creative and industrious ants of society for the coming bad economic times and the ravenous horde of grasshoppers headed their way.

Our hope is this book helps prepare productive elements of our society for the endgame when the mathematical certainty of unfunded liabilities born of unachievable social goals cannot be papered over.

Daxton Brown

Financial Future

1   Economic Armageddon

Nearly every nation in the world is now facing serious financial and social collapse – Great Depression II. If only a few nations were involved, it might be possible to contain the economic avalanche to a few specific geographical areas as has been successfully done in the past. However, since the entire world is currently on the edge of the cliff, as the meltdown develops it will impact almost everyone on the face of the earth. This is the New Normal.

Your financial future is at risk and will need serious restructuring. The old ways will not work as fiat currencies are debased and collapse. Your goal is to at least make it through the collapse with your financial situation intact, and better still, to be in position to profit from the opportunities that present themselves even in imploding markets. It won't be easy, but it is doable and the purpose of this book is to get you to the other side of the financial abyss (which may last a decade or more).

The meltdown is unavoidable because the world is a giant economic Ponzi scheme with the wheels fast coming off. The governments of the United States, Europe, Japan and their financial institutions are massively in debt and no longer in control of their financial futures, nor able to kick the can further down the road. However, to keep the system working just a little longer, our political and financial elite have maintained an illusion that they know how to pull all the correct levers, hence the continuing stream of lies about "green shoots" and recovery.

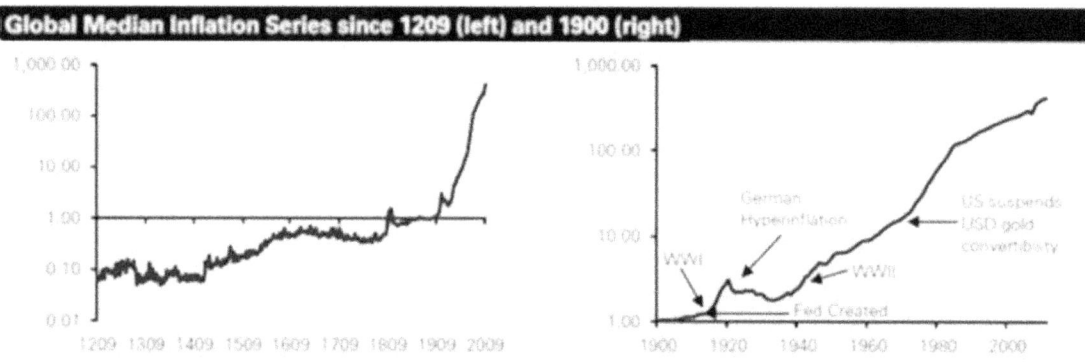

Despite what government propagandists claim, inflation is not under control. A massive restructuring of the economic system is needed to give people the ability to earn money to buy the things being produced. In the West, where people demand high living standards and don't let people starve, we have been making up the slack between production and expectations with "free money" in the public welfare sector. This involves borrowing money, lots of it, from places like China, or having the Federal Reserve print it (part of the same scheme of taking from one pocket to put in the other) and spreading it like fertilizer on a growing parasite class of the unemployable and government bureaucrats. But the bill is coming due for our politician's largesse and a huge realignment of currencies through sovereign defaults is now in swing. For you and your family, debating the morality of the welfare state is no longer the point; instead you need to focus on surviving as this system collapses.

When the lifeboat is full, the best use of the oars may be to beat away those hanging on, lest everything is lost.

The prognosis for America is especially discouraging. We have relied too heavily on surplus savings from abroad buying our Treasury bonds, on top of running massive current account deficits. Until recently, deficits of this order were only incurred when we were engaged in global war;

otherwise we attempted to balance budgets over a complete business cycle. But now we run annual deficits in the $600 billion to $1 trillion dollar range, as much as 10 percent of the total economy. We have compounded the deficits we accumulated over the last decades, so they now are well over 80% of GDP, perhaps as much as 100% or even 200% depending on how hidden liabilities are counted.

Only once before has the ratio of federal debt to GDP come in above 60 percent and that was after World War II. Even worse, our reported federal debt ratio today doesn't even take into account Social Security and Medicare. Total liabilities and unfunded mandates for Medicare and Social Security and other promises are now over $100 trillion (some account $200 trillion), tripling from the year 2000 to 2010. This unfunded liability is above $200,000 per person and $500,000-plus for the average household. The problem with these trust funds is they're not funded and should be counted as a liability, bringing the debt-to-GDP ratio well above 100%.

The system is broken, it can't be fixed for decades and everyone knows it. Two reasons explain why the system can't be fixed:

- It has grown beyond its own capacity to support itself – you can't tax and spend your way to prosperity based on an economy strangled by regulation and welfare.
- It has become so bureaucratically complex that no one can do anything significant to fix it because it is hemorrhaging in too many different places.

Even the poorest poor of the nations on the face of the earth know we are in a meltdown. Wealthy people know it. Poor people know it. Politicians know it. Nobody wants it to happen. But almost everyone is fatalistically waiting for it to be over, just hoping that it doesn't expand too far before they can squirrel away survival money.

Worst Case Scenario

As bad as the financial disaster already has been, an even larger economic tsunami can quickly spiral out-of-control. Having survived years of a "rolling recession", most people don't realize a collapse could overwhelm the world economy in a span of just a few weeks. Most expect a gradual meltdown (if not a recovery!). However, once the avalanche begins it can quickly escalate far beyond anyone's ability to control or manage it on a worldwide basis. Five basic reasons we are at a tipping point are as follows:

1. Banks: The financial institutions around the world cannot withstand a full-scale worldwide bank run - most are already bankrupt holding worthless collateral. Therefore, they already have plans to shut down in the event of runs on the bank. The European Central Bank is essentially using one credit card to pay another. Our Federal Reserve has already fired its bullets.

2. Governments: Leaders around the world understand the ramifications of a "bank holiday" in our computer controlled financial economy. It isn't hard to imagine government officials emptying their buildings and locking their doors. Any governmental transactions in progress, including trials, would be halted and postponed until some future date. High-level government officials, including judges and tax officials, could easily disappear to unknown remote locations. The Federal Reserve knows it would be targeted.

3. Retail Businesses: Since they might be unable to process even simple transactions during a bank holiday, retail establishments, large and small, would lock their doors. If possible, they will complete transactions for customers who have enough cash to pay for their purchases, but those wishing to pay by check or credit card or debit card will find the verification system down and transactions can't be completed. In a manner similar to what happened during the World Trade Center meltdown, store management may demand that employees remain at their stations until further notice or they will lose their jobs , but the more intelligent employees will leave at the same time as the store's last few remaining customers. The security guards might remain to protect the stores, but since

most of them are not paid exceptionally well, they would likely return home and protect their own families instead.

4. Criminals: Anyone who has any criminal background would immediately see the collapse as a once-in-a-lifetime opportunity to improve their financial situation. Career criminals already have plans that include exactly which businesses they are going to rob first, second, third, and so on. Any business with substantial amounts of cash-on-hand will be high on every criminal's list. Jewelry stores, pawn shop and coin shops that have any silver or gold jewelry, or precious stones (diamonds, rubies, emeralds, etc.); will be very high on every criminal's list. Mini-warfare would break out at these establishments between competing criminals.

5. Normal People: Even average people would begin looting (to keep from being left behind). Grocery stores would be broken into and emptied from wall-to-wall. Stores with firearms, ammunition, appliances, clothing, shoes, or anything else needed by the average citizen, will be emptied. The reality is that there are not are not enough police and law enforcement personnel to protect everyone and everything. Although the military would be ordered to protect specific high priority establishments and resources, there will simply not be enough military personnel to protect individual civilians or businesses. In skirmishes over the few remaining resources, normal average people would go to extremes if they perceived their very survival to be at stake.

Paranoia Or Reality?

Is the above scenario exaggerated? Perhaps. Is it out of the realm of possibility? A few years ago, we would all have thought it crazy talk, but now the reported debt and default numbers are so astronomical that the chorus of fear is quite widespread. The crash of 2008 brought us far closer to a systemic failure than anyone realized. Only with great reluctance was the Federal Reserve forced to divulge the extent of its multi trillion dollar international intervention, but now the monetary silver bullets have been shot, not only in the U.S. but Europe and Japan as well. So called Quantitative Easing has now been extended to perpetuity.

Are you prepared for the stampede when everyone is headed to the exits at the same time? You need to be structuring your financial holdings such that they can weather even the most extreme downturns. This could certainly turn out to be an act of paranoia. But on the other hand, you will be one of the few with your head above water if a financial panic comes.

The federal fiscal gap is the present value today of the difference between future spending (including servicing the debt) and projected revenue in future years.

The International Monetary Fund in a recent annual review of U.S. economic policy noted that "a larger than budgeted adjustment would be required to stabilize debt-to-GDP". This was a polite way of pronouncing the U.S. bankrupt. The U.S. federal fiscal policy required to run sustainable budgets and close our fiscal gap necessitates a permanent annual fiscal adjustment equal to about 14 percent of U.S. GDP. Putting 14 percent of gross domestic product in perspective, current federal revenue totals 14.9 percent of GDP. Consequently, closing the U.S. fiscal gap would require an immediate and permanent doubling of our personal-income, corporate and federal taxes as well as the payroll levy set down in the Federal Insurance Contribution Act.

The IMF 14% prescription is designed to create a huge surplus equal to 5 percent of GDP, rather than a 9 percent deficit, because this is what is necessary to pay for the spending to come. That assumes that such surpluses would not also be spent. Clearly, the longer the country waits to make tough fiscal adjustments, the more painful they will be. Sadly, those adjustments will not be made.

The Congressional Budget Office in its Long-Term Budget Outlook, shows an even larger problem. Some economists have used that data to calculate 'Unofficial' Liabilities of as much as $200 trillion, or more than 15 times the official debt. This gargantuan discrepancy between our "official" debt and our actual net indebtedness reflects that our Congress has labeled most of its liabilities "unofficial" to keep them off the books and far in the future.

Social Security FICA contributions are currently called taxes while future Social Security benefits are considered transfer payments. The government could equally well label our contributions "loans" and called our future benefits "repayment of these loans less an old age tax," where the old age tax makes up the difference between benefits promised and the real principal-plus-interest on the contributions.

However, the true fiscal gap isn't affected by using misleading labels. The only correct measure of our long-run fiscal condition is to consider all spending streams, no matter how labeled, and equate them to their present value – what they will cost each and every one of us stated in current dollars.

When you use sound accounting, the annual costs of future entitlements will total about $4 trillion in today's dollars. How can this fiscal gap be so enormous? First, we have 78 million baby boomers who, when fully retired, will collect benefits from Social Security, Medicare, and Medicaid that, on average, exceed per-capita GDP. While our economy will be bigger in 20 years, it won't be big enough to handle this size load year after year.

The Inflation Threat

Sarah Palin made a speech at a trade-association convention in Phoenix in 2010 urging Federal Reserve Chairman Ben Bernanke to "cease and desist" his "pump priming". Palin said the United States "shouldn't be playing around with inflation." She went on to say, "All this pump priming will come at a serious price. And I mean that literally: everyone who ever goes out shopping for groceries knows that prices have risen significantly over the past year or so. Pump priming would push them even higher."

Love or hate Sarah Palin, if even she could forecast where monetary policy was taking us, why couldn't the geniuses at the Federal Reserve? Critics like the Wall Street Journal's Sudeep Reddy questioned Palin's comments about food inflation, saying that, "Grocery prices haven't risen all that significantly, in fact. The consumer price index's measure of food and beverages for the first nine months of this year showed average annual inflation of less than 0.6%, the slowest pace on record." Alternative organizations tracking inflation, most notably www.shadowstats.com, paint a different inflationary picture and have been justified by time. It is now clear that the government's consumer price index (CPI) numbers are phony, as any trip to the grocery will confirm. Our own government spokespeople have lost credibility when they tell you the economy is on the mend, especially as it required many trillions in bailouts since 2008 which have still not cured that blowout.

Fudging The Numbers

The U.S. Bureau of Labor Statistics (BLS)'s CPI is no longer a reliable indicator of U.S. food inflation or any type of price inflation. Estimates are that the real rate of annual food inflation in the U.S. is already 5% and this rate will likely rise above 10%. The BLS has been using both geometric weighting and hedonics to artificially manipulate the CPI downward. The U.S. government has a strong motivation to keep CPI increases as low as possible because since the year 1975, retired Americans receive annual Social Security payment increases that are tied to the CPI. Calculated accounting for the way the BLS's CPI understates the real rate of price inflation, Americans on Social Security should be receiving COLA payments that are nearly double what they receive today. Food and energy inflation can easily become a larger crisis than the mortgage crisis.

When calculating food inflation, the government gives a lower weighting to goods that are rising in price and a higher weighting to goods that are falling in price. Perversely , the CPI will give a lower weighting to steak and a higher weighting to hamburgers if the price of steak is rising while the price of hamburgers is falling. The government prevaricators justifies this by claiming expensive steak prices mean Americans are more likely to eat hamburgers. Therefore, the CPI no longer accounts for the price to maintain the same standard of living. The CPI is now effectively calculated based on the bizarre theory that America's standard of living is in decline and an expectation that it will decline perpetually in the future.

Americans subconsciously realize it is becoming harder for them to make ends meet, but they don't realize inflation is a root cause. While we've all heard stories about how a gallon of gas used to cost a quarter and we are subliminally aware that the U.S. is currently experiencing heavy price inflation, Americans haven't viewed inflation as a problem because increases have occurred over long time periods and been offset in part by wage increases. However, the U.S. price inflation that occurred over the past 100 years now seems likely to occur again over just the next 10 years as the Federal Reserve's money printing causes the world to lose confidence in the U.S. dollar.

Another misconception is that American wages have risen at the same rate as inflation. The median household income in the U.S. was $11,800 in 1975 and in 2011 is $49,777. Going by the government's CPI, $11,800 in 1975 dollars equals $47,208 in today's dollars. If the government's CPI is to be believed, Americans are earning higher real incomes today than 35 years ago. However, once you discount the effects of geometric weighting and hedonics, the median household income in 1975 of $11,800 actually equals $154,000 in today's dollars. In 1975, a father was able to support his family on just one income while college students could afford their own tuition on a part-time summer job. Today, families go deeply into debt even with both parents working just to survive.

In short, for political reasons founded in a fear of its own citizens, headline government economic statistics like GDP, inflation and unemployment can no longer be trusted. When that happens, it is time for common men to head for the economic exits. The purpose of this book is to provide alternatives to help you survive the coming perfect economic storm government officials are so eager to hide from you.

The U.S. Government Is Currently Printing Money Just To Survive

The Federal Reserve held the Fed Funds Rate at 0-0.25% in 2010 and promised little change in the future (also called ZIRP, Zero Interest Rate Policy). There is little doubt that multiple versions of Quantitative Easing (QE1, QE2, QE3, QE4 . . .), otherwise known as money printing, will follow. This monetary debasement is necessary not because of a need for stimulus, but because Federal revenues only cover 57% of expenditures. In other words, the government is bankrupt and will need to be continuously propped up with funny money.

Increases in commodity prices have risen dramatically over the last decade, despite what a skewed Consumer Price Index claims. Agricultural and energy commodity price increases will begin to work their way into grocery stores nationwide in the weeks, months and years ahead, as food manufacturers and retailers are forced to raise their prices. Food manufacturers and retailers who don't raise prices and pass their rising costs on to U.S. consumers will go out of business.

Canaries In The Coal Mine

In 2010 Federal Reserve Bank of Dallas President Richard W. Fisher admitted the Fed's debt laundering, saying in a statement, "For the next eight months, the nation's central bank will be monetizing the federal debt." That monetization process will not stop for eight years much less eight months.

The U.S. has no way of paying off its $15.7 trillion national debt and $100 to $200 trillion in unfunded liabilities without printing the money and creating massive price inflation!

Fed Chairman Ben Bernanke testified under oath on June 3rd, 2009 in front of Congress that, "The Federal Reserve will not monetize the debt." This must be viewed as perjury, because certainly the man pulling the monetary levers realizes the United States is bankrupt and the only way to paper over the debt is through inflation

The government's $700 billion 'Emergency Economic Stabilization Act of 2008', clearly did not "jump-start" the economy, but what it did do was jump-start a massive biflationary monetary crisis. American families now spend 13% of their annual expenditures on food and 34% on housing. These two numbers will increase and may even reverse order as the Federal Reserve monetizes debt by plan, creating massive price inflation. For every 1% rise in consumer wages, expect to see about a 4% rise in food prices. There are currently 47.4 million Americans on food stamps, up 50% from the pre recession days (32 million to 47 million). The government does not have the resources to make these entitlement payments without printing the money and creating massive food price inflation. Unsurprisingly, food stamps are addictive and make those who receive them need them even more.

While the U.S. government may be able to technically avoid going bust by creating a worthless U.S. dollar, it is unlikely that the average middle-class American will be so lucky and in turn will become dependent on the government to survive. The Progressive's strategy to get re-elected is to make as many Americans as possible dependent on social welfare. Because of systemic inertia, there is faint hope the conservative opposition can hold the fiscal line any better even if they do take control. There is no white knight to dramatically reduce government spending in an attempt to prevent hyperbiflation.

Demographic Destiny

At least 10,000 Baby Boomers retire every day. This will happen day after day, month after month, year after year until 2030. this is a demographic tsunami in the United States, and we are totally unprepared. Financial promises made to Baby Boomers worth tens of trillions of dollars cannot and will not be kept. Even without all of the other massive economic problems we are dealing with, this retirement tsunami will destroy our economy all by itself. The number of senior citizens in the United States will more than double during the first half of this century. Where in the entire world are we going to get the money to take care of all of these elderly people when we are already drowning in debt?

The Baby Boomer generation is so massive it has fundamentally changed America with each stage that it has passed through. When Baby Boomers were young, sales of diapers and toys skyrocketed. When they became young adults, they pioneered social changes that permanently altered our society. Often, these changes were for the worse.

Overall household spending peaks when we reach age 46, and 2008 was the same year the peak of the Baby Boom generation reached that age.

People tend to buy houses at about the age 31 or so. People tend to buy their luxury cars around age 53, after kids have finished college and before old age. Demographics even tell us when household spending on potato chips peak, when the head of the household is about 42.

The US economy is simply the total of what we all spend, and overall household spending hits a high when the average age is 46. The peak of the Baby Boom (1961) plus 46 suggests the high point in the US economy should be about 2007, with a long, slow decline to follow for years to come.

Thus the Congressional Budget Office cannot be far off when it projects that an aging population will lead to diminished economic growth in coming years.

Lost in the discussion over a 2014 Congressional Budget Office report which said 2.5 million fewer Americans would be working because of Obamacare, was a prediction that aging will be a major drag on growth: CBO expects economic growth beyond 2017 will diminish to a pace that is well below the average seen over past several decades due to slower growth in the labor force because of the aging of the population.

We face an inbuilt intractable problem creating a permanent New Normal economy. Our rapidly aging population will need an immense amount of economic resources to care for them, all while our economy is steadily declining. Some hard numbers about the demographic tsunami now overtaking us follow:

1. There are now around 40 million senior citizens in the United States. By 2050 that number is projected to balloon to 89 million.

2. According to the Employee Benefit Research Institute, 46 percent of all American workers have less than $10,000 saved for retirement, while 29 percent of American workers have less than $1,000 saved for retirement.

3. As much as 26 percent of all Americans in the 46 to 64-year-old age bracket have no personal savings whatsoever.

4. 60 percent of American workers say the total value of their savings and investments is less than $25,000.

5. 67 percent of American workers believe they are behind schedule on saving for retirement".

6. A study conducted by Boston College's Center for Retirement Research found American workers are $6.6 trillion short of what they need to retire comfortably.

7. In 1991, half of all American workers planned to retire before they reached the age of 65. Today, that number has fallen to 23 percent.

8. 70 percent of all American workers expect to continue working once they are "retired".

9. 56 percent of American retirees still had outstanding debts when they retired.

10. Americans 55 years of age or older now account for 20 percent of all bankruptcies in the United States. They only accounted for 12 percent of all bankruptcies in 2001.

11. Only 10 percent of private companies in the U.S. now provide guaranteed lifelong pensions for their employees.

12. Total unfunded pension and healthcare obligations for retirees for state and local governments across the United States stand at 4.4 trillion dollars.

13. Americans spend 2.8 trillion dollars on health care per year. This will rise to 4.5 trillion due to our aging population health care spending by 2019.

14. The United States spends more on health care than China, Japan, Germany, France, the U.K., Italy, Canada, Brazil, Spain and Australia combined.

15. If the U.S. health care system were a country, it would be the 6th largest economy on the Earth.

16. We were told Medicare would cost $12 billion a year by 1990 after it was first established. Instead, the federal government spent $110 billion on the program in 1990, and approximately $600 billion on the program in 2013.

17. It is projected that Americans on Medicare will grow from 50.7 million in 2012 to 73.2 million in 2025.

18. Medicare faces unfunded liabilities of more than 38 trillion dollars over the next 75 years. That is $328,404 for every household in the United States.

19. There were 42 workers for every retiree receiving Social Security benefits in 1945. Today, there are only 2.5 workers. If you eliminate paper pushing government workers, only 1.6 private sector workers remain for every retiree receiving Social Security benefits.

20. 63 million Americans now collect Social Security benefits. By 2035, that number will soar to 91 million.

21. The Social Security system faces a 134 trillion dollar shortfall over the next 75 years.

22. The U.S. government faces up to 222 trillion dollars in unfunded liabilities during the years ahead, with Social Security and Medicare making up the bulk.

So where will we get the money to diffuse the demographic time bomb? Generations following the Baby Boomers will have to navigate this crisis, likely by defaulting on many promises made to older generations. Their bright future has been destroyed by our foolishness and our reckless accumulation of debt. They do not deserve to spend their years slaving away to support previous generations in their golden years. .

But Isn't America Different?

Everyone is aware Europe is in deep economic trouble, and has a major fiscal deficit issue. Half of the Eurozone is effectively locked out of the capital markets and Europe's debt/GDP is very high. The Eurozone only has funding courtesy of various back door Ponzi schemes funded by the European Central Bank. But the truth is that at least Europe is taking small steps to rectify its historic profligacy and is at least pretending to be implementing austerity (in some cases actually doing so). How about the US? Well, the chart below shows precisely where the differences lie and should answer that question. While the consolidated GDP of the US and Europe are nearly identical, they differ materially in terms of both fiscal deficit, and total Debt/GDP.

Hint: higher and right on the graph are bad.

Spot the looming crisis
Gen govt gross debt vs budget deficits, sized by GDP

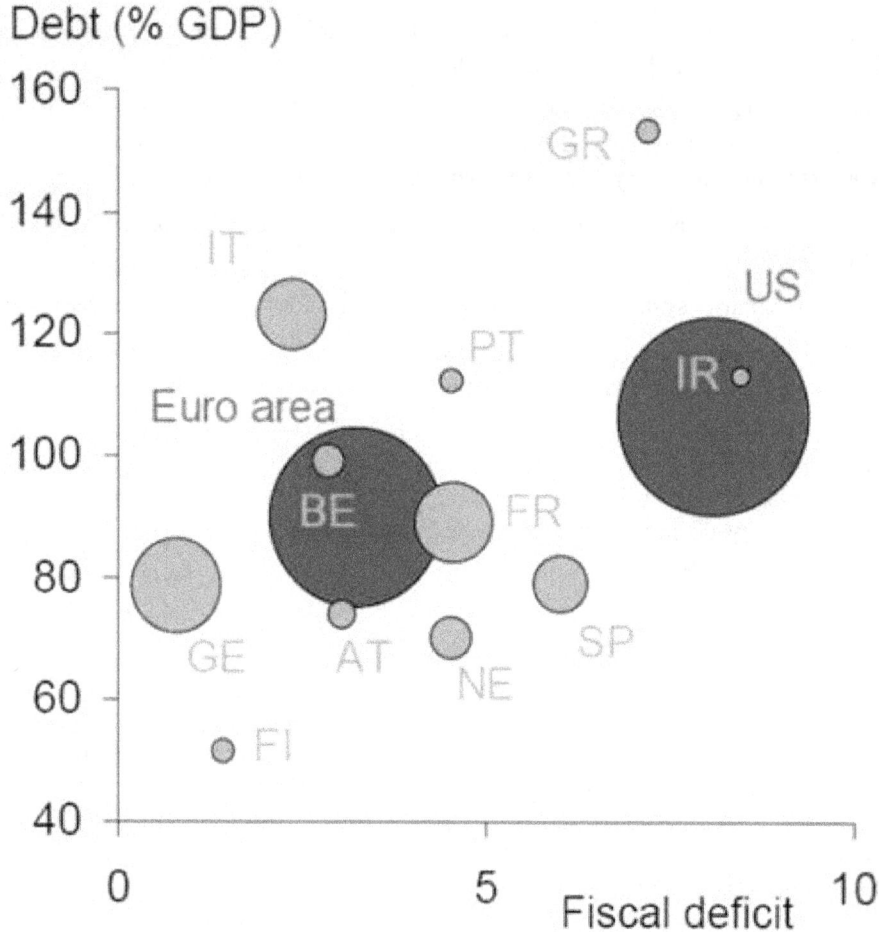

Ironically while the financial sectors of both the US and the Euro Area are nearly identical in their liability composition, where they differ is in the amount of deposit buffers backing the financial system: in Europe deposits are nearly three times greater than the US! This is of course a double edged sword. On one hand it means banks have a greater cash-based capital buffer - US banks would *die* to have the nominal amount of European deposits - but it also means that European banks have a far greater propensity to bank runs since in Europe the shadow banking system is far less developed. This implies Inflation in Europe is a far, far greater risk. The Bundesbank, for all the criticism it gets day in and day out, is spot on in its unwillingness to cede to the ECB's endless money printing demands.

Overbanked?

Financial sector liabilities, % GDP

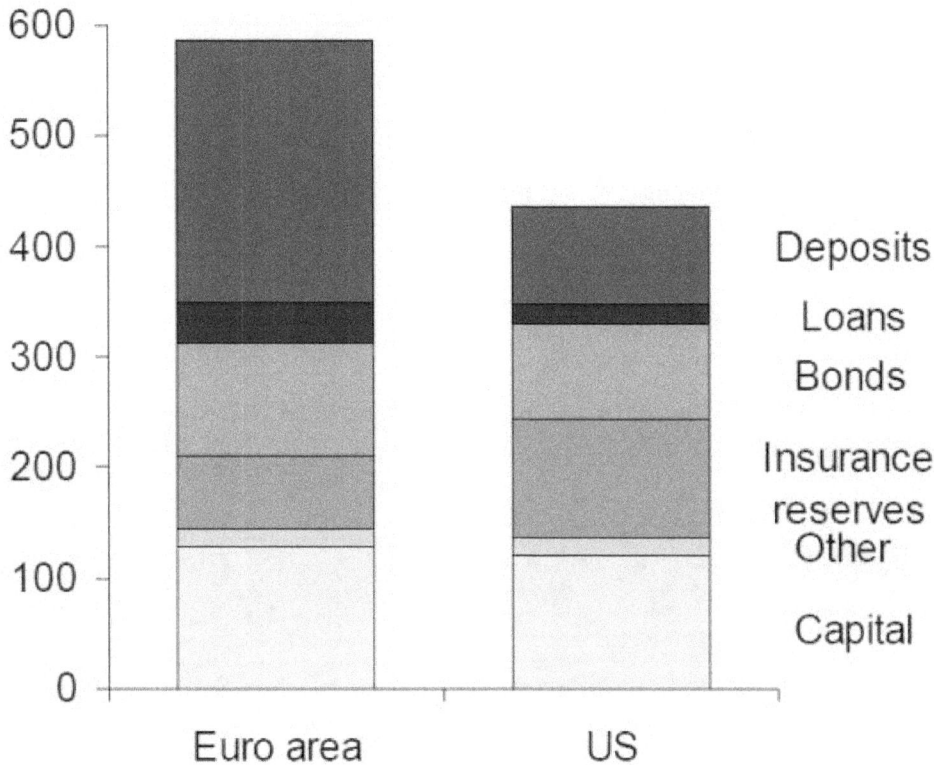

Source: OECD, ECB.

Surviving The New Normal

Despite these dire facts (we'll present even more later), Americans have taken few steps to prepare for an economic disaster, much less natural disasters, terrorist attacks and other emergencies. Part of the reason is that we have been well off in the United States for 100 years, and we trust in our bank accounts to sustain us. Unfortunately, money sitting in savings and investments is useless if you become stuck in a perfect storm and the stock market crashes, or the Chinese stop propping up Treasury bond sales.

So what this book will provide you with is financial survival strategies and tactics designed to shelter the funds you still have while building a more solid financial base to be able to profit even during coming hard times. But to do so you will need more than just a few traditional stock tips, you will need to know why the entire system is broken – you have to learn the nuts and bolts of 'the New Normal'. That requires you to understand a lot of economics and financial history that you haven't been getting from academia or the news media, much less from politicians who have a vested interest in the status quo Ponzi game. That is why this book is dense with facts and filled with non-mainstream economic analysis that keeps its eyes on the fundamentals. But it will be worth stepping outside the box; it is your financial survival at stake.

2 Timeline

To be able to plot your financial future, you need to understand what the inevitable timeline of collapse we are on will look like. Our crystal ball for the timing *details* may be no better than anyone else's, but there are certain elements that are inevitable.

The United States and much of Europe are borrowing an extraordinary amount of money now just to pay interest on the money they've already borrowed. They cannot even self-fund their mandatory entitlement programs without going into the hole, and their options are limited. While social issues are intimately wrapped up in our problems, economic issues will dominate the timeline and thus give us some insight into how the economic collapse will unfold:

Stage 1: Continue borrowing, keep the party going.

This is the stage we are currently in, in Europe, Japan and America. As long as governments CAN do this, they WILL do this. Regardless of their intentions, though, more debt only worsens the situation, creating higher borrowing costs in the long run, and even more debt. As this happens, the pool of sovereign debt buyers begins to dry up, especially from overseas piggybanks like China. Consider this the first stage of the collapse.

Stage 2: Biflation

The more buyers stop purchasing Treasury securities, the more the ECB and Federal Reserve will themselves mop up the excess liquidity. In doing so, the Fed essentially conjures up money and loans it to the government, like paying off one credit card with another. No matter what governments say, this is inflationary for commodities and essentials, *but it is deflationary for assets* as money velocity falls in businesses built on trust. This causes a dual inflationary and deflationary economic swamp – a biflationary depression. The more money central banks print, the greater the level of biflation in the long-term. Meanwhile, as foreigners simultaneously reduce their US dollar holdings, inflation of necessities will become more acutely felt throughout the US even as assets and wages are depressed.

Stage 3: Austerity

There's will come a time when the US government is forced to face its economic reality and make some incredibly deep cuts that would be felt across society, from Wall Street and the military industrial complex to project housing on the other side of the tracks. This will happen either through good government accountability, or through the collapse of bad government when the bills aren't paid. Feeble attempts at reform started during the "Fiscal Cliff" legislation of late 2012 solved nothing. Government revenues are now only 57% of expenditures – bridging that gap will inevitably cause pain.

Stage 4: Default

Eventually, the debt burden is simply going to be too much, and the most obvious solution will be to default. Politicians will make China out to be the enemy. Who knows, they may even invent a war just to have an excuse to default on Chinese owned debt. Americans will wave the flag and celebrate defaulting on their enemies. But whatever happens, default is inevitable, we are only debating how large and when, not if.

Stage 5: Economic and Social Cannibalism

In the best traditions of Atlas Shrugged, the government will continue its persecution of the productive class– professionals, investors, entrepreneurs, and skilled workers. Existing taxes will rise, new taxes will be created, trade barriers will be enacted, and a maze of cost prohibitive regulations will be passed. This will happen no matter whether politicians of the left or right are in charge because there is no simple way to correct our financial problems. The two political parties now only differ in the degree to which they must appropriate the wealth of citizens. Add on to this the unleashed furry of pent up social problems which have been festering for decades and you understand why you need to planning your finances as though your life depended on it. Everyone becomes a potential financial cannibal in a long term depression economy, including private business partners.

Where We Are And Where We Are Headed

The first stage option (keeping the party going) is what has been happening since the 1970s. Politicians have made small concessions to show they're "serious" about fiscal discipline, cutting laughably small programs while dumping hundreds of billions of dollars into entitlement programs and wars. The worse the debt situation becomes, the higher the borrowing costs become, and the worse the debt situation becomes. Existing lenders will continue backing away from the US Treasury market as the hollowness becomes evident.

In the longer term, only options 2-5 remain: biflation, austerity, default, and cannibalism. Each of these remaining options will shake the financial and social system to its core. When inflation eats away at a family's already meager standard of living and deflation destroys assets and earnings, when austerity eliminates the benefits to which recipients have grown accustomed, when default vanquishes a retiree's savings and a country's sovereign debt becomes toilet paper, when high taxes make workers feel like they're just government serfs– this is when an economic civil war begins:

- Rising crime: devoid of a job or means to support their families, people will turn to crime out of desperation
- Class warfare: with dividing lines drawn between have's vs. have-not's, it will become unpopular and even dangerous to be successful
- Corruption: low-level public service officials will look to supplement their income through bribery and kickbacks
- Black economy: An underground, cash-only (probably gold or foreign currency) economy will emerge with people getting paid in envelopes
- Censorship: Of course they'll blame it on national security, but the idea will be to prevent public disparaging of government policy
- War: The government may need another major event to distract people from the real problems
- Protests/Riots: This is when things turn bloody
- Police state conditions: The government will close ranks and send the cops out to show all the little people who's really in charge

The US and European police states are alive and well. In Europe, the police are doing battle in the streets with their citizens. For those who think it can't happen in the US, remember the LA riots, remember New Orleans and remember any number of G8/G20 protests? Occupy Wall Street could become the new normal.

International headlines show what happens when you strip people of their livelihood, of their ability to put food on the table for their families. The US has been able to kick the can down the road simply because the country benefits so much from a US-oriented international financial system. This is coming to an end very, very quickly. As a rule of thumb, the greater the economic distortion, the harder the collapse. The US economy has been in a fantasy world for so long, that when its dominant primacy is yanked away, the collapse will be at freefall speed.

The Eurozone and its monetary system will be in a state of collapse for years. Japan is in even worse straits. While this will strengthen the dollar in the short term, we will soon join their pain.

We have not put dates on these events because that would be impossible. What we do know is that nothing can even begin to heal until there has been a political purge in the United States, Japan and Europe. That means you have to be prepared to survive several years, if not decades, through oscillating binges of deflationary liquidity traps in some sectors conjoined with high inflation in other areas.

Not predicting an exact timeline is however in itself a prediction – that anyone who does try to tell you how to market time everything is nuts. However, this does lend itself to other coping strategies that revolve around flexibility. That is the edge we will be presenting in coming chapters.

3 Economic Collapse

- America will cut back its spending, innovate, and pay off its debts. We will earn our way out. It's just how we do it. -

The above generic optimistic statement is typical of the type one has often heard in the financial media in the years since the 2009 Crash. However, this country has never come back from anything like the combination of economic problems it faces now. Moreover, our problems are coupled to worldwide problems in the Eurozone, Japan, China and elsewhere due to massive deleveraging needed to wean the world of the welfare state.

How Economic Collapse Shapes Your Investments

This chapter is a tour through the dismal statistics of our economy. The purpose is not to cause mental despair, but to give you a clear idea what needs to be done before a robust recovery can begin. Until you see signs that a structural correction has begun, there is no need to shift to an aggressively optimistic portfolio. Good luck with that.

The only way for the nation to rise above its troubles will be through experiencing a terrible financial calamity, to bring the reality home to the population that we have to give up our protections and entitlements and return to our roots. Risk taking, production, work ethic and personal self-reliance will not come back without first experiencing the shock of real hardship of a magnitude similar to the Great Depression. Unfortunately, we appear to be well on our way down that path.

This time *is* different. Holding a pile of U.S. Treasuries won't save you when we head into a currency crash or inflationary spiral. Because of the Fed's zero interest rate policy, bond yields may not even rise even given monetary debasement. Even if America somehow "muddles along" indefinitely with slow growth and high inflation, Treasury bonds at artificially low rates will bring you only losses, tears and poverty. Owning expensive real estate that will not appreciate is not an investment. Other traditional avenues of economic escape are similarly clouded.

From high unemployment, to low GDP growth, to current and future liabilities, there are fundamental problems that will not be resolved anytime soon – in fact, they're likely to get worse for a decade or more. One end result could even be a hyperinflationary worldwide great depression, or at best lost economic decades similar to what Japan has experienced. A more likely future is a Biflationary Depression, in which goods you need inflate while assets and wages deflate.

It isn't clear whether deflation or inflation will rule in any given sector of our economy, but in terms of maintaining the purchasing power of your own wealth, you will want to put *some* of your dollars into hard assets like physical gold and silver, or exchange US dollars for other currencies such as the Canadian dollar, Australian dollar, Norwegian kroner, Swiss francs, etc. Other inflation hedged investment strategies are also possible, and might include investments in stocks in the food industry or in rail transportation, both of which are so critical that their values should float along with the tsunami of money printing. Timing is critical, so anything we write needs to be judged against current events. We will discuss all these avenues in later chapters.

Zimbabwe had the worst hyperinflation anyone's ever seen. Zimbabwe survived because they had an ongoing economy based on a black market in US dollars, but in the US we don't have a backup system. We don't have a sizeable black market in the US and there's no backup to our system since the dollar is the reserve currency. While this is a problem for people who live in a US dollar denominated world – Australia, Canada, Singapore, Chile, Norway and others are unlikely to have this problem.

It will get very difficult if food starts to disappear from food shelves. It's a good idea to store goods that you would normally consume for several months, just to protect yourself, your family and to have goods for barter. A bag of rice, bottled water, or roll of toilet paper stored in your garage will be worth its weight in silver if goods start flying of the store shelves. We address these 'Prepper' avenues in our book, "Going Galt: Surviving Economic Armageddon".

Signs Of A Major Collapse

Look for what governments have historically done when they go bankrupt - debase their currencies. What the Federal Reserve hopes for is an inflationary spiral to cancel astronomical debt. Current monetary policies of our Federal Reserve are clear omens; they are creating money out of thin air out of desperation. More money chasing fewer goods inevitably leads to higher prices as seen the world over in commodities and other assets. However, money printing also leads to a loss of faith in business transactions which crushes wage and is deflationary. We've all seen the ramp up in commodity prices hit store shelves and gas stations. Home prices and wages have on the other hand collapsed. This creates a raisin muffin economy, the conditions for a Biflationary depression. In such a chaotic economic soup, stocks and commodities will crash and boom in cycles, but across the board price increases simply cannot be avoided long term.

The Hail Mary the Federal Reserve is trying to complete to save our economic system is to export US inflation to China and developing countries. Significant increases in the BRIC (Brazil, India, Russia, and China) domestic stock market prices and real estate values are signs that this is occurring, but the Fed strategy relies on these nations remaining ignorant to their monetary fate. The Chinese have already taking steps to curb this inflationary bubble and the Russians have completed non dollar denominated transactions with the Chinese. Uncontrolled spending of Federal, State and local governments will lead to new fiscal problems, which ultimately lead to more monetary quantitative easing policies in a vicious cycle. As the US government wastes more money, more needs to be printed to "monetize" the debt that no one else wants to buy.

Weakness in the dollar will not save us; it will kill the system no matter what politicians say. When our creditors start offloading US Treasuries and stop buying new debt issues, the game is over. Watch the dollar for the early signs of hyperinflation and panic. If it gets out of control you'll see massive dumping of dollars. Deflationary pressures will on the other hand grind down wages and profit margins. The Fed will be intervening even more than it does now as people turn dollars over as quickly as they can – they're not going to want to hold them. Gasoline and food prices will sky rocket even as income falls.

The Austrian Economics School's Commandments

1) You cannot spend your way out of a recession.
2) You cannot regulate the economy into oblivion and expect it to function.
3) You cannot tax people and businesses to the point of near slavery and expect them to keep producing.
4) You cannot create an abundance of money out of thin air without making all that paper worthless.
5) The government cannot make up for rising unemployment by just hiring all the out of work people to be bureaucrats or send them unemployment checks forever.
6) You cannot live beyond your means indefinitely.
7) The economy must actually produce something others are willing to buy.

8) Every government bureaucrat should keep the following motto in mind when attempting to influence the economy: "First, do no harm!"
9) Fractional reserve banking supported by central banks is economy distorting and ethically questionable activity. In particular, no government should ever do anything to save any bank from the full consequences of a bank run, no matter what the short-term consequences.
10) Gold is God's money.

We are in a period in which many developed economies of the world will either willingly deleverage or be forced to do so. Deleveraging will produce a fundamentally different economic environment, which might last four to six years – but could last twenty. Whether this deleveraging is orderly, as appears to be the case in Britain, or more resembles a chaotic default as in Greece, will create a profoundly different economic world from the one we have lived in for 60 years which has been defined by ever-increasing amounts of leverage. Economically speaking, outright reductions in leverage or even a significant slowing of the rate of growth creates a whole new ballgame.

Whether we get Crisis Lite or Crisis Depression is up to us and the politicians we elect. Leaders in many countries think that with the right policies they can grow (export) their way out of the problem. But not everyone can grow their way out of a crisis at the same time - Someone has to buy. While the right policies will help, growth will be severely constrained for years to come.

How Did We Get Here?

In the late '40s after World War II, the US and the developed world began a cycle of ever-increasing debt both in the private and public sectors. Government began to grow as a percentage of overall GDP, especially later in this cycle as politicians created huge entitlement programs of pensions and health-care benefits that require significant unsustainable taxes.

There is a limit to how much money an individual, business or country can borrow. If your debt grows faster than your income and your ability to service the debt, people will eventually stop loaning you money. The end result is a restructuring of the debt, through default or serious inflation, or through a reduced standard of living in order to service the debt. For individuals, that may mean cutting off the cable TV, no eating out, no vacations, etc. For countries it means reduced government programs and benefits, and higher taxes.

It will seem like the end of the world for the unprepared as jobs and safety nets evaporate. Fiscal sanity requires the growth of the debt to be below the growth rate in nominal GDP. Without proper restructuring the US will suffer much as Greece, Spain or Ireland. Yet, in your personal microeconomy there will be opportunities for the nimble who can sell short this tumbling house of cards.

The 2008 banking crisis showed the limits of how much individuals can borrow, especially against their home equity as evidenced by millions of foreclosures. In the US, private debt began to shrink after the crash except for student loans. Based on formulistic neo-Keynesian policy, governments worldwide stepped into this credit contraction by massively borrowing. However, all governments have limits to how much debt they can carry, including the US. The debt crisis has continued to unfold in Greece, Ireland, Portugal and Spain because they refused to deleverage their entitlement economies. Japan's economic collapse is not far down the road and will shake the world.

The economic environment in which individuals and governments either willingly or are forced by the markets to reduce their borrowing and debt is significantly different from the period where they could create ever-increasing amounts of leverage. What we think of as normal gets turned upside down. Volatility increases, and for many people this will qualify as a true crisis. However, volatility and crisis also mean there will be opportunities for those prepared for them.

The next graph shows the rise of debt in the US. Even with the recent pullback in consumer debt the rise is tremendous because of enormous government deficits. This chart only goes to 2011 but little has changed since (we present a more updated version later). Most importantly this chart shows just how astronomic our debt run up has been considering this is a time of relative peace and is unrelated to the debt spike of World War II.

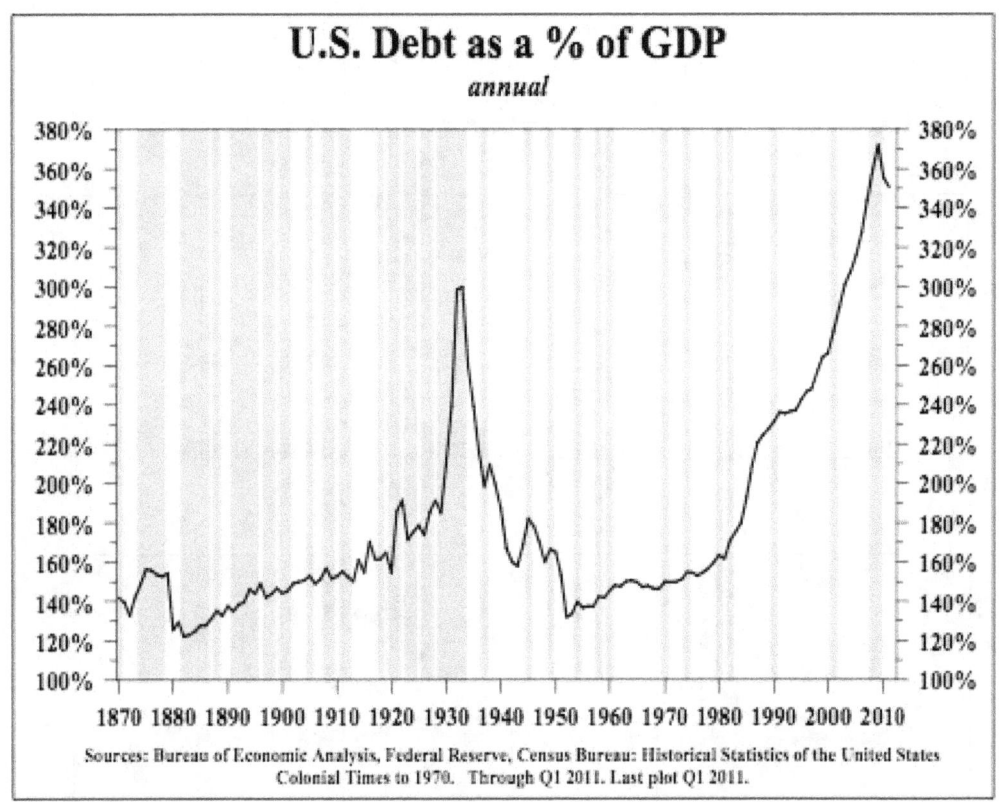

Two charts from the Bank of International Settlements outline what happens for 12 countries in terms of the debt-to-GDP ratio: if current spending and tax rates remain unchanged (the top dotted line), if there are efforts to rein in spending with small gradual spending cuts and tax increases (middle line), and what with serious spending cuts and significant tax increases (the lowest line).

Public debt/GDP projections

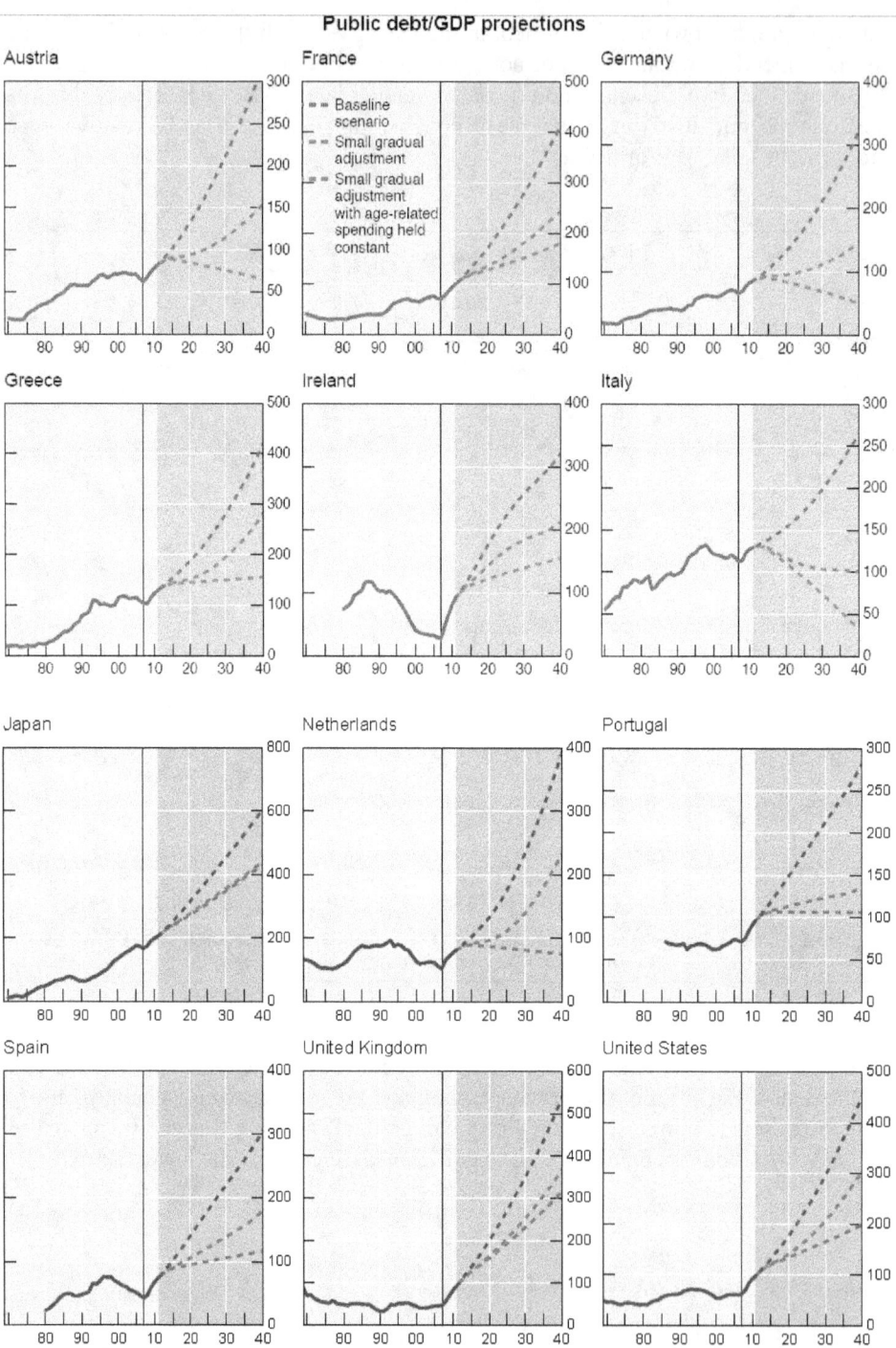

The horizontal axis represents the years between 1970 and projections until 2040. If age-related spending is held constant, seniors will get ever-smaller pensions and health care that would be drastically reduced. Some countries simply do not recover even with draconian measures.

The only historical example of a country that saw its debt-to-GDP rise over 150% and did not default is Britain. However, Britain was then at the height of its empire and power, with long-term rates at a very low level and a completely different investment and bond climate. Many of the countries are now on a path to twice that level in the very near future.

The rule in economics is: if something can't happen, it won't happen. Many believed the linear trend of real estate and stock market gains would go on forever as debt climbed stratospherically, but we should all have known that couldn't happen. Many expect a typical recovery despite rising debt, but this time is different, because so many things are on unsustainable paths that changes in present trends are inevitable. So what we must think about is what will happen when unthinkable change is forced on not only our country, but most of the countries forming Western civilization.

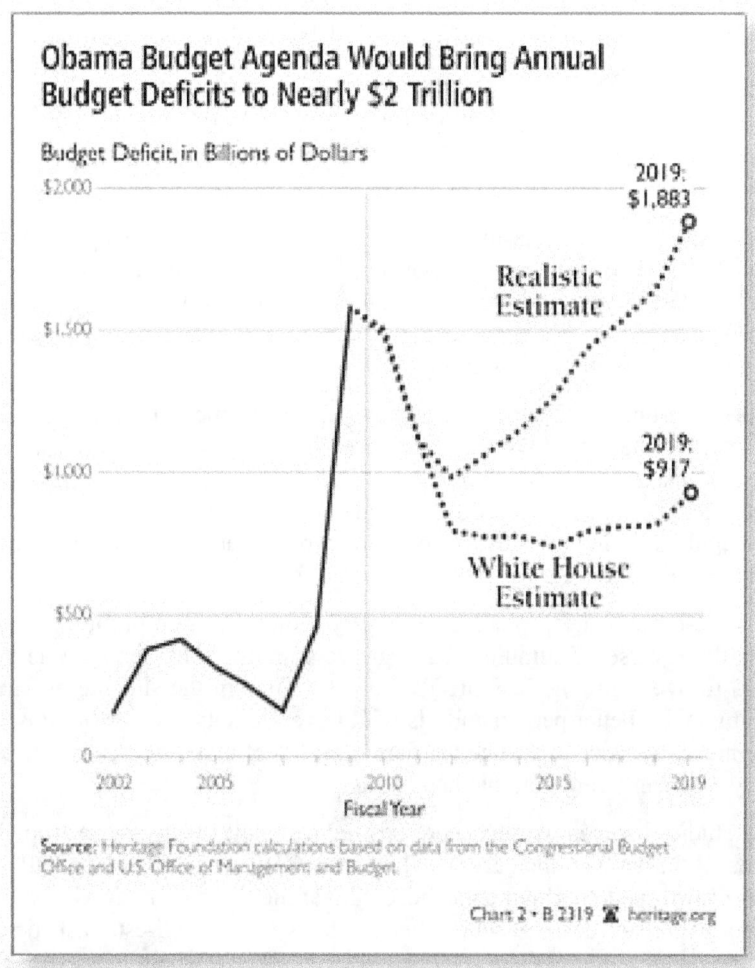

The chart of projected debt for the US, compiled in 2010 by the Heritage Foundation, is a chart of something that *will not and did not happen*. Administration budgets are all held somewhat in check by the fact we are broke. Long before we ever get ten years of multi-trillion-dollar debt, the bond market will require much higher rates, driving up interest-rate cost as a percentage of tax revenues to stratospheric levels, forcing cuts in things like military, education, and Medicare spending which we think are absolutely necessary. We can proactively deal with the deficit problem, or we can wait until there is a crisis and be forced to react. Budget deficits are *going* to come down one way or another, either through fiscal discipline or collapse. Both options constrict your financial future.

All our problems are dwarfed by two basic root questions: 1) how much health care do we want and 2) how do we want to pay for it? We can radically cut health care and other discretionary budget items, we can radically raise taxes, or we can pursue some combination, but not without major consequences. Polls say a bipartisan majority of people want to maintain Medicare and other health programs (perhaps reformed), yet a large bipartisan majority does not want tax increases.

To survive, the nation must reduce the deficit over 5-6 years below the growth rate of nominal GDP (excluding inflation). A country can run a deficit below that rate forever, without endangering its economic survival, though it may be wiser to run some surpluses and pay down debt. If you keep your fiscal deficits lower than income growth, the debt becomes less of an issue over time. However, raising taxes or cutting spending have side effects. Either one will make it more difficult for the economy to grow. Let's review a few basic economic equations.

GDP = C + I + G + Net Exports

Or in words the Gross Domestic Product (GDP) is equal to Consumption (Consumer and Business) + Investment + Government Spending + Net Exports (Exports – Imports). This is true for all times and countries.

In typical business-cycle recessions, as businesses produce too many goods and start to cut back, consumption falls. The Keynesian response is to increase government spending in order to assist the economy to start buying and spending. The theory is that when the economy recovers you can reduce government spending as a percentage of the economy. It also presupposes governments are capable of creating worthwhile goods or services.

Of course government spending reductions never happen, outlays just keep going up. Government (both parties) increased spending massively in response to the Great Recession of 2008. While GDP increased marginally (as expected) because Government is part of the GDP equation, positive effects were less than anticipated (also expected by anyone who understands economics 101). The stimulus was applied to increase the absolute size of government, not to add to productivity. Government malinvestment should actually be *subtracted* from GDP!

Thus, massive deficits are projected for a very long time. The problem is that taking away deficit spending is the reverse of stimulus – a negative stimulus. The economy is not growing fast enough (<2%/year) to overcome the loss of QE 2-3-4 stimulus in the short-term. However the only way for the economy to get better permanently is with lower deficits and smaller government. To get the deficit under control, we need to reduce the deficit by 1% of GDP every year for 5-6 years. Given our political history, you can't count on that happening.

Academic studies have shown tax increases reduce GDP by anywhere from 1 to 3 times the size of the increase. Large tax increases will reduce GDP and potential GDP proportionately, including a cost to growth and employment. Those who argue that taking away tax cuts will have no effect on the economy are not dealing with either the facts or the well-established research. If you propose to reduce potential nominal GDP by 1% a year in a world where massive Qualitative Easing only resulted in 2% GDP growth, the future looks bleak for long periods and the incentives for revolt become significant.

Increasing Productivity

There are only two ways to grow an economy. You can increase the working-age population or you can increase productivity. Short of becoming a baby factory, the key is to increase productivity.

The "I" in our GDP equation is investments. That is what produces the tools and businesses that make "stuff" and buy and sell services. Increasing government spending, "G," does not increase productivity, it simply transfers taxes taken from one sector of the economy to another, less a substantial cost of transfer. While people who get transfer payments and services are better off, those who pay taxes have less to invest in private businesses that actually increase productivity.

Over the last two decades, net new jobs in the US have come from business start-ups while small and large businesses have been a net drag. The only way to solve the unemployment problem is thus through investment in startups, hiring 5-10-50-100 people, with the cumulative effect being growth in the economy and productivity.

Returning to our equation, we find: *Savings = Investments.* If the government "dis-saves" or runs deficits, it takes away potential savings from private investments and that money has to come from somewhere. Through 2011, it came from QE2, but further easing is problematic because of the inflation threat. QE3 in 2012 has been a decided flop, QE4 no better establishing a trend. A better option is private investment that increases productivity, adds to real growth and produces jobs. When the government takes money from one group and employs another, those are best viewed as virtual jobs because that money could have been put to use in private business. Government cannot create jobs better than the taxpayers and businesses they take the taxes from.

There are costs to large government involvement in the economy, so the question is how much government do we want? This depends on how large a drag government creates. The following chart using data between 1960 and 2006 correlates the rate of growth of GDP in OECD countries versus the size of government. The larger the percentage of government in the ratio, the lower the growth.

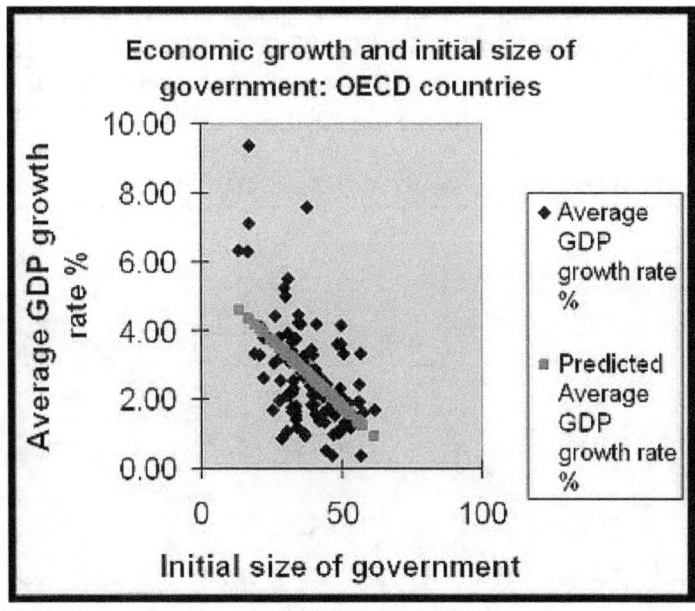

A clear correlation exists worldwide between the size of total government and structural growth. Going from a government that consumes fifty percent of the economy to one that consumes twenty percent reduces the time needed to double the economy from roughly 35 years to 17 years, swamping the tax revenue lost with higher growth.

Unlike niche anarchist libertarians or radical progressives, most people recognize there are tradeoffs and a just place for government. A professional military seems irreplaceable, as do courts, highways and transportation projects, border enforcement, etc. Clearly, society functions better with some government services which increase productivity. We "buy" these services collectively with tax dollars because they are seen as essential public goods which could only be offered by private companies with difficulty.

However, government ownership of steel mills, airlines, energy production and other industries (GM? Amtrac?) has rapidly approached state socialism (perhaps fascism is the correct term) where the trains really don't run on time. Even the Chinese and Russians have given up on the infallibility of centrally planned economies. Government-run businesses are rarely as efficient as private ones and that efficiency is a direct component of productivity.

Remember, the C in the economic equation is private and business consumption. The G is government, but G unfortunately now makes up a large portion of overall GDP and represents consumption rather than production. The larger G is, the harder it is to find private sector productivity gains. One might even argue that GW (Government Waste or misallocation) should be subtracted from GDP because it is wasteful consumption. That is:

GDP = C + I + G + Net Exports – *GW*

Is it any wonder that we have no net new jobs over the last decade? In an effort to appear to be "doing something," to "feel your pain," government is sucking the investment money out of the economy. This shows up in worker pay where the average worker has not seen their pay rise in real terms in almost 15 years- if they have a job. In fact, they *lost* 5% the last decade.

The next chart shows the contribution of the private sector and the public sector to GDP. The top line is real GDP per capita. The next line shows what GDP would have been without borrowing. So a very real portion of GDP is coming from government debt. The line below that is private-sector GDP and shows the private sector, per capita, is roughly where it was in 1998. Sadly, the growth of the "economy" has been in government circuses rather than productive enterprise.

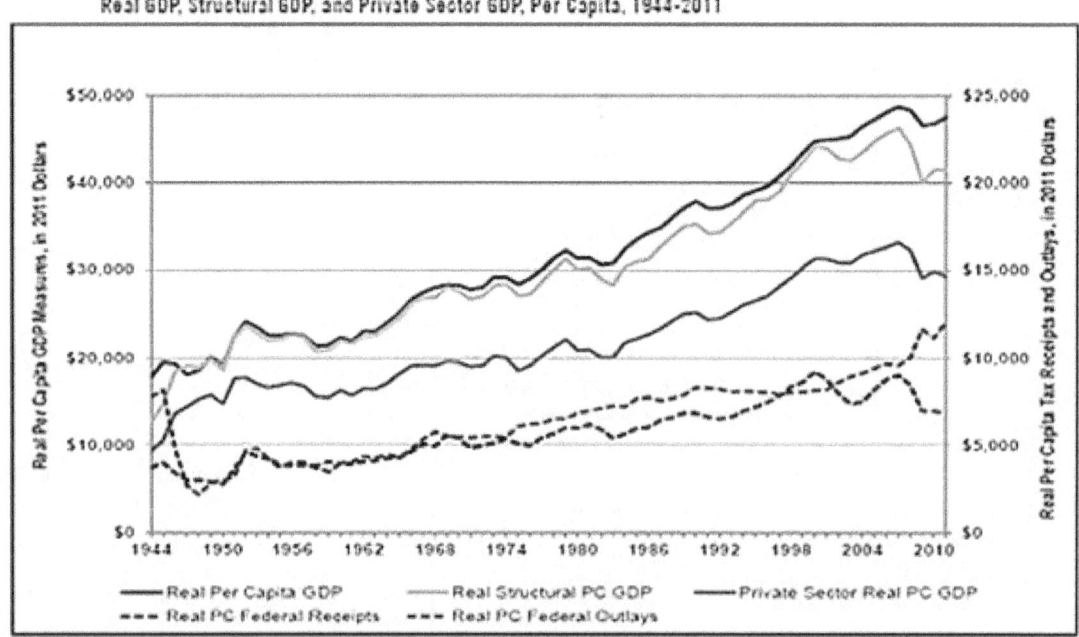

Real GDP, Structural GDP, and Private Sector GDP, Per Capita, 1944-2011

Do we want to grow the private economy? Or do we want more tax revenues so we can have more government services like healthcare? If we tax the private economy we will reduce economic growth and the growth of jobs. Thus our fiscal deficit and the national debt are an economic cancer that threatens to destroy our republic. The ever expanding role of government has in fact caused real wages to stagnate since 1995.

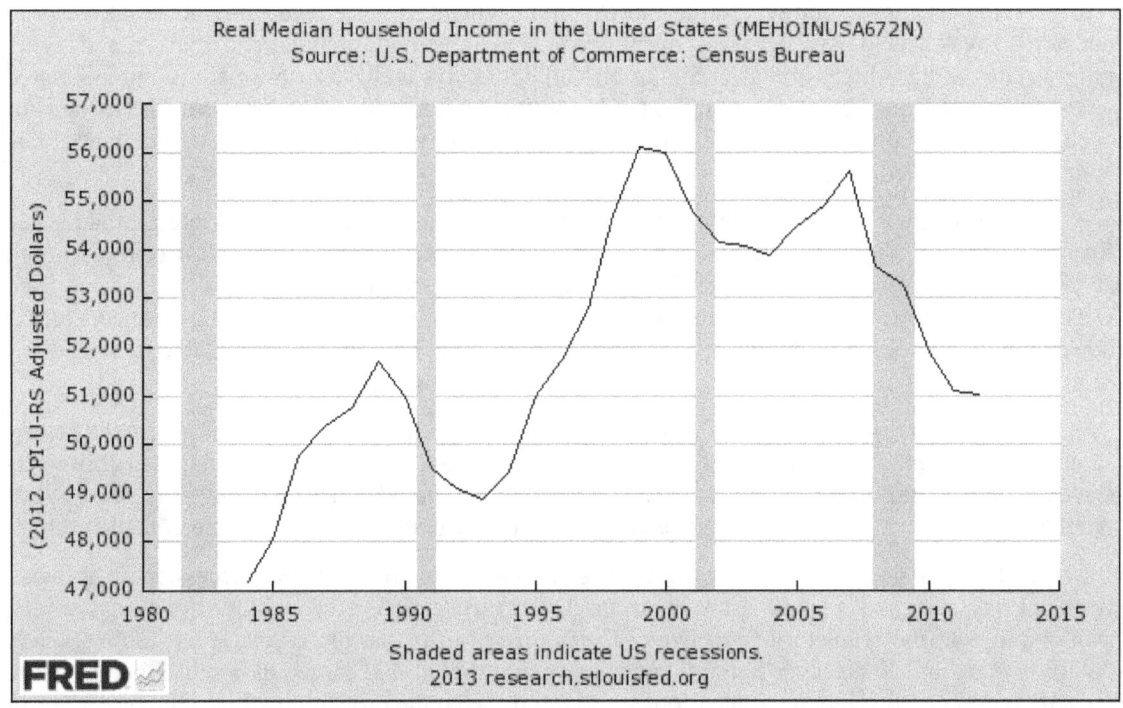

Sane people all know the dire straits we are in. One can only conclude that we are being run over an economic cliff for political purpose. This purpose may be some crazy form of socialist utopianism that believes in a future modeled on the economic model of North Korea. Or we may just be led by a gaggle of nihilist lemmings who want to take us all over the edge for no purpose. It hardly matters; you have to get off the freight train before it hits the mountain.

We now have a population grown dependent on myriad expensive government entitlements which are beyond our productive ability to pay for, but are politically impossible to eliminate. We have an aging population with a massive wave of retirements just beginning to occur, coupled with a workforce participation rate that is the lowest in decades. A further burden is overzealous government regulators and a runaway civil tort system which has sent much of our industrial base fleeing the country. We no longer have a natural competitive advantage, as the fall of the iron and bamboo curtains has unleashed powerful competitor countries that were for decades hobbled by communist ideology. On top of this, we have an expansive military budget driven by little wars that seem to grow like a cancerous tumor.

The result is national debt that has grown exponentially faster for decades. Politicians now posture about cutting a few $billion from the budget when our problem is measured in tens of $trillions. Added up, it means economic collapse is inevitable because the government needs everything you own to stay afloat. It hardly matters whether this economic war on the people is premeditated, or simply the end wages of greed, for the devastation is the same. No individual can stop this whirlpool; but you can shape your finances to avoid the riptide.

4 Cyclical Financial Implosion

Even changes in political leadership which implement an austere econo-political climate will not stop an avalanche of new debt, vast quantities of additional digital fiat dollars, inflation and higher interest rates. Credit-driven financial implosion will come in waves because we are riding a hundred years of central bank Ponzi schemes abetted by political bread-and-circus largesse. The ravages of cyclical economic upheaval cannot be completely avoided, but you can financially survive them if you understand what is coming.

The collapse of the US subprime mortgage derivatives in 2007 morphed into a broad-based financial crisis in the fall of 2008 which gradually spread to most other first-world advanced economies. The collapse did not wreak the same havoc on emerging markets and second and third world nations because those economies were insulated from the folly of first-world finance - credit, borrowing, overwhelming debt and interest payments. They did not qualify for the intoxicating elixir of massive credit.

Varied opinion has been offered to explain what went wrong - Wall Street greed, crony capitalism, deficient and inadequately administered regulations, a credit and debt engorged consumer-driven economy, imprudent lending standards, negative real interest rates and negligible savings. All rationalizations inevitably rest on the excessive availability and abundance of cheap credit and cash.

Measures designed and implemented since the onset of the Great Recession to mitigate financial risk, such as the Dodd Frank Financial Reform legislation, have merely institutionalized the shortcomings of the regulatory framework. The 'too big to fail' private financial institutions which qualify for unlimited taxpayer bailouts are more concentrated and larger today than before 2008. Indeed, the supposed solutions to the problem exemplify what the problem really is – big government entwined with the central bank!

Deficits are exploding rapidly leading inexorably to massive debt at all levels of government from local to state to federal governments. US sovereign/federal debt is now over $16 Trillion and is expanding at over $1.5 Trillion per year - over three times greater than just a few years ago. Over 40 percent of all federal spending comes from borrowing, which means more magic money created by the FED to service the ballooning beast.

But hat is just the start of the problem. Added to this witches brew are the unfunded and underfunded obligations of the social safety net represented by Social Security, Medicare and Medicaid, all conveniently excluded from the federal government's annual operating budget. Depending on what assumptions are made for future inflation, eligibility, program utilization and related issues, further unfunded liabilities of between $60 Trillion and $110 Trillion must be added to the US federal government's debt tab. State and local governments contribute a further $3.87 Trillion in unfunded liabilities attributable to employee pensions and health insurance benefits. State and municipal employees agitating for retention of the unsustainable status quo highlights their bloated pension and health benefits.

Based on several hundred years of economic history, a debt to GDP ratio of 90 percent seems to be a nation's tipping point. The USA, United Kingdom, Japan and others are lined up to join Greece, Ireland, Italy, Portugal staring at a financial abyss. Fundamentals are therefore in place for more waves of financial collapse. This time governments will join private financial institutions heading toward the debt wall, unable to perform their previous role of bailing out ailing financial institutions since government itself is now in dire need of rescue.

There is no institution big enough to bail out all failing governments. European nations sharing the Euro currency can't help since they occupy an equally impecunious perch on the financial cliff. Only advanced nations supported by a strong natural resources sector (Canada, Australia) or high productivity manufacturing (Germany) will avoid financial catastrophe.

Financial Crisis Triggers

Rising interest rates are all that is necessary to trigger the second round of collapse in the ongoing financial crisis. Current interest rates are lower than the early 1950's and real interest rates are perilously close to being negative. With rapidly growing price inflation on the horizon, interest rates will be forced northward to stave off inflation.

Until recently foreign purchasers have been the largest buyers of US Treasury debt, with China and Japan in the lead. Japan now has other priorities following its lost decades and highly destructive tsunami. China has already substantially reduced its purchases of US Treasuries citing lack of confidence in the declining value of the United States dollar, instead spending on minerals and energy. Sixty year low interest rates on US Treasury bonds, less than the rate of inflation, make them risky and unattractive investments.

In the absence of enough foreign or private sector purchasers; the US central bank has been 'monetizing' federal government debt through its own purchases of Treasury bonds. The process is dubbed Quantitative Easing, by which the FED creates money out of thin air and allows the FED to become the purchaser of last resort of government debt. The FED is expected to purchase 50 percent or more of all new and maturing Treasury bonds because there are not enough foreign or domestic, private sector or government buyers at current rates of interest and levels of systemic risk.

The most telling portent came in 2011 when PIMCO, the largest private bond fund, sold its entire US Treasury bond holdings. PIMCO head Bill Gross cited risks associated with near negative interest rates and the declining value of the US dollar stemming from excessive money creation. Knowing that institutional money managers representing pension funds and insurance company investment pools frequently follow industry leaders, at some point Billions and Trillions of Treasury bonds will be dumped into the sickly bond market. As this process plays out, FED money creation and debt monetization will go into overdrive even as price inflation explodes and the dollar devalues.

America's Political Process Guarantees Financial Crisis

To the extent America is a democracy rather than a republic, continuing serious financial crises are guaranteed. Salient factors include:

- The magnitude and momentum of expanding government deficits, debt and unfunded liabilities cannot be reversed without severe austerity measures.
- The monetization of Treasury debt by the Federal Reserve Board using manufactured money acquired through the mystical process labeled 'Quantitative Easing' cannot be reversed or rolled back.
- The inevitability of eventual higher interest rates brought on by a policy of devaluing the currency followed by long term price inflation.

The political process guarantees that no essential, measures will be undertaken by political decision makers to stabilize the financial system. Politicians and government bureaucrats are, like most people, ambitious ladder climbers who work hard to preserve their careers and associated benefits, including the cushiness of defined benefit, inflation protected pensions and gilded health insurance. Preservation of the status quo is their top priority. Politicians across the partisan spectrum and range of ideologies have learned that the voting public does not want to hear about emerging or imminent problems. They want reassurance, not anxiety and when a crisis blindsides them, they want immediate action from their government. Voters expect their elected politicians to 'do something' when a crisis strikes, whether it helps the situation or not.

There is no incentive to scan the horizon and to implement tough measures designed to head off the mounting financial crisis. Until the crisis arrives, politicians who assume leadership roles as educators and disseminators of serious policy options will be branded messengers of mayhem for calling for belt tightening and sacrifice. The default is for voters point to government waste and target 'rich people' for austerity and additional revenue. Messenger politicians are chastised by losing their next election while candidates who ignore the storm clouds and promise good times will be rewarded with the vote. Political will wilts in this kind of hostile electoral environment – the electorate soon votes themselves the treasury. The voting public hears what it wants to hear and gets what it richly deserves.

Politicians in power know that the public can be bribed with their own money - actually borrowed Chinese money. Presidential election years are thus awash with positive investment environments. Voters enjoy their virtual prosperity and the general feeling of financial wellbeing as the propaganda mills churn. Incumbent Presidents, legislators, lobbyists all do well in such an environment. If our politicians were to act like adults with pragmatic economic deficit reduction, financial collapse could be delayed and perhaps avoided. Unfortunately the challenge is insurmountable as the political will too feeble to inflict the necessary bloodletting.

A bread and circus scenario will play out well into the future with artificially low interest rates. Large institutional Treasury bond purchasers such as pension funds and insurance companies will leave the Treasuries market. The dollar will plummet with excess of FED money printing. Emerging price inflation in food and energy will make for a grouchy voter and eventually interest rates will rise again. Can governments keep the lid on, or will the global financial pressure cooker explode? The odds are not in our favor.

The Perfect Financial Storm

Buying time by creating ever more magic money, which inevitably results in price inflation, overheated stock and commodities markets and devaluation of the currency - will work until it doesn't. When the perfect storm of collapsing economic fundamentals arrives, the financial earthquake will rapidly demolish the existing highly precarious financial system. Governments will stand by helplessly, unable to shield themselves much less their vulnerable citizens and private financial institutions from the tsunami of debt and fiat currency implosion.

Alternatives

There are two competing theories for how to solve this economic mess:

1) The US should pursue a strong growth and jobs policy through monetary easing as its #1 goal.

2) The US should pursue a combination of spending cuts and tax increases to reduce government crowd-out of the private sector, reviving the productive economy and solving the budget deficit.

However, both goals can't be pursued at the same time given Keynesian policies. If you increase government spending it will increase GDP in the short term, but this effect only lasts about 4-5 quarters and further balloons the long term debt. The real solution is to reduce government spending, but that will reduce the GDP and jobs in the short term with high political instability.

Thus, following popular Keynesian policies means the US will be growth challenged for years to come as the level of debt overwhelms productive pursuits and generates crises like those endured by Europe and Japan. It is known that tax cuts produce a growth in GDP of roughly 1 to 3 times the total amount of the cut. It follows that increasing taxes will have a negative effect of roughly the same amount. The penultimate goal is thus to reduce the deficit below the nominal growth rate of GDP without increasing tax rates.

If you reduce government spending you are going to reduce GDP *over the short term* by a rough equivalent (GDP = Consumption (C) + Investments (I) + Government Spending (G) + (Net exports)). Therefore, economic growth will slow if we become serious about reducing the deficit. And we are going to need to cut government spending by about 1.5% of GDP per year every year for five years (allowing for some growth) to get the deficit to a manageable level.

As government spending comes down we will see overall real GDP shrink unless it is accompanied by private-sector growth. With Keynesian nostrums proving a failure, the only way to speed economic growth is to decrease regulation, and/or decrease energy and commodity costs, solutions we are only now contemplating. With time, smaller government expenditures and a smaller deficit would mean more money for private-sector investment and productivity growth, but getting the deficit under control will mean slower growth near term.

Voting pro-business Republican or Tea Party will not provide a quick fix, even if it is the long term solution. The policy choices made in the second Obama administration will not be met with a return to the 4% growth; employment levels may not improve for a decade. It will take a lot of education to convince voters that there is no magic bullet spending cuts or tax increases and that we will need to stay the course, even while there is a general malaise in the economy. Economic headwinds we will be facing for years include:

- In 2013, trickle down tax increases for almost everyone, as we lose parts of the Bush tax cuts. This means less money in the pockets of everyone, even those below $100,000. This will be a significant drag on the GDP.

- The stimulus package of 2009 has faded from view along with QE1, QE2, QE3, QE4, etc. with nothing at all to show for it. Economic growth will be perpetually below 2%. There is no multiplier effect and economic growth as the Keynesians promised. It actually seems to be a negative multiplier, which von Mises and Hayek style Austrian economics suggested it would be.

- The delusion at the Fed was that the economy could take over after QEn, but there was no acceleration in growth. Europe and Japan hint at our slow growth future where benefits of any austerity measures are slow to be felt, if tried at all. When the Fed sees the economy slip into recession, they will use the only real tool they have left, and again inject liquidity into the economy which will again depress progress towards a recovery.

- The aftereffects of debt crises in numerous countries that require deleveraging shows that for the first two years there is a significant slowing of GDP, and the slower growth does not dissipate for 4-6 years. We have not started deleveraging as a nation so the real work will not be done until at least 2016.

- The real unemployment level may be 20% if you count people who were in the work force as recently as 2008. Many of the nation's workers are not paying income, Social Security or Medicare taxes. Many of them are on food stamps and unemployment, which exacerbates deficits at the federal and state levels. A robust economy would drive the unemployment level down, yet the needed economic growth of 3% or more seems unobtainable.

- Private-sector wages have gone nowhere and actually declined for 12 years. But transfer payments as a percentage of private-sector income and wages have risen inexorably for the past 50 years.

All these problems combined mean we aren't coming out of the Great Recession of 2007 any time soon and we are really in the eye of the storm of Great Depression II. The following graph, using Bureau of Economic Analysis data, is a ratio of 'BEA's government social benefits to persons' divided by 'BEA's wages and salaries. While wages and salaries are about 50% of total personal income (other sources of personal income are benefits, interest, dividends, etc.), it is the largest bucket of income that produces revenue for the government via our tax structure. Therefore wages and salaries are currently the engine of support for the government's social programs. The BEA's definition of government 'Social Benefits to Persons' includes Social Security, Medicare, Medicaid (the biggies), unemployment insurance, supplemental nutrition (SNAP, formerly food stamps), veteran's benefits, etc.

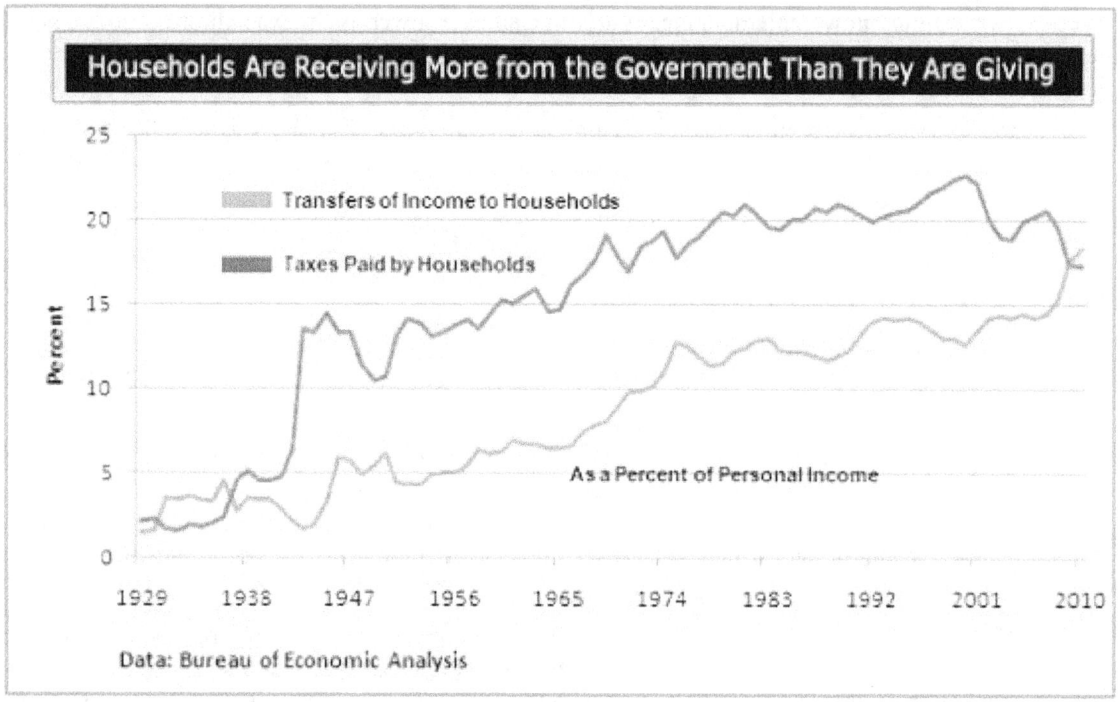

For the ratio to go back to something sustainable, e.g. 15%, either wages and salaries need to rise, benefits need to be trimmed, or taxes need to go up. A useful analogy is the train engine (wages and salaries) pulling rail cars up a hill. In those cars are the Defense Department, the EPA, government social benefits to persons, etc. Since 1938, the size of the social benefits rail car has grown from 5% the size of the engine, to now 20%. The 'Little Engine that Could' is rapidly becoming the 'Little Engine that Couldn't.'

- At some point the size of government becomes a drag on the economy and it acts as a headwind to growth. That contradicts the Keynesian idea that reducing government spending reduces GDP, which while technically correct is a short-term effect. The economic drag due to the size of government is the longer-term effect.
- As the debt-to-GDP level of a country approaches 90%, the data shows a slowing of potential GDP growth by about 1%. We have passed this level, and that is before we include state and local debt.
- Most worrisome is that our debt is now at levels not seen since World War II and it is accelerating (see below).

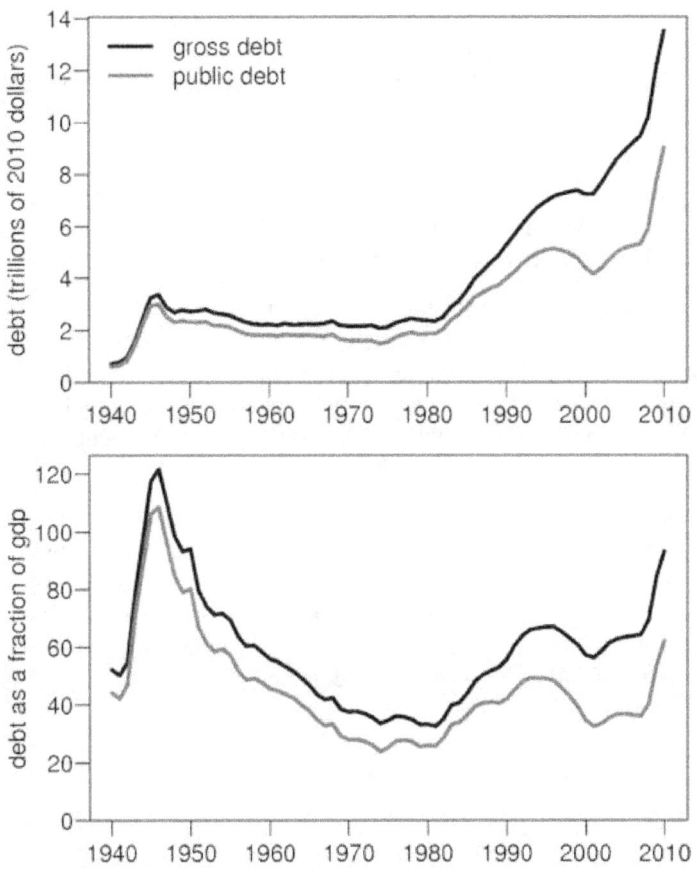

Economic Future

Where are we headed the next decade? Betting against the power of the free-market US economy has been a bad idea in the past. However, we are now not a free market economy but a crony capitalist system. We have just experienced a slow-growth economy from 2000 to 2012, only growing at 1.9%, the worst performance since the Depression. We can deal with the deficit proactively and restore a free market where companies are not too big to fail, or we can wait until the next inevitable crisis to react. Much of this decision is out of our hands and depends on how much debt the market will let us have.

Deficit control is the best-case scenario, but it means a slow-growth, economy for perhaps as long as 5-6 years. It also means at least one recession during that period, as growth will be close to "stall speed" and any exogenous shock could tip us into recession. Recessions mean higher unemployment, lower tax revenues, and an even deeper hole that will require more fiscal discipline and work. A recession will mean (on average) a 40% retrenchment of US equities. It will also mean another deflation scare and likely QEn.

Crisis Scenario

If we don't deal with the deficit in a meaningful way, the debt will rise to epic, Greek proportions and the bond vigilantes will rise to push up interest rates. Interest as a percentage of government spending will rise, crowding out other government expenses or increasing the debt still further. Then we have a crisis where the bond market will force us to get the deficits under control. Health care will have to be slashed, tax increases will be brutal. Even Social Security is not untouchable in a crisis world. Means testing and spending freezes will be the rule of the day. Military cuts will be draconian. Our allies who depend on us for a defense shield will be disappointed. Education will be on the chopping block. The economy will be in Depression 2.0 with unemployment north of 15%.

This scenario has played over and over historically in various countries in ancient and modern times. While we may be the world's superpower, we are not immune to the laws of economic reality. In such a scenario, the Fed will try to monetize the debt with QE 3-4-5-6. What has been seen as normal economically will no longer be the reigning paradigm.

The US may have a couple years before the bond markets call the deficit hand, if they see a serious move to control the deficit. If not, a crucial point will be reached as we see a push-back on rates. Bond investors are going to be watching the slow-motion train wreck in Europe and Japan. It is one thing for tiny Greece to default, yet another for Japan to do so, which would spook the bond market. Overnight, the normal indulgence that a superpower and reserve-currency country like the US is accorded will become strained - Lehman Brothers on steroids.

Politicians may be forced to do the right thing because not doing so is such a horrific outcome. Winston Churchill said "You can always depend on the Americans to do the right thing, after they have exhausted all the other possibilities.", but this may no longer apply. Politicians on the right understand the severity of the problem but can't run on an austerity platform. Fixing our problems will mean spending cuts that will be excruciating. We have made bad economic choices as a country for decades, and now we have to take the medicine.

5 How Life Will Change

Collapse of the Middle Class

In political science one learns about the different kinds of social pyramids. The first pyramid is the basic society - a pyramid with two horizontal lines, dividing those on top (high social class) those in the middle (middle class) and the bottom of the pyramid (the poor, proletarian). The middle of the pyramid, the middle class, acts as a cushion between the rich and the poor, a buffer for social stress.

The second pyramid example has a big middle section, and represents 1st world countries in which the bottom is very thin and arrows show there is a possibility to go from low to middle class, and then from middle class to the top of the social pyramid. This is the classic, democratic capitalist society. In countries such as socialist European ones , the pyramid is similar but a little more fat, meaning that there is a big middle class section and smaller high and low class.

The third pyramid shows a communist society. Arrows from the low and middle class try to reach the top but bounce off the line. A small higher social class and one big lower social order, cushioned by a minimal middle class. Venezuela is the current Petri dish for this pyramid while Cuba has perfected the art. North Korea has reached the ultimate end point. Only the insane now ascribe to this model.

Unfortunately there is also a fourth pyramid. This one has arrows from the middle class dropping to the lower, poor class. This is a collapsing country, a country that turns into a 3rd world country where there is almost no middle class, one huge low, poor class, and a very small, very rich, top class. The arrows going from the middle to the bottom of the pyramid represent the middle class turning into poor. The income from the middle class is not enough to function as a middle class any more. Some from the top class fall to middle class, but the vast majority of the middle class turns into poor.

We now have in our own country a middle class that is suddenly confronted with becoming poor. They may not be confronted with third world poverty, but our middle class has suddenly discovered that they are either overqualified or unskilled for the few jobs they can find and settle for anything they can. Not only has unemployment sky rocketed, but take home pay has dropped and temporary jobs are displacing permanent jobs.

Just as disturbing is the generation gap: no matter how hard upcoming students study many are preparing for jobs they are not going to get. Eventually the number of students dropping out of college will increase as students either see no point in studying something that will not make much difference in their future salaries, or they have no money to keep themselves in college, or they simply have to drop college to work and support their families. Productive jobs have for two decades been outsourced to China or India, or are now taken by "undocumented workers".

Humans adapt when they have no other choice, but Americans are not now used to adversity. We haven't suffered through civil wars, dictators and dirty social wars since our own Civil War. Can we survive the coming collapse? Of course we can, it's just that many won't be prepared. Those are the ones who will be responsible for social unrest once the economic system flatlines; those that were too lazy to take care of themselves, or have gone soft believing that the government will "take care of them because they are tax payers". Those who don't adapt to the New Normal will die young and live unfulfilling lives.

You can avoid being a statistic by aggressively adapting your finances to the new environment.

A Different Mentality

A different mentality refers to thinking of a practical use for money, the money we used to throw away. We have become used to living in an affluent society. Once the overhanging world debt collapses, money is no longer measured in diversions and entertainment, but in terms of the necessary goods it can buy. Stuff like food, medicine, gas, or private medical care suddenly become very important. Spending 500 dollars on beauty products or a ball game no longer works.

Things may not get economically better for a long time – perhaps twenty years (see Japan's lost decades). But even though humans have a capacity to "get used to it" doesn't mean your own life can't get better even as the ship of welfare state takes on water.

Once you experience the lack of stuff you took for granted, like food or medicines, your priorities suddenly change. For example, say you have two wisdom tooth removed and you are prescribed antibiotics along with Hydrocodone for the pain. Now you take the antibiotics, but buy two boxes with the same prescription and keep one box just in case. You don't use the Hydrocodone, adding it to your pile of medicines.

Why? Because medicines may not always be available in a new price regulated world that will come from a nationalized health system – you may not be able to get drugs even if you have money to purchase them. Going without painkillers may hurt, but making sacrifices to ensure survival is the mentality you should have if you want to be prepared. The stuff that is "nice to have" has to be sacrificed to get what is indispensable.

Of course, there are things that are not "basic need stuff" that are important in other ways. Going to the hairdresser once every month or two fits in that category. It's not life or death, but it boosts morale. Buying a movie to watch won't burn a hole in your pocket. It is just that someone who can't survive a week without a credit card, doesn't have the mentality to survive Great Depression II. Addictions such as alcohol, drugs or even cigarettes should be avoided by the financial survivalist. Not only are they bad for your health and expensive, but they create an addiction to something that may not be available in the future. In short, you have to grow up, hunker down and cut out vices.

How Does Life Change In The New Normal?

Everything changes!

The streets will become more dangerous, thanks to general poverty. Education will suffer, in the worse case with kids working, or stealing to survive instead of going to school. Tools become expensive, as does food and housing. But you can thrive in your own micro-economy.

The self destructive economy created by the stupidity of our presidents and politicians, is a formula for disaster. After years of closing factories and the destruction of our national industry, with extremely low wages, people will get fed up, they will Go Galt. We are already suffering currency devaluation against the Canadian, Australian, Chinese and Russian currencies. The only reason we are doing well against the Euro is because the European Union is in even worse shape than we are, starting with the PIIGs (Portugal, Italy, Ireland, Greece and Spain) but extending throughout the entire socialized system.

Then comes the devaluation. What happens if one day the Secretary of the Treasury declares that no one can withdraw more than 100 bucks a day from the ATM, nor close out accounts? Imagine what your life will be like if you go to your local market and everything has gone up 200%. How will you survive with your pay check? Eventually, the sheep will get desperate. First, the banks won't return their money to people, then those with the lowest income will find out their salaries aren't high enough to buy the minimum food to survive. Banks would be destroyed by people who want their hard earned money back, FDIC or not. Supermarkets and shops will be looted, as well as regular homes. The chaos will spread all over the country, concentrated in the largest cities. Everything you need, from food and gas to TVs and refrigerators will rise in price, inaccessible for most people. Things you own and are part of your net worth, like cars and real estate will drop in value.

Impossible? Look at Argentina and its collapse. More recently, look at Greece, where there are accounts of the woods being stripped for firewood.

Food

Keep in mind that if society collapses, food will always be in your thoughts. If you don't have it you'll do ANYTHING to get it, and even if you are prepared you'll worry about being able to get more for the future. Once food prices rise between 200% and 300%, or food simply disappears from store shelves, you'll realize what a valuable commodity food really is.

To those that think that food will never be a problem in USA: visit a country like Argentina or Venezuela. Just after WWII Argentina practically fed Europe and was known in Europe as "the world's granary". Cattle and wheat production was enough to feed not only their own country but another continent. After the 2001 Argentinean crisis people in Buenos Aires, the capital city and the richest province, didn't realize how bad things actually were in the other provinces. This was until teachers noted that kids had problems with education - they had problems concentrating, fell asleep, and found it difficult to resolve mathematical equations. They later found out that this was due to malnutrition; kids were not receiving the minimum amount of nutrients for a healthy working body.

Will we see people eating out of trash cans in the United States? In the Third World every night entire families, wife, husband and 2 or 3 kids go through trash cans in search of food. At every stoplight dirty and skinny little bare foot kids are begging. It's one thing to see those terrible images of a little kid starving in Africa, but now imagine that that kid speaks English, with an American accent, and you see the Hollywood billboard in the background. Both cases are terrible, but the one that looks as if he could be your son and not some kid in Africa or Mexico hits a nerve. Because "those things don't happen here".

Because the entire world economy is now so fragile, it won't take much to cause sections of our country to go third world. It could be a hurricane, economic collapse, an earthquake or a meteor hitting earth, you need to be prepared for hard times because there will be little you can do once they arrive.

Monetary Theory

6 Physics of Money and Value

To secure your financial future in the New Normal, we need to do some foundation building and make sure you understand what money is. This is a much more elusive quantity than most people realize. Economists have a vested interest in confusing you because they get paid on the basis of consulting on a subject they make needlessly arcane. Politicians babble on endlessly about the Keynesian pump priming (legal counterfeiting) needed to keep full employment, though this makes no sense. Fortunately we have an alternative explanation of wealth based on physics that will give new insight into what constitutes money and value for even sophisticated readers.

One standard definition of Money is that it is any object or record generally accepted as payment for goods and services and repayment of debts within a country or other socio-economic context. The main functions of money are as:

- A medium of exchange; a unit of account
- A store of value
- A standard of deferred payment

Any kind of object or secure verifiable record that fulfills these functions can serve as money.

That is the standard definition, but what is important to you is not the preservation of money, but the preservation of *value*. Money itself is a human construct; even according to the standard definition it is dependent on the humans using it to give it definition within some economic context dependent on time and place. What we need if we are going to break free of the rhetorical manipulations of economists, the Federal Reserve, the bankers and politicians is to clear our heads of anthropocentric definitions of money and look to the solid foundations of physics which provide less subjective definitions of value. It turns out this isn't as hard as it might seem and rest assured that this will be more common sense than hard work. First, let's modify the standard definition of money by stating that:

Money is a method of measurement of value.

But what is value?

Value is the potential to do useful work.

You use money to make things happen. To move yourself into a house, to get food, to pay for heating and cooling your home. Physics and thermodynamics give us a way to understand what *useful work/value* is objectively rather than through the distorted lens of anthropocentric economic theories. There is no concept known as 'money' in physics, but there are measurements and laws which govern the fundamental units of the physical world, the real world in which you and I live and what is necessary to accomplish useful work.

While 'money' can be made worthless in the blink of an eye through human whim (through currency devaluation, or by changing the exchange rate of that preferred money, gold), the laws of physics are conservative, eternal and give us a more solid foundation. Bear with us through some science 101 so we can get to some underlying economic truths you will find nowhere else. We promise to translate the science into plain English quickly. There are two universal Laws of Physics that cannot be broken and provide physical relationships that must apply to any theory of money:

1) **First Law Conservation of Mass-Energy:** Matter and energy is neither created nor destroyed. Mathematically this is expressed as:

$$dM + dE = 0$$

(where M is the mass and E is the Energy). The little 'd', for those not mathematically inclined, is the symbolic way of saying differential change.

2) **Second Law of Entropy:** Within a closed system, order can only degrade (or stay the same for a reversible process) but not improve without an outside energy source.

$$dS >= dQ/T$$

(where **S** is the entropy, **Q** is the energy per mass and **T** is the reference temperature)

3) **Gibb's Free Energy Equation:** Nothing happens in the world without a negative change in Free Energy. This isn't a law, but really a mixture of the first two laws.

$$dG = dH - T\ dS$$

(Where **G** is Free Energy and is understood to mean energy that is free and available to do work, **H** is the enthalpy or internal energy, **T** is the reference temperature and **S** is the entropy)

Until we translate these formulas, the above will be confusing to the non-technically minded. Just keep in mind that the **G** term, Free Energy, is what is important and represents value both in the world of physics and in economics, *the ability to make things happen*! Now we need to translate these three physical concepts into plain English that you can understand. This will give you a common sense concept of value which will help you preserve your assets and income within an economic situation spiked with fraud and statistical noise generated by politicians with agendas, bankers creating money out of thin air and economists milking a job. Here are the same laws simplified:

1) **First Law:** Mass and Energy are valuable commodities that will always have some intrinsic value because they can't be destroyed. The prime example of this is gold, which is valued for its mass physical properties, rarity, density etc. Oil is another example, which has value both as mass (carbon and hydrogen) but more importantly as an energy source. Even bare dirt can have value as real estate. So the First Law of Physics is the first approximation we have to value (going back to the age old adoption of gold as a monetary standard and the definitions of real estate). But this First Law isn't sufficient to bring us into the modern age because we know most of our personal wealth is not tied up in gold or oil or even in physical commodities like bushels of corn. We know even solid physical assets like real estate can be devalued as they have been since the 2007 subprime crisis, so while the First Law is important it cannot be the sum total Law of Value; *we have to account for the information value of money*.

2) **Second Law:** the Law of Entropy and Disorder. It turns out that the Second Law of Physics, the law of entropy, is also the Law of Information because the opposite of disorder is order, or information. Negative entropy, negentropy, or order evolving systems are all different

expressions for information. We won't go into all the history of how information was tied to entropy through the field of statistics, other than to say there is a vast science called information theory based on this Second Law Thermodynamics.

The physics definition of entropy is at first confusing to laymen because it says in a nutshell that everything falls apart eventually. The way we get around the disorder predicted by the Second Law is to use the sun (or occasionally nuclear energy) to reverse the effects of decline. That's why trees grow in sunlight as energy is used to displace the disorder caused by cellular processes to the universe, turning disassociated dirt, water and CO_2 into complex plant tissue. That's also why we can use the power from electrical plants to run our computers and concentrate ever greater amounts of valuable information.

But you don't care about the physics of information or about growing trees, what you care about how this affects your portfolio and the value of money. What is important to notice is that the Second Law is an inequality. That is, $dS >= dQ/T$. What that means to you in a practical sense is that unlike a fixed element like gold, or a barrel of oil, the amount of information in a system is dynamic and relative. Information has no fixed value, and what value it does have tends to degrade with time. That means money can have both a fixed First Law mass/energy commodity component as well as a variable Second Law entropy informational component, both in varying proportions. It is the variability of the informational component that subjects your finances to the greatest risk of theft by the state.

Unfortunately and by political design our money is now for the most part pure information, fiat money, created from the ether. We barely even bother with flimsy paper money anymore, but rely on digital bits of information in bank computers and cyberspace. Our Federal Reserve created a half trillion dollar in currency to backstop European banks with a keystroke in 2011. Unlike commodity money, digital fiat money (information money) can appreciate, or depreciate, on the whims of the Federal Reserve and Central Banks as they 'print' more Greenbacks or Euros (though they often don't even bother to print bills anymore). Our money can also change value based on rumors and regulations – all disturbances in the 'informational' force.

In normal situations, when Central Banks aren't printing money to prop up failing sovereign debt and private banks, the market works out the informational value of money on a daily basis through free transactions, currency Fx markets and stock markets. However, intervention by politicians and central banks disrupts this value discovery process as they attempt to create money by fiat rather than through price discovery.

Our conundrum is that we know commodity money like gold, oil, real estate and even bushels of corn have value, but our bankers have convinced us that pure information in the form of digital accounting entries is real money in the modern age. So which type of money, commodity or informational, is right?

Well they both are, but to nail this down in terms of physics we need to explore the final relationship, which is sometimes called a third law.

3) **Gibb's Free Energy Equation**: also called by other names in chemistry and other fields. This states that no reaction occurs unless there is a negative change in the Free Energy of the system, defined as a change in the energy per unit mass plus the change in information content. This is something you haven't read in an economics book, but is critical to your financial understanding of inflationary processes. In essence, it is the addition of the first two laws:

*Nothing happens unless there is a negative change in the mass **and/or** energy **and/or** information of a system.*

Putting this in plain English, value is the ability to exchange some combination of physical commodity (gold), energy (oil) and/or information (perhaps an engine design, digital data, etc.) to make things happen. The negative change element is just a way of saying there has to be a profit margin, a cost. All we're doing here is formalizing what you knew intuitively already, but that bankers and politicians have tried to obscure by claiming they can pull levers in the financial markets to make prosperity magically appear.

Another way to say this is there is no free lunch; you have to expend resources, energy and brains to make things happen. It is the difficulty in pinning down the informational value component that makes things so slippery, and is why institutional thieves in the banks and governments would love you to believe that money has no physical component and that gold is worthless as a currency. We can demonstrate the concept that value can have a variety of physical and informational components quickly:

If you wanted to feel rich in these uncertain times, which would you rather have?

- $250,000 in the Treasury Bills drawing .25% interest, or
- $50,000 in cash, a paid off home, a basement of groceries, a bunker of heating oil, a book copyright and a small pile of gold, the total valued at the same $250,000?

Now, each individual situation is different, but what is clear is that the person who owned a mix of mass and energy commodities, information copyrights and cash could logically lay claim to having the same wealth as the person with just cash. Who is in reality better off is subjective (the subjective Second Law inequality relationship). But what we have just shown you is that your wealth can be a combination of Mass (like gold), Energy (fuel oil) and/or Information (a digital bank account). This is just a restatement in economics terms of the Gibb's Free Energy equation; you can make things happen if you have a gradient of wealth made of mass, energy and information that you can 'spend'. No big deal you may think, but it leads to a Eureka moment when it comes to the practical question of how to preserve your wealth.

Wealth is the ability to make things happen. It can be composed of elements of mass/energy, and elements of information. *The mass/energy elements of your wealth are relatively hard to steal, but the informational wealth in the form of fiat money and paper financial instruments can be stolen at the whim of government, by the Federal Reserve, or by digital thieves in a nanosecond.*

Which type of wealth would you rather have in uncertain times?

Flation

Now that we have a basic definition of what money is as a representation of wealth, both in terms of physics and economics, we can discuss how governments and central banks steal your wealth through various forms of monetary manipulation – or what we will call 'flation'. The information portion of monetary value, fiat money, is subject to manipulation and theft from a distance – it can be stolen without someone ever entering your safe. Since the Federal Reserve and other national banks are not fully regulated, and government debt is not easily constrained by requirements for balanced budgets (laws are ignored even when present), both bankers and politicians will gravitate towards stealing everything you have through various forms of inflation and deflation.

Governments around the world have gotten tricky with time, so now you need to know about multiple flavors of 'flation' to keep your head above water. In ancient times, coins would be clipped or metal debased to defraud the citizenry, but now one faces multiple forms of inflation, deflation, stagflation and biflation – all of which can negatively affect your financial health. The reason to understand this subject thoroughly is so that you can avoid at least some of the devastating consequences and not be impoverished by stealth fraud as the black hole welfare state implodes around us.

We have shown that money is a symbol of value and is a measure of the physical property called Free Energy, the ability to do useful work. That value is determined by the sum of the fixed mass-energy of a system plus the information content. So where do inflation and deflation come in? Time for some more basic math.

One way to look at the Gross National Product (GDP) of a country is given by the following equation:

GDP = M * V

This just says that the productive income of the nation can be measured by the amount of money in circulation times its velocity (the number of times that money turns over in economic transactions). So, if you have a $15 trillion GDP and say $1 trillion in currency, that would imply a velocity of 15 transactions per year for each dollar. So now the question is what happens when the Federal government, through its partner in crime the Federal Reserve, dumps another $X trillion into the system (as a sophisticated form of legalized counterfeiting).

Keynesian economists (the type favored by institutions and governments) will claim that through some magic multiplier affect money injection will cause an increase in GDP that is a multiple of the added money. Of course, you know from your personal experience of 2008 and 2009 and during later QEn stimulus that nothing of the sort happens. While no doubt some transitory jobs were created with bailout money, you just can't fool Mother Economic Nature. If you aren't providing new physical resources to the system, and you aren't providing quality new information (how would monopoly money improve the market knowledge base?), all you are doing is pushing on a string. You can't just create wealth out of thin air by snapping your fingers, though that is the essence of Keynesian theory.

If an economy is working at full capacity in a given environment (everyone is producing what they believe is prudent, not every useless item they might be tricked into producing), the GDP can be considered essentially a constant. Then additional money created by the Federal Reserve *may* end up as inflation, as most of us have been taught to expect. This is the classic case of more dollars chasing the same number of goods that most people are aware of, where sellers eventually wise up to the fact that they are not getting a fair deal with the new monopoly money and raise prices accordingly. But another result is also possible.

Trust is lost when people realize they are being presented with worthless script created out of the ether. This can result in a drastic *decrease in the velocity of money* as sellers refuse to do transactions based on what they expect will be a devalued currency. One manifestation of this effect in recent times is that although the banks have been flush with bailout money, they have been loath to lend to customers they believe unlikely to pay back loans on any terms. But the effect of lost faith in the currency happens at much smaller transaction levels as well, showing up in the fear of small businesses to add workers and increase wages, even though their particular business may be doing well.

This loss of trust in the currency leads to *deflationary* pressures throughout the economy as credit collapses, even at the same time there are classic inflationary pressures. The insidious part is that these 'flations' can cancel out in the official statistics, as product prices rise while wages and home prices (the essence of most people's assets) fall. So this leads to a new understanding of why one needs to view the economy as a raisin muffin filled with local pockets of inflation AND/OR deflation all caused by the Federal Reserve's multiple shell game operations which create money to paper over the Federal deficits. This is the essence of a Biflationary economy.

The reason this is so important to the individual is that it explains why both the inflationist and deflationist prognosticators over the last number of years have been so far off base. Because the equation GDP = M * V has two independent variables (M and V), predicting whether inflation or deflation will predominate is like pushing on a balloon. If the real production of goods and services is constant, if you increase M (money) you would get inflation, but just as likely you would get a decrease in velocity V and deflation, or some combination of the two.

That's why despite seemingly tame aggregate inflation numbers, consumers never see long term price declines. Your own pocketbook tells you the price of food, gasoline, clothing, energy, etc. have all increased, but these increases are nulled out in the government statistics. We are all painfully aware of decreases in the value of assets like 401ks and homes. Real wages declined nearly 10% between 2001 and 2011. So, it is obvious just through casual observation that what we have currently is **biflation** instead of inflation or deflation. Biflation is a state of the economy where ***inflation and deflation occur simultaneously***.

The price increase of commodities is caused by the increased money flow (via loose monetary policy) chasing them. On the other hand, the growth of the economy is tempered with high unemployment and decreasing purchasing power. This has resulted in a greater amount of money directed toward essential items (inflation) and away from non-essential items and things requiring credit to buy such as houses and used cars (deflation).

7 Biflationary Misery Index

Given the fact that the state of the economy is masked during our Biflationary era by deflationary statistics canceling out inflationary increases, what is needed is a new Biflationary Misery Index akin to the Misery Index that was popularly quoted during the Carter years. First some historical background.

Stagflation Misery Index

In economics, stagflation is a situation in which the inflation rate is high and the economic growth rate is low leading to high unemployment. It raises a dilemma for economic policy since actions designed to lower inflation may worsen economic growth and vice versa. The term stagflation is generally attributed to British politician Iain Macleod, who coined the phrase in his speech to Parliament in 1965. The following chart shows recent estimates worldwide.

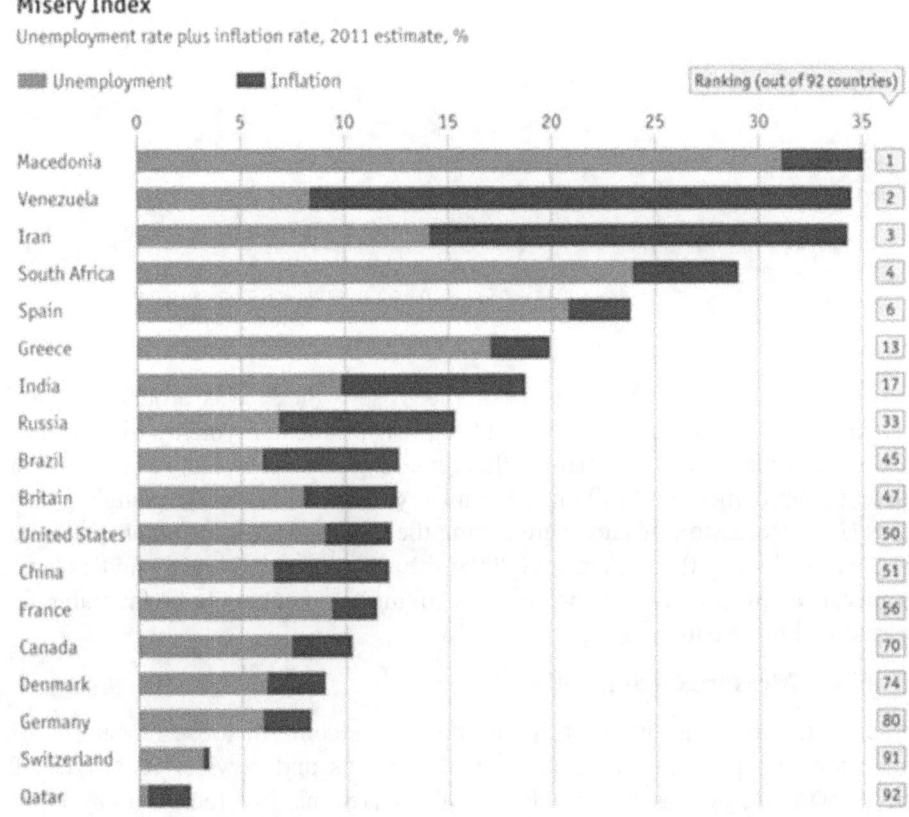

In Keynesian postwar macroeconomic theory, inflation and recession were regarded as mutually exclusive. Anomalous stagflation has thus proven very costly to eradicate once it starts, both in human terms as well as budget deficits, because it is outside standard Keynesian theory.

The most notable example of inflation fighting is in the early 1980s when Paul Volker, with Ronald Reagan's blessing, allowed interest rates to climb above 15% to successfully reduce inflationary pressures.

In fact, Reagan had come to power in part because of the political impact of one measure of stagflation termed the Misery Index. Derived by the simple addition of the inflation rate to the unemployment rate, the Misery Index reached 21% under President Carter and was used to swing the presidential elections in the United States in 1980.

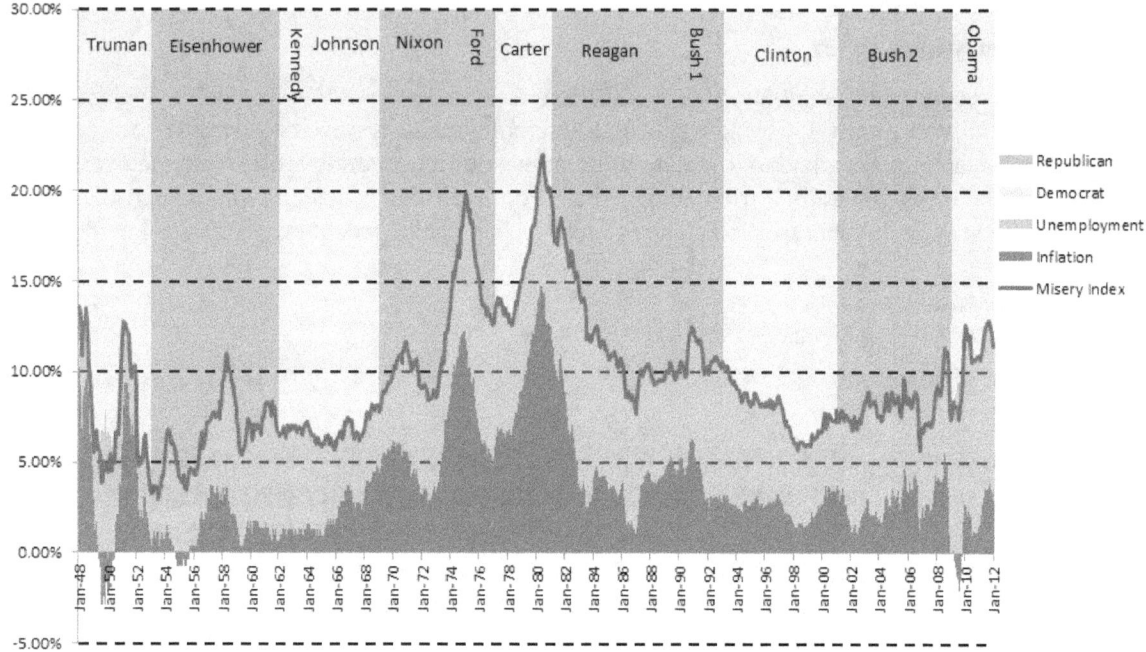

As shown above, the 2012 value of the Misery Index was around 12% using current official estimates of low inflation (~3%) and improving unemployment (~7.5%). Not much has changed since 2012 and we will remain in this rut a long time. However, using pre-1980 formulas to calculate unemployment and inflation, the misery index has reached as high as 25% since the start of this Great Recession (what we are calling the Biflationary Depression). Despite showing a worsening Misery Index after the crash of 2008, the above chart obviously understates our current problems because government statisticians are cooking the numbers to be favorable to continuing spending and Fed intervention.

Misery Index Is Measure Of Stagflation

Stagflation, not pure inflation, is the normal outcome of loose monetary policy. At the same time monetary pumping increases prices of goods and services it weakens the pace of economic growth and decreases the velocity of transactions. For loose money policy to work, people would need to be fooled into thinking any increase in money was the same as prosperity, but that game soon wears thin. The creation of new money ex nihilo (out of nothing) benefits the creators and early recipients of the new money relative to late recipients. Money creation is not wealth creation; it merely allows early money recipients to outbid late recipients for resources, goods, and services. Since the actual producers of wealth are typically late recipients, increasing the money supply weakens wealth formation and undermines the rate of economic growth. Of course that is exactly the plan our Federal Reserve has been following and the only surprise is that anyone is surprised that stagflation has been the result

An increase in the money supply rate of growth coupled with a slowdown in the rate of growth of goods increases the rate of price inflation (especially necessaries like fuel and food) while causing a decline in the rate of growth in the production of goods leading to unemployment. This fits the standard definition of stagflation, i.e., an increase in price inflation and a fall in real economic growth. But clearly the summation of inflation plus unemployment does not capture the full extent of the economic chaos which also includes depreciation of assets and the lowering of wages.

Thus the stagflation Misery Index model breaks down because loose money also leads us to experience massive deflation from credit collapse, most notably in housing and other malallocation of resources. This leads to the need for a new index.

Biflationary Misery Index

What is needed is a Biflationary Misery Index which builds on the earlier stagflation misery index but isn't quite as susceptible to political manipulation.

The Stagflation Misery Index (SMI) was a function of unemployment + inflation, which we can write as:

$$SMI = U3 + I$$

The first enhancement we can make is to change from the unemployment rate, which is grossly distorted by the lack of reporting of those who have been discouraged, to either the broader U6 numbers or better still the employment participation rate. Even the U6 broad unemployment numbers are subject to manipulation by government statisticians, so our preference would be to use the participation numbers, as shown below.

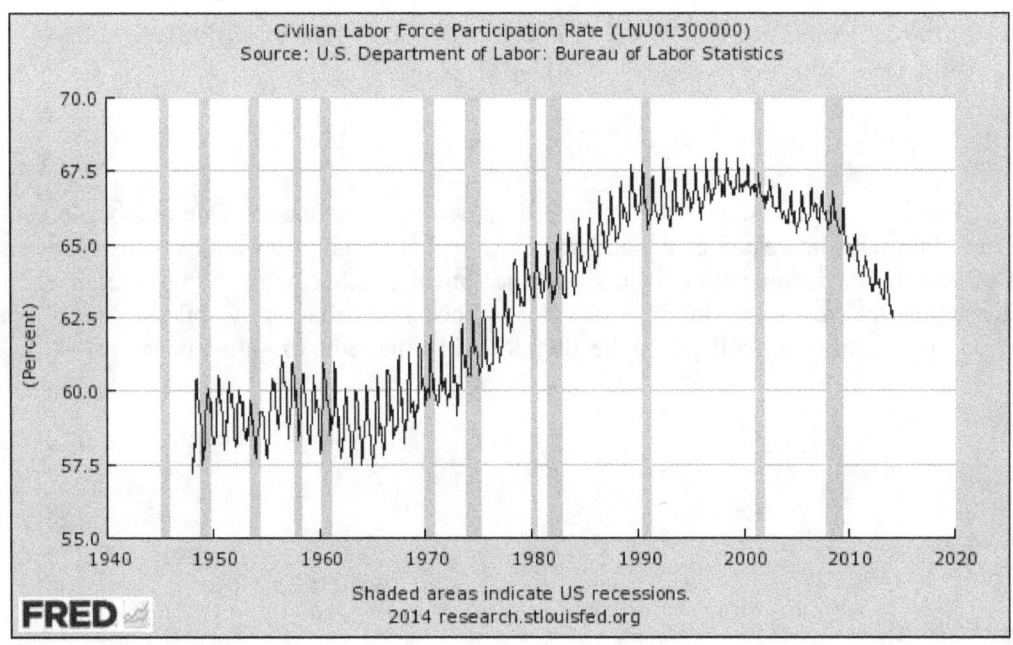

Civilian Labor Force Participation Rate (LNU01300000)
Source: U.S. Department of Labor: Bureau of Labor Statistics

Shaded areas indicate US recessions.
2014 research.stlouisfed.org

A second improvement is to change from the Consumer Price Index as the measure of inflation to changes in the price of gold. While gold is admittedly subject to price speculation and changes in production, it can't be manipulated by government selection of index numbers nor by the substitution effects that plague the CPI. It peaked in 2012, dropped, but is now returning to a long tem appreciation trend as fiat money is debased.

Third we need a number that reflects deflation in the economy. One number to consider might be short term interest rates which have been kept artificially low and actually represent the theft of wealth and income from savers. Another broad number might be changes in the Case Schiller residential real estate index which clearly shows an inflationary spike in housing prices followed by a deflationary collapse in the 2000 to 2011 timeframe (biflation in action).

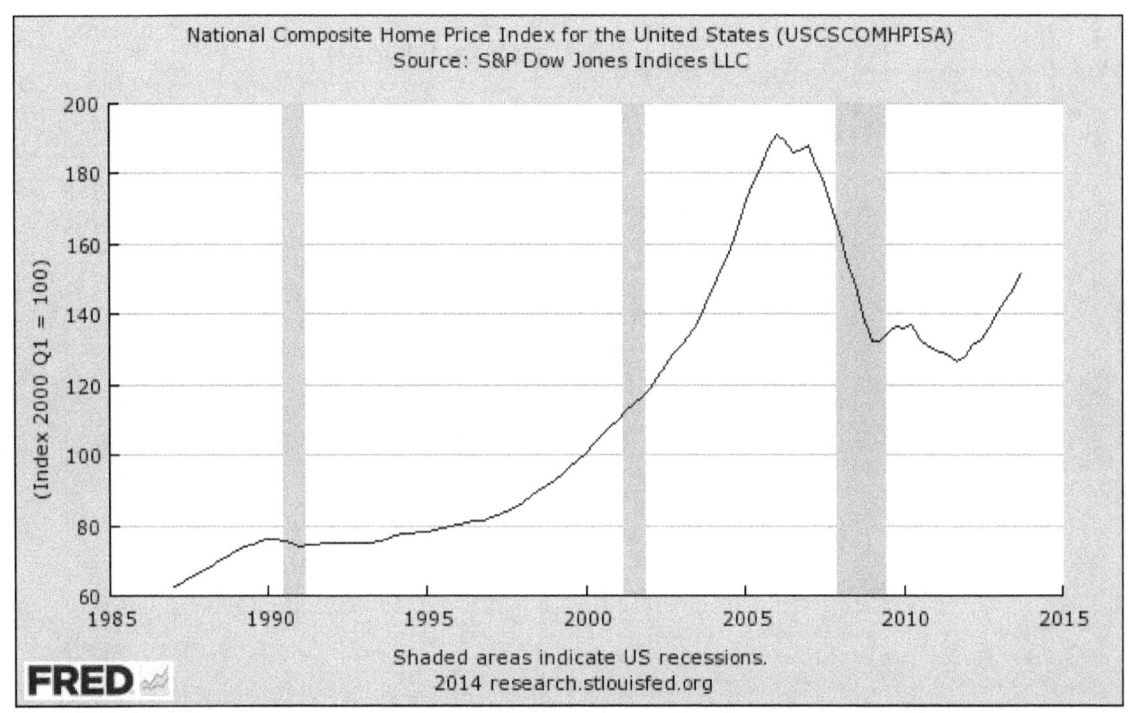

National Composite Home Price Index for the United States (USCSCOMHPISA)
Source: S&P Dow Jones Indices LLC

Shaded areas indicate US recessions.
2014 research.stlouisfed.org

The end result after some manipulation is a Biflationary Misery Index, as presented in the following chart. We are leaving some of the math unresolved for the reader on purpose because they involve proprietary methods. We will however be publishing our Biflationary Misery Index with regular updates on our website at:

www.futurnamics.com/biflationindex.php

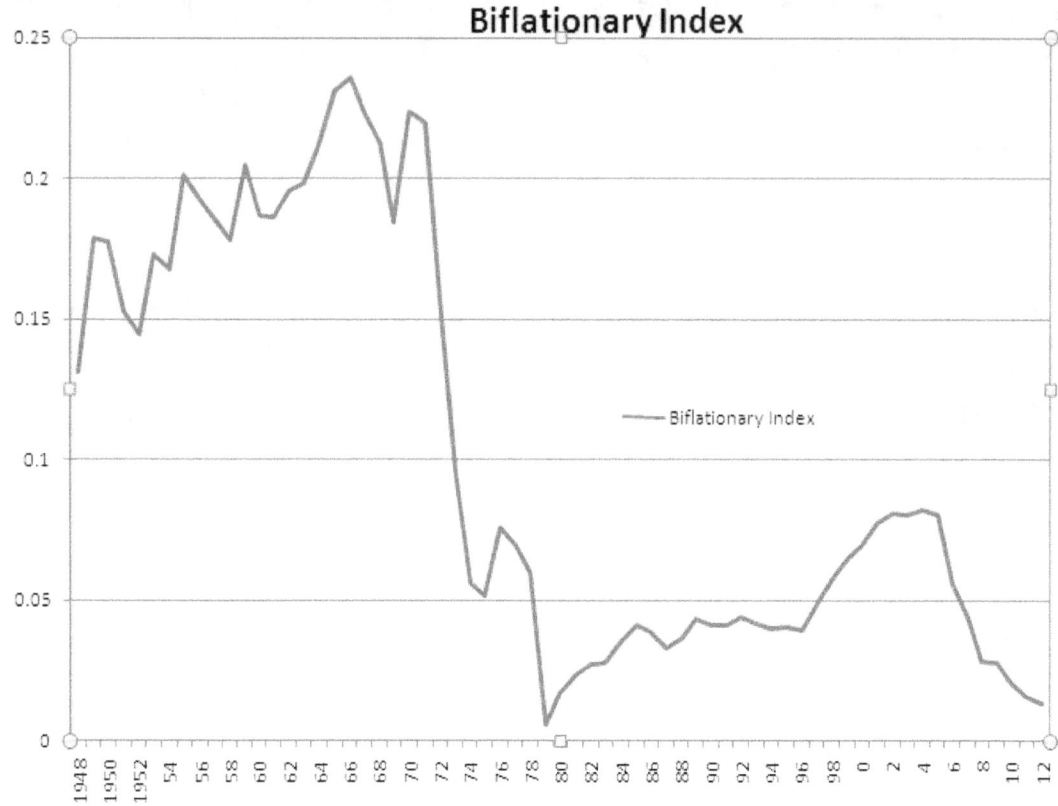

Biflationary Index

The most important thing to note about this chart is that it predicted the current economic collapse to have started in 2005, well before most economists thought we were in trouble. The older Misery Index was ramping up in this period but wasn't predictive of the size of the slump.

The second thing to note is that while we seem to be headed towards a bottom at the beginning of 2014, the end is not yet in sight. We devote a number of the following chapters to showing you how to weather this deep Biflationary Depression. However, this chart alone should give you confidence that you need to move to a biflationary model of investing. The unemployment and inflation numbers published by the government and which make up the traditional Misery Index are clearly incapable of giving you a usable financial direction.

8 Stagflation Biflation Inflation Deflation

Bluntly, your government is trying to steal your livelihood. Where the theft comes in is that instead of sending you a bill for services (taxes), it instead just inflates (or deflates) away the value of what you own. They have gotten tricky with time, so now you need to know about all the flavors of 'flation' to keep your financial head above water.

Despite the seemingly tame headline CPI inflation numbers, consumers never see long term price declines in food, energy, education and health. However home values (most people's nest egg) and wages are deflating. So, it is pretty obvious what we have here--**biflation**--instead of simple inflation or deflation. Biflation is a state of the economy where **inflation and deflation occur simultaneously**.

The increased price of commodities is caused by increased money flow due to loose monetary policy and fiat dollars chasing them. On the other hand, the growth of the economy is tempered with high unemployment and decreasing purchasing power. This results in a greater amount of money directed toward essential items (inflation) and away from non-essential items and things that required credit to buy such as a house and cars (deflation).

Keynesian Stagflation

In economics, stagflation is defined as a situation in which the inflation rate is high and the economic growth rate is low. It raises a dilemma for economic policy since actions designed to lower inflation may worsen economic growth and vice versa. The term stagflation is generally attributed to British politician Iain Macleod, who coined the phrase in his speech to Parliament in 1965. In neo-Keynesian postwar macroeconomic theory, inflation and recession were regarded as mutually exclusive.

Stagflation has proven very costly to eradicate once it starts, both in human terms as well as budget deficits. A notable example is the early 1980s when Paul Volker, with Ronald Reagan's blessing, allowed interest rates to climb above 15% to successfully reduce inflationary pressures. In fact, Reagan had come to power in part because of the political impact of the measure of stagflation termed the Misery Index. Derived by the simple addition of the inflation rate to the unemployment rate, the Misery Index reached 21% under President Carter and was used to swing presidential elections in the United States in 1980. The 2011 value of the Misery Index using pre-1980 formulas to calculate unemployment and inflation, reached 25%.

Adherents to the Austrian School maintain that creation of new money ex nihilo (out of nothing) benefits the creators and early recipients of the new money relative to late recipients. Money creation is not wealth creation; it merely allows early money recipients to outbid late recipients for resources, goods, and services. Since the actual producers of wealth are typically late recipients, increasing the money supply weakens wealth formation and undermines the rate of economic growth.

An increase in the money supply rate of growth coupled with a slowdown in the rate of growth of goods increases the rate of price inflation by definition. What we have currently is a fast increase in price inflation (especially fuel and food) and a decline in the rate of growth in the production of goods leading to unemployment. This is the definition of stagflation, i.e., an increase in price inflation and a fall in real economic growth and employment. But stagflation is an obsolete Keynesian concept because what we are also experiencing is a deflationary collapse of wages and assets making stagflation a subset of much worse biflationary depression.

Stagflation is the normal outcome of loose Keynesian monetary policy, not an anomaly. Stagflation is the natural result of monetary pumping which weakens the pace of economic growth and at the same time raises the rate of increase of the prices of goods and services. For loose money policy to work, people would need to be perpetually fooled into thinking the increase in money was the same as prosperity, but that game soon wears thin. Where the stagflation model breaks down is that loose money has also led us to experience massive deflation from credit collapse, most notably in housing (inflation + deflation). As people lose faith in the currency, they stop spending and giving credit. This leads to a refinement in terms called biflation.

Biflation

Biflation (sometimes mixflation or even screwflation) is when the economy experiences both inflation and deflation simultaneously. The term differs from stagflation in which there is low growth with inflation alone, and thus is outside traditional economic analysis. The concept of Biflation was first introduced by Senior Financial Analyst Dr. F. Osborne Brown, of the Phoenix Investment Group.

During Biflation, there's a rise in the price of commodity/earnings-based assets (inflation) and a simultaneous fall in the price of debt-based assets (deflation). Insidiously, this is what the Federal Reserve is shooting for with its loose money policies because it:

1) Bails out banking interests and Wall Street by inflating asset prices. It also bails out the Federal government by providing free money beyond tax revenues.

2) Screws Main Street and individuals by devaluing the currency, devaluing their wages, devaluing personal assets like homes awhile conversely inflating the cost of food and energy essentials.

The inflationary aspect of biflation comes when an over-abundance of money is injected into the economy by the central bank. Since essential commodity-based assets (food, energy, clothing) remain in high demand because they are the basis for survival, their price rises with the increased volume of money chasing them. The increasing cost of purchasing essential assets is the price-inflationary arm of Biflation.

The deflationary aspect of biflation comes because the economy is tempered by increasing unemployment, decreasing purchasing power and the decreased velocity of money. Bluntly, no one trusts anyone else in business transactions because of bankruptcies and institutional fraud normalized by the government. As a result, money is directed toward buying essential items and directed away from buying non-essential items. Debt-based assets (homes, high-end automobiles and other typically debt based assets) become less essential and increasingly fall into lower demand. Consequently, their prices fall due to a decreased volume of money chasing them. Decreasing costs to purchase non-essential assets is the price-deflationary mechanism of biflation.

Biflation Is Worst Of All Worlds

If you were a statist government and you wanted to crush a rebellion of the lower classes, certainly you would employ Biflation as a weapon of war. It allows you to support the bureaucracy and the bankers and corporatist hangers on who milk government contracts, while simultaneously economically crushing those civilians leading the rebellion. As such it is a modern siege tactic, somewhat akin to poisoning wells and food supplies as performed by our ancestors.

Since geographic boundaries have been supplanted by ideological and political boundaries of the state in this age of the Internet and Social networking, Biflation acts as a much more effective economic weapon than burning food supplies and polluting the drinking water; it is sort of the neutron bomb of destructive economic policy.

Don't expect this biflationary period to blow over anytime soon. U.S. debt levels are so astronomical that the Federal Reserve cannot increase interest rates without collapsing our system because of the increased interest payment that would be needed to service this debt. Loose money guarantees inflation, but it also induces debilitating deflation as businesses realize the game is fixed and transactions grind to a halt. Loose monetary policy is the only option left, but it guarantees a slowing economy as money velocity falls.

Consequently, you couldn't pick a better weapon of war than biflation to demoralize a population and crush its economic base; it is better than even bombing the industrial structure of a country. If the Federal Reserve and President don't know this, they are idiots. If they do know they obviously are at war with the people they are supposed to protect.

9 Money In A Collapse

In today's Western economies, "Banking" has degenerated into a monopoly-distribution point for disseminating of fiat currency. The situation is incredibly destructive, ruinous and benefits only people who are the most direct beneficiaries of central bank funding stream. Central banks have to distribute money through private banks because the alternative – simply distributing it to people – would reveal the scam for what it is. Filtering money-printed-from-nothing through banks gives the process a mysterious quality and renders it more complex, which is necessary when one is promoting a Ponzi scheme.

Given that the Federal Reserve's money printing process, coupled with profligate government spending, has lead us to worldwide financial ruin, your survival depends on your ability to make an end run around the monetary system. This can be done in a number of ways, the most obvious being through owning precious metals, but also through barter and investment strategies that focus on commodities and self investment. But first, you need to understand just how fragile the current monetary system is.

Who Really Has Money? Most people currently thought of as wealthy have their wealth tied up in credit-related investments of one kind or another—the stock market, bonds, CD's, real estate, etc. Few people keep piles of cash around because there's been no need for large stacks of bills to consummate transactions in a long time (unless you are a drug dealer). All these currently wealthy people could suddenly become poor if a financial tsunami were to hit. This doesn't mean metaphorically poor, it means freezing, starving poor, broke, destitute. All their resources will be in the wrong form for the new conditions. Survival after a national disaster; requires cash. Only those with cash will be wealthy.

Wouldn't the government simply print paper money to replace electronic money if there were a financial run on the banks? The answer is that is simply impossible. The presses at the Bureau of Engraving and Printing run at capacity 24 hours a day just to replace the paper money that wears out each year. To replace just the paper currency currently circulating would take years at the current BEP printing capacity. It would take decades to replace the entire $1 trillion in what is called the M0 money supply.

Cash For Survival The answer to the money dilemma is a simple one: Have Cash—coins and green pieces of paper with pictures of dead presidents on them. Convert at least some of your credit investments and electronic forms of money into cash. If you have cash after an economic Armageddon, you will be one of the few wealthy people in your neighborhood. Those with cash will not only survive disastrous times, but will be able to use that cash to build a prosperous future. But be warned: you must keep a low profile both now and in the future because times have changed. You want to attract as little attention as possible, both while you convert to cash and later when you use your cash, for two different but equally vital reasons.

First, awhile you have every right to convert all investments and savings into cash, doing so will invite the attention of the government. DEA agents may think you're some kind of drug dealer. Drug laws are so powerful regarding confiscation of suspected drug dealers' assets that you could find yourself in a protracted legal battle to get back perfectly legitimate money that belongs to you. But also be aware that the government is so broke it must eventually confiscate even legitimate wealth (see Cyprus as an example of what can happen). You want to avoid attracting the attention of bank tellers or branch managers who might report to the DEA or other agencies that you are withdrawing large sums of cash.

Secondly, when everyone is impoverished and hungry, it's prudent to keep your wealth out of sight. A desperate man will go to extremes to feed his family and keep them sheltered and warm; a hungry man will do whatever is necessary to procure food. Someone who flashes wads of cash is courting danger. Keep cash in smaller denominations of tens and twenties and a few fifties. If you receive any crisp new bills, stop off at a convenience store and buy a candy bar, hand the clerk a new bill and receive older, worn bills in change. Anyone with brand new currency invites envy as a hoarder and can become a target for thieves. You want to avoid attracting attention to yourself both now and in the future. After a disaster, you will need ones and fives, but cashing a large check and asking for a lot of small bills is too conspicuous.

Gold And Silver Gold and silver coins are real money, based on their standard precious metal content; they have always been a historical refuge in times of crisis. Because of increased public awareness about possible disasters, gold and silver coins have become more desirable, as evidenced by all the advertisements by people who want to buy your gold jewelry. You are not interested in numismatic collectible coins; you're only interested in gold and silver coins for their precious metal content. Perhaps the cheapest way to hold silver coins is by buying junk silver dimes and quarters minted pre-1965.

It is impossible to predict the value ratio of silver coins to copper-clad coins after a disaster (our currently circulating ones), but silver coins will undoubtedly be worth considerably more than clads. You pay a higher premium for silver dollars than you do for silver dimes and quarters, but it would be wise to have some silver dollars on hand as part of any survival plan. Siler dollars are bigger and more impressive looking than dimes and quarters. Even though a silver dollar generally has the same metal content as ten silver dimes or four silver quarters, it simply looks more valuable. One alternative is new American Silver Eagles which are current pure Silver coins manufactured by the US Mint. Though not common in circulation, they are worth far more than their face value and are legal tender.

The most desirable and valuable form of real, hard money is Gold coins. The reasons are multiple:
- Gold is scarce
- Gold does not rust or corrode
- Gold is beautiful to look at,
- Gold is highly desirable as jewelry
- Gold has industrial uses
- Gold has a long, long monetary history in many cultures worldwide.

Gold is the real deal. Currently the price of gold is higher than it's been for 25 years, even though there have been retrenchments. The rise in Gold prices is a warning that inflation is on the way (Inflation or the threat of inflation causes an immediate rise in the price of gold). American coins in one oz., 1/2 oz., 1/4 oz. and 1/10 oz. denominations are the best gold coins to own. People have no experience with real gold money and they will probably more readily accept U.S. gold coins than foreign coins. The U.S. 1 oz. Liberty coin is somewhat more expensive to buy than South African Kruger Rands,.it is easier to move the American coins when you exchange your gold to spend. Buy more 1/10 oz. coins than 1/4 oz. coins, and more 1/4 oz. coins than 1/2 oz. coins because smaller denomination gold coins are preferred.

For its size and weight, gold is an immense store of value but you can't take a one oz. gold coin to a local flea market or general store and buy loaves of bread and cheese. How will the store owner make change for such a high value coin? Instead, that's when you use the fraying fiat paper money, followed by clad coins, then silver coins before you exchange any gold. A small gold coin will be of far greater use even on large purchases than a larger one. Purchase major items with your 1 oz. gold coins.

Every pawnbroker wants to buy gold! "I buy gold. Pay cash" signs are everywhere! Most of those buyers deal with junk gold, like jewelry, either stolen or being sold because the owner needs the money, not the gold coins that investors talk about. Be forewarned, no dealer pays the true value of junk gold, unlike people buying gold coins or bullion.

Small shops and dealers will pay for gold as regular jewelry when they can since it is impossible to determine the true mineral percentage of gold, Besides gold coins, buy small gold rings and other jewelry which are less expensive than gold coins. That way you won't be losing money selling premium quality gold coins for the price of junk gold. Buy a small bag worth of gold rings. Small time thieves will snatch gold chains right off of your neck and sell them at these small dealers found everywhere. This will become common at train stations, subways and other crowded areas.

Coins You also need regular coins. Gold and silver are useful during the rebuilding stage after a financial crisis, but dimes and quarters, nickels and pennies will always be the most easily traded money even in difficult times. A financial crash creates massive deflation making real hard money far more valuable. A loaf of bread that now costs $1.25 may cost 5 cents after a deflationary depression, assuming there's any bread to be had. People are completely used to ordinary pocket change coins, so that's what they will most readily accept for local transactions—and nearly all transactions will be local after a major national disaster. Start saving a coin stash. Take a few $20 bills to a bank in which you do not have an account once a month to trade them for rolls of quarters or dollar coins. Most bank exchange paper for coins without question.

Storing Cash Now that you have some spendable currency, you need to find a safe place to hide it. First, tell no one that you have a load of cash, except possibly your spouse, and don't tell your spouse unless absolutely certain of the strength of your marriage. Hard times drive people to do things they would not ordinarily do, and if the economic hammer hits hard enough, these may be the hardest times in our country's history. If your spouse is fully trustworthy, consider yourself fortunate and keep no secrets; otherwise, be careful. Money spent on that loser brother-in-law can come back to haunt you in multiple ways.

If you plan to hide your cash somewhere in your house, you want to make sure to protect it from fire, so go to a Wal-Mart or discount store and buy a fireproof storage box, usually available for under $40. It will protect your cash from burning for a half hour of direct flame. Store paper money, gold and silver in the box. If and buy another bos if you fill the first one up. Change electronic credit wealth into cash, gold and silver so your money is fully under your control. In hard times, hard money will always be there for you as long as you keep it safe.

Barter Another way to get around the money problem is through barter. Barter is a means of exchange in which goods or services are directly traded for other goods or services without an intermediary medium such as money. It is usually bidirectional, but may be multilateral. Barter usually runs parallel to monetary systems even in developed countries, though to a limited extent. However, in times of monetary crisis barter replaces money as the method of exchange as a last resort, when fiat currency is unstable and devalued by hyperinflation.

An increasingly prevalent informal bartering system is Swapping, in which Internet communities trade items of comparable value on a trust basis. A disadvantage of electronic barter is the lack of trust in Internet commerce. Consumers have limited guarantees they will receive what they bargained or paid for. Although the Internet based consumer market has demonstrated that it works, there is never a guarantee of satisfaction in consumer to consumer transactions and no absolute defense against fraud. However, when a person barters there is less incentive to deliberately mislead. Neither party is paid cash in a barter transaction; each party receives something that may never be converted to cash.

In the United States, the sales a barter exchange makes are considered taxable revenue by the IRS. The gross amount of a barter exchange member's sales are reported via a 1099-B form to the IRS. Barter exchanges are required to report members sales by the Tax Equity & Fair Responsibility Act of 1982. According to IRS regulations, "The fair market value of goods and services exchanged must be included in the income of both parties."

Because barter is taxable, it is unlikely to play as large a part in economic survival-plans as one might assume. More likely will be grey and black markets.

MOVING MONEY TO OTHER COUNTRIES

While gold is a great store of value, you can't barter it at a supermarket because you would lose too much money as an exchange premium. You could wait until things settle down and change your gold for Dollars/Euros or whatever stable paper money is left standing and save yourself from devaluation. But in the end, you may have to get out of Dodge with your gold and deposit it in a safe country. Foreign accounts should be safe since they are protected by another country's law and aren't affected by national executive orders.

But beware, it is not currently easy to move investment size amounts of money out of the United States, and the situation will only get worse. Nations to consider are:

Canada	**Singapore**	**Sweden**
Australia	**South Korea**	**Chile**
New Zealand	**Norway**	

Make sure to understand that such transactions don't happen over night because foreign banks are now wary of coming into conflict with US taxation, money laundering and banking laws. So getting out of Dodge will take time and effort because the Federal government doesn't want you to leave, it needs you to stay here so it can help prop up the collapsing Federal government welfare state and our devalued currency.

10   The Fed &Monetary Collapse

US tax receipts have been running at 57 percent or less of outlays since 2011 and are unlikely to recover anytime soon. This obviously cannot be supported long term except through the printing of money, enabled by the Federal Reserve. The active destruction of a country's currency for political motive creates an underclass of have-nots by stealth confiscation of working-class assets while protecting the bankers and Wall Street. Thus you need to know how the Fed became the engine for the destruction of American wealth for you to avoid being sucked into the suicidal financial consequences.

The Federal Reserve is a wealth transfer machine designed to skim wealth from the productive many to transfer it to the parasitic few.

We have reached a unique junction of American history: the confluence of Big Lie economic propaganda, neo-feudalism and the worship of false financial gods. Corporate media and the Central State have combined to perfect Orwell's nightmare vision of centralized media and a fascist centralized State which turn lies into self-serving "truth."

The Federal Reserve is expected to "save" this crumbling, exploitative Status Quo. The propaganda machine would have us believe that the Federal Reserve, the privately owned central bank of the U.S., has "saved" the Status Quo from financial ruin on numerous occasions by "smoothing out" the business cycle (credit expands and contracts) and by "stimulating aggregate demand" by lowering interest rates and pumping money into the economy (quantitative easing).

We are constantly prompted to worship the Federal Reserve's supposedly god-like powers to rescue a corrupt and venal Status Quo from the black hole of recession and collapse. But the Fed has no ability to add positive information to the financial system, unless you assume they have god like powers of analysis unavailable to the rest of the market.

The Fed is the "enforcer" of neo-feudalism in America: the feudal Lords of Finance control the for-sale political system and skim tribute from the 99.5% toiling in the fields below their castles. The Fed enforces this parasitic transfer of wealth by manipulating interest rates to enrich the banks and provides "free money" to the Financial Lords which they then use to buy assets and lend at interest.

Parasitic Money Creation

The mechanisms of the Fed's parasitic transfer of wealth are well-known. For example, the Fed "loans" money to the Feudal Bank Lords at 0% interest. The Lords then loan this free money out to peasants, students and other debt-serfs at high rates of interest. The interest lenders "earned," courtesy of the parasitic Fed, is theirs to keep.

If the banks can't find enough debt-serfs who can pay more interest, they can always deposit the free money back at the Fed and earn interest from the Fed itself.

Another example: the Fed "loans" free money (0% interest) to the major banks, who then buy low-risk long-term U.S. Treasury bonds paying 3%. When these crony bankers spot a better skimming opportunity, they sell the bonds to the Fed, who buys the bonds as part of its "Operation Twist" or other Qualitative Easing program.

Peasants who have arduously saved up capital (cash) earn next to nothing as a result of Fed policy, but the Fed ensures Feudal Bank Lords earn a guaranteed return on money they have obtained for free. The suppression of interest income to near-zero (a negative return once inflation is factored in) is a massive transfer of wealth from savers to Fed-backed speculator and banks.

As a direct and intentional result of the Fed's quantitative easing, huge sums of "free money" slosh into the "risk-on" stock market, where the money provides liquidity for the investment bank's high-frequency trading (HFT) skimming operations. The losers are the peasants who have been locked into 401K plans that divert their earnings into the stock market, where HFT can skim billions from the 401K plans.

The Fed guarantees the Bank Lords free money, and also supports their speculative bets in the stock market. Whenever the market threatens to swoon, the Fed intervenes to manipulate the market up to levels where the High Frequency Trading automaton machines will trigger momentum buying.

A power center that enables and enforces neofeudal exploitation and predation can only be called evil and the Federal Reserve must eventually be abolished, though it would be unwise to count on this anytime soon. Its purpose--enabling and enforcing a neofeudal transfer of wealth from the productive many to the unproductive, parasitic few--is evil.

Un-tethering the monetary system from the checks and balances of loss has much greater negative impacts than on the core financial system. The loss of trust in the financial markets leads to a society and culture that loses its moral compass. A culture of greed, self-serving lies and corrupt vested interests grows as manipulation of the system becomes the proven way to success. No one has gone to jail in the real estate collapse (despite massive mortgage fraud), nor in the banking and derivatives scandals.

Anyone daring to label the widely worshipped Federal Reserve as a false god, a purveyor and enforcer of predation and exploitation, will also be mocked by "sophisticates" of finance who depend on the neofeudal skimming, exploitation and lies for their share of the spoils. Their survival demands obedience to the Fed's godlike power to skim from the many and distribute to the few.

Since the banks are among the few, they will do anything for their Master, the Federal Reserve, for it has the power they worship: the power to transfer vast wealth from the productive many to the parasitic few.

Should we be surprised that sycophants in the media, academia, politics and finance support the evil that enables their own predation and exploitation? Of course not, for self-service and self-justification are natural. What is unnatural is believing that this Ponzi scheme can continue indefinitely.

The Federal Reserve Is The Problem, Not The Solution

Central banking has always been characterized by mystique. The central bank elders have cultivated the impression they have god-like omnipotence. There was a time when the Fed didn't bother to announce its policy decisions at all – not letting the public know was very much a part of its modus operandi. The central bank portrayed itself as a Delphic oracle, dispensing judgments and interventions it claimed were necessary for the very survival of the nation. Lesser mortals were invited to believe in the wisdom of these judgments, but they were not allowed to understand them. The Federal Reserve dominates the field of economics through its extensive network of consultants, visiting scholars, alumni and staff economists, so real criticism of the central bank is a career liability for economics professionals.

Alan Greenspan, Fed chairman from 1987 to 2006, may have been speaking with his tongue in his cheek when he said, "if I turn out to be particularly clear, you've probably misunderstood what I've said",

So don't count on the Federal Reserve to fix America's financial problems - THEY ARE THE PROBLEM. The Fed has had a conflict of interest with that of U.S. citizens since their inception in 1913. The Federal Reserve System is not federal, it has zero reserves and it is not a system. Their deceptive name hides the fact they are a privately owned, central bank, with no reserves. They are not a part of the Federal government and Congress has as little control over them as it does of Federal Express. The Federal Reserve is a privately owned corporation, a private banking cartel who has a total monopoly on "creating" money for the U.S. government.

The average person believes the Fed is an agency of the U.S. government that stabilizes our economy by controlling interest rates and providing liquidity when in times of crisis. In practice, the Fed "creates" money and then loans it to our government. In practice, the Fed actually exchanges money for U.S. bonds, which creates a perpetual cycle of national debt. This creation of money from thin air is a way to "monetize the debt," that is, to pay for government spending in excess of tax receipts through inflation. While this may avoid raising visible taxes, it is a stealth tax none the less which erodes the standard of living for all Americans.

A currency based on the "full faith and credit" is a recipe for slavery at the hands of an oligarchy. It's no accident that the federal Income Tax amendment was passed at about the same the Reserve bank was created: the latter depends on the former for its collateralization. The collateral is us and our labor. But we don't get to decide how much we get mortgaged for: the bank and its private owners do. We just get handed the bill, called "income taxes".

The FED doesn't actually print money. Instead, U.S. currency is printed by the Bureau of Engraving and Printing (BEP). The Fed is the master distributor of the money, which they "create" by executing a simple computer entry in their accounting system. This immense power leads to the accusation that the Fed's only real agenda is to turn a profit. Conspiracy theories abound, which revolve around two different ways the Fed can manipulate the economy for benefit of elites:

- They can manipulate interest rates to create "boom-bust" cycles which work out to the advantage of "insiders".
- They increase the money supply by "creating" money through their lucrative "sweet heart" deal they've had with the U.S. government. Debasing the currency is a form of theft.

When the U.S. Government needs money, they go to the Fed to borrow it. The Fed then instructs the Treasury to print X amount of Federal Reserve Notes (FRN) in units of one hundred dollars. Treasury then charges the Fed 2.3 cents for each note printed. The Federal Reserve then lends that fiat money to the federal government at face value plus interest. In exchange, the government issues a bond for the loan amount as security.

The government owes the privately owned Federal Reserve the face value of the bonds plus interest. The Fed earns interest by "loaning" money it has created to the U.S. government. They earn interest by loaning money, which is not even theirs to loan, and which they just created out of thin air. So essentially every bill they "create" has a debt associated to it and if the debt is not paid they have only one option - create more Federal Reserve Notes. When you have perpetual deficits, the Fed can perpetually loan more money to the government in exchange for U.S. bonds to pay off that debt, growing the national debt even more.

This is what is referred to as a debt monetary system. Our currency has debt attached to it before any of us spend any of it. We can never get out of debt because it is a self propagating, vicious cycle, that ultimately ends with the destruction of our currency and bankruptcy of our nation. Under debt based monetary systems, money is backed by debt, not by a commodity that is in demand like gold or even oil. Ultimately it is the debt of the United States government that backs our currency. Since we are the government in the United States, it is our own debts that back our currency. Our printed fiat currency has no intrinsic value other than what comes from our obligation to pay back our own debts. And that debt will be paid, either through taxes, or inflation.

This sounds circular, confusing and insane, because it is. The monetary system is meant to be as opaque as mud so that you don't understand it. It was this realization that led Henry Ford to proclaim, 'It is well enough that people of the nation do not understand our banking and monetary system, for if they did, I believe there would be a revolution before tomorrow morning.'

When money is deposited in a bank, it is eventually lent to another person. If the initial deposit was $100 and the bank lends out $100 to another customer the money supply has increased by $100. However, because the depositor can ask for the money back, banks have to maintain minimum reserves to service customer needs. If the reserve requirement is 10% then the bank can only lend $90 and thus the money supply increases by only $90. The reserve requirement therefore acts as a limit on this multiplier effect. Because reserve requirements apply only to more narrow forms of money creation corresponding to M1 but not to deposits such as time deposits, reserve requirements only play a limited role in monetary policy.

Money Creation

Currently, the US government maintains over 800 billion US dollars in cash money (primarily Federal Reserve Notes) in circulation throughout the world, up from a sum of less than 30 billion dollars in 1959. Theoretically, the amount of money in circulation is increased to accommodate money demanded by the growth of the country's production. In reality, since tax receipts lag expenses by near 40%, the monetary base must be expanded to pay for profligate government spending. The process is as follows:

Of the total money deposited at private banks, predictable proportions remain deposited and are referred to as "core deposits." Banks use the bulk of "non-moving" money (their stable or "core" deposit base) to loan it out, with a legal obligation to keep a fraction of bank deposit money on-hand at all times (fractional reserve banking).

In order to raise additional money to cover excess spending, Congress increases the size of the National Debt by issuing securities typically in the form of a Treasury Bond. It offers the Treasury security for sale, and someone pays cash to the government in exchange. Banks are often the purchasers of these securities, and these securities currently play a crucial role in the process.

The 12-person Federal Open Market Committee, which consists of the heads of the Federal Reserve System (the 7 Federal governors along with 5 bank presidents), meets eight times a year to determine how they would like to influence the economy. They create a plan called the country's "monetary policy" which sets targets for interest rates and monetary growth.

Every business day, the Federal Reserve System engages in Open market operations. When the Federal Reserve wants to increase the money supply, it buys securities such as US Treasury Bonds from banks in exchange for dollars. If the Federal Reserve wants to decrease the money supply, it will sell securities to the banks in exchange for dollars, taking those dollars out of circulation. When the Federal Reserve makes a purchase, it credits the seller's reserve account (with the Federal Reserve). The money that it deposits into the seller's account is not transferred from any existing funds; therefore it is at this point that the Federal Reserve has created high-powered money.

By means of open market operations, the Federal Reserve affects the free reserves of commercial banks in the country. When the Federal Reserve increases reserves, banks loan out the money up to the amount of these excess reserves, because holding the money would amount to accepting the cost of foregone interest. This creates an equal amount of deposits as the granted money is added to bank account balances.

The Federal Reserve's high-powered money is thereby multiplied through bank loans into a larger amount of broad money. As banks increase or decrease loans, the nation's (broad) money supply increases or decreases. Because account-holders may request cash withdrawals, banks must keep a supply of cash handy. When banks need more cash than on hand, they can make requests for cash with the Federal Reserve. The Federal Reserve takes these requests and orders printed money from the US Treasury Department. The Treasury Department sends these requests to the Bureau of Engraving and Printing (to make dollar bills) and the Bureau of the Mint (to stamp the coins).

The US Treasury sells this newly printed money to the Federal Reserve for the cost of printing. Aside from printing costs, the Federal Reserve must pledge collateral (typically government securities such as Treasury bonds) to put new money, which does not replace old notes, into circulation. Printed cash is then distributed to banks, as needed.

Though the Federal Reserve authorizes and distributes the currency printed by the Treasury (the primary component of the narrow monetary base), the broad money supply is primarily created by commercial banks through the money multiplier mechanism. The Fed" controls the money supply in the United States by controlling the amount of loans made by commercial banks. New loans usually take the form of additions to checking account balances. Check deposits are an integral part of the money supply, so the money supply increases whenever new loans are issued.

Deposit money is convertible into cash when depositors request cash withdrawals. Withdrawals of cash in turn require banks to limit or reduce lending. The majority of broad money supply worldwide us the result of current outstanding loans of banks to debtors.

Fractional Reserve Banking and the Debt Money System

Our money is created out of debt and is a debt money system. Our money is initially created by the purchase of U.S. bonds. Purchasers of bonds include the public which buys savings bonds and some Treasuries, but bigger buyers include banks, foreigners and the Federal Reserve itself when it wants to create more money. The difference is the Fed pays for bonds with a simple bookkeeping entry created out of digital nothing. This new Fed created money is then multiplied by a factor of 10 by the banks through the fractional reserve principle.

Banks don't create currency, but by making new loans they do create checkbook money or deposits. In turn, over 1 trillion dollars of this privately created money has been used to purchase U.S. bonds on the open market, which provides the banks with roughly 50 billion dollars in interest, risk free, each year, less the interest they pay to depositors. In this way, through fractional reserve lending, banks create over 90% of the money and therefore cause over 90% of our inflation.

The Fed has a vested interest in favor of bailouts because they are in the business of creating money. The bailouts call for spending hundreds of billions of dollars that our government does not have and the Fed will earn billions in interest by creating all of this money. These bailouts will ultimately fail even as our national debt and inflation grow. Banking "insiders" profit enormously as the Fed creates deliberate boom-bust cycles, while our currency becomes more and more worthless. Sadly, today's dollar is only worth four cents compared to its value in 1913, when the Federal Reserve was first chartered.

Even worse, the Fed cannot be audited and does not answer to the President or anyone for that matter. The president appoints the Board of Governors but has no control over their activities. Congress knows nothing of the plans, and actions taken in concert with other central banks. We get less and less information regarding the money supply each year, and M3 money supply numbers are no longer reported.

The law enabling the Federal Income tax law was by necessity enacted the same year as the equally disruptive Federal Reserve Act. Prior to this, the U.S prospered and the government paid its bills without needing revenue from income tax, but that ended with the enactment of the Federal Reserve Act of 1913.

U.S. Central Bank History

In 1690, the Massachusetts Bay Colony became the first in the United States to issue paper money, but soon others began printing their own money as well. Scarcity of coins in the colonies drove the demand for currency, the primary means of trade. Paper currencies were used by the Colonies to pay expenses, as well as lend money to citizens. The primary means of exchange quickly became paper money and began to be used in financial transactions with other colonies. However, some currencies used were not redeemable in gold or silver, causing them to depreciate with time.

During the American Revolutionary war a first attempt at a national currency was made. In 1775 the Continental Congress began issuing its own paper currency, calling their bills "Continentals". Backed only by future tax revenue, Continentals helped finance the Revolutionary War. Lacking a captive tax foundation, the value of Continental diminished rapidly over time. This experience led the United States to be skeptical of unbacked currencies, which were not issued again until the Civil War.

Our founding fathers were on balance vehemently opposed to a central bank, though Alexander Hamilton and other "federalists" were in favor. It was Thomas Jefferson who famously stated:
"I believe that banking institutions are more dangerous to our liberties that standing armies."
"The central bank is an institution of the most deadly hostility existing against the principles and form of our constitution. I am an enemy to all banks, discounting bills or notes for anything but coin. If the American people allow private banks to control the issuance of their currency, first by inflation and then by deflation, the banks and corporations that will grow up

around them will deprive the people of all their property until their children will wake up homeless on the continent their fathers conquered."

James Madison opined "History records that the money changers have used every form of abuse, intrigue, deceit, and violent means possible to maintain their control over governments by controlling the money and its issuance."

Andrew Jackson added his weight in opposition; "It is not our own citizens only who are to receive the bounty of our government. More than eight millions of the stock of this bank are held by foreigners... is there no danger to our liberty and independence in a bank that in its nature has so little to bind it to our country? ... Controlling our currency, receiving our public moneys, and holding thousands of our citizens in dependence... would be more formidable and dangerous than a military power of the enemy."

Abraham Lincoln is quoted as saying "The government should create, issue and circulate all the currency and credit needed to satisfy the spending power of the government and the buying power of consumers ... The privilege of creating and issuing money is not only the supreme prerogative of Government, but it is the Government's greatest creative opportunity. By the adoption of these principles, the long-felt want for a uniform medium will be satisfied. The taxpayers will be saved immense sums of interest..."

Thomas Jefferson's views found articulation in Article 1, Section 8 of the US Constitution which specifically states Congress is the only legitimate body that can "coin money and regulate the value thereof." No amendment to the US Constitution allows anyone to coin and regulate currency other than Congress. Yet, throughout our history, several central banking systems have been implemented.

First Bank of the United States: Alexander Hamilton, as Secretary of the Treasury, made a deal in 1791to support transferring the capital from Philadelphia to the waterlogged banks of the Potomac in exchange for southern support for his groundbreaking Bank project. The First Bank of the United States was chartered by Congress in that same year and operated between 179 and 1811. Modeled after the Bank of England, The First Bank of the United States was differed from today's central banks. Most glaring is that it was partly owned by foreigners, who shared in its profits. Only 20% of the country's money supply was under its control, with private banks accounting for the rest. The First Bank was bitterly opposed by a number of founding fathers, including Thomas Jefferson and James Madison, who viewed it as a source of corruption, speculation and financial manipulation.

Second Bank of the United States: The Federal government waited five years before chartering the Second Bank of the United States whose existence spanned the years (1816-1836). A copy of the First Bank, the Second Bank opened branches throughout the country. After becoming president in 1828, Andrew Jackson denounced it claiming it was an engine of corruption that benefited his opponents. His dismantling of the Second Bank in the 1830s inspired the Second Party System, as Democrats opposed banks while Whigs supported them.

"Free" Banks: While state-chartered banks had always existed in the United States, after the loss of the Second Bank's charter, a need for more banking arose. The era from 1837 to the Civil War is commonly known as the free banking era. States enacted "free bank laws," which allowed the creation of banks under less onerous charters. Although banks were still regulated, they could enter banking simply by depositing government bonds as a reserve with state auditors.

The bonds as collateral backing the notes issued by the free banks. Free banks were further required to redeem notes on demand in specie. Hundreds of banks opened doors as a consequence of the free banking laws and free bank notes circulated nationally. Such bank notes were often circulated at a discount depending in part on the distance from the issuing bank and based on the soundness of the bank.

The Suffolk Bank in New England, a private institution, took over some of the roles typical of a central bank during the free bank period, exchanging notes, clearing payments, and disciplining banks that over-issued notes. In 1853, the New York Clearinghouse Association was established to process the rising volume of note and check transactions, allowing banks to exchange notes and checks and to settle accounts.

National Banks: The outbreak of Civil War and the need to finance the army led to interest in creating a new national bank. Learning lessons from the Second Bank, the new model was based on the free banking system and the "national banking system" was established in 1863. Banks were allowed to choose between a national charter or a state charter. Nationally chartered banks were required to issue government-printed bills as their notes, which were backed by Federal bonds that funded the war effort. This created a uniform national currency in the United States. By 1865, state bank notes had been taxed out of existence.

Creation of the Fed

1900, the U.S. had had tried several central banking systems, all sharing the flaw of being dominated by banking interests. The Rockefellers, the Morgans, and the Rothchilds came to be synonymous with big banking. "The Panic of 1907", also known as the 1907 Bankers' Panic, provided the impetus for new banking legislation the New York Stock Exchange fell close to 50%. Panic and numerous runs on banks and trust companies exacerbated a nationwide economic recession as many state and local banks and businesses were forced into bankruptcy. Loss of confidence among depositors coupled with a retraction of market liquidity by some New York City banks and side bets by so called bucket shops all added to the Panic.

The crisis was triggered by the failed attempt in October 1907 to corner the market on stock of the United Copper Company. When this bid failed, banks that had lent money to the cornering scheme suffered runs that later spread to affiliated banks and trusts, leading a week later to the downfall of the Knickerbocker Trust Company—New York City's third-largest trust. The collapse of the Knickerbocker spread fear throughout the city's trusts as regional banks withdrew reserves from New York City banks and vast numbers of people withdrew deposits from their regional banks.

The panic was deepening when financier J. P. Morgan intervened by pledging large sums of his own money while convincing other New York bankers to do the same, to shore up the banking system. Some question whether Morgan acted out of altruism or self interest, but at the time, the United States did not have a central bank to inject liquidity back into the market. By November the financial contagion had largely ended, yet a further crisis emerged when a large brokerage firm borrowed heavily using the stock of Tennessee Coal, Iron and Railroad Company (TC&I) as collateral. Collapse of TC&I's stock price was averted by an emergency takeover by Morgan's U.S. Steel Corporation—a move approved by anti-monopolist president Theodore Roosevelt. The following year, Senator Nelson W. Aldrich established and chaired a commission to investigate the crisis and propose future solutions, leading to the creation of the Federal Reserve System. The Aldrich commission recommended a central bank should be implemented so that a panic like 1907 could never happen again, but questions remain whether this benefited the people or bankers more.

Aldrich met with prominent banking firms at a secret meeting in 1910 at J.P. Morgan's Jekyll Island estate off the cost of Georgia. Attendees included Henry Davison (J.P. Morgan Company senior partner), Frank Vandelip (National Bank of New York President, associated with the Rockefellers), Charles D. Norton (president of First National Bank of New York dominated by the Morgans), Benjamin Strong (J.P. Morgan representative), and Paul Warburg (representing Kuhn, Loeb & Co.), who was the Act's primary architect.

Over a period of ten days these bankers drafted the Federal Reserve Act, which it then handed to Senator Nelson Aldrich to push through congress. The Federal Reserve Act of 1913 was voted on and passed through the Senate two days before Christmas, between the hours of 1:30 A.M. and 4:30 A.M., when much of Congress was at home with their families for the Christmas holidays.

Woodrow Wilson was elected president in 1912 with heavy political sponsorship by the bankers after agreeing to sign the Federal Reserve Act. Wilson signed the bill into law on December 23, 1913, unconstitutionally transferring control of the money supply from Congress to the private banking elite. Woodrow Wilson later wrote in regret "I am a most unhappy man. I have unwittingly ruined my country. A great industrial nation is now controlled by its system of credit. We are no longer a government by free opinion, no longer a government by conviction and the vote of the majority, but a government by the opinion and duress of a small group of dominant men"

The Federal Reserve act of 1913 was an easy sell to the big US bank because they could sell all the loans they wanted by fixing prices. Knowing in advance when interest rates would be lowered or raised let them speculate with foreknowledge of the boom/bust cycles. Many small banks lacking inside information were wiped out.

The public was told the Federal Reserve was an economic stabilizer and that inflation and economic crisis were a thing of the past, but history has shown nothing is further from the truth. From 1914-1919 the Fed increased the money supply by nearly 100%, resulting in extensive loans from small banks to the public. Then in 1920, the Fed called in mass percentages of the outstanding money supply, resulting in supporting banks having to call in huge numbers of loans. Just like in 1907 bank runs, bankruptcy and collapse occurred and over 5400 competitive banks outside of the Federal Reserve System collapsed, further consolidating the Fed monopoly.

The Federal Reserve System was adopted by the United States in 1913. Milton Friedman and Anna Schwartz, in *A Monetary History of the United States*, identify mistakes in Federal Reserve policy as a key factor in the 1920 crisis. At the end of the war the Federal Reserve Bank of New York began raising interest rates sharply. In December 1919 the rate was raised from 4.75% to 5%. A month later it was raised to 6% and in June 1920 it was raised to 7% (the highest interest rates of any period except the 1970s and early 1980s). This reduced the amount of bank lending, both to other banks and to consumers and businesses. In the latter half of 1921, the New York Federal Reserve reduced rates in successive half-point moves during the July- November period from the 7% high to 4.5% on November 3, 1921 and the depression ended.

Congressman Charles Lindbergh said in 1921 "Under the Federal Reserve Act, panics are scientifically created. The present panic is the first scientifically created one, worked out as we figure a mathematical equation."

Did the Fed Cause the Great Depression?

From 1921 through 1929 the Fed again increased the money supply, this time by 62%, resulting once again in extensive loans to the public and banks while also stoking inflation as the price for an economic boom. A new type of loan in the stock market called the margin loan allowed investors to put down only 10% of a stock's price with the other 90% loaned through the broker. A person could own $1000 worth of stock with only $100 down, making margin loans popular in the roaring 1920's as everyone seemed to make money in the market. However, margin loans could be called in at anytime to be paid within 24 hours, typically resulting in the sale of the stock purchased with the loan.

"Greedy speculators" are often blamed for causing the Great Depression. Yet, with artificially low interest rates, it made sense to borrow and buy assets, no different than today. If interest rates are 2% and inflation is 10%, then borrowing to invest is sensible. The Federal Reserve and zero or negative interest rates were the real culprit. False signals sent by the Federal Reserve through artificially cheap interest rates mislead speculators then as now.

U.S. monetary policymakers were guilty of four major errors that helped lead to the Great Depression. The Fed's first mistake was the tightening of monetary policy in the spring of 1928 that continued until the stock market crash of October 1929. This monetary tightening did not seem particularly justified by the macroeconomic environment: The economy was only just emerging from a recession, commodity prices were declining sharply, and there was little hint of inflation. The Federal Reserve raised interest rates in 1928 because of their concern about speculation on Wall Street. Drawing a sharp distinction between "productive" (that is, good) and "speculative" (bad) uses of credit, Fed policymakers were concerned that bank lending to brokers and investors was fueling a speculative wave in the stock market. Attempts to persuade banks not to lend for speculative purposes were ineffective, so Fed officials dissuaded lending directly by raising the policy interest rate.

The market crash of October 1929 showed that the Fed can bring down stock prices. But the cost of this "victory" was very high, the Fed's tight-money policies led to the onset of a recession in August 1929. The slowdown in economic activity, together with high interest rates, was the most important source of the stock market crash that followed in October. The market crash, rather than being the cause of the Depression, was in fact largely the result of an economic slowdown and the inappropriate monetary policies that preceded it.

The second monetary policy action occurred in September and October of 1931. The United States and the great majority of other nations were on the gold standard, where central banks stood ready to maintain the fixed values of their currencies by offering to trade gold for money at the legal exchange rate.

The fact that the value of each currency was fixed in terms of gold implied that the rate of exchange between any two currencies was likewise fixed. The gold standard is subject to speculative attack, as is any fixed exchange rates system, if investors doubt the ability of a country to maintain its currency at the legally specified parity value., Following financial upheaval in Europe and concerns about British investments on the European Continent, in September 1931 speculators began presenting pounds to the Bank of England demanding gold in return, which attacked the British pound. The Bank of England depleted its gold reserves and left the gold standard unable to support the pound at its official value, allowing the pound to float freely.

After the English pound collapsed in 1931, speculators turned to the next currency in line for devaluation, the U.S. dollar. In September and October of 1931, central banks and private investors converted substantial dollar assets into gold from the Federal Reserve's gold reserves. Panic ensued as the speculative attack in the U.S. banking system created fear of imminent devaluation of the dollar. Depositors, both domestic and foreign, withdrew funds from U.S. banks to convert into gold and other assets.

The Federal Reserve ignored the assault on the banking system to focus on stopping the gold reserves losses and protect the dollar. This flew counter to long-established practice that required the Fed to respond both speculative attacks on the dollar and to domestic banking panics. The Fed again raised interest rates sharply to stabilize the dollar on the theory that currency speculators would stop liquidating dollar assets if they could earn a higher rate of return on them. The Fed's strategy worked and the attack on the dollar subsided. U.S. commitment to the gold standard had been successfully defended, but the Fed had chosen to tighten rather than ease monetary policy despite the fact that macroeconomic conditions included accelerating decline in prices, output and money supply.

The third policy action occurred in spring of 1932 when Congress began to place considerable pressure on the Federal Reserve to ease monetary policy. The Board was reluctant to comply, but nevertheless conducted open-market operations from April to June of 1932 to increase the national money supply. This reduced interest rates on government bonds and corporate debt, giving the appearance that the decline in prices and economic activity had been stooped. However, Federal Reserve members were ambivalent about monetary expansion. Some viewed the Depression as the necessary purging of financial excesses built up during the 1920s and slowing the economic collapse by easing monetary policy only delayed the inevitable adjustment. Other officials, noting the very low level of nominal interest rates, concluded monetary policy was in fact already quite easy and that no more should be done. These policymakers did not appreciate that, even though nominal interest rates were very low, ongoing deflation meant the real cost of borrowing was very high because any loans would need to be repaid in dollars of greater value. Thus despite the very low level of nominal interest rates, monetary policy was not in fact easy. Fed officials were convinced the policy ease advocated by the Congress wouldn't work and reversed the policy when the Congress adjourned in July 1932. The economy relapsed dramatically.

The fourth and final policy mistake was the Fed's ongoing neglect of problems in the U.S. banking sector. As depositor fears about the health of banks grew, runs on banks became increasingly common. Bank panics spread across the country, often affecting all the banks in a major city or even an entire region. President Roosevelt declared a "banking holiday" between December 1930 and March 1933, shutting down the entire U.S. banking system. Nearly half of U.S. banks eventually closed or were merged with other banks. Surviving banks retrenched sharply rather than expanding their deposits and loans to replace those of the banks lost to panics.

Removing The Gold Standard

The bank panics of February/March 1933 created foreign exchange movements that put the Fed in danger of exhausting its holdings of gold. Removing the gold standard would allow the Fed to create more money, but to do this they needed to acquire the remaining gold in the system. Under the pretence of helping to end the depression, came the 1933 gold seizure.

In January of 1933 Hoover was a lame duck republican president with a democratic congress. FDR had been elected and was waiting to be sworn in early in the month of March.

Hoover started the Reconstruction Finance Corporation in an attempt to restore confidence in the banking system and save banks that were threatened with runs with emergency funds. Very little of the cash deposits made at a bank are actually on hand given fractional reserve banking.

At the beginning of February [1933], Herbert Hoover proposed to the Federal Reserve Board that every bank in the country should be closed for just one day. Each bank would then submit a statement of its assets and liabilities. It would list its live assets and its dying or dead assets separately. The Federal Reserve would accept the banks' own statement. The next day all solvent banks would be opened and the government would declare them to be solvent. Ogden Mills, head of the Federal Reserve, reported to Hoover that he learned that the men around Roosevelt believed that the worse the situation got the more evident to the country would be the failure of the Republican Party. 'In other words,' Mills said, 'they do not wish to check the panic.'"

Executive Order 6102 by President Franklin D. Roosevelt ended the gold standard in the U.S. by "forbidding the Hoarding of Gold Coin, Gold Bullion, and Gold Certificates" by free U.S. citizens. Signed on April 5, 1933, the order criminalized the American public's ability to own gold as an investment vehicle and required U.S. citizens to deliver to the Federal Reserve by May 1, 1933, all but a tiny amount of gold coin, gold bullion, and gold certificates in exchange for $20.67 per troy ounce,. This essentially robbed the public of the little wealth they had left. Violation of the order was punishable by fines up to $10,000 ($167,700 if adjusted for inflation as of 2010) or up to ten years in prison, or both as specified by the Trading With the Enemy Act of October 6, 1917, amended on March 9, 1933.

The Gold Reserve Act of 1934 raised the price of gold from the Treasury to $35 an ounce ($587 in 2010 dollars) for international transactions. The Exchange Stabilization Fund was funded by the profit the government realized by confiscating gold at $20.67 and increasing the pegged rate to $35 per ounce. The Gold Reserve Act made gold clauses unenforceable, and by increasing the exchange value of the dollar in gold from $20.67 to $35 per ounce, decreased the real value of the dollar overnight by 40.94%. $35 per ounce remained the gold price until August 15, 1971, when President Richard Nixon abandoned the gold standard for foreign exchange by announcing the United States would no longer exchange dollars for gold at a fixed value.

President Gerald Ford repealed the limitation on ownership of gold coins, bars and certificates by an act of Congress which went into effect December 31, 1974. Codified as Pub.L. 93-373[5][6], contracts remained unenforceable if they used gold monetarily rather than as a commodity of trade. The act did not repeal the Gold Repeal Joint Resolution, which outlawed contracts that specified payment in a fixed amount of money or a fixed amount of gold. However, the Act, Pub. L. No. 95-147, § 4(c), 91 Stat. 1227, 1229 of Oct. 28, 1977 amended the 1933 Joint Resolution and made clear that parties could once again include gold clauses in contracts formed after 1977.

A dollar bill minted before 1933 says it is redeemable in gold. While a dollar bill today says it is legal tender, it is worthless paper backed by nothing more than faith. All that gives our money value is how much is in circulation. Since the dollar was no longer redeemable in gold, this allowed a further increase in the money supply and an even more devalued dollar. Loan contracts which contained "gold clauses" requiring payment to be increased if the dollar were devalued relative to gold were declared invalid by Congress, defrauding creditors and providing a massive subsidy to debtors.

Politically connected insiders greatly profited from all three periods of the Great Depression. First they were able to profit by being positioned to borrow and buy assets at the start of the boom. They were also first in line to buy assets with the newly created money, so were the primary beneficiaries of inflation. They profited again by being able to foresee the crash coming due to their political connections and converted their holdings to cash before the inevitable crash. At the bottom of the Depression, the bankers and those connected to Federal Reserve inside information were able to borrow and buy assets at a discount. Later, they effectively defaulted on these loans via inflation; inflation meant these loans could be repaid with devalued dollars.

Nothing has changed. Manipulation of bailout money, interest rates and the value of the dollar allow the Goldman Sachs of our times to profit immensely.

Louis McFadden and the Fed

On June 10, 1932, Congressman Louis McFadden, a long-time adversary to the Federal Reserve and a lifelong banker himself, made a 25-minute speech before the House of Representatives, accusing the Federal Reserve of deliberately instigating the Great Depression. McFadden introduced House Resolution No. 158 in 1933, Articles of Impeachment for the Secretary of the Treasury, the Comptroller of the Currency, and the Board of Governors of the Federal Reserve. McFadden charged criminal acts, including fraud, conspiracy, unlawful conversion, and treason.

The following are some quotes from McFadden's 1933 speech and resolution:

"Mr. Chairman, I see no reason why citizens of the United States should be terrorized into surrendering their property to the International Bankers who own and control the Fed. The statement that gold would be taken from its lawful owners if they did not voluntarily surrender it, to private interests, show that there is an anarchist in our Government."

"The statement that it is necessary for the people to give their gold- the only real money- to the banks in order to protect the currency is a statement of calculated dishonesty!"

"By his unlawful usurpation of power on the night of March 5, 1933, and by his proclamation, which in my opinion was in violation of the Constitution of the United States, Roosevelt divorced the currency of the United States from gold, and the United States currency is no longer protected by gold. It is therefore sheer dishonesty to say that the people's gold is needed to protect the currency."

"Roosevelt ordered the people to give their gold to private interests- that is, to banks, and he took control of the banks so that all the gold and gold values in them, or given into them, might be handed over to the predatory International Bankers who own and control the Fed."

"Roosevelt cast his lot with the usurers. He agreed to save the corrupt and dishonest at the expense of the people of the United States. . . . ."

"By his action in closing the banks of the United States, Roosevelt seized the gold value of forty billions or more of bank deposits in the United States banks. Those deposits were deposits of gold values. By his action he has rendered them payable to the depositors in paper only, if payable at all, and the paper money he proposes to pay out to bank depositors and to the people generally in lieu of their hard earned gold values in itself, and being based on nothing into which the people can convert it the said paper money is of negligible value altogether."

"It is the money of slaves, not of free men. If the people of the United States permit it to be imposed upon them at the will of their credit masters, the next step in their downward progress will be their acceptance of orders on company stores for what they eat and wear. Their case will be similar to that of starving coal miners. They, too, will be paid with orders on Company stores for food and clothing, both of indifferent quality and be forced to live in Company-owned houses from which they may be evicted at the drop of a hat. More of them will be forced into conscript labor camps under supervision."

Were McFadden's accusations the rantings of a lunatic? He had been president of a bank and spent ten years on the House Banking Committee, so his words are difficult to dismiss, especially since they parallel much of what is going on today. At least partial vindication is found in the current value of gold which has gone through the roof as people lose faith in our fiat currency. While it may be wide of the mark to accuse international bankers of a conspiracy to steal the world's wealth, the collapse in the value of the dollar makes the debate moot. Our currency is headed towards irrelevance and the only ones being bailed out are the large banks who are too big to fail, but have contributed mightily to the explosion of the debt bomb. Louis McFadden warned about the same cronyism that bailed out the banks and Wall Street back in 1933.

Federal Income Tax Intertwined With The Federal Reserve

The Federal Reserve act was not the only destructive bill pushed through congress in 1913. Also passed was the Sixteenth Amendment, which gave Congress the power to collect taxes, based on income, without regard to the States or the Census. If every dollar created is an instrument of debt in the Federal Reserve System, this requires the collection of massive sums of money from citizens to make the interest payment. The new income tax was needed in order to guarantee repayments on the Federal Reserve debt. It is a direct unapportioned tax and therefore theoretically unconstitutional. In order to be constitutionally legal, all direct taxes have to be apportioned (equal for every person).

Being unconstitutional doesn't mean you don't have to follow the law as currently enforced because many people have spent jail time arguing the merits of tax avoidance. What you need to understand is that the entire system is corrupt, but it is collapsing of its own weight. Your goal is to survive, not to waste energy debating with IRS auditors and judges how many years you are willing to stay in jail for a lost cause. Pay your taxes and live to fight another day.

The 16th amendment and the Federal Reserve Act are functionally equivalent to a surrender treaty. The Federal Reserve Act surrendered control of the monetary system to the banking cartel, guaranteeing the eventual abandonment of the gold standard. The debt-based money created by the Federal Reserve's guarantees the enslavement of every living and future American under a crushing debt burden.

The income tax enabled politicians to greatly increase the size of the government and their personal power. At present, roughly 35% of the average worker's income is taken from them via this tax, requiring 4 months of work out of the year to fulfill this tax obligation. A good chunk of this money goes to pay the interest on the currency being produced by the Federal Reserve Bank, not to any government program.

Bretton Woods Agreement

The United States emerged as a dominant world power after World War II, both militarily and economically. By 1945, the U.S. was producing half the world's coal, two-thirds of the oil, and better than half of the electricity. U.S. manufacturing produced massive quantities of machinery, including airplanes, ships, vehicles, machine tools, armaments, and chemicals. America held 65% of the world's gold reserves and was sole possessor of the atomic bomb.

In July 1944, delegates from 44 Allied nations came together for the United Nations Monetary and Financial Conference at the Mount Washington Hotel in Bretton Woods, New Hampshire. The conference objective was to establish rules for commercial and financial relations between the world's major industrial nations. The conference agreements became the basis for the Bretton Woods Monetary System.

Bretton Woods established a pegged rate currency exchange system with the U.S. dollar functioning as the reference currency. Signatory nations agreed to peg their currencies to the U.S. dollar and buy and sell U.S. dollars to target market exchange rates within trading bands of plus or minus 1% from the initial ratio. U.S. dollars were to be convertible into gold at a rate of US$35 per troy ounce. The U.S. dollar in essence became a proxy for gold, replacing the physical metal which had anchored the previous international gold standard financial system.

The U.S. has enjoyed an enormous advantage from this system because we are the only entity legally capable of creating more of the reserve currency, the U.S. dollar. This forced other nations to maintain large reserves of U.S. dollar to equilibrate their currency within the trading band.

JFK and the Fed

John F. Kennedy signed a virtually unknown Presidential decree, Executive Order 11110 on June 4, 1963, four months before his assassination on November 22, 1963. This decree returned the Constitutional right to create and *"to issue silver certificates based on any silver bullion, silver, or standard silver dollars in the Treasury."* to the Federal government.

This meant the government could introduce new money based on the amount of physical silver held in the U.S. Treasury's vault. $4 billion in"Kennedy Bills" in $2 and $5 denominations were put into circulation by the U.S. Treasury and. $10 and $20 United States Notes (USN) printed by the Treasury Department after Kennedy was assassinated were never put into circulation.

Kennedy must have known that if the silver-backed USN were widely circulated, they would eliminate the demand for Federal Reserve Notes (FRN). The USN was backed by silver while the FRN was backed by nothing of intrinsic value, and was also an instrument of debt. Executive Order 11110 should have prevented the national debt from reaching its current level of nearly $15 trillion, all created since 1963.

Had LBJ or any subsequent President enforced Kennedy's Executive Order 11110, the U.S. Government would have been able to repay its debt without going to the private Federal Reserve Banks where it is charged interest to create new "money". However, Lyndon B. Johnson surrendered to the banking interests in 1964, declaring, "Silver has become too valuable to be used as money." Kennedy bills were subsequently removed from circulation.

Nixon Unilaterally Closes Gold Window

The escalating costs of the Vietnam War and domestic social programs led to increasing creation of U.S. dollars to fund the shortfall. In the early 1970's the United States began running trade deficit for the first time in the twentieth century. Foreign holders of U.S. dollars rightly questioned the U.S. government's ability to reduce budget and trade deficits. Foreign countries began to redeem U.S. dollars in gold as entitled under the Bretton Woods Agreement signed in 1944. The French under Charles de Gaulle were particularly aggressive in exchanging dollars for gold.

To prevent the U.S. Treasury from being drained of gold, President Richard Nixon unilaterally closed the gold window on August 15, 1971. Nixon made the dollar inconvertible to gold except on the open market. The world's currencies now "floated" against one another without reference to gold. The inevitable result was gold soared from US$35 to US$195 an ounce by the end of 1974. In abandoning the gold standard, central banks now only had the public's perception of inflation holding them back from creating as much money as they desired. The U.S. was now on a paper money system - fiat money.

Abolishing The Federal Reserve

Is it even possible to get off the Federal Reserve merry-go-round? There may be a way to fix the problem within a few short years without causing financial collapse by paying off U.S. Treasury bonds and other debt instruments with debt free U.S. notes in the same manner president Lincoln issued notes. That would create tremendous inflation since our currency is now multiplied by the fractional reserve banking system, but there is an ingenious solution advanced in part by Milton Friedman to maintain a stable money supply while avoiding both inflation and deflation as the debt is retired.

As the Treasury Department buys bonds on the open market with U.S. notes, the reserve requirements of local banks would need to be raised proportionally so the amount of money in circulation remains constant. As those holding bonds have them exchanged for U.S. notes, they deposit this money, making available the currency needed by the banks to increase their reserves. Once U.S. bonds are replaced with U.S. notes, we would be at 100% reserve banking instead of the fractional reserve system currently in use.

The Federal Reserve Act would no longer be necessary and could be repealed. Monetary power could be transferred back to the treasury dept and there would no further creation or contraction of money by banks. Our national debt could be paid off in a single year. The Fed and fractional reserve banking could be abolished, without national bankruptcy, financial collapse, inflation or deflation or any significant change in the way the average American goes about his business.

Pay off the national debt with debt-free U.S. notes.- If the United States can issue dollar bonds it can issue a dollar bill. Both dollar bonds and bills have value based purely on the faith and credit of the U.S. government. Paying off U.S. bond debt with U.S. notes amounts to a straightforward substitution of one form of government obligation for another. U.S. bonds bear interest while U.S. Notes do not.

Abolish fractional reserve banking. - As the debt is paid off, the reserve requirements of all banks and financial institutions would be raised proportionally at the same time to absorb the new U.S. notes, which would become the banks increased reserves as they were deposited. Towards the end of the transition period, the remaining liabilities of financial institutions would be assumed or acquired by the U.S. government in a onetime operation, and/or paid off in debt free U.S. notes to keep the money supply stable. The national debt would be paid and the Fed would become an obsolete anachronism.

Repeal the "Federal Reserve Act of 1913" and the "National Banking act of 1864" --These acts delegate money power to a private banking monopoly. No banker or person affiliated with financial institutions should be allowed to regulate banking. Money power should be in the hands of the Department of Treasury, as it was under President Lincoln.

Withdraw the U.S. from the IMF, the BIS (bank of international settlements) and the World Bank.-Institutions like the Federal Reserve centralize the power of the international bankers over the world's economy.

Monetary reform would guarantee the amount of money in circulation would stay very stable causing neither inflation nor deflation. For decades the Fed has doubled the American money supply every 10 years. That fact and fractional reserve banking are the real causes of inflation and a reduction in our buying power, a hidden tax.

The money supply should increase slowly to keep prices stable, roughly in proportion to population growth (about 3% per year), which is similar to what growth in our GDP has also been. Monetary regulators and the treasury dept should have absolutely no discretion in this matter except in time of declared war. Money supply should not be at the whim of a group of bankers meeting in secret. Decisions on how much money will be in the American economy need to be made based on the statistics of population/GDP growth and the price level index. You would then have open and honest monetary policy with all deliberations in public, not secret meetings of the Fed board of governors as today.

11   Where Central Banks Are Taking Us

Financialization's Self-Destruct Sequence

Financialization is a term that describes an economic system or process that attempts to reduce all value that is exchanged (whether tangible, intangible, future or present promises, etc.) either into a financial instrument or a derivative of a financial instrument. The original intent of financialization is to be able to reduce any work-product or service to an exchangeable financial instrument, like currency, and make it easier for people to trade these financial instruments.

Financialization is what led to the increasing dominance of the finance industry in economic activity, of financial controllers in the management of corporations, of financial assets among total assets, of marketised securities and particularly equities among financial assets, of the stock market as a market for corporate control in determining corporate strategies, and of fluctuations in the stock market as a determinant of business cycles.

The disturbing features of financialization are the development of overleverage (more borrowed capital and less owned capital) and, as a related tool, financial derivatives. Derivatives are financial instruments, the price or value of which is derived from the price or value of another, underlying financial instrument. Those instruments, which initial purpose was hedging and risk management, became widely traded financial assets in their own. The most common types of derivatives are futures contracts, swaps, and options. In the early 1990s, central banks around the world began surveying derivative market activity, and report the results to the Bank for International Settlements.

The problem with global financialization, which affects your individual financial health, is that the multiple layers of financial repackaging separate the base economic assets from the value floating in the system of derivatives. In short, the whole system is subject to collapse if any part of this ballooning virtual financial turns out to not have true underlying assets. In this case, an avalanche of defaults occur which can rip through the entire global economic system.

We are in the latter stages of financialization's self-destruct sequence.

Like all systems that follow an S-curve of growth and decay, in the New Normal financialization cannot return to its growth phase. Reflating asset and credit bubbles is not possible once everything has already been financialized.

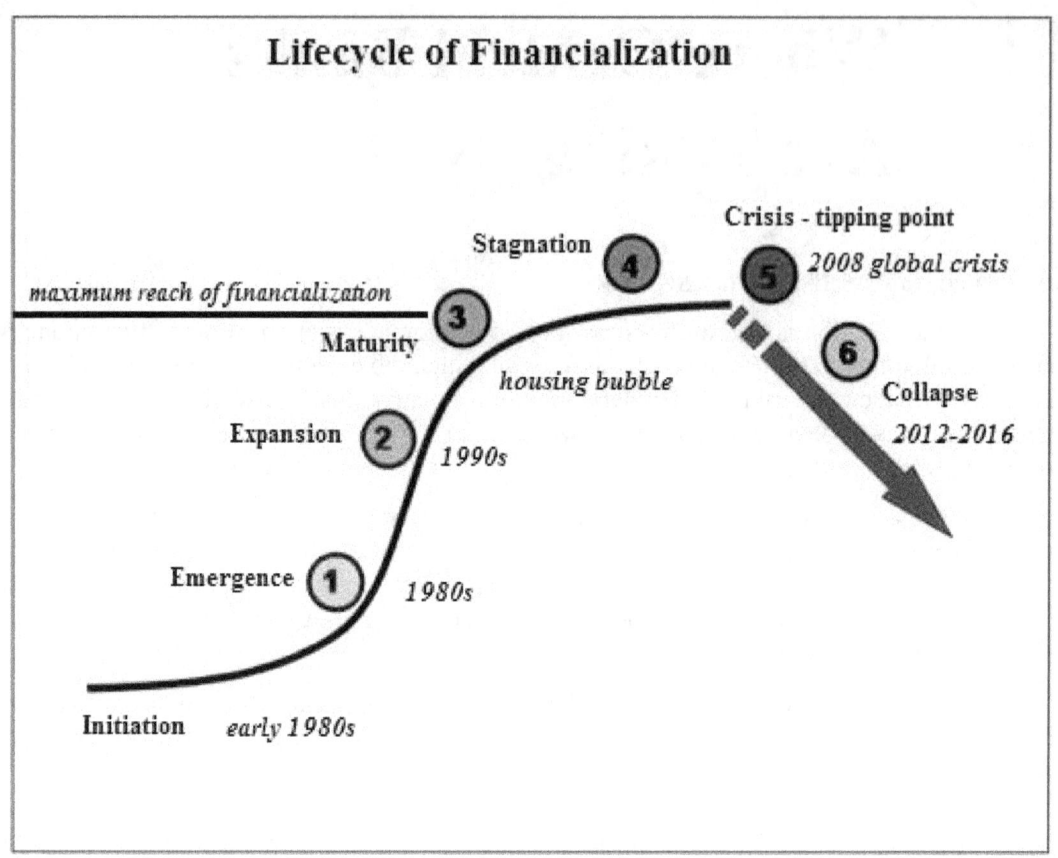

Lifecycle of Financialization

Crisis - tipping point
2008 global crisis

Stagnation (4)

(5)

maximum reach of financialization

(3)

Maturity

housing bubble

(6)

Collapse
2012-2016

Expansion (2)

1990s

Emergence (1)

1980s

Initiation   *early 1980s*

The dynamic at play is a self-destruct sequence triggered by central bank and Central State efforts to reflate asset and credit/leverage bubbles. All central bank and State policies aimed at driving capital into risk assets boil down to reflating phantom assets purchased with debt by issuing more debt that is based on newly issued phantom assets.

Phantom assets purchased with debt cannot be reflated by issuing more debt that is based on newly issued phantom assets. Piling more debt/leverage on a sandpile of phantom assets (CDS, bonds that cannot possibly be paid back, empty condos in the middle of nowhere, etc.) only heightens the probability that the unstable pile will collapse.

The implicit Central Planning campaign to trigger "mild" inflation is part of the self-destruct sequence. Central planners metaphorically fight the last war, or at best the last two wars, and remain blind to any dynamics that did not exist in their case studies.

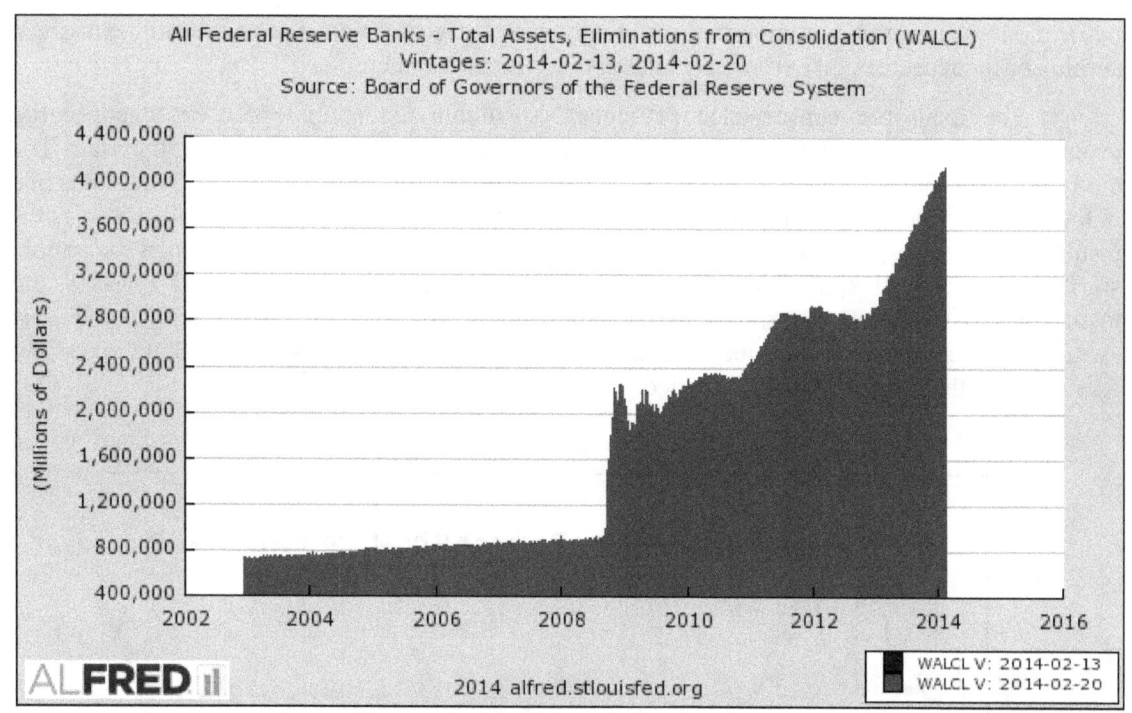

In the 1970s, central bank easing and Central State stimulus sparked accelerating inflation. This reduced the weight of debt because wages inflated along with goods and services. Now that labor is in surplus globally, wages are not keeping pace with inflation. This completely changes the dynamic of "mild" (3%) inflation: as the purchasing power of earned income declines, servicing debt becomes more burdensome. Inflation only renders debt less burdensome if wages rise at the same rate as the cost of goods and services.

In a decade of "mild" inflation and stagnant wages, households will experience a very real-world 30+% decline in their income even as their debt payments remain unchanged. In other words, "mild" inflation in an era of stagnant earned income crushes households, forcing either liquidation or renunciation of debt. What happens as debt service costs rise as a percentage of real net income? There is less cash for consumption, and so the consumer-dependent economy spirals down. Credit is poured into the banking sector, but little trickles down to high-debt, stagnant-income households. This is deleveraging writ large.

What happens when central bank financial repression--lowering the yield on cash to near-zero--causes pension plans to fail and savings to earn negative real returns? Households must save more income to compensate for the destruction of yield by Central Planners.

These mutually reinforcing dynamics feed the self-destruct sequence's inevitability. Add up the self-destructive forces: declining purchasing power, negative real returns on savings, rising debt based on newly issued phantom assets, and promises unbacked by real assets or based on declining national surpluses.

As central planning fails to reinflate phantom assets, the credibility of the status quo institutions that promised success crumbles. In the euphoric blow-off top phase of financialization, expectations of security and wealth were raised by political Elites anxious to mask their systemic looting of national wealth. Political promises are even easier to issue than paper money. However, issuing promises, credit and leverage does nothing to expand the national surplus or the resources that ultimately back those promises and credit.

The explosive convergence of fantasy (phantom assets and promises) and reality eventually comes no matter how clever the central bankers and politicians think they are. The entire goal of Central Planning (central banks and States) is to "extend and pretend" the status quo in the hope that the gargantuan divergence between fantasy and reality will magically close as the result of "aggregate demand" or a new business cycle, or some other version of renewed "animal spirits." But "animal spirits" require trust in the transparency and fairness of markets and institutions. As markets are rigged and manipulated to manage perceptions and enable vast skimming operations to continue, the credibility of the markets, politicos, State oversight agencies and the financial sector is eroded.

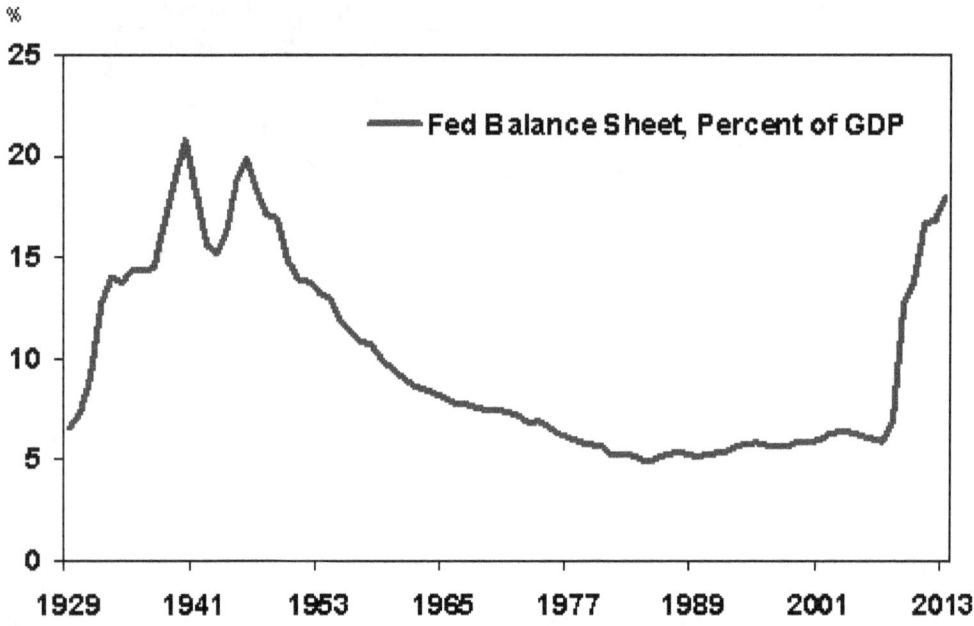

Not since World War II has the Fed balance sheet been this high. As central bank/State reflation of phantom assets fails, the credibility of the entire political/financial elite and the institutions they control will be irrevocably lost.

Financialization's self-destruct sequence has been triggered, leaving us with no way to stop it. Yet, the workings of the machine are opaque, and the interactions complex. We cannot know when the sandpile will collapse, or what the proximate cause of the collapse will be, but we can know that the unstable pile will collapse under the weight of the system's illusory assets, fraud, collusion, embezzlement, corruption and corrosive dependence on artifice and lies.

Vested interests will continue their pillaging until the destruct sequence's final implosion brings the entire rotten edifice down in heap of empty promises. Your personal financial goal for the next decade(s) is to avoid that collapse.

12   The Rise of Cybercash

Are we forever shackled to the theft of our wealth through the devaluation of our currency? The traditional solution has been to buy gold and silver, which while proven as stable proxies for wealth have the problem of being bulky, not easily transported and not easily exchanged. Counterfeiting problems also crop up and there have been rumors of tungsten being salted in with gold bars.

A disruptive alternative technology called cryptocash however now exists. If individuals could circumvent the government monetary system, then it would be possible to contest the legitimacy of a central government which can only run socialist schemes by confiscating wealth through manipulating fiat currency. Enter Bitcoin.

Bitcoin is one of the first implementations of a concept called 'cryptocurrency', first described in 1998 by Wei Dai on the Cypherpunks mailing list. Bitcoin is a digital currency created in 2009 by Satoshi Nakamoto. Bitcoin also refers to the open source software he designed to implement it, and the peer-to-peer network that it is formed from these software nodes which are used to verify transactions. While there have been ups and downs, there is much to learn from Mr. Nakamoto's virtual monetary system, and this first online success story in the world of stateless currencies.

Whether Bitcoin itself succeeds or fails is not critical to your financial future. What is critical is that some such distributed cybercash system will eventually succeed and you need to be prepared for the both the positive and negative changes this upheaval will bring. Therefore, read this not so much as an endorsement of Bitcoin itself, but as providing an outline of the coming disruptive paradigm shift of cybercurrency.

The elusive Satoshi Nakamoto published a research paper in November 2008 outlining the structure for an Internet-only currency he dubbed Bitcoin. Confidence in global currencies and financial system were at low points around the world. Satoshi Nakamoto only uses that nom du guerre when writing research papers; no one knows his real name. And he isn't so much a central banker as a technologist and architect of Bitcoin.

Rather than have one central database of user balances and transaction history, Nakamoto's design distributed the database to a network of third parties. Each one keeps the "Ledger" of owners and also runs hugely complex programs to solve cryptographic puzzles. If you crack the puzzle, you are rewarded with new Bitcoin currency, but the puzzles are so complex that people working them now band together online to share computing power. The overall supply of Bitcoin in the system therefore grows at a slow and pre-ordained rate. Bitcoin is two things:

- It is a **digital currency unit**

- It is the **global payment network** with which one sends and receives those currency units.

Both the currency unit and the payment network share the same name: Bitcoin.

Unlike most currencies, Bitcoin does not rely on trusting any central issuer. Bitcoin uses a distributed database spread across nodes of a peer-to-peer network to journal transactions, and uses cryptography in order to provide basic security functions, such as ensuring that Bitcoins can only be spent by the person who owns them, and never more than once.

Bitcoin's design uses encrypted anonymous ownership and transfers of value. Bitcoins can be saved on a personal computer in the form of a wallet file or kept with a third party wallet service, and in either case Bitcoins can be sent over the Internet to anyone worldwide who has a Bitcoin address. Bitcoin's lack of central administration and peer-to-peer topology make it difficult for any authority, governmental or even criminal entity to manipulate the value of Bitcoins and/or induce inflation by producing more of them. Difficult but not impossible, at least in this iteration.

By May 2011, there were over 6 million Bitcoins in existence. By 2014 nearly 13 million Bitcoins were in the system, all set to mathematically cap out at 21 million coins. Valued at 2014 prices, the total value of the Bitcoin economy is about $10 billion USD. While the Bitcoin economy is small relative to established economies, real goods and services, such as used cars and freelance software development contracts have been traded. Unfortunately, illegitimate goods such as drugs and services such as money launder have also occurred. Given the exponential rise of Internet giants like Google and Facebook it is possible Bitcoin presents a formidable challenge to the US and foreign governments and worldwide central banks as they try both to increase taxes and devalue their currencies as a means of stealth taxation.

Q: Is Bitcoin particularly vulnerable to counterfeiting?

A: The Bitcoin network works by harnessing individuals' greed for the collective good. Tech-savvy users, called miners, devote computing power to a blockchain, a global running tally of every Bitcoin transaction. The blockchain prevents the same Bitcoin from being spent twice. Miners are rewarded for their computing efforts by being gifted with an occasional Bitcoin. Counterfeiting shouldn't be an issue as long as miners keep the blockchain secure.

Q: What is the probability of fraud?

A: Bitcoin occurs is vulnerable where people store their digital cash or exchange it for traditional currencies, like dollars or Euros. If an exchange has sloppy security, as did the Mt Gox exchange, or if an individual's electronic wallet is compromised, money can easily be stolen.

Monetary Differences

In many ways, Bitcoin is like other currencies. The world has Euros, dollars, yen, gold and silver ounces, and now it has Bitcoin as well.

However, as opposed to conventional fiat currency, Bitcoin differs in that no overseer can control the value due to its decentralized nature, mitigating possible instability caused by central banks. This poses a threat to the Federal Reserve and other central banks which claim the right to determine the money supply. There is a limited controlled inflation hardcoded in the Bitcoin software, but it is predictable and known to all parties in advance. Inflation cannot therefore be centrally manipulated to effect redistribution of value from general users. In other words, Bitcoin cannot be manipulated to impose a hidden tax on its users and is therefore disruptive to traditional state structures which count on the theft of wealth to maintain their bureaucracies.

Bitcoin transfers and transactions are facilitated directly without the use of a financial processor between nodes which fortunately or unfortunately makes chargebacks impossible. The Bitcoin client broadcasts the transaction to surrounding nodes which propagate the payment across the network. Corrupted or invalid transactions are rejected by honest clients. Transactions are mostly free; however a fee may be paid to other nodes to prioritize transaction processing.

The total number of Bitcoins tends to 21 million over time. As it approaches that mark the value of Bitcoins will likely increase in real value (price deflation) due to the lack of new introduction. However, Bitcoins are divisible to eight decimal places, which removes practical limitations to downward price adjustments in a deflationary environment.

Bitcoin is not only a currency unit, but a payment network and replaces the function not only of banks, but also the Federal Reserve and central banks. The huge advantage this brings is that money creation is not at the whim of any person nor group. It also replaces inter-bank funding networks (like SWIFT and SEPA), payment processors (like PayPal) and remitters (such as Western Union). The entire banking industrial complex devoted to the creation, storage, accounting, and transfer of money is usurped by Bitcoin. If Bitcoin succeeds, PayPal and Western Union would be removed from the marketplace. The Federal Reserve (and every central bank) would be made redundant. "Disruptive technology" is an understatement.

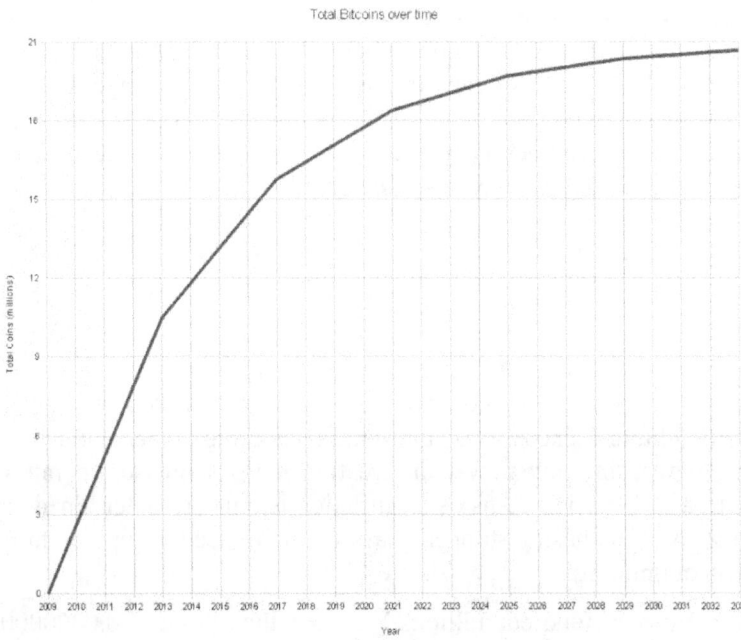

Primer

The best performing currency year-to-date has no home country, no central banker and no physical scrip; it is the online-only Bitcoin and it is becoming more mainstream. BTC, as the currency is known, up 130% year to date in dollar terms, thanks to rising demand from a wide variety of adherents, which includes libertarian activists, small businesses, online drug dealers and gambling sites.

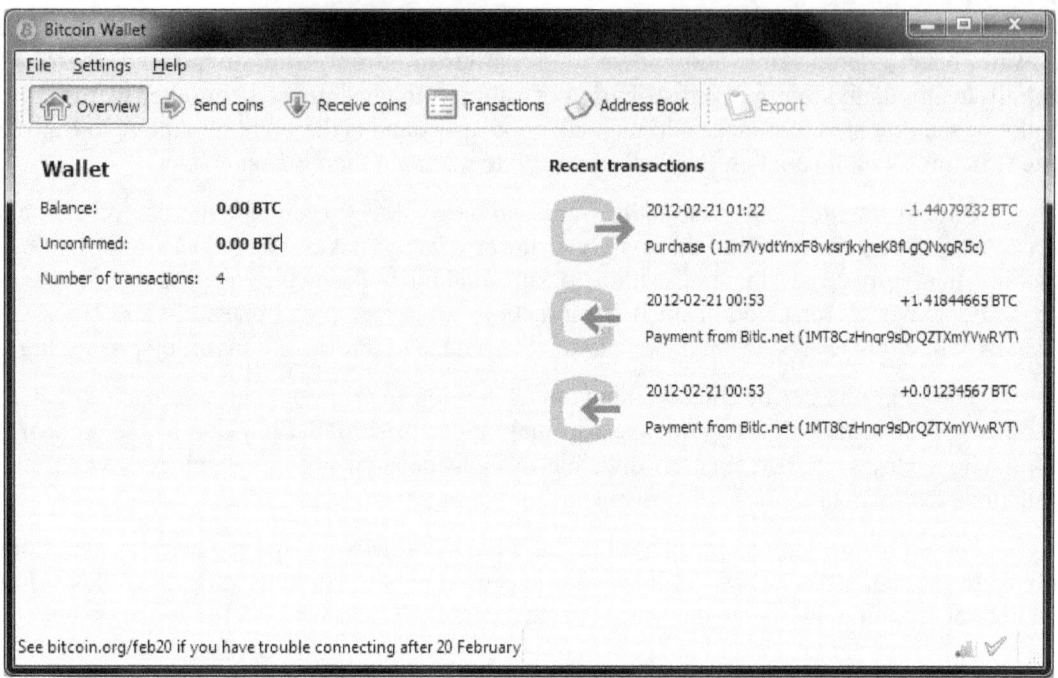

Bitcoin can be complicated; it is after all an entirely new global monetary system. It is both a currency and a payment network for that currency. It is a powerful game changer and it is important for anyone interested in Bitcoin to do their due diligence. However, no deep knowledge is necessary for a typical and it readily becomes easy and comfortable to use. Learning the physics that enable it might on the other hand require years of devotion.

The properties of the Bitcoin currency unit are as follows:

- There will never be more than 21 million in existence, and they are released over time at a declining rate.

- As new coins are released on the set schedule, they are given at random to those who contribute computing power to securing the network. This is called "Bitcoin Mining", or more accurately "Bitcoin Auditing." Those who contribute computing power to this have better odds of receiving new coins, but new coin creation never increases in rate, it diminishes over time until all 21 million coins exist. Inflation is thus pre-determined and ever-decreasing toward zero. That hasn't stopped massive high speed computer farms from being devoted to Bitcoin mining.

- Each Bitcoin is divisible by one hundred million. You can thus possess 0.00000001 Bitcoins.

- Bitcoins are divided and combined seamlessly in your account and are perfectly fungible.

- Because of advanced mathematics and cryptography, it is theoretically impossible to make a counterfeit Bitcoin.

- Bitcoins exist in a perfect free market and always have a market price. In early 2013, this price was about $31.00 each, but rose to over $1,000 before falling back.

- There are global market prices for Bitcoin in every major national currency from yen to Brazilian Reals.

- Bitcoin market price is established by being traded like other currencies on exchange websites. The most prominent exchange is MtGox.com which failed in early 2014 due to some undetermined combination of fraud and incompetence.

How It Works

To use Bitcoin, you need a Wallet (software) which allows you convert your local currency into BTC and back again. There are many available options online, as well as BTC Exchanges to execute the conversions. A network distributed database manages the system anonymously, so no central record of what you own or where you spent your money exists. This carries obvious advantages and disadvantage. Bitcoin is therefore a stateless currency, with essentially no government oversight.

Traditionally you download the Bitcoin software, though you can also use an "ewallet" system. The software acts as your "bank account." and stores a secret code on your computer which enables funds to be paid to and spent from your bank account. This Bitcoin bank account is called your "wallet" and sits on your computer or other storage device (like thumb drives). As soon as one has this wallet software one can receive and send Bitcoins to other wallet-holders anywhere in the world. It is as fast and easy as sending an email.

You don't need a name, an address, a Social Security number, or any personal information of any kind. Nobody "approves" you for Bitcoin. It's free and open-source software. You get it from Bitcoin.org.

Transactions are sent and accounts are secured using what's known as "public key cryptography." Every account has a *public key* and a *private key* - both of which are long strings of numbers and letters. Your wallet software knows your *private* key, and this allows it to send money. To send money to someone, you merely need to know their *public* key (basically their bank account number). If you have your private key plus their public key, a transaction can be created and the funds are deducted from your account and credited to the receiver's account, without outside intervention.

Your account is defined as a long string of numbers and letters:

1PGFCtrJHUsc7fs4LGWLmXUEwuKyDaHuRa

Thus, your account has no personal information attached to it. You do not need to divulge any information whatsoever in order to obtain a Bitcoin account. This means you can receive, store, and spend Bitcoins with *relative* anonymity. The anonymity is relative because your address can be posted anywhere (like on your Facebook page), where others could see that that account belongs to you, and money is going to it.

Bitcoin is a peer-to-peer network, which means account holders can transfer Bitcoin currency between accounts instantly and with relative anonymity. So long as an account holder protects their *private key*, their funds remain secure and only they can send them to someone else (and nobody can stop them).

The decentralization and anonymity embodied by Bitcoin is in part a reaction to the U.S. government's prosecution of digital currency companies like e-Gold and Liberty Dollar. However, the cat is out of the bag, no matter how government lawyers and economists struggle with the issue. If our government were truly providing a valuable return on its services, we would be experiencing a deflationary environment. As time passed, government would become more efficient rather than growing larger and greenbacks would become more valuable, benefiting all citizens. That the greenback is in decline suggests Bitcoin will take a central role in future monetary reform.

Getting Bitcoins

There are three ways to obtain Bitcoin currency:

- Selling goods and services for it
- Buying it at an exchange
- Mining Bitcoins

"Exchanges" are websites where buyers and sellers can trade one currency for another. If you have an account at an exchange, and fund the exchange with dollars, you can buy Bitcoins.

The practical steps for doing this are as follows:

1. Create a free account at a trustworthy exchange. Since the massive failure of MtGox.com this is no longer as straightforward an option. Mainly for Europeans is BitStamp.net.

2. Put money in the exchange by using an intermediary like Dwolla.com or BitInstant.com. Dwolla will link to your bank account and takes 3-5 days to move money from your bank to the exchange. BitInstant, comparatively, allows anonymous cash deposits up to $500 at a time and takes under an hour. These cash deposits are made by you at any major bank branch (you don't even need a bank account). Within 30-60 minutes of your cash deposit, BitInstant will credit your exchange account with your USD. You can literally have your first Bitcoins 30 minutes after reading this article.

3. Once your funds are at the exchange, you can buy Bitcoins at the current market price. The coins then stay at the exchange in your account until you send them somewhere else (to your personal wallet or someone you'd like to pay, etc). If you want to sell Bitcoins for dollars, you simply do the process in reverse - send the Bitcoins to an exchange, sell them at market price, and transfer the USD to your bank.

The Bitcoin market is fully-liquid and operates 24/7 with no holidays. The exchanges are accessible from any country in the world and support all major national currencies. Currency traders will understand that there are interesting arbitrage opportunities and means of acquiring currencies in countries with capital controls via Bitcoin.

The second way to get Bitcoins is to sell goods and services just as you sell goods or labor for dollars. To receive Bitcoins, put the Bitcoin address you received automatically when you opened your Bitcoin wallet account on your webpage. There is no "sign up" or "approval" to accept Bitcoin and no age, financial or geographic restrictions. Just get the wallet software (from bitcoin.org) or use an "ewallet" such as Paytunia.com, and post a Bitcoin address for the universe to see. Anyone can send you Bitcoins instantly with your Bitcoin address.

For small businesses who would like a more advanced way to accept and track Bitcoin payments for website orders, there are a few good merchant solutions. Paysius.com will plug into your site (using common shopping cart plugins) and enable your customers to select "Bitcoin" as payment during checkout instead of credit card or PayPal, etc. Few businesses can pay for salaries or suppliers in Bitcoin, so systems like Paysius offer the ability to auto-convert Bitcoins into US dollars for deposit in a corporate bank account. Fees are lower than credit card processing, and Bitcoin payments have zero chargebacks or reversals (it's impossible to reverse a

Bitcoin payment) Merchants can securely accept payment from any country with no more risk of reversal in contrast to by PayPal or those hit by credit card fraud. Bit-pay.com is another option for merchants to accept Bitcoin.

Mining Bitcoins

Mining Bitcoins is to mathematically compute what is known as a SHA-256 hash that is numerically below a set threshold value (i.e. the first bits must be all zero). It's like randomly drawing 256 bits and hoping that the first N bits are all zero. With each additional zero bit, the chances go down by 50%.

Imagine you have a hat with 100 pieces of paper in it, numbered 1 to 100. You pull out a piece of paper every minute and look at what you got (then put it back and shake up the hat). If the number drawn is lower than 20, you win, something that would occur on average every five minutes. If you started checking numbers faster than every minute, you could slow down how often you win by making the highest winning number 15 instead of 20. Bitcoin mining is similar but instead of 1 to 100 numbers, there are 1 to $1.1579E+77$ possible numbers that you get when you take the hash of some data.

Bitcoin awards you 50 BTC if you find a hash of the current transaction block that is $1.7248E+61$ or smaller. A SHA hash is a complex mathematical formula that is a filter for some original data which seeds it; the formula creates a number on the other side which is a 'signature' of the original data. Other hashes familiar in the computer world are MD5 or CRC. Hashing the same transaction block would always give the same SHA hash, so your computer adds random data (called a nonce) to the end of a transaction block to change the hash that comes out. It is impossible to tell what the hash will be from the nonce you add, so SHA is cryptographically secure and there is no shortcut to generating billions of different test nonces to check for a valid hash.

Market Risk

When incremental adoption meets relatively fixed supply, prices go up. That is what has happened to BTC prices. BTC prices do sometimes plummet, which has sometimes been caused hack attack on Bitcoin Wallet companies. In the cyber and real worlds, confidence in money as a store of value is the ultimate driver of its value.

Failure Modes

Bitcoin could fail through normal processes like currency devaluation or a declining user base. However, a more realistic threat is a global governmental crackdown on the software. Bitcoin is not the only cryptocurrency system possible though, so this is an unwinnable battle for the state. It will be possible to ban all crypto-cash variations, much less Bitcoin. This means traditional taxation, traceable through bank accounts, as well as taxation through inflation, are vulnerable to technological obsolescence.

There are no centrally controlling powers in the Bitconomy, but a core group of developers work on the mainline bitcoin.org client. If co-opted, they could cause havoc ranging from releasing poorly implemented code to hiding backdoors in clients.

Another attack mode would be to purchase more computing power than the entire network and compromise block contents. Such a disrupter could use a Distributed Denial Of Service attack on the Bitcoin peer-to-peer network by refusing to record other people's transactions in the blocks they mine, or by double spending their own coins.

The Bitcoin developer group is thus a weak point, and the FBI has already paid them visits. However, Bitcoin is an open source project which makes it hard to hide backdoors. Any poorly implemented versions would be shunned by the Bitcoin community. Nothing gives the current developers sole rights to the software. If Bitcoin users come to believe they are untrustworthy, a new group of developers would be created and the software would fork down a new, trusted path.

There are hurdles to true anonymity with Bitcoin, and governments/regulators will fight anonymity with the claim that it hides criminal activity. While Bitcoin exchanges can be built with no intermediary and relative anonymity, fiat money is usually involved at some point, usually to buy the Bitcoin in the first place. This is the Achilles heel to Bitcoins anonymity until there is no longer a need or desire to convert back and forth with fiat currencies.

The only truly anonymous Bitcoins are those mined by their possessor (with a TOR proxy) rather than those exchanged for fiat money. New anti-money laundering laws (AML) require exchanges to maintain account holder information, so all exchange transactions can be tracked back to the names of people on both sides of a transfer. You cannot create an account with CryptoXChange, Dwolla, etc. without providing your name and other identifying information. If you transfer any significant amount of fiat money you need to provide additional ID, i.e., passport number, social security number, etc. With BitInstant you can deposit cash into a bank, but banks will start asking for ID to make these kinds of deposits.

Then there is your own bank account from which your fiat money originates which definitely has your personal information. If you used an electronic means to transfer your account balance to an exchange then your name is once again tagged to the funds and everything you buy with it. In fact, if at any point along the line you used an account associated with your name then your name becomes traceable throughout the entire chain of events. From your bank, to the exchange, to the public key in your Bitcoin wallet there will be a record trail, especially as exchanges must record the public key of every Bitcoin deposit and withdrawal. So in practice the Bitcoins in the wallet on your home computer likely have a fiat money rail and are traceable to your name for months or years after you acquired them. Thus, most Bitcoins in circulation today are traceable back to an individual, making anonymity a challenge.

One way to break this chain once one has some Bitcoins is to transfer the coins to a new wallet. A new different public/private key pair breaks the direct chain of information pointing to the holder and it appears as though an exchange was made to someone else. No intermediary is needed as one acts as both the sender and receiver. Just as a fiat dollar bill finds itself in hundreds of different hands over its lifetime, so will Bitcoin value be transferred and dispersed. The person who held a Bitcoin yesterday is no more responsible for it today than someone who never held it before. Making a phantom transfer to a new wallet obfuscates the fact that you once openly possessed it; however, there is still al permanent record in the Bitcoin block chain that you once possessed coins via the public key tied to your name. But no one knows who controls the newly created public key generated out of thin air by your Bitcoin client which was never associated with your name.

After the transfer, it is no longer possible to prove with certainty that you still have the Bitcoins, short of your new wallet being confiscated. One other way the exchange can be traced though is by your computer's IP address. If the sender and receiver IP's are the same, it's pretty obvious the exchange occurred between one person. A way to eliminate this is by using a TOR proxy, which Bitcoin clients allows you to setup once you're running the TOR client (www.torproject.org). A TOR proxy makes it extremely difficult to determine either the sender or receiver's IP address. Making several wallet to wallet transfers, with the sending and receiving wallets on different computers, both running TOR, would make even NSA tracking problematic.

After transfers, it would take considerable effort, through a surveillance operation at the time of transfer to determine you still possess the coins and make tracing transactions difficult. The more bit coiners employing these techniques, the more anonymous the Bitcoin network will become despite the amount of information the exchanges gather. Anonymity tools do add overhead and tedium to using Bitcoin, but future Bitcoin clients will likely have such devices built-in.

Are Bitcoins Valuable?

For Bitcoin to be a virtual currency, Bitcoin must have value.

Financial privacy has long been symbolized by the "Swiss bank account" which was trusted by clients to retain their anonymity. Even in Switzerland "bank privacy" has become a myth as banks have bent to the will of the US government and now divulge customer information. Bitcoin is equivalent to having a private, numbered Swiss bank account, but without having to bother with the Swiss bank itself. Instead of trusting a regulated bank governed by fallible humans, your trust is in an unregulated cryptographic environment governed by infallible mathematics. You will have to decide on your own who you think more likely to fail your needs.

A major reason Bitcoin is revolutionary is that it has no counter-party risk to hold and to transfer funds, an advantage unique to cybercurrencies. Physical gold and silver bullion have no counter-party risk, but only if stored in your own home. Once stored in a vault or bank there is counter-party risk requiring trust in numerous intermediaries to transfer your gold somewhere else or spend it across a distance.

Bitcoin allows complete ownership of money for both storage and transfer. Even if one's home is broken into, or the government issues a "confiscation order" (as done with gold in 1933), one's Bitcoins are safe as long as your wallet is hidden. In times of chaos, fleeing a country with $1,000,000 in bullion is impossible without the government knowing about it. With Bitcoin, $1,000,000 of Bitcoin can exist on a USB drive. Or the private key can be written on a piece of paper. Or you can email the wallet file to yourself to be retrieved outside the country.

Never in the history have individuals had this ability to hold and transfer currency without interference. But what gives Bitcoins their initial value? Why do they have a price?" Bitcoins have value because:

1. They are useful

2. They are scarce

These two attributes combined in any asset give it a price. Once the first Bitcoin was traded in exchange for something else, an exchange rate (market price) was established. Subsequent exchangers agreed or disagreed with that rate, and made further trades in a truly free market. Bitcoin thus spontaneously developed a price, unlike national currencies which are manipulated by central banks. All things develop and exchange price in an open market if they are sufficiently useful and sufficiently scarce.

There are many notable financiers and economists including Paul Krugman and Warren Buffet who do not believe Bitcoin has value and is no more than a speculative bubble fad.

However, any follower of gold or silver as money understands why metals function as money and how Bitcoin has similarly derived value mechanisms:

- They are chosen in an open marketplace as money,

- Their properties make them useful as a means of exchange

The properties of gold and silver which make them excellent as money: They are scarce, fungible, uniform, transportable, have a high value-to-weight ratio, are easily identifiable, are highly durable, and their supplies are steady and predictable. Contrast this to other goods like chickens, or seashells, or sand, and you discover none of them combine the same favorable attributes as precious metals. Chickens can't be cut in half or recombined and retain value. Seashells are not uniform. Sand is too plentiful to be used as money. Other metals, such as iron not scarce enough to use as money and you'd need carts of it to go shopping.

As per the Austrian school of economics definition, money is merely any commodity in an open market which satisfies the properties necessary for useful exchange. Gold and silver have been the premier stores of value historically, but they are not perfect, infallible money and practical problems remain. Silver coins can't be easily divided and combined to make change. It is difficult to send large values of gold across a distance without hiring security and waiting for transport. Precious metals incur storage fees, risk theft at home and it is possible (though difficult) to make fake gold and silver ingots.

Though gold and silver have been the best money historically, they are not perfect. Bitcoin is an experiment in whether a better form of money can be invented than what the marketplace currently enjoys or what the state enforces by fiat. If Bitcoin's attributes make it excellent money and it thrives in an open free market, then it will be increasingly used over time and replace less efficient monetary vehicles.

So far, Bitcoin has found more and more niches for early adoption, despite colossal failures like MtGox. Fluctuations in its market price have been at times severe, but have returned to the trend line even after severe disruption, providing confidence to holders that it will retain value. It is thus likely that with time Bitcoin and other cybercurrencies will used for still more purposes in a trial and error process, full of innovations and failures. But a resilient cybercash economy is being built, voluntarily - not by decree of central banks, but by spontaneous, self-interested private economic interest. It would thus be unwise to remain ignorant of this trend for one's own financial survival.

Bitcoins Are Pure Fiat

The argument that "nothing backs Bitcoin" is true and Bitcoins cannot be redeemed for any fixed value, nor is it traded at any fixed exchange rate for existing currencies or commodities. However, neither are precious metals backed by anything, their value comes because they are useful and scarce. All goods (food, housing, cars . . .) have value in proportion to their usefulness and scarcity. It is the usefulness of Bitcoin which gives it value, without any backing from any government or corporation, without being tied to any fiat currency or existing commodity. Bitcoin commands a price on the market because it is a useful store of value without the myriad problems of traditional moneys.

Security

Bitcoin requires a high degree of personal responsibility, so users need to know the basic rules to use it safely. If you are careless, you can lose money and never get it back. However, with a few basic pointers you can use Bitcoin securely, without fear of loss.

1. Bitcoins are like cash and are stored in a specific physical place. You must be mindful of where your Bitcoins are, and any risks that location poses. If your coins are on your computer, and you don't back them up elsewhere and the computer crashes, your money is gone, lost to the ether. If you store your coins with an online service (like an ewallet or exchange), then you are trusting that service to hold your coins safely. That has turned out to be a bad bet with the $500 million collapse of Mt Gox. You wouldn't give 10 bucks cash to someone you don't trust and the same is true with Bitcoin. Back up all Bitcoins kept on your computer or Smartphone and keep your systems secure. It isn't wise to completely trust anyone who holds coins, disperse your assets.

2. Bitcoins are protected with passwords. If someone learns your wallet password and they obtain your wallet file, they can spend your coins! Similarly, if someone learns your login information to a service provider they can steal your coins. Use strong passwords with Bitcoin (more than 12 characters) and keep them in a safe place. Bitcoin funds are not protected by government-mandated and taxpayer-subsidized FDIC insurance. Bitcoin banks cannot just type in digits to replenish funds stolen by fault of your own carelessness.

3. When using the wallet software from bitcoin.org, the first time you open your wallet software you need to make a password to encrypt your wallet. After making this password, you need to **backup your wallet file** in another different location. This file is where your money is stored. The file name is "wallet.dat" and backing it up is as simple as copying the file and putting it somewhere else.

4. Locating the wallet.dat file:

   On Windows, you must first tell your computer to "Show hidden files and folders" - look up how to do this online. Then, find your wallet here:

   C:\Documents and Settings\YourUserName\Application data\Bitcoin (XP)

   C:\Users\YourUserName\Appdata\Roaming\Bitcoin (Vista and Windows 7)

   On a Mac, it is found here:

   ~/Library/Application Support/Bitcoin/

   If you back up the wallet properly your likelihood of losing your Bitcoins will be low. Put this wallet.dat file on a USB drive in your safe. Or mail it to family member. Put it on a different computer. Burn it to a CD and put it in a bank safety deposit box. You can even email the file to yourself. Better yet, do two or three of the above..

5. Bitcoin-based companies don't need to be registered anywhere. They don't need a business checking account or an IRS EIN number. Bitcoin enables unregulated free trade on a global scale, but Bitcoin users need to be careful. The only thing protecting you are mathematical algorithms that define its encryption and growth plus your password and location secrecy. Only buy things from companies or websites you trust because otherwise you may never see your money again and there is no way to "reverse" a payment. Reputation and history are everything with Bitcoin.

6. Bitcoin will remain an experiment for many years. As resilient as the system is, the value of a Bitcoin could drop to zero on any bad news. Do not invest money in Bitcoin you

cannot afford to lose. Bitcoin is a highly volatile commodity with an extremely uncertain future. Do not put retirement money into Bitcoin.

Bitcoin Uses

Bitcoin can enable any kind of trade or business one can imagine, but because it is relatively new, much infrastructure still needs to be designed. Entrepreneurs have been testing Bitcoin-systems for a couple years, but the vast majority its global potential remains untapped.

One can buy goods and services from anyone who will accept Bitcoins. A list of some businesses can be found here: https://en.bitcoin.it/wiki/Trade

Donations to worthwhile causes are made very efficient via Bitcoin. Indie film companies and animal shelters may accept Bitcoin donations. Bitcoin is great for donations because micro-transactions are possible. You can't send $0.10 via PayPal to a charity because the fees are larger than $0.10. To accept donations, simply put a Bitcoin address on your website.

Gambling is also possible with Bitcoins being used for online poker. Sites such as SealsWithClubs.eu are gaining popularity, with larger casinos being built.

Sending money to friends or family overseas is especially efficient with Bitcoin instead of paying Western Union $40. Remittance markets are an area where Bitcoin excels, because it passes across borders instantly and without regulation or interference. If you're in places like China or Belarus with capital controls, if you can immediately transfer wealth outside the country to other currencies. Bitcoin transcends borders and regulations so your wealth doesn't sit in an account that can be frozen or seized.

To convert Bitcoin to gold or silver to store value try a site like Coinabul.com

Anything you can do with "money", you can do with Bitcoin, but free of governmental restriction upon that activity. This obviously opens up large areas for abuse, which we do not advocate. However, cybercurrency is here to stay with all its flaws and advantages no matter how much oversight government entities may want.

The Future Of Bitcoin & Cybercash

Government doesn't regulate Bitcoin yet, but they eventually must! Janet Yellen testified to a Senator Manchin in early 2014 that the Federal Reserve does not have jurisdiction over Bitcoin, but that will certainly change. Governments have no option but to try to regulate and crush cybercurrencies because they sidestep taxation, currency inflation and money laundering interests. However, world government will have a near impossible task trying to do so because they are up against the laws of mathematics on which Bitcoin is built.

The FBI and various U.S. legislators are paying close attention. Since Bitcoin has no sovereign sponsorship, it works outside any nation's security apparatus. Illegal drugs, online casinos, money laundering are all made easier because the anonymity of the currency.

Being known as a currency for illegal drugs and gambling is problematic, but don't forget that the U.S. Treasury printed 3 billion $100 bills in 2012 and the Federal Reserve estimates 80% of those bills go overseas, often to facilitate the global drug and arms trade, tax evasion and human trafficking. So Bitcoins growing role in worldwide currency markets only parallels the same types of legitimate and illegitimate business activities the dollar already enables with its "Reserve Currency" status. Bitcoin is just a more honest reflection of what already exists.

The Federal Reserve and modern central banks inevitably led to inflate away the value of their currencies as a methodical means of theft to benefit the political and banking classes. As the Euro and dollar fail over coming years or decades, attempts to move towards cybercash will become irresistible. Just as foreseeable is that governments will need to make these sound but unpilferable currencies illegal. The creator of Liberty Dollars has now spent substantial jail time for attempting to distribute alternative gold backed coinage.

We don't advocate using cybercash as a means of avoiding the devaluation of your currency, or for the illegal practice of avoiding taxes. However, a prudent citizen will be aware that this is a disruptive and likely unstoppable financial technology. Unfortunately, citizens may be caught between a rock and a hard place, as their wheelbarrows of Dollars or Euros are unable to buy food, but they still have hungry mouths to feed and the only money of value is cybercash.

Long term, competition from cybercurrencies may force governments to impose either gold backed currencies, or at least fixed rule monetary policies that will give their citizens an even break over fiat money. However, that also implies a necessary default on the current unfunded financial pyramid is necessary to allow the creation of a stable currency which is not purposely debased to fund government largesse. The grinding forces of monetary instability will make it inevitable that citizens consider an alternative path that preserves their wealth. This makes it just as inevitable that governments will try to shut down Bitcoins.

Private websites on a hosted server can be taken down by a government even before any trial or finding of criminal activity, as shown when MegaUpload was taken down by the US government. It should be assumed the government can take down any site it wishes, with or without the legal cover of legislation like SOPA and PIPA. Websites that deal in Bitcoins could be removed and shut down and the exchanges would be the first targets. One might even conjecture some of the failures of exchanges in 2014 were government orchestrated.

Yet, websites can be mirrored, copied, and hidden easily, so taking down Bitcoin websites is like cutting the heads off a Hydra - publicity and the profit motive compel more sites to spring up. The demise of the notorious SilkRoad as an exchange for illegal drugs and services certainly did not stop that activity.

While taking down websites is an inadequate strategy for the government if it wishes to impede Bitcoin, they have other options.

A government could prohibit individuals and businesses from openly accepting Bitcoins within one. If the US Government banned the acceptance of Bitcoin: it would mean Bitcoin could only be accepted in secret. This might not harm the economy significantly, but neither would it stop Bitcoin. Unless every government followed suit, Bitcoins could be openly accepted in other countries. The end result would be capital flight which create pressure on governments to legalize Bitcoins.

A more direct attack method might be for governments to attempt to shut down Bitcoin transfers. Centralized systems like PayPal, Visa, or even e-gold are vulnerable to state intervention because the Feds can simply confiscate the servers, and throw the owners in jail. Centralized systems must inevitably bend to the government's will, or be shut down. This also puts at risk the private financial information of their clients as well.

Because there is no central point of failure, Bitcoin is not as vulnerable to governmental financial repression. There are no Bitcoin offices, central servers, CEO or employees to arrest or harass. There is no controlling authority to jail or sue, though the Federal government will eventually attack users by claiming they are unpatriotic. Bitcoin has no home country, it is licensed nowhere. It is a distributed network, a protocol that can operate as long as the internet exists and even without the internet. Transactions occur peer-to-peer, meaning no governing body approves them. No one has authority or a mechanism to freeze accounts.

Bitcoin is like a virus which, so long as a few hosts survive somewhere in the world, can perpetuate itself and regrow at the speed of information. It cannot be turned off.

The final power the governments wields is via their ability to print, regulate, and control the nation's money. When a state currency is challenged, the state itself is challenged. Market forces move swiftly in the digital world and the Federal Reserve will become less and less important as the currency they print is used in narrower and narrower circles. Bitcoin enables individuals to sidestep the government - to ignore it to a large degree - instead of fighting it head on. Bitcoin, paired with the free flow of information on the internet, provides a mechanism to create a stable monetary system immune to the pilfering of politicians.

The Zimbabwe government would have been powerless if its people had had Bitcoin in their communities - money they could hide and spend via cell phones and email accounts. The same applies to Venezuela where Hugo Chavez stole billions. Why would Greeks need to riot at the ECB mandates when the country could abandon the Euro in favor of a money that each individual controls. Where would the US get the resources to deficit-finance its welfare programs when it no longer has the ability to print money and pay back debt with debased currency?

Like a gold standard, Bitcoin shackles a government and forces it to subsist only on what it can tax openly and legitimately borrow. Unlike a gold standard, Bitcoin doesn't require official status to become a standard. The market arrive at the conversion price without government approval or manipulation because Bitcoins are not only a means for storage and transfer of wealth, but also an honest broker of information on inflation and economic activity. And it cannot be stopped because it exists in digital decentralized form.

Bitcoin's growth and adoption curve create revolutionary possibilities, despite the birthing pains. Instead of trying to change governments with a diluted vote, one simply abandons obedience to the government's powerbase - power derived from control of exchange and currency. This cuts the umbilical not only to the political aristocracy, but to tribute exacted by the banker class. The growing pains of this new cybercurrency monetary system are far outweighed by the gift of liberty it can bring.

Disruptive Technology

Once one realizes the government is quite powerless to stop Bitcoin, other ramifications spring to mind. If Bitcoin doesn't fail outright and succeeds even marginally, it will replace many institutions.

Money transfer mega-companies like PayPal and Western will discover they have to compete with a system that transfers money at practically zero cost. The "service" these companies provide becomes obsolete, and can be replaced by frictionless Bitcoin global transfers.

Humanity will be billions of dollars per year richer if we eliminate companies that are providing a service which can be done for free. Email made humanity richer by enabling communication at lower cost, and Bitcoin can make the world richer by enabling monetary transfers at lower cost.

If Bitcoin grows large enough to start replacing financial transaction networks, its value will stabilize further and more confidence can be imbued in the long-term price. Subsequently, Bitcoin will become an increasingly better (more stable) means of value storage, which threatens banks first and then national currencies second.

All the work done by banks to hold and account for money (and transfer it between individuals and companies) can be done natively by Bitcoin. And so just as the payment services become redundant, so too do many services provided by banks, shrinking the banking sector down to those areas where it still serves useful value.

A Bitcoin world would still have banks, but the banks would be properly placed into those market roles where they do useful work. People don't necessarily want to store value on home-based PC's, and a bank with security staff and safe systems may make a smart place to hold funds (but instead of everyone *having* to hold funds at the bank, it would be their option based on their risk-profile). Similarly, there will always be a need in a capitalist system for loans and interest paid on deposits. Banks would enjoy this ability with Bitcoin so long as they were efficient and could compete in the open market.

As we move further along the adoption and growth curve of a Bitcoin monetary system, we will see national currencies themselves become challenged. Why would people hold Euros or Dollars or Yen which are perpetually debased when an alternative exists that enables easier payments and cannot be debased by central banks? If Bitcoin proves itself over the years as a solid store of value, what rational reason would one have to use national currencies at all? Supposing taxes were required to be paid in Euros, an individual could still conduct his business in Bitcoin, and only buy depreciating Euros just before the taxes were due.

We don't see the adoption of gold as an alternative currency today because gold has no good payment system built into it. Physical bullion is not efficient for daily trade, and digital vaults backed by gold have all come under fire from governments. Transfer systems of companies like GoldMoney have been pressured into shutting down; GoldMoney discontinued its account-to-account transfers.

Bitcoin makes storage *and* transfer of funds easy, secure, private, and instantaneous. With a history of price stability earned over time, or in conjunction with gold and silver as an even more reliable combined store of value, why use state fiat at all?

A prudent person should assume Bitcoin will fail, but, there is a real chance it will succeed, a chance which increases with every new user, every new business, and every new system developed within the Bitconomy. The ramifications of success are extraordinary, and can affect the course of liberty around the world.

Financial Strategies

13 Financial Survival Basics

If you have your money invested in 401ks or other standard investment vehicles you already realize that you have been made a sucker. The government not only wants your tax money, it wants ALL your money because it is flat broke. Fortunately, here are some ways to protect your money and income that are still legal:

1 Don't invest all your money in one country. Don't put all your eggs in the same basket, just in case any economy goes to hell. Invest in countries like Canada, Australia, Singapore, Chile, Scandinavia; anywhere their debt to GDP ratio is low.

2 Buy Commodities, solid things like gold, or stocks in mining or manufacturing companies. Most banks and financial institutions are currently bankrupt.

3 Keep cash. Some dollars and Euros but also Canadian and Australian dollars. There are obvious risks in currencies like the Dollar or Euro, but cash diversity is the only way you have to cover all contingencies. It's possible for our national paper money to lose 1/3 of its worth from one day to another.

4 Keep your passport and cash ready. If you can't afford to live in this country, the best thing to do may be getting the hell out of it! Maybe you have family somewhere else, keep in touch just in case.

5 If you have land, have some animals, a garden and fruit trees. Raising a few chickens and rabbits makes a huge difference and complements your staple food storage.

6 People will be fixing things in the future instead of buying new ones. A handyman will always find a way to survive, no matter what your primary job is.

7 Downsize as much as possible and reduce debt!

Until costs and inefficiencies resulting from overly-generous pensions, early retirements, union work rules, long vacations, escalating health care costs, government bureaucracy and inflexible hire-and-fire rules are seriously dealt with, financial problems will continue to fester in one form or another. U.S., voters are not yet ready to accept the major changes needed because so far money can be printed and borrowed to put off the day of reckoning. Eventually that will no longer be possible and then the hard choices will have to be made.

Economic Depression Survival Tips

It hardly matters whether we are in a deflationary, inflationary or biflationary economy, what we know for certain is that we are in an economic depression. So, what do you need to do to survive financially? Here are some fundamentals:

Keep That Income If *you can k*eep your job or other income, tough times aren't so tough. In fact, if you are still making the same money when prices are dropping, homes cost less and stocks are on sale, a depression can be an opportunity. So find ways to preserve and protect any income you already have. Make sure that the boss knows you are a great worker. Transfer to areas of the company less likely to face layoffs. Work overtime or extra shifts and save the money.

Find better employment in a more secure industry. Of course that isn't easy, if even possible.

Cut costs in your small business. As soon as sales start to drop, don't hesitate to use the axe. The workers, clients and suppliers you will retain will appreciate your remaining in business.

Find a second job if you have the time. Consider starting a low-investment low-risk business on the side to develop an alternate source of income.

Get Ready Whatever you do, in this New Normal there is always a chance you will lose your primary income. This is true in good times and bad, but in tough times it may be a long time before you can replace that income. This makes preparation in your personal life very important.

Cut fixed expenses, like payments for rental furniture or appliances. Obviously you can stop trips to the movies or bar the moment that you hear you are losing a job, but other fixed expenses are harder to quickly reduce and will drag you down fast. Get rid of the extra car you don't need, or the unused boat that costs maintenance and insurance. List all of your household expenses and find ways to reduce each one if possible, but start with those that would be the most difficult to reduce quickly when hard times come.

If you are in particularly insecure industry (auto worker, real estate agent, mortgage broker, etc.), seriously consider downsizing your life in more drastic ways. A $600-per-month apartment in place of a $1,200 one means you can set aside an additional $9,000 in 15 months to be ready for whatever comes your way. It also means you'll have a much easier time finding a way to pay that rent if you lose your job. A nice $3,000 used car (they exist if you look) in place of a payment of $500 per month on a newer one means another $7,500 saved in 15 months, and no repossession risk if your income is lost.

Develop other sources of income to the extent possible. Have a side business that makes a few hundred dollars per month, buy some dividend-paying stocks that generate regular checks for you, sell something on Craigslist. Diversify and it's unlikely that you will lose all sources of income at once.

Surviving an economic depression means having contingency plans. What is the least amount you can live on if you lose your primary income, and how will you do it? You may want to try living on that for a week to see if your plan is realistic. Can you sell some of your things if necessary, and do you know what they'll bring in a fast sale? How quickly can you find another job if you lose your current one? Make a list of possible jobs and who you'll need to contact. Have those numbers ready.

Lower your regular expenses, develop other income, have plans in place and money in the bank. Take those steps and you'll be better prepared than most for recessions, depressions or other tough times.

14   Bankruptcy & Strategic Default

In the event of an economic collapse, you may very well find yourself bankrupt and forced to seek protection for the sake of survival. The moral issues of bankruptcy that bother honest people – defaulting on debts you legitimately owe – may not even apply in a collapse. If you are self employed or a business owner, long chains of defaults by your business suppliers and accounts receivables will be completely out of your control. If you are employed by a business, whole economic sectors can suddenly vaporize, especially in financial service industries. At that point, survival trumps moral guilt. Therefore you need to be aware that there are a number of different bankruptcy strategies.

There are six types of bankruptcy under the Bankruptcy Code, in Title 11 of the United States Code:

- Chapter 7: basic liquidation for individuals and businesses; also known as straight bankruptcy; it is the simplest and quickest form of bankruptcy available
- Chapter 9: municipal bankruptcy; a federal mechanism for the resolution of municipal debts
- Chapter 11: rehabilitation or reorganization. This chapter is used primarily by business debtors. It is sometimes used by individuals with substantial debts and assets. Known as corporate bankruptcy, it is a form of corporate financial reorganization in which companies are allowed to continue operating while they repay debts under a court approved plan
- Chapter 12: rehabilitation for family farmers and fishermen;
- Chapter 13: rehabilitation with a payment plan. Generally used by individuals with a regular source of income; this Chapter enables individuals with regular income to develop a plan to repay all or part of their debts. Chapter 13 is also referred to as Wage Earner Bankruptcy
- Chapter 15: ancillary and other international cases; provides a mechanism for dealing with bankruptcy debtors and helps foreign debtors to clear debts.

The most common types of personal bankruptcy are Chapter 7 and Chapter 13. Chapter 7 cases account for as much as 65% of U.S. consumer bankruptcy filings. Corporations and other business entities file under Chapter 7 or Chapter 11.

Chapter 7

A Chapter 7 bankruptcy is designed to eliminate unsecured debts (including credit cards), store cards, payday loans, medical bills, utility bills, and other debt not tied to property. A debtor surrenders non-exempt property to a bankruptcy trustee who liquidates the property and then disburses any proceeds to the debtor's unsecured creditors. The debtor is entitled to a discharge of some debt as long as they are not guilty of inappropriate behavior. Concealing records relating to ones financial condition abrogates the bankruptcy agreement. Certain debts also are given special treatment, such as spousal and child support, student loans and some taxes which are not discharged. Exempt property such as clothes, household goods or an older car do not have to be surrendered to the trustee. The amount of property that may be exempt varies state to state. Chapter 7 relief can only be taken once in any eight year period. Generally, secured creditors retain their rights to collateral even though the debt is discharged. For example, a creditor with a security interest in a debtor's car can repossess the vehicle even if the debt has been discharged.

An eligibility "means test" was introduced in the 2005 amendments to the Bankruptcy Code for Chapter 7. Individual who fail the means test will have their Chapter 7 status revoked or may need to convert to Chapter 13.

Trustees generally sell most debtors' assets to reimburse creditors. Some assets are protected: Social Security income, unemployment compensation, and limited equity in a home, car, or truck. Household goods and appliances, trade tools, and books are also protected, though these exemptions can vary from state to state. An experienced bankruptcy attorney may be needed for advice.

Chapter 13

Chapter 13 is designed to stop foreclosure and to reorganize debts into affordable monthly repayment. The debtor retains ownership and possession of all their assets, but must devote some portion of his or her future income to repaying creditors, generally over a period of three to five years. The plans vary in the amount of payment and period of payment. The value of the debtor's property and their income and expenses also are factored into the plan. Secured creditors are theoretically entitled to greater payments than unsecured creditors.

If you're an individual or a sole proprietor, you are allowed to file for a Chapter 13 bankruptcy to repay all or part of your debts. Only individuals with regular income whose debts meet certain limits can file for relief under Chapter 13. Plans run for three years if the debtor's monthly income falls below a state's median income, unless the court finds "just cause" and extends the plan. Plans are generally five years for debtor's whose monthly incomes are greater than a state's median income and cannot exceed the five-year limitation.

Unlike Chapter 7 bankruptcy, in Chapter 13 the debtor keeps all of their property. If the plan appears feasible, the bankruptcy court confirms the plan and the debtor and creditors are bound by its terms. Creditors have the option to object to the plan the grounds it doesn't comply with statutory requirements, but otherwise have no say in its formulation on. Payments are generally made to the trustee who disburses funds in accordance with the terms of the bankruptcy plan.

Once the court confirms the plan, debtors must make the plan succeed by making regular payments to the trustee directly or through payroll deduction. With the plans confirmation, the debtor is entitled to retain property but only as long as payments are made. Debtors may not incur new debt without consent of the trustee, because new debt compromises the debtor's ability to fulfill the plan

When the debtor completes payments fulfilling the terms of the court plan, the debtor is granted a discharge of the debts outlined in the plan. The discharge releases the debtor from all debts provided for by the plan with the exception of certain debts including long term obligations (home mortgage), alimony or child support debt, certain taxes, debts for government funded educational loans, debts incurred from death or personal injury caused by driving while under the influence, and debts for criminal restitution. If the debtor fails to make payments or fails to gain court approval for a modified plan, the case will be dismissed by the bankruptcy court on the motion of the trustee. On dismissal, creditors will generally pursue remedies through state law for unpaid debts.

Chapter 11

The debtor In Chapter 11 bankruptcy retains control and ownership of their assets and is redefined as a *debtor in possession* ("DIP"). While creditors and the debtor work with the Bankruptcy Court to negotiate a plan, the debtors in possession runs the day to day operations of the business. On meeting requirements for fairness and priority among creditors, creditors are vote on the proposed plan. If the terms of the plan are confirmed, the debtor continues to operate as long as they pay their debts.

Chapter 7, a "straight bankruptcy", and Chapter 13, an affordable plan of repayment, are the chapters which almost always apply to consumer debt. In all types of bankruptcy filings an automatic stay means the request for bankruptcy protection automatically stops most foreclosures, evictions, utility shut-offs, lawsuits, repossessions, attachments, garnishments, and debt collection harassment.

15   Financial Repression

"Financial Repression", is the ominous-sounding name for government theft of the citizens' wealth through monetary manipulation. It is what we are now experiencing in America and is the means by which the state funds explosive entitlement society. It will accelerate as the financial situation deteriorates (see Greece) and you need to understand both the mechanisms and the ways to avoid at least some of the financial pain.

Monetary manipulation allows governments to issue debt at lower interest rates than would otherwise be possible. Low nominal interest rates help governments reduce debt servicing costs, while high negative real interest rates liquidates or erodes the real value of government debt. Thus, financial repression is most successful in liquidating debts when accompanied by a steady dose of inflation, and can be considered a form of stealth taxation.

Stanford economists Edward S. Shaw and Ronald I. McKinnon first introduced the term financial repression in 1973 to describe emerging market financial systems in the 1960s-80s. Similar techniques were also used in developed economies, after World War II until the 1980s, when such direct government intervention in markets fell out of favor. However, these techniques are back in vogue because they are the only stop-gap measures standing between us and financial collapse. Financial repression incorporates the following key elements:

- Explicit or indirect capping or control over interest rates, particularly those on government debt.
- Government ownership or control of domestic banks and financial institutions while placing barriers to entry before other institutions seeking to enter the market.
- Creation of a captive domestic market for government debt requiring domestic banks to hold government debt via reserve requirements, or by disincentivising or prohibiting alternative options.
- Government restrictions imposed on the transfer of assets abroad through capital controls.

Repression Taxation

Unlike income, consumption, or sales taxes, the "repression" tax rates are determined by financial regulations and inflation performance that are hidden in the highly politicized realm of fiscal measures. Given that deficit reduction usually involves highly unpopular expenditure reductions and/or tax increases, the 'stealthier' financial repression tax is more politically palatable to governments faced with the need to reduce outstanding debts. That it is a theft of wealth by the banking and political class is obvious. That it is also a means of political repression also follows as night from day.

In financial repression governments use banks as vehicles to squeeze more indirect tax revenue from citizens by monopolizing the entire savings and payment system. Governments force local residents to save in banks by giving them few other options and then stuff debt into the banks via reserve requirements. Financial repression constitutes a form of taxation allowing the government to finance its debt at very low interest rates. Governments make the financial repression tax even larger by maintaining interest rate caps while creating inflation.

Directed lending to government by captive domestic audiences (such as pension funds), explicit or implicit caps on interest rates, regulation of cross-border capital movements, and a tighter connection between government and banks are all subtle types of debt restructuring that are forms of "financial repression."

Financial repression is most successful in liquidating debts when accompanied by a steady dose of inflation. Inflation need not be high to liquidate sovereign debt. For advanced economies real interest rates were negative roughly half of the time during 1945-1980. For the United States and the United Kingdom the annual liquidation of debt via negative real interest rates averaged from 3 to 4 percent of GDP a year, or a 30-40% GDP debt reduction over the decade. For Australia and Italy, which recorded higher inflation rates, the liquidation effect was larger (around 5 percent per annum).

Investment Implications

The international financial system will be forced to implement long term financial repression because of the irresolvable mass of debt it has accumulated. This will require governments to institute capital controls to avoid capital flight, which unsurprisingly was a hot topic at the 2011 INET Bretton Woods conference attended by Paul Volcker, Larry Summers, Gordon Brown, Adair Turn, George Soros, and others influential in the financial sphere.

It takes significant time to coordinate international effort to restrict capital flows, so investors may have time to take action - barring a sudden financial panic or collapse. However, for investors in European countries with acute debt problem (i.e., Greece, Ireland, Portugal, Spain, Italy, etc.), time has run out. Leaving the euro zone, as Greece is being forced, means imposition of immediate capital controls. Investors don't receive advance notice of capital controls as the goal is to prevent capital flight.

To protect capital from financial repression, investors need to hedge inflation and avoid fixed rate government bonds. However, the track record of equities during higher-inflation periods is mixed. Investing in domestic equities is no solution if private sector institutions are forced to hold more bonds. Large cash hordes of corporations have not gone unnoticed by the Federal Government. Multinational firms (like Coca-Cola or McDonalds) may offer some safety because their assets and income are spread worldwide among many currencies.

As financial repression grows, investors could reallocate assets offshore, though dodging wide international efforts to restrict capital flows will be difficult for retail investors. Some capital controls already are imposed by the United States, which has clamped down on offshore accounts by forcing foreign banks to act as reporting agents to our IRS. These controls have been couched as attempts to curtail scofflaw tax cheats and money launderers, which they do. But their real purpose is to stop the potential panic flight of larger sums as citizens desert a sinking economic ship. Traditionally investors have established accounts in countries like Switzerland; proven through the decades to be a safe haven for free capital, but Switzerland's banks no longer can protect depositors. Australia and Canada have shown currency resiliency of late. Even countries like Chile and Brazil are mentioned but caveat emptor.

Taking physical possession of precious metals, such as gold and silver is yet another way for investors to protect wealth from the effects of financial repression. Commodity based investments like mining and food stocks may also show some resiliency. Where possible, buying securities which have a large international presence and which can cushion themselves against dollar losses are also attractive.

While both commercial and residential real estate has taken tremendous hits since 2008 and price recovery may take a decade, physical assets always have some intrinsic value. Buying property at prices below replacement cost which have rents that can sustain mortgage costs is possible even in this Great Recession.

Finally, one can also invest in oneself. Adding to your skills through education creates assets that cannot be inflated away by the government. Purchasing equipment like drill presses and sewing machines can also add to your self sufficiency and avoid the inflationary trap. This author has also written a book titled "Going Galt: Surviving Economic Armageddon" which is a preparedness book that goes extensively into how to move as much as your life off-grid as possible. It is extremely difficult to completely drop out of society and fully avoid government financial repression, but it is relatively easy to reduce your dependence by half.

In a sense, all attempts to mitigate the effects of inflation and economic controls are stealthy but effective acts of civil disobedience. The tomatoes you produce in your garden are not now taxed (though legislation has been attempted that would regulate home gardens by the FDA!). The classic car that you repair and upgrade is a loss of a taxable income stream to the government.

Capital Flight

Capital flight and capital controls are two signs that fear and instability are nearing critical mass. Capital flight is people and enterprises moving their capital (cash and liquid assets) to an overseas "safe haven" to avoid devaluation of the currency or confiscation of their capital/assets. (Devaluation can be seen as one method of confiscation; high taxes are another.) . A good example to watch is France, which enacted a 75% tax on the income of the wealthy, only to see those citizens flee to tax havens.

Capital controls are the Central State's way of stemming the flood of cash leaving the country. Why do they want to stop money leaving? If we think of each Central State as a neofeudal fiefdom, we understand the motivation: citizens are in effect serfs who serve the State and its financial nobility. If the serfs move their capital out of the fiefdom, it is no longer available as collateral for the banks and a source of revenue for the State.

Capital controls include such measures as limiting the amount of funds that can be transferred out of the country; limiting the amount of gold that can be taken out of the country; barring all transfers of funds overseas; limiting all IRA, 401K and retirement funds to owning government Treasury bonds, and so on.

The U.S. banned private ownership of gold above a few ounces in 1933 as a form of capital control, forcing citizens to keep their capital in cash that could circulate and boost economic activity. Did it work? Obviously not.

Once capital has drained away, borrowing and lending shrink, cutting off the revenue source of the banks (financial nobility). Since financial activity declines as cash is withdrawn from financial institutions, the State's "skim"or "vigorish" of sales taxes, VAT taxes, transaction fees, income taxes, wealth taxes, etc.--also declines. Both the State and its financial nobility are at increasing risk of decline and eventual implosion as capital flees the fiefdom.

Those in the know transfer their wealth into another currency before it's illegal, and once the devaluation makes everything in the country much cheaper, they transfer their wealth back into the new currency and buy up all the assets on the cheap. Watch Greece and Spain to see how this is unfolding in real time.

Changing The Rules

The State will "change the rules" overnight to protect itself and its Elites.

Central State bureaucracies and Elites can become very creative at expropriating citizens' cash and assets once they feel threatened by a loss of faith in their legitimacy and competence, i.e. capital flight. For many decades, a Swiss bank account was the standard way that the wealthy hedged the risks of capital controls. As a result of the Federal government's efforts to catch tax cheaters and money laundering, Swiss bank accounts are no longer easily available to Americans.

The US is working on inter-governmental engagements worldwide to check non-compliance by American taxpayers using foreign bank accounts in their jurisdictions. Through engagements with more than 50 countries, the US is implementing information reporting and withholding tax provisions, commonly known as the Foreign Account Tax Compliance Act (FATCA). Enacted in 2010, FATCA aims at checking non-compliance by US taxpayers using foreign accounts by requiring foreign financial institutions to report information about accounts held by US taxpayers to the US tax department, or by foreign entities in which they hold a substantial ownership interest.

Concerns have been raised by foreign banks and financial institutions about the FATCA provisions that lead to increased compliance costs and infringe upon the local financial secrecy laws of the jurisdictions concerned.

The jurisdictions with which Treasury is working to explore options for inter-governmental engagement include the UK, Bermuda, Brazil, the British Virgin Islands, Chile, the Czech Republic, Gibraltar, India, Lebanon, Luxembourg, Romania, Russia, Seychelles, Saint Maarten, Slovenia, and South Africa. It is in the process of finalizing agreements with France, Germany, Italy, Spain, Japan, Switzerland, Canada, Denmark, Finland, Guernsey, Ireland, Isle of Man, Jersey, Mexico, the Netherlands, and Norway.

Jurisdictions where Treasury is actively engaged in concluding intergovernmental agreements include: Argentina, Australia, Belgium, Cayman Islands, Cyprus, Estonia, Hungary, Israel, Korea, Liechtenstein, Malaysia, Malta, New Zealand, the Slovak Republic, Singapore, and Sweden.

Negotiations with many of these jurisdictions are expected to be concluded by early 2013. Working cooperatively with foreign governments and financial institutions, the IRS is intensifying its war on tax evasion. What it is really doing is setting the stage for worldwide wealth confiscation

Hedging Against Capital Controls

As financial insecurity and instability rise, hedging becomes increasingly important as a means of capital preservation. There is no perfect hedge. Every hedge has risks. Physical gold can be stolen, expropriated at the border, etc. Any currency can be devalued. Property held overseas can be expropriated by a "new" government. The list is endless.

A hedge is not the same as a speculation, though each has risk. All hedges are imperfect, and so diversification is a key strategy in hedging. The purpose of a hedge is to preserve capital, not score speculative gains.

The two most basic hedges against capital controls and devaluation are:

1) **Owning physical gold/silver (discussed in other chapters)**

2) **Diversifying holdings to other currencies held in overseas "safe havens"**

Hedges against instability and insecurity can be seen around the globe: wealthy Chinese are transferring capital overseas at a furious pace and buying gold. Greek and Spanish citizens have been flying to London to open bank accounts so they can transfer their money out of Spain and Spanish banks. Should Spain or Greece leave the euro, the transfer into their traditional currency would amount to a forced devaluation of their cash. Even the French rich have been moving assets after the imposition of a 75% tax on income.

Massive capital flight out of these countries has been widely reported in the financial media, and it raises an important question for anyone with cash to safeguard: what happens if capital controls become possibilities in the U.S. or Canada?

The idea that the amount of money that could be withdrawn or transferred from your private accounts might seem farfetched at the moment, but if history teaches anything about financial crises, it is that the rules are changed overnight to protect the Central State and vested interests. We cannot control economic, financial and political instability; all we can do is hedge the risks by diversifying our assets and taking control of what we can control.

Hedging and local control are essential strategies for individuals in the New Normal. Having capital that is liquid (easily converted into legal tender or moved to safety) and income streams that are reliable, i.e. that are not speculative or dependent on the Central State and are under your own control, are key assets that cannot be replaced.

Foreign Bank Accounts

Foreign bank accounts can also provide a hedge against capital controls. These accounts are not free to set up, but very little of financial value is free. They are however the type of hedge that is available to "the rest of us," i.e. the bottom 99.5%. However, an overseas account is a utility, not a means of wealth creation.

As with any financial decision or transaction, do your due diligence. This means understanding all the risks and all the potential benefits. Read financial statements, obtain regulatory filings, ask questions, verify what you are told, and so on. Each nation's banking laws and legal system are different. Assume nothing.

U.S. citizens are required to disclose foreign accounts and report all income regardless of its origin, i.e. all income earned anywhere on the planet must be reported to the IRS. The purpose of an overseas account is not tax evasion, it is capital preservation/hedging, and so having accounts in nations that have tax treaties with the U.S., transparent reporting and rule of law is a definite plus in terms of compliance.

Holding cash in an overseas account in another currency exposes you to the risks of foreign exchange (FX) fluctuations. It is possible to hold other currencies in the U.S., and U.S. dollars in a foreign account. "Overseas" and "foreign" are used interchangeably, though an account opened in North America may be foreign but not overseas. The point is having a foreign account offers a different sort of hedge than owning a foreign currency.

Few financial pundits consider the topic of moving away from troubled banks or economies, but parrot the party line that central planners are currently coming up with a painless solution.

Having the option to leave the country requires setting up a new foreign bank account, though you might want to fund it with a minimal amount so as to limit taxable income. That way, you have the option to quickly transfer funds in the event of any concerns over the US monetary system. Having a financial exit is something you'd prefer wasn't ever needed, but as we are seeing in Greece and Spain, it is becoming all too necessary. The purpose of the account has nothing to do with total return and more to do with having a lifeboat.

There are two primary challenges to opening up a foreign bank account. The first challenge is proof of ID. Many banks require that you be physically present to open the account. This can take time to work around through extra credentialing steps and in the end, there is no need for air travel provided you meet certain criteria.

The second is compliance via Foreign Bank and Financial Accounts Registration (FBAR) as well as compliance issues under the Foreign Account and Tax Compliance Act (FATCA). These two entities leave one with the impression of complexity and risk, but once you file these documents there is little else required from you. You just have to let the U.S. Government know you have an account if the value exceeds an aggregate of $10,000 USD during the tax year, and if the value is over $50,000.00 you must file an additional form.

Are Foreign Accounts Like a U.S. checking account?

Most are like regular bank accounts as if you walked into a local branch within the US. You are given an account manager who discusses the banking services being offered. The banks offer checking, savings and investment accounts, and usually you can access U.S. ATMs for your funds.

The US has tax treaties with most countries, ostensibly so that you are not double taxed. A year end statement of income earned is provided to you by the bank and it is your responsibility to include this on your US Tax form, much as you would from other financial institutions you deal with. In reality, the Federal government is so cash strapped that it must take its search for revenue global, hence foreign banks are being brought under scrutiny by the IRS.

Does The IRS Look Down On Offshoring Of Assets?

The IRS is not interested in your assets, at least not yet. They are interested in the interest income and capital gains on those assets. If you have a 100% transparent account that the IRS understands you are not using as a form of sheltering or secrecy, you should be fine. Of course, this is all subject to a stable economy; everything said here goes out the window if we take on aspects of the Weimar Republic

.

16   Retirement & Pensions

Planning Your Non-Retirement

Let's face it; most of us are destined to live too long. By that we mean we are likely to outlive a good quality of life in a peaceful, well-funded retirement. That means the handwriting is on the wall, it is now self delusional to think in terms of a secure retirement. That means you should perhaps be making some major adjustments in your long term planning.

The Federal Reserve has made it incredibly difficult to save for your own retirement. Baby Boomers who diligently saved money for retirement are finding that their savings accounts are paying next to nothing thanks to the ultra-low interest rate policies of the Federal Reserve. At current near zero interest rates, you need $2 million plus to retire comfortably.

You can understand the impact of the invisible tax on the elderly by watching the decline of interest income from $50,000 invested in a five-year Treasury obligation. As recently as the year 2000, this would have returned a yield of about 6.15% , resulting in interest income of $3,075 a year. The same obligation yielding 0.7 percent or less returns an interest income of $350 a year. This is the lowest yield on Treasury debt since the Federal Reserve began keeping a yield index in 1953.

But the problem goes far beyond just a low interest rate. This represents an income decline of nearly 89 percent in just 12 years. After you account for inflation, those that put money into savings accounts today are actually losing money.

Americans have not saved up much money for retirement anyway. Statistics from the Employee Benefit Research Institute show 46 percent of American workers have less than $10,000 saved for retirement. A horrendous 29 percent of workers have less than $1,000 saved for retirement.

A study conducted by Boston College's Center for Retirement Research discovered that American workers are $6.6 trillion short of what they need to retire comfortably. Baby Boomers are just starting to retire and the Social Security system is still solvent at the moment, and yet the number of elderly Americans that are experiencing financial problems is already soaring.

For example, between 1991 and 2007 the number of Americans between the ages of 65 and 74 that filed for bankruptcy rose by a staggering 178 percent. One of every six elderly Americans is living below the federal poverty line.

There may be no such thing as retirement in your future. That doesn't mean you can't slow down, as is inevitable with age and declining health, but you are going to have to remain economically active to the end, as insurance both for yourself and your younger family.

The Retirement Dilemma

Most people will have to forget retirement because there will be no guaranteed income to sustain a viable lifestyle. The problem is that income and asset values have plateaued over the last decade, while pension and entitlement programs are underfunded. In the past many retirees could count on accumulated stock market wealth to help fund retirement. For over 12 years the major stock averages have gone nowhere in nominal terms and have declined significantly in real (inflation adjusted) terms. The dream of becoming rich from investments has crashed.

Even the supposedly safest asset of all - a retiree's home – is not a rising asset and will indeed be stagnant for decades. Despite a misguided faith that real estate prices could never fall, according to S&P/Case-Shiller, the National Home Price Index has declined some 30% to levels not seen since the middle of 2002. This means that only those retirees who have owned their homes for at least 10 years have any hope of selling at a profit. Ownership over significantly longer periods may be needed to build up significant equity.

That leaves public and private pension plans. Here again there are serious issues; state public pension are seeing shortfalls. According to the American Enterprise Institute for Public Policy Research, "States report that their public-employee pensions are underfunded by a total of $438 billion, but a more accurate accounting demonstrates that they are in fact underfunded by as much as $3 trillion. The accounting methods that states currently use to measure their liabilities assumes plans can earn high investment returns without risk." Huge returns without risk simply do not exist and bond yields are the lowest they have been in nearly a century.

Private pensions, while not as badly underfunded, never were as generous and so offer little relief either. Americans have negligible savings, the real estate market is still in secular decline or a standstill, stock prices are volatile and suspicious given a lack of volume, real incomes are falling, public pension plans are insolvent and our entitlement programs are bankrupt. None of this bodes well for dreams of a bucolic retirement.

How to Change Your Retirement Strategy

The preceding dismal diagnosis of our long term investment alternatives is at least something honest you can attempt to deal with. A short list of strategies to survive a perpetually dismal economy includes:

- Delaying retirement as long as possible
- Downsizing ruthlessly (home, cars, vacations, clothes, etc.)
- Taking your money to countries like Canada, Australia, Brazil and Chile which offer real rates of return instead of pension robbing zero rates.
- Investing in multinationals that can outsource their profits and hedge their dollar losses with foreign currencies.
- Minimizing your tax exposure.
- Becoming self sufficient through gardening, doing your own mechanical work or otherwise bringing economic activity in house.
- Taking advantage of the welfare state as a patriotic duty to accelerate its collapse.
- Considering strategic defaults where necessary (the banks were bailed out, why not you)
- Moving to a less expensive country like Mexico, the Philippines, etc.
- Focus on maintaining your health. If you are going to live to a hundred, you better figure out how not to be slobbering in your soup.
- Since your health and energy are going to diminish as you get into your 80s, 90s, even 100s, you will need to plan to be in occupations that will allow slowing capacity and are actually beneficial to your health.

None of this is particularly pleasant advice to be giving, but we will all soon be in survival mode as the second leg of the Great recession turns into Great Depression II.

The Social Security Train Wreck

The Social Security trust fund needs to earn interest to achieve levels that will preserve it till 2033; with interest rates close to zero, the trust fund is projected to be depleted ten years earlier - by 2023. By law, the money deposited in the SS trust fund must be invested in U.S. government securities, so it cannot just be thrown into the stock market. In order for the Social Security Ponzi to work, the trust fund, invested in government securities, needs to produce healthy returns. It won't generate those returns thanks to QE-genie Bernanke.

The Federal Reserve is systematically destroying both Social Security and the retirement plans of millions of Americans. The QE to Infinity policies the Federal Reserve is pursuing are devastating for senior citizens. By keeping interest rates at exceptionally low levels, the Federal Reserve is absolutely crushing savers and is systematically destroying Social Security.

Meanwhile, the inflation that QE causes is crippling retired Americans on fixed incomes. Sadly, most elderly Americans have no idea what the Federal Reserve is doing to their financial futures. Most Americans approaching retirement age have not adequately saved for retirement, and the Social Security system that they are depending on is going to completely and totally collapse in the coming years.

The trustees of the Social Security system had projected that the Social Security trust fund would be completely gone by 2033, but because of the Fed policy of keeping interest rates exceptionally low for the foreseeable future it is now being projected by some analysts that Social Security will be bankrupt by 2023. **Social Security is facing a 134 trillion dollar shortfall over the next 75 years.** The collapse of Social Security is thus inevitable long term, and the foolish policies of the Federal Reserve are going to make that collapse happen much more rapidly.

The only way that the Social Security system can stay solvent is for the Social Security trust fund to earn a healthy level of interest. Income to the trust funds must by law be invested, on in securities in which both principal and interest are guaranteed by the Federal government. Securities held by the trust funds are "special issues" of the U.S. Treasury and are available only to the trust funds.

The trust funds have in the past held marketable Treasury securities available to the general public. Special issue securities, unlike marketable securities, can be redeemed at any time at face value. However, marketable securities are subject to the open market and may suffer either a gain, or a loss if sold before maturity. Special issues give trust funds the same flexibility as holding cash.

Those investments in government securities would need to produce healthy returns to be viable. Unfortunately, the indefinite ultra-low interest rate policy of the Federal Reserve is making this impossible. The average rate of interest earned by the Social Security trust fund has declined from 6.1 percent in January 2003 to 3.9 percent in late 2012, and will continue to go even lower as long as the Fed continues Qualitative Easing.

$135 billion of old bonds matured in 2012. This money was rolled over into new bonds with a yield of only 1.375%. The average yield on the maturing securities was 5.64%. The drop in yield on the new securities lowers SSA's income by $5.7B annually. Over the fifteen year term of the investments, that comes to a lumpy $86 billion.

So what happens when the Social Security trust fund runs dry? All Social Security payments would immediately be cut by 25 percent. Based on current law, all SS benefit payments must be cut by 25% when the Trust Fund is exhausted. This will affect 72 million people with severe economic consequences.

According to a Gallup survey, 67 percent of all Americans believe there will be a Social Security crisis within 10 years. The Social Security trust fund might not even make it into the next decade. Most Social Security trust fund projections assume that there will be no recessions and that there will be a very healthy rate of growth for the U.S. economy over the coming decades. So what happens if we have another major recession or worse?

There are way too many people retiring and not nearly enough workers to support them. Right now, approximately 56 million Americans are collecting Social Security benefits. By 2035, that number is projected to grow by 35 million to a whopping 91 million. Back in 1950, each retiree's Social Security benefit was paid for by 16 U.S. workers. But according to new data from the U.S. Bureau of Labor Statistics, there are now only 1.75 full-time private sector workers for each person that is receiving Social Security benefits in the United States.

Another major problem is the growth of the Social Security disability program. Since 2008, 3.6 million more Americans have been added to the rolls of the Social Security disability insurance program. Today, more than 8.7 million Americans are collecting Social Security disability payments. Back in August 1967, there were approximately 65 workers for each American that was collecting Social Security disability payments. Today, there are only 16.2 workers for each American that is collecting Social Security disability payments.

The Social Security Ponzi scheme is rapidly approaching a crisis point. So how bad are things going to be when Social Security collapses? Things are tough for retirees right now, but they are going to get a lot tougher.

Americans who are living on fixed incomes are going to be absolutely crushed by the inflation that QEn is going to cause. Just like we saw with QE1 and QE2, a lot of the money from QE3 has ended up in agricultural commodities and oil. That means that retirees (and the rest of us) are going to end up paying more for food at the supermarket and gasoline at the pump. But those on fixed incomes are not going to see a corresponding increase in their incomes. That means that their standards of living will go down.

America now has around 40 million senior citizens. By 2050 that number is projected to increase to 89 million. How will our society cope with more than twice as many senior citizens? The truth is that our system is going to totally collapse long before then. We are rapidly approaching a financial crisis unlike anything we have ever seen before in U.S. history, and the foolish policies of the Federal Reserve just keep making things even worse.

That means unless you are quite wealthy (with a net worth over $2 million) you have to plan your financial future as though retirement isn't going to be an option. Since you can't avoid getting old, you need to scale back to enjoy living in your golden years.

17　New Normal

We are on a bumpy journey to a "new normal". Developed countries worldwide will see sluggish economic growth, high structural unemployment, increased regulation, and constant pressure for private sector deleveraging. Engage in "constructive paranoia" and structure your portfolio to take advantage of these changes, rather than fall victim to them. While investing will be more difficult, new businesses that will dramatically change our lives are being formed every day. There will be opportunities for business and investment, perhaps just not the traditional ones we are used to.

Only Emerging economies have a chance to maintain the breakout stage of their development phase. Those that are unburdened by stifling deficits, welfare and regulations will deliver high economic growth, strong currencies, and increasingly close the income gap with the developed world. Many emerging market currencies will appreciate. We have suggested some countries to watch, but you will have to do your homework because any advice we write can be quickly made obsolete

The Federal Reserve and financial policymakers have artificially boosted asset prices through loose monetary policy, divorcing them from economic fundamentals. Main Street has suffered in the process. Interest rates have been repressed, which has adverse effects on those on fixed incomes. The dollar has also seriously weakened and will fall further. The net effect is a double edged sword. "Good" asset price inflation has created a hugely positive wealth effect beneficial to bankers and Wall Street, while "bad" inflation has created a new tax on individuals in the form of higher commodity and energy prices. On the whole, this is a raw deal for the American public and the world.

We will see an uneven and faltering economic recovery over the next decades. Long term the growth rate for the US will be subpar at 2% or less, depending on whether anyone believes the economic data. Investors face an even bigger challenge in that much of our past returns have already been borrowed from the future. Inflation has already returned. Commodity prices will rise. Yield curves will steepen while high dividend stocks will prosper.

Hedging Your Bets

Your biggest single risk is actually due to political upheaval and the uncertainty this causes in markets. The major hedge you can make to protect your investments is thus to diversify politically. This means in part moving investments either out of country, or to multinationals which are insulated against the political risks in America. It also means distancing yourself from our political hierarchy. For example, why would anyone invest in our government's promise of green jobs appearing? Believing in our government's economic predictions is simply not wise, their own economic statistics don't add up. Diversifying politically also may mean investing in foreign countries, especially those whose debt to GDP ratios are low and are therefore likely to survive a global economic collapse.

Australia, New Zealand, Canada, Chile, Switzerland and Singapore all come quickly to mind as places where their fiscal houses are in much better order and their economies offer a hedge against our collapsing dollar. Second tier countries which are more risky but also help distribute your political risk might include Brazil, Mexico, South Korea and Argentina – though with the caveat that *buyer bewares*. Something like investing in cattle herds in Argentina might make more sense than you think.

Commodities in general are thought of as a hedge against inflationary pressures, though they aren't without risks. Food is not likely to go out of style any time soon and many are playing the agriculture markets as a hedge. Shares in oil stocks also seem likely to avoid price collapse, though there may not be meteoric gains that peak oil enthusiasts suggest. Mining companies in general will hold long term value.

The biggest reason to stay in gold, silver and precious metals is because central banks around the world can see the writing on the wall long term. They understand the dollar will be devalued one way or another. Moreover, the US Congress has no appetite for hard decisions which would be deflationary in nature.

Be aware of opportunities to short the system. For example, those who go short government bonds, may make a killing. Many areas of the government subsidized Green Energy scam are also ripe for plucking.

However, there currently are no real bargains because everyone is scouring the planet for a safe haven. Real estate does not look like it will recuperate for years. Equities have been floating on the thin vapors of Federal stimulus and can't be trusted. What we can be sure of is that the dollar will reach its intrinsic value. The European Union will fall apart and go away within years. So be careful to pick and choose any investments you make and stay diversified. Trust and verify because there are no longer any sure deals.

Some other investible ideas…

•Everyday essentials. Energy is the classic essential. Sure, energy use and prices will ebb and flow with the economy, but ultimately everyone uses energy every day, and the people in emerging markets want to use a lot more of it. Carefully thought-out investments in energy, ideally bought on the dips, belong in everyone's long-term portfolio.

•Breakthroughs to a brighter future. Throughout modern history, companies that make significant technological advances transcend bad economic times. Do you think that the company that finds a cure for a common variety of cancer will be weighed down, even by a stock market crash? Hardly. In cautious amounts, these sorts of potential breakthrough stocks belong in your portfolio.

•Investing in the inevitable. A ton of charts and data point to just how unusual and unsustainable today's low, low U.S. interest rates are. When these sorts of baseline trends eventually change direction, they tend to move in the new direction for years, and even decades. It is extremely difficult to pick a bottom, but anyone who is paying even a little attention can and should be getting positioned to profit from a sea change in U.S. interest rates while they still can.

•One foot over the border. History has shown that having even one foot over the border can make the difference between losing everything and coming out just fine. Internationalizing your assets is not always easy or convenient, but that doesn't make it any less urgent that you do so.

18   Internal Exile

As the American, European and Japanese systems collapses on multiple economic, political and social fronts, people will naturally look for places to run. Leaving the country is an unlikely option given the logistics, but it may be possible to insulate yourself from events either by making a fortress with what you now have, or by moving to places within the country more likely to weather the approaching ten to twenty year storm.

Because of the growing economic problems that the United States is experiencing, millions of American families are considering a move to another part of the country. In the past, most Americans would just ride recessions out and safely assume things would get back to "normal" sooner or later, but this time is different. Unemployment has never stayed this high for this long since the Great Depression. Thousands of our factories and millions of our jobs have been shipped overseas, and many of our formerly great cities (such as Detroit) have been turned into deindustrialized wastelands. The federal government and most state governments are essentially bankrupt and continue to slide into more debt.

Meanwhile, Helicopter Ben Bernanke and Janet Yellen, his replacement, and their cohorts at the Federal Reserve have fired up the printing presses in a desperate attempt to revive the U.S. economy. Many believe that by flooding the financial system with paper money they are setting in motion a series of events which will eventually lead to the death of the dollar. With so much wrong with our economy, is it any wonder why more Americans are deeply concerned about the state of the economy today than at any other time since World War II?

If the economy continues to crumble and millions of Americans find it nearly impossible to find a good job, many will begin wondering if things are any better in other parts of the country. Without a doubt, some areas of the U.S. are complete and total disaster zones at this point. For example, so many houses have been abandoned in Detroit that the mayor has proposed bulldozing one-fourth of the city. In Las Vegas, it was estimated that approximately 65 percent of all homes with a mortgage were "underwater" at the height of the housing crash. The number of people unemployed in the state of California is approximately equal to the populations of Nevada, New Hampshire and Vermont. Unfortunately, there are indications that the U.S. economy is going to stagnate long term. It may even get worse.

In choosing a place to live, the following are some other factors that you will want to consider:

#1 You Need To Make Money

Unless you are independently wealthy or you work for yourself, you are going to have to find a way to make money. For most people, that means getting a job. Unfortunately, jobs are only going to become harder and harder to get in the years ahead. In fact, right now there are not a lot of areas in the U.S. where jobs are plentiful. There is some work up in Montana, Texas and the Dakotas because of all the oil that has been found there, but other than that there are not a whole lot of bright spots out there. Many Americans are trying to become independent and build their own businesses, but that is not always an easy thing to do either.

#2 Low Tax States

One of your primary goals in the New Normal is to lower your tax burden. While the natural beauty of states like California can't be denied, their high tax burdens to fund large welfare entitlements makes it prohibitively expensive to live there. The following chart and list ranks tax burdens by state. You will have to carefully weigh whether the benefits of where you live now, if in a high tax state, outweigh the benefits of living in states with low or even zero income taxes. Here are some comparisons among the states by tax burden.

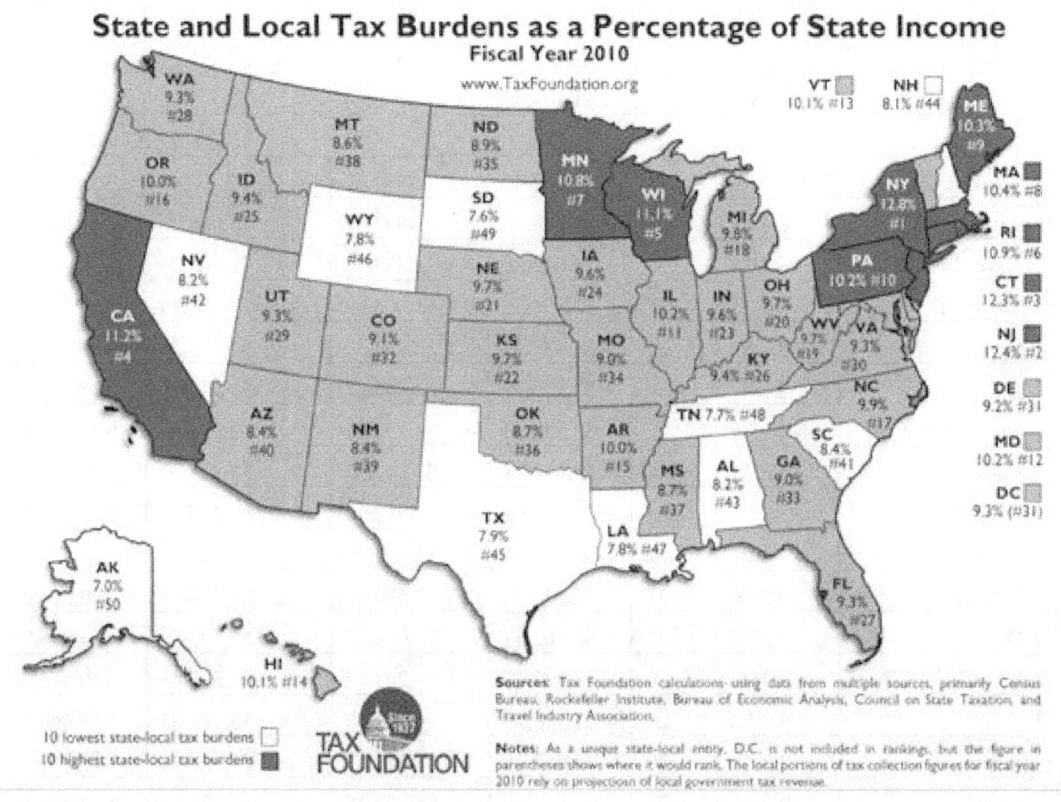

State-Local Tax Burden Compared to U.S. Average

State	Rate	Rank	Per Capita Taxes Paid to Own State	Per Capita Taxes Paid to Other States	Total State and Local Per Capita Taxes Paid	Per Capita Income
United States	9.86%		$3,055.18	$1,056.38	$4,111.55	$41,145.78
Alaska	6.97%	50	$2,150.48	$1,063.05	$3,213.53	$46,098.24
South Dakota	7.58%	49	$1,856.89	$1,178.42	$3,035.31	$40,017.82
Tennessee	7.72%	48	$1,844.24	$862.53	$2,706.77	$35,078.49
Louisiana	7.75%	47	$1,899.64	$951.44	$2,851.08	$36,776.18
Wyoming	7.77%	46	$2,074.57	$1,646.92	$3,721.48	$47,899.73
Texas	7.93%	45	$2,221.39	$882.30	$3,103.69	$39,141.66
New Hampshire	8.11%	44	$2,210.33	$1,506.99	$3,717.32	$45,863.77
Alabama	8.18%	43	$1,849.85	$890.24	$2,740.08	$33,498.69
Nevada	8.24%	42	$2,089.46	$1,207.27	$3,296.73	$40,023.03
South Carolina	8.37%	41	$1,909.40	$851.07	$2,760.47	$32,961.73
Arizona	8.42%	40	$2,068.48	$937.87	$3,006.35	$35,726.09
New Mexico	8.44%	39	$2,022.06	$883.68	$2,905.74	$34,413.60
Montana	8.61%	38	$2,005.39	$1,083.62	$3,089	$35,870.61
Mississippi	8.69%	37	$1,837.97	$787.30	$2,625.27	$30,210.85
Oklahoma	8.73%	36	$2,125.47	$935.02	$3,060.49	$35,049.74
North Dakota	8.91%	35	$2,540.33	$1,192.55	$3,732.88	$41,910.02
Missouri	8.95%	34	$2,310.21	$1,017.57	$3,327.77	$37,178.77
Georgia	8.96%	33	$2,309.03	$912.96	$3,222	$35,945.83
Colorado	9.10%	32	$2,910.14	$1,194.06	$4,104.20	$45,124.87
Delaware	9.20%	31	$2,137.27	$1,590.45	$3,727.71	$40,516.26
DC	9.25%	-31	$3,965.77	$2,024.79	$5,990.56	$64,755.78
Virginia	9.25%	30	$3,131.65	$1,204.77	$4,336.42	$46,872.28
Utah	9.29%	29	$2,226.25	$954.80	$3,181.05	$34,260.30
Washington	9.29%	28	$3,087.95	$1,173.47	$4,261.43	$45,853.81
Florida	9.31%	27	$2,620.78	$1,107.45	$3,728.23	$40,053.19
Kentucky	9.36%	26	$2,216.42	$811	$3,027.42	$32,355.75
Idaho	9.37%	25	$2,118.23	$982.95	$3,101.18	$33,081.88
Iowa	9.58%	24	$2,658.15	$1,001.57	$3,659.72	$38,199.59
Indiana	9.59%	23	$2,428.04	$866.45	$3,294.48	$34,348.16
Kansas	9.65%	22	$2,637.91	$1,164.08	$3,801.99	$39,389.23
Nebraska	9.70%	21	$2,768.62	$1,084.86	$3,853.48	$39,741.90
Ohio	9.71%	20	$2,719.82	$843.19	$3,563.01	$36,693.54

West Virginia	9.71%	19	$2,222.32	$806.43	$3,028.75	$31,182.11
Michigan	9.84%	18	$2,693.85	$809.10	$3,502.95	$35,587.98
North Carolina	9.91%	17	$2,647.68	$887.39	$3,535.07	$35,658.58
Oregon	9.96%	16	$2,755.07	$973.88	$3,728.96	$37,432.04
Arkansas	10.03%	15	$2,410.44	$874.98	$3,285.42	$32,768.16
Hawaii	10.10%	14	$3,367.49	$1,029	$4,396.49	$43,508.92
Vermont	10.11%	13	$2,905.92	$1,247.88	$4,153.80	$41,080.84
Maryland	10.20%	12	$3,855.02	$1,379.14	$5,234.16	$51,329.23
Illinois	10.20%	11	$3,387.70	$1,124.28	$4,511.99	$44,224.20
Pennsylvania	10.24%	10	$3,117.68	$1,065.43	$4,183.11	$40,860.62
Maine	10.26%	9	$2,859.91	$946.82	$3,806.73	$37,101.09
Massachusetts	10.43%	8	$3,987.42	$1,434.77	$5,422.19	$51,990.93
Minnesota	10.79%	7	$3,639.94	$1,087.04	$4,726.98	$43,789.78
Rhode Island	10.85%	6	$3,318.04	$1,308.87	$4,626.90	$42,627.72
Wisconsin	11.07%	5	$3,413.90	$964.69	$4,378.59	$39,536.04
California	11.23%	4	$3,953.46	$980.56	$4,934.02	$43,919.29
Connecticut	12.27%	3	$4,966.25	$2,018.24	$6,984.48	$56,914
New Jersey	12.42%	2	$4,853.37	$1,835.68	$6,689.05	$53,868.50
New York	12.77%	1	$5,150.94	$1,223.99	$6,374.92	$49,934.62

#3 Lower Housing Prices And A Lower Standard Of Living

Many Americans are packing up and moving from states that have a very high cost of living (such as New York or California) and are moving to areas where housing is cheaper and where it doesn't take as much money to live. After all, why pay half a million dollars for a house when you can get the same house for $200,000 in another part of the country? Many people are discovering that a lifestyle with fewer bills and a smaller monthly budget can be extremely liberating.

#4 Food And Water Independence

Food and water independence can also be liberating. After all, if the U.S. economy does totally collapse someday, how will we all feed our families? 100 years ago, most Americans grew at least some of their own food. Today, very few Americans do that. Fortunately, a growing number of Americans have started to grow "survival gardens" and/or have started to store up emergency food supplies. If the inflationary policies of the Federal Reserve do end up totally trashing the U.S. dollar, the food that you and your family have stored up will end up being a **great** investment. Owning a fertile piece of land is going to be a great asset to have in the years to come, so think about finding a place where it is possible to grow food and where water is plentiful when picking out a new area to move to.

#5 Community And Crime

If the U.S. economy does collapse, rioting and gang violence may turn many American cities into war zones. Just remember what happened to New Orleans after Hurricane Katrina hit. That was a Sunday picnic compared to what could happen if the U.S. economy falls apart. Many Americans can see what is coming and they are moving out of the big cities. But wherever you move to, you will not be alone, so do your research ahead of time. Are you moving to an area where the people are friendly and helpful? Will you have family and close friends in the region? It is always good to have a support system around you - especially when times get hard.

#6 During Hard Times Weather Makes A Difference

During good times one can live anywhere you choose, but if the economy fails the weather and nature becomes a bigger factor. For example, if you plan to totally rely on the power company, do you really want to live some place where it gets down to 20 or 30 below on a regular basis? What is your backup plan if basic services shut down for an extended period of time? How will you provide power and heat for your family? In addition, do you want to move some place incredibly hot if you can't always count on having air conditioning? Weather will make a huge difference in your lifestyle. The desert or the mountains may sound appealing now, but when you are trying to grow food they may not seem so great then.

There are many things to think about when choosing a new place to live. But the time to think about these things and prepare is now - not later. If and When the U.S. economy does collapse, millions of American families will be scrambling to come up with a plan, but by then it will be too late.

#7 Walled Communities and Homes

Even if you can't move to another state, it might be possible to move to gated communities in your area that offer protection. The number of gated communities has risen dramatically over the years in response to rising insecurity. Indeed, this is how third world or developing countries like Mexico have long dealt with having huge populations of dispossessed; they simply walled themselves off from the less affluent areas.

Even homes can be walled off with high walls, security gates and invasion detection. Your own need for security will depend on the community in which you live, but the point is that it is difficult to take these measures in the midst of a general collapse, one needs to prepare well in advance.

#8 Going Suburban/Rural

While there are advantages to living in a city with services and police during an upheaval, you still may prefer to distance yourself from areas that are sympathetic to progressive politics. You will likely benefit from lower crime rates, from less necessity to bribe officials to conduct business, from not schooling your children in a melting pot of dysfunction. Moving to a home that has at least some land allows you the option to stockpile, to have worksheds and to have space for cars, boats and RVs. Rather than luxuries, consider these items that allow you to go off grid

#9 Gardening

Starting your own victory garden may also be useful. While yields from amateur gardeners may be low, they may be sufficient to sustain a family over a short critical period. Protecting your food from being pilfered will be a concern, so an ostentatious garden may not be wise. A garage full of canned vegetables can't hurt.

For a guide to food gardening, we have prepared a comprehensive reference titled "*Going Galt: Survival Gardening*". More information is here:

http://www.futurnamics.com/garden.php

#10 Backup Energy

Solar photovoltaic might be an option for some, but the expense can be from $10,000 and up for a home installation. Fortunately, the price for solar panels has been falling sharply. The problem with most systems is that they use the power grid as their backup battery and would thus be useless in a brownout, so be prepared to spend a lot of money if you truly want to get off the power grid completely with a battery system. Consequently, a generator would be useful with enough fuel to last a week. Speaking of fuel, gasoline supplies may evaporate, so being able to fill 5 gallon jerry cans would be wise.

#11 Stockpiling

Water is the first essential item that you need to survive, so having a fifty gallon drum or two, or various other survival containers would be smart. Regarding food, there is everything from bags of rice and beans, to cans of chili that can be stored for great periods of time. There are many survivalist manuals that will help. (See our book "Going Galt: Surviving Economic Armageddon").

#12 Transportation

Have reliable transportation that can carry a load if you have to leave town (like an SUV or pickup). Some of the older classic cars should also be considered if you are trying to harden your family for survival because they are infinitely repairable. There is a reason you see 1950s Chevies still running in Cuba.

Bugging Out

Suppose you are right smack in the middle of one of the worst-hit cities in the country as the welfare state collapses. The looting is out of hand, power has been sporadic for two weeks, and water supplies are running low. You've changed your mind about this 'living in the city' thing and you still have enough gas in your truck to make it out of town… if you can get past the gangs, that is.

You've decided to *BUG OUT!*

Some basic pointers:

- Don't try to bug out in a Chevy Geo. You will want a big heavy 4x4 truck to go off-road and around stalled vehicles
- Get something that can carry at least 1000 pounds of supplies. Big 4x4 pickups require more fuel, but they can carry fuel as cargo.
- Don't bug out unless you can have someone ride shotgun, literally. You will want an armed passenger in the likely case you run into not-so-nice people.

WHAT TO TAKE

We have written an extensive disaster preparation book titled *Going Galt: Surviving Economic Armageddon*, which goes into the details, so this is just a synopsis. Here's what you should take if you're preparing to bug out with two people; all this will fit in your truck:

- Your 96 hour kits for each person in the vehicle
- 20 gallons of water
- 40 gallons of extra fuel or more (and a full gas tank)

WHERE TO GO

If you have a designated place of refuge (Grandma's house, a cabin in the woods, etc.), head straight for it. If not, you're basically driving anywhere you can go, so try to head for an area that is forested and near a creek or river where you can get some water.

Choosing to remain in the city is a rational choice in many situations. However, the further away you can get from the population centers in general, the better your chances of surviving. Perhaps you have a difficult time actually accepting that a major disaster is going to be as bad as described. And after all, if you leave the city, sell out, quit your job, and move to the country – and then nothing bad happens – you will have disrupted your life, and you may find yourself jobless, broke and homeless. You COULD assume it will be a mild event, which is also a credible possibility. In that case, surviving in the city will be quite feasible, especially if you have neighbors that can support your efforts and you don't live in a dangerous city with high racial tensions.

However, the very nature of a major disaster means that if only one or two major infrastructure components fail, the ripple effect will quickly create a much worse scenario. It seems there is very little room for "mild" effects unless they are miniscule. As shown by Katrina, Sandy and the Fukushima tsunami, an all too possible scenario includes massive disruptions, severe shortages in food and water, loss of power in some areas, and a breakdown of social order in areas where the population density is high. But you can survive anything with an open mind, practice and good planning. Why not start now as part of your holistic plan for financial survival?

So if the economy does collapse, where should you go? What would be the best U.S. state to move to? The following are some of the states that Americans have been moving to in an attempt to insulate themselves from the coming economic problems

Preferred States For Relocation		
Montana	Nebraska	Tennessee
Idaho	Kansas	Kentucky
North Dakota	Alaska	West Virginia
South Dakota	Oklahoma	Maine
Wyoming	Arkansas	Washington
Colorado	Missouri	Oregon
New Hampshire	Vermont	Virginia
Texas	North Carolina	

19   Foreign Exile

It may also come to the point where you just can't make it in the United States any more. There are no perfect options for exile; there is no place to run where you can be totally safe. That said, there are some countries which make sense as targets for emigration. Nations to consider are (though not an exclusive list):

- Canada
- Australia
- New Zealand
- Singapore
- Switzerland
- Norway
- Sweden
- Chile

One key figure to look at when deciding where to go given a coming debt collapse is the Debt to GDP ratios of various countries, as well as their political and economic climate. In 2011 Bill Gross of PIMCO described a "Ring of Fire" that is still relevant.

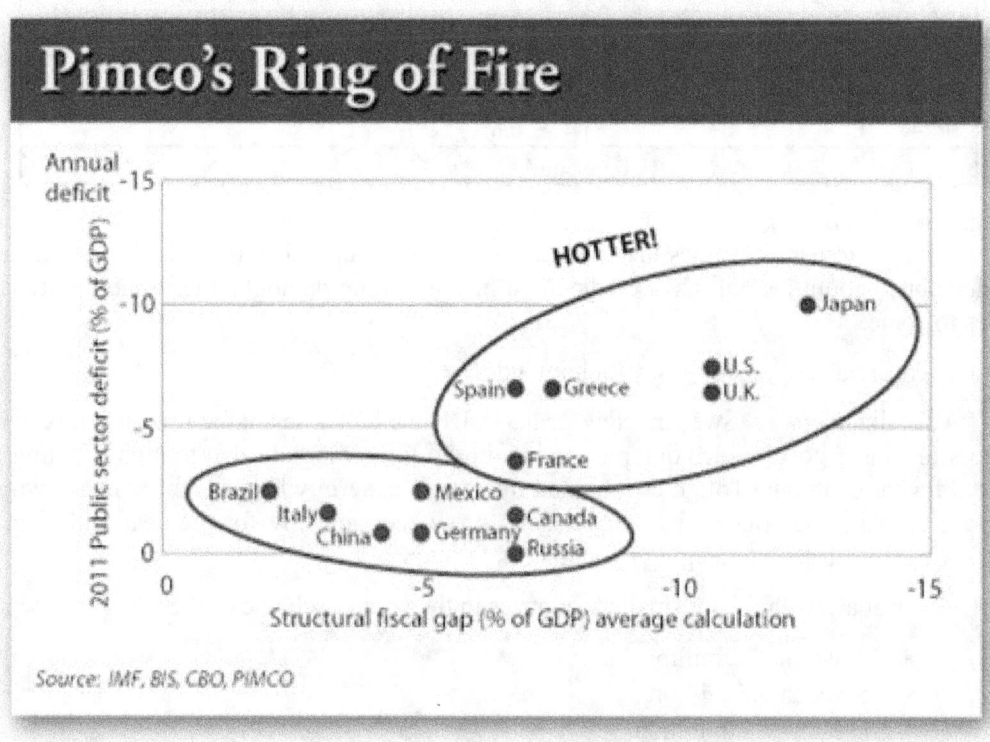

Another indicator is the direction of the percentage of the world economy represented by a country over the last decade.

Countries representing more than one percent of World GDP as of 2011	Percentage of World GDP 2001	Percentage of World GDP 2011	Percentage Change 2001 - 2011
United States	31.8%	21.6%	-32.3%
China	4.1%	10.5%	153.6%
Japan	12.9%	8.4%	-35.2%
Germany	5.9%	5.1%	-12.8%
France	4.2%	4.0%	-4.9%
Brazil	1.7%	3.5%	105.4%
United Kingdom	4.6%	3.5%	-24.1%
Italy	3.5%	3.1%	-10.3%
Russian Federation	1.0%	2.7%	178.2%
India	1.5%	2.6%	72.3%
Canada	2.2%	2.5%	11.4%
Spain	1.9%	2.1%	12.4%
Australia	1.2%	2.0%	65.6%
Mexico	1.9%	1.7%	-14.7%
Korea, Rep.	1.57%	1.59%	1.6%
Indonesia	0.5%	1.2%	142.3%
Netherlands	1.2%	1.2%	-4.2%
Turkey	0.6%	1.1%	81.1%
Data source: World Bank			

Demographic Trends

With the lower birth rates that come from increasing urbanization, wealth, and education, most developed countries will have mediocre at best to falling demographic economic trends for decades to come.

There are a few exceptions, which include:

Australia. Norway. Sweden. New Zealand. Denmark. These are the few currently wealthy countries that have positive demographic trends in the future, largely due to higher immigration rates and higher birth rates (often encouraged by greater maternity benefits for working women). These are the few countries which are likely to grow economically for the near and even long term, lacking the burden of an aging population

Unfortunately, these are smaller countries in the greater scheme of the developed world.

- Australia 23 million
- Sweden 9.5 million
- Denmark 5.6 million
- Norway: 5 million
- New Zealand: 4.5 million.

The combined population of these countries is only a little larger than California.

Given the demographic trends, expect the developed world to split into three segments:

#1: Marginally positive growers.

#2: Treading water economic survivors — the U.S., Canada, France, and the U.K.

#3: Economic shrinkers — Japan, Germany, Portugal, Greece, Austria, Switzerland, Italy, Spain, Taiwan, South Korea, Singapore, East Europe, Russia. Even China faces demographic upheaval after 2025.

Between 2023 and 2070 worldwide demographic growth will come from emerging countries that are still urbanizing. They will be generating middle-class consumers, though because of energy limits they may not become as affluent as their developed-world counterparts.

Survivors such as the U.S., Canada, France, and the U.K. will remain steady or stagnant because of a previous history of higher immigration and birth rates (though births are in decline), and their still-high productivity. The U.S. and Canada will do better than the U.K. and France in coming decades because of higher productivity and the fact that they're less entwined in the economic whirlpool of Europe.

The large category of shrinking economies will face long term declining demographic trends made worse by low birth rates and xenophobic immigration policies. They cannot grow with both their workforce and population in decline.

Moving Money Out Of The Country

Foreign accounts may be safe since they are protected by another country's law and aren't affected by national executive orders. But beware, it is not currently easy to move investment size amounts of money out of the United States, and the situation will only get worse. Such transactions don't happen over night because foreign banks are now wary of coming into conflict with US taxation, money laundering and banking laws. So getting out of Dodge will take time and effort because the Federal government doesn't want you to leave, it needs you to stay here so it can help prop up the collapsing Federal government and devalued currency.

Moving bars of gold could be quite a trick. While gold is a great store of value, you can't barter it at a supermarket because you would lose too much money. You can wait until things settle down and change your gold for Dollars/Euros or other stable paper money and save yourself from devaluation. But in the end, you may have to get out of Dodge with your gold and deposit it in a safe country.

Index of Economic Freedom

Every year, the Heritage Foundation along with the Wall Street Journal, publishes their Index of Economic Freedom which ranks countries by their adherence to free market principles and honest government. Investors wishing to broaden their foreign exposure would do well to keep this index in mind and note that of late the United States has been moving in the wrong direction from year to year towards less economic freedom.

#1 Hong Kong
#2 Singapore
#3 Australia
#4 New Zealand
#5 Switzerland
#6 Canada
#7 Chile
#8 Mauritius
#9 Ireland
#10 United States

Financial balances & economic performance compared

2012 % GDP (unless otherwise stated)	US	Japan	UK	Can.	Euro	Belg.	France	Germ.	Greece	Ire.	Italy	NL	Port.	Spain
Government finances														
1 Government gross debt (2012)	107	237	89	88	94	99	90	83	171	118	126	58	119	91
2 Government gross debt (2017 est.)	114	250	94	77	90	91	86	74	153	108	121	75	115	101
3 Government net debt (2012)	84	135	84	36	73	83	84	58	171	103	103	35	113	79
4 General government balance*	-9.4	-8.8	-6.9	-3.8	-3.7	-2.9	-4.5	-0.4	-8.9	-8.3	-2.6	-4.5	-4.9	-7.0
5 Required fiscal adjustment[2]	12.8	20.3	9.4	4.3	5.0	5.7	5.8	0.9	10.5	11.4	3.3	4.5	6.2	10.6
6 Req'd fisc.adj't (inc. age costs)[3]	19.6	21.1	13.1	8.2	6.8	10.1	7.4	3.0	13.9	12.9	4.6	9.5	10.4	12.7
Private sector finances														
7 Households' gross debt	86	76	99	91	71	55	67	58	59	117	51	131	104	87
8 Non-fin. corporates' gross debt[4]	89	145	115	54	138	186	134	64	73	269	114	114	158	186
External finances														
9 Current account*	-3.1	1.2	-1.7	-2.1	1.2	0.8	-2.4	6.2	-3.6	3.8	-0.9	9.0	-1.1	-1.9
10 Net external assets	-26	57	-9	-12	-12	65	-16	38	-96	-99	-24	35	-108	-92
Economic growth														
11 Real GDP growth, 2001-11 % ar*	1.6	0.6	1.6	1.9	1.1	1.5	1.1	1.1	1.0	2.1	0.2	1.3	0.1	1.7
12 Real GDP growth, 2012-17 % ar*	3.0	1.1	2.2	2.3	1.7	1.1	1.3	1.2	1.2	2.5	0.9	1.5	1.1	0.5
13 Population growth 2012-17 % ar*	1.0	-0.3	0.7	1.2	0.2	0.8	0.5	-0.2	0.1	0.6	0.4	0.2	0.1	0.4
Credit ratings														
14 S&P	AA+ (neg)	AA- (neg)	AAA	AAA		AA (neg)	AA+ (neg)	AAA	CCC (neg)	BBB+ (neg)	BBB+ (neg)	AAA (neg)	BB (neg)	BBB- (neg)
15 Fitch	AAA (neg)	A+ (neg)	AAA (neg)	AAA		AA (neg)	AAA (neg)	AAA	CCC	BBB+ (neg)	A- (neg)	AAA	BB+ (neg)	BBB (neg)
16 Moody's	Aaa (neg)	Aaa	Aaa (neg)	Aaa		Aa1 (neg)	Aaa (neg)	Aaa (neg)	C	Ba1 (neg)	Baa2 (neg)	Aaa (neg)	Ba3 (neg)	Baa3 (neg)

121

Investing Your Money

20 Stocks

The billion dollar question is which way will the stock market go long term in a broken biflationary economy? When both the Federal government as well as the Federal Reserve are out of control, trust is lost in all sectors because winners and losers are then chosen by random acts of bureaucrats rather than by market forces. While it is clear that the Fed has gone to extraordinary lengths to prop up the stock market after the 2008 crash, it is also clear that their ability to paper over the losses is not infinite.

The rule is to be wary of an overly bullish view of stocks and an impending recovery. Investors are being forced into the equities market by Federal Reserve policy, implemented in part by creating artificial low returns on bonds and other assets. In such a rigged environment, one goal is to preserve wealth in any repeat of the 2009 crash.

As a warning note, good news during the initial 1929-33 depressions/recession triggered "euphoric response." The 1929-33 recession saw six quarterly GDP bounces with an average gain of 8 percent. This sent the stock market to a 50 percent rally in early 1930 and investors thought the worst had passed. Optimism is intrinsic to human nature. However, in the financial survival game, we have a fiduciary responsibility to ourselves and our families to be as realistic as possible about the outlook for the economy and the market at all times.

In 2012, PIMCO's founder and co-CIO Bill Gross penned a piece on "the death of the cult of equities." It doesn't take a financial wizard to figure out the validity of the Fed's long-term malevolent effects on markets--but it is nice to hear someone with clout actually come out and speak the truth. *The S&P over 20 years: Empirical evidence that Old Wall St.'s "buy and hold" strategy died in 1999.*

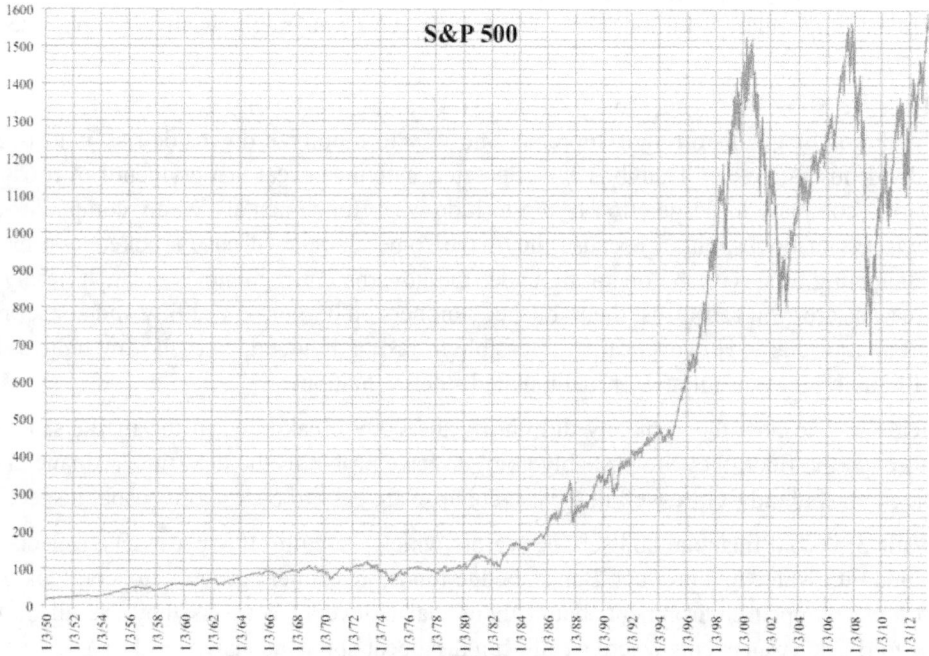

The sit-back-and-relax "buy and hold" strategy that unqualified portfolio managers banked on for so many years has indeed perished in this volatile, highly leveraged, central banking dominated environment. There is also an interesting coincidence between the departure from the old-school investing strategy, and the corporate consumer-engineering that began in 1999.

Yet there is an argument to be made that the stock market has a use as an inflation hedge. Many multinational stocks derive large percentages of their profits from overseas ventures and have insulated themselves from currency swings. Equities in countries that have their currencies under control can provide some protection from inflation (see Australia, Canada, Norway, Singapore, Hong Kong). Also stocks that are based on necessities like food, mining, transportation, and mundane products like cleaning and laundry soaps can also avoid being devalued.

Reasons For Stocks Resiliency

There are a number of reasons stocks may beat expectations at least short term during a biflationary collapse:

- Large companies have the means to adapt and offload their costs to either cheaper foreign countries or through automation.
- The Federal Reserve for better or worse will intervene through POMO (Permanent Open Market Operations by the US federal Reserve Board) to prop up the market. In other words, the Federal Reserve rigs the market to the upside.
- We are the prettiest horse in the glue factory. Europe has dismal prospects so there is some flight to safety in US stocks as long as markets are weak elsewhere.
- There's no place left for cash to hide with Treasury yields kept artificially low, forcing cash into the stock market.

Consequently, despite the gloomy economic prospects of our economy, you probably have no option but to keep a good percentage of your assets in the market, and perhaps in U.S. equities. Since you presumably are not a speculator and are reading this book to preserve capital in cloudy times as much as make a speculative killing, there are certain rules you might want to emphasize in your choice of stocks.

Rule 1: Show Me The Money: Since you cannot trust your government or the Federal Reserve, and crony capitalism reigns supreme, one way to minimize downside risk is to find stocks that give dividends. A Rule of Thumb is 3% or greater, with the caveat that dividends over 6% may be indicative of a company in desperation trying to hide weak fundamentals. Many companies are now running two sets of books, either because they have some element of base crookedness, or because they are attempting to survive by operating under the government regulator's radar. It hardly matters what the reasons are, you can't trust the published numbers on corporate viability and stock prices can be pumped up artificially. However, it isn't possible to fake a dividend, so cash flow reduces some of your risk of buying into speculative or manipulated stock valuations.

Rule 2: See how the company did during the 2009 breakdown in the markets. If it nearly dropped through the floor, they are probably going to have problems the next time a financial tsunami hits. Stock charts that didn't fare well in the last collapse are easy to pick out by visual inspection.

Rule 3: Avoid financial and service sectors which are built on paper assets, especially those areas that add little value to a product. Banks, hedge funds, investment groups, etc. con look great in a Federal reserve pumped environment, but without real unleveraged assets they are all particularly vulnerable to Black Swan events where wealth can disappear spontaneously.

The above rules may not make you rich, but they are meant to keep you solvent during the random fluctuations that come during a biflationary economic breakdown. You can then apply some of the more traditional investing tactics, but with modifications to better cope with a dual inflationary and deflationary environment.

Buy and Hold

Buy and hold is the traditional long-term investment strategy based on the view that in the long run financial markets give a good rate of return despite periods of volatility or decline. This viewpoint also holds that short-term market timing, i.e. the concept that one can enter the market on the lows and sell on the highs, does not work. The theory is that timing gives negative results, at least for small or unsophisticated investors, so it is better for them to simply buy and hold.

The antithesis of buy-and-hold is the concept of day trading, in which money can be made in the short term if an individual tries to short on the peaks, and buy on the lows with greater money coming with greater volatility.

One of the strongest arguments for the buy and hold strategy is the efficient-market hypothesis (EMH): If every security is fairly valued at all times, then there is really no point to trade. Some take the buy-and-hold strategy to an extreme, advocating that you should never sell a security unless you need the money. The efficient-market hypothesis (EMH) says that market-timing strategies cannot work. It says that investors can't "beat the market"; interestingly, it says that investors can't do worse (on average) than the market either.

One can also argue for buy-and-hold on purely cost-based grounds, without resort to the EMH. Costs such as brokerage and bid/offer spread are incurred on all transactions, and buy-and-hold involves the fewest transactions for a given amount invested in the market, all other things being equal. Warren Buffett is an example of a buy-and-hold advocate who has rejected the EMH in his writings, and has built his fortune by investing in companies at times when they were undervalued. Some may argue that Warren Buffett is a long-term market timer.

Unfortunately, given that we are now in an era of crony capitalism and Federal Reserve intervention, the traditional buy-and-hold strategy may not work as well in practice as in theory. If markets no longer reflect underlying valuations but instead reflect corrupting influences from governmental intrusion and crony capitalism, then holding good stocks with solid financials may not mean anything in the face of market manipulation. Some ways to modify your buy and hold strategy during biflationary times:

- Internationalize your holdings across countries with stable currencies. We provide a list of countries with the best Debt-to-GDP ratios and best adherence to free market values.
- Avoid sectors based on paper financial gains. While these sectors may offer greater speculative gains, they will be subject to rapid collapses as seen by Lehman and MF Global as unbacked assets are exposed as worthless paper.
- Buy and Hold but regularly cull the worst of the herd. This might be described as buy and hold with an eye for the exit door.
- Buying securities which pay dividends can even out some of the speculative nature of many stocks which are otherwise priced on the subjective evaluations of the market herd.

Market Timing

Market timing is the strategy of making buy or sell decisions of financial assets by attempting to predict future market price movements. Predictions may be based on technical or fundamental analysis derived from market or economic conditions. This is an investment strategy based on the outlook for an aggregate market, rather than for a particular financial asset. During this biflationary period, timing will be highly dependent on pronouncements by the Federal Reserve and the release of unemployment and other numbers by the Bureau of Labor Statistics. Those with inside information or exceptional economic insights will have an advantage, but none of this is straightforward because we have entered an era of expert liars.

Moving Average: Market timing often looks at various moving averages. Popular are the 50- and 200-day moving averages. Some consider it bullish if the market has gone above the 50- or 200-day average, or bearish if below. Some consider it significant when one MA crosses over another. Market timers make predictions based on the idea that trends will, more likely than not, continue into the future. Others say, "nobody knows", and that world economies and stock markets are of such complexity that market timing strategies are unlikely to be more profitable than buy-and-hold strategies. Armed with the biflationary perspective you are gaining, there might be instances where market timing would work as your predictions would seem contrarian.

Differing Views On The Viability Of Market Timing: Is market timing a viable investment strategy or gambling based on pure chance? The efficient-market hypothesis claims financial prices always exhibit random walk behavior and cannot be predicted with consistency. However, market timing can be sensible in certain situations, such as an apparent bubble. Because the US economy is now dominated by Federal Reserve and regulatory intervention necessary to prop up the collapsing welfare state, one can guarantee with certainty that we are experiencing bubbles in multiple sectors.

However, because the economy is a complex network system, even at times of significant market optimism or pessimism, it remains difficult to pre-determine the local maximum or minimum of future prices with any precision. Bubbles can last for many years before inflated prices collapse. Likewise, a crash can persist for extended periods before deflated prices, like housing, reinflate. Stocks that appear to be "cheap" at a glance can often become even cheaper before either rebounding at some time in the future or heading toward bankruptcy – a course often repeated during multiple aftershocks following the first crash of the Great Depression.

Yet, market timing is fundamentally just another name for trading. Attempting to predict future market price movements is what all traders do, regardless of whether they trade individual stocks or collections of stocks (aka, mutual funds, ETFs or indexes). Market timing may well be possible especially if one bases the timing on the somewhat predictable efforts of the Federal Reserve to print money and then cover their inflationary trail causing boom and bust patterns. For those without particular inside information into market movements, a buy-and-hold strategy with periodic "rebalancing" may well outperform trying to guess at the timing of what are essentially irrational monetary policy adjustments.

Brokerages Favor Institutional Investors: Market timing is difficult enough to carry out on a consistent basis for individual investors unschooled in technical analysis. Retail brokers also generally lack the mind set and tools to successfully time the market; most brokerages discourage their brokers from moving their clients in and out of the market. However, as market makers, many of these same brokerages take the opposite approach with their large institutional clients, trading various financial instruments for these clients in an attempt to "predict future market price movements" and thereby make a profit for the institutions. This disconnect in the treatment of institutional vs. retail clients suggests retail brokers and their clients are discouraged from market timing, not because it doesn't work, but because it would interfere with the brokerages' market maker trading for their institutional clients. More insidiously, retail clients may be encouraged to buy and hold so as to maintain market liquidity for the institutional trading. This would suggest a conflict of interest, in which the brokerages are willing to sacrifice potential returns for the smaller retail clients in order to benefit larger institutional clients.

The 2008 decline in the markets is instructive. While many retail brokers were instructed by their brokerages to tell their clients not to sell, but instead "look to the long term", the market makers at those same brokerages were busy selling to cash to avoid losses for the brokerages' large institutional clients. The result was that the retail clients were left with huge losses while the institutions fled to the safety of short term bonds and money market funds, thereby avoiding similar losses.

Curve Fitting And Over-Optimization: A major stumbling block for many market timers is the phenomenon of curve fitting. This means that a given set of trading rules has been over-optimized to fit the particular dataset for which it has been back-tested. In other words mathematical formulas which attempt to predict the future based on historical data are notorious for diverging wildly from reality even while perfectly modeling past behavior. Over-optimized trading rules often fail to work on future data, just as bettors often fail to predict Super-Bowl contestants based on the previous year's results, even using massive databases and sophisticated algorithms. Market timers attempt to avoid these difficulties in a number of ways. One is by looking for clusters of parameter values which work particularly well. Another is using out-of-sample data, which ostensibly allows the market timer to see how the system will work on unforeseen data. However, once the strategy has been revised to reflect such data it is no longer "out-of-sample".

Independent Review Of Market-Timing: Several independent organizations (e.g., Timer Digest and Hulbert Financial Digest) have tracked some market timers' performance for over thirty years. These organizations have found that purported market timers in many cases do no better than chance, or even worse. However, there are exceptions, with some market timers over the thirty year period having performances that substantially and reliably exceed those of the general stock market or the sectors in which that the market timers invest. Jim Simons' Renaissance Technologies Medallion Hedge Fund has consistently outperformed the market. The fund allegedly uses mathematical models developed by Elwyn Berlekamp.

Evidence Against Market Timing: Mutual fund flows are published by organizations such as Investment Company Institute and TrimTabs. These show that flows generally track the overall level of the market. For example, in the beginning of the 2000s decade, the largest inflows to stock mutual funds were in early 2000 while the largest outflows were in mid 2002. It is good to note that these mutual fund flows were near the start of a significant bear (downtrending) market and bull (uptrending) market respectively. A similar pattern was repeated near the end of the decade.

This mutual fund flow data seems to indicate that most investors (despite what they may say) actually follow a buy high, sell low strategy. Studies confirm that the general tendency of investors is to buy after a stock or mutual fund price has already increased. This creates a surge in the number of buyers which then drives the price even higher. However, eventually, the supply of buyers becomes exhausted, and the demand (supply and demand) for the stock declines and the stock or fund price also declines.

A key premise of this book is that we are in a biflationary depression, which is the result of the breakdown of honesty (both in terms of monetary policy and crony capitalist behavior). This suggests not that market timing would fail, but that you would need to track variables beyond economic fundamentals, specifically political cronyism.

Indexes And Exchange Traded Funds

The famous Dalbar study found that the average investor's return in stocks is much less than the amount that would have been obtained by simply holding an index fund consisting of all stocks contained in the S&P 500 index. Recent studies suggest that corporations and investment banks cannot time the credit markets. They show that investment banks such as Goldman Sachs do as poorly as firms like Ford when it comes to timing the issuance of their bonds.

The best predictor of a fund's consistent outperformance of the market is more likely low expenses and low turnover, not pursuit of a value or contrarian strategy. However, other studies have concluded that some simple strategies will outperform the overall market. One market-timing strategy is referred to as Time Zone Arbitrage.

Foreign Equities

Given the possibility of an economic crash in the United States, it seems wise to look towards foreign markets to diversify one's investments. Because markets are so fluid, it wouldn't make sense to suggest specific companies to buy stock in simply because such suggestions would be outdated by the time you read them. But as far as picking countries there are long term trends visible and we provide a chart in a following chapter which outlines some of the economic fundamentals of countries worldwide (such as Debt To GDP ratios) that might influence your selections.

The ease of buying foreign stocks and bonds may also depend on your brokerage. Well known market guru Peter Schiff runs EuroPacific Capital as a brokerage that specializes in being able to make foreign transactions, but there are others. You may also have to set up accounts in foreign countries through banks like the Royal Bank of Canada which will also give you exposure to their markets and currency.

Another way to diversify into foreign investments is by buying multinationals. Every investor has to do their own due diligence, but the benefit of buying multinationals is diversification of risk both in regards to currency fluctuations and political instability.

Top 100 Multinationals

Rank	Multinational	Origin	Sector
1	HSBC Holdings	United Kingdom	Banking
2	General Electric	United States	Conglomerates
3	Bank of America	United States	Banking
4	JPMorgan Chase	United States	Banking
5	ExxonMobil	United States	Oil & Gas Operations
6	Royal Dutch Shell	Netherlands	Oil & Gas Operations
7	BP	United Kingdom	Oil & Gas Operations
8	Toyota Motor	Japan	Consumer Durables
9	ING Group	Netherlands	Insurance
10	Berkshire Hathaway	United States	Diversified Financials
10	Royal Bank of Scotland	United Kingdom	Banking
12	AT&T	United States	Telecommunications
13	BNP Paribas	France	Banking
14	Allianz	Germany	Insurance

Rank	Multinational	Origin	Sector
15	Total	France	Oil & Gas Operations
16	Wal-Mart Stores	United States	Retailing
17	Chevron	United States	Oil & Gas Operations
18	American Intl Group	United States	Insurance
19	Gazprom	Russia	Oil & Gas Operations
20	AXA Group	France	Insurance
21	Banco Santander	Spain	Banking
22	ConocoPhillips	United States	Oil & Gas Operations
23	Goldman Sachs Group	United States	Diversified Financials
24	Citigroup	United States	Banking
25	Barclays	United Kingdom	Banking
26	EDF Group	France	Utilities
27	E.ON	Germany	Utilities
28	ENI	Italy	Oil & Gas Operations
29	Petrobras-Petróleo Brasil	Brazil	Oil & Gas Operations
30	PetroChina	China	Oil & Gas Operations
31	Procter & Gamble	United States	Household & Personal
32	Deutsche Bank	Germany	Diversified Financials
33	UniCredit Group	Italy	Banking
34	Telefónica	Spain	Telecommunications
35	Mitsubishi UFJ Financial	Japan	Banking
36	Volkswagen Group	Germany	Consumer Durables
37	IBM	United States	Software & Services
38	ArcelorMittal	Luxembourg	Materials
38	Daimler	Germany	Consumer Durables
40	BBVA-Banco Bilbao Vizcaya	Spain	Banking
41	Wells Fargo	United States	Banking
42	ICBC	China	Banking
43	Credit Suisse Group	Switzerland	Diversified Financials
44	HBOS	United Kingdom	Banking
45	Crédit Agricole	France	Banking
45	Nestlé	Switzerland	Food Drink & Tobacco
47	Fortis	Netherlands	Diversified Financials
48	Verizon Communications	United States	Telecommunications
49	France Telecom	France	Telecommunications
50	Siemens	Germany	Conglomerates
50	Wachovia	United States	Banking
52	Sinopec-China Petroleum	China	Oil & Gas Operations
53	Hewlett-Packard	United States	Technology Hardware &
54	Lloyds TSB Group	United Kingdom	Banking
55	Royal Bank of Canada	Canada	Banking

Rank	Multinational	Origin	Sector
56	Bank of China	China	Banking
57	Pfizer	United States	Drugs & Biotechnology
58	Johnson & Johnson	United States	Drugs & Biotechnology
59	Samsung Electronics	South Korea	Semiconductors
60	StatoilHydro	Norway	Oil & Gas Operations
61	Generali Group	Italy	Insurance
62	CCB-China Construction Bank	China	Banking
63	Microsoft	United States	Software & Services
64	Suez Group	France	Utilities
65	Zurich Financial Services	Switzerland	Insurance
66	Nippon Telegraph & Tel	Japan	Telecommunications
67	Sanofi-aventis	France	Drugs & Biotechnology
68	Honda Motor	Japan	Consumer Durables
69	Nokia	Finland	Technology Hardware &
70	Munich Re	Germany	Insurance
71	Mizuho Financial	Japan	Banking
72	Novartis	Switzerland	Drugs & Biotechnology
73	MetLife	United States	Insurance
74	Roche Holding	Switzerland	Drugs & Biotechnology
75	Morgan Stanley	United States	Diversified Financials
76	Vale	Brazil	Materials
77	Rio Tinto	United	Materials
78	China Mobile	Hong Kong/China	Telecommunications
79	GlaxoSmithKline	United Kingdom	Drugs & Biotechnology
80	BASF	Germany	Chemicals
81	RWE Group	Germany	Utilities
82	Sumitomo Mitsui Financial	Japan	Banking
83	BHP Billiton	Australia/United	Materials
84	Time Warner	United States	Media
85	Banco Bradesco	Brazil	Banking
85	KBC Group	Belgium	Banking
87	Dexia	Belgium	Banking
88	Altria Group	United States	Food Drink & Tobacco
89	National Australia Ban	Australia	Banking
90	Cisco Systems	United States	Technology Hardware &
91	Manulife Financial	Canada	Insurance
92	Bank of Nova Scotia	Canada	Banking
93	Intel	United States	Semiconductors
94	Unilever	Netherlands/United	Food Drink & Tobacco
95	Toronto-Dominion Bank	Canada	Banking
96	Nissan Motor	Japan	Consumer Durables

Rank	Multinational	Origin	Sector
97	Lehman Bros Holdings	United States	Diversified Financials
98	Carrefour Group	France	Food Markets
99	Commonwealth Bank	Australia	Banking
100	Boeing	United States	Aerospace & Defense

Finally we should mention that Exchange Traded Funds (ETFs) are available that are market baskets for different countries. The stock-like features of an ETF is perhaps their most important benefit. ETFs trade on the market, which allows investors to make the same types of trades they can with stocks.

For investors looking for international exposure in their portfolios, there are a lot of options. Foreign currency ETFs, emerging market funds, international bond ETFs and even broad foreign market ETFs.

High Frequency & Algorithmic Trading

One reason it has become increasingly difficult for small investors to rely on the stock market is because of the rise of computer trading. High Frequency Trading (HFT), related to algorithmic trading, are trading systems that utilize advanced mathematical models for making transaction decisions in the financial markets through high speed computer connections. The rules built into the model attempt to determine the optimal time for an order to be placed that will cause the least amount of impact on a stock's price. Large blocks of shares can be purchased by dividing the large share block into smaller lots and allowing the complex algorithms to decide when the smaller blocks are to be purchased.

The use of algorithmic trading is used by large institutional investors and hedge funds due to the large amount of shares they purchase every day. Complex algorithms allow these investors to obtain the best possible price without significantly affecting the stock's price and increasing purchasing costs. Trading platforms use powerful computers to transact a large number of orders at very fast speeds and analyze multiple markets. Traders with the fastest execution speeds will be more profitable than traders with slower execution speeds. It is estimated more than 50% of exchange volume comes from high-frequency trading orders.

The reason we are discussing HFTs is that the odds are you will not have access to High Frequency Trading platforms, though you may be able to purchase some algorithmic software. This means the market is severely rigged for short term small investors, especially anyone trying to day trade. While it is theoretically possible to be smarter than the computer trading platforms in day trading and short term transactions, it isn't likely. That's why we have suggested dividend bearing stocks as an alternative to playing a market which will be roiled both by computer trading and Federal Reserve intervention well into the future.

Diversification

Stock diversification is obviously a high priority in a world in which certainty has evaporated. A rule of thumb has been that to average out the statistical noise in a portfolio you need to own at least ten different stocks spread across perhaps five economic sectors. That rule of thumb now seems dated. The minimum number of stocks is likely closer to twenty stocks and ten sectors. It may actually be tat forty stocks is needed because as everyone moves to index funds, we no longer have a re market based on the collective wisdom of thousands of individual investors.

We would avoid sectors that are subject to the collapse of paper assets (banks and financials), or at least monitor those stocks closely. Also important is diversification not only among market sectors but also currencies and geographical regions. It is clear the Euro, Yen and Dollar are being destroyed to support collapsing welfare states, but what is not clear is where to run. We can suggest Canada, Australia, Hong Kong, Singapore and the Scandinavian countries as possible refuges, but the relative strengths can turn on everything from wars to petroleum shortages to worldwide collapse of commodity economies. In short, diversify to lower risk but be aware that the situation will remain fluid.

Beware the POMO

POMO stands for permanent open market operations by the US Federal Reserve Board. With a POMO, the Fed buys the US Treasury debt and pumps liquidity into the system. The idea is that the money freed-up from holding US Government bonds will be put into use boosting spending and the economy. In the summer of 2009, the Fed did a series of POMOS which boosted the stock and bond markets rather than giving any significant lift to the economy, all part of its effort to reinflate the economy.

The Fed will continue to do POMOs in overdrive. For example, Tue, Oct 05 2010 the Feds bought nearly $5 billion in treasuries. Where did that money go? You guessed it, the stock market. Stocks of Netflix, Apple, PriceLine were being bid to insane levels. Not that there is anything wrong if the stock prices go up on their own fundamentals. But the problem is the freed-up money from POMOs is used to buy a few specific stocks, often by increasingly small number of players in the market, these players being computers. So called robo-trading pumped up by Federal Reserve POMO operations makes the market a dangerous place for small investors when the inevitable Black Swans make their return.

The Fed is essentially a private bank controlling the entire banking system of the largest economy in the world. This leads to uncomfortable questions. Who is Ben Bernanke and now Janet Yellen really propping up through these POMOs? The economy? The stocks? Their Goldman Sachs Wall Street buddies? Or, President Obama as a Quid-pro-Quo for appointment?

What we might further wonder here are three things:

1) How would the stock markets have behaved without the massive daily additions of billions of dollars?
2) When the stock market turned around in advance of the initiation of the POMO purchases, did major bank holding companies, such as Goldman Sachs, effectively front-running this flood of money?
3) Even when the stock market rose 40% by early 2012 and green shoots were everywhere, why did the Fed continue to pour gasoline on the fire?

Part of the answer may lie in the observation by the somewhat conspiratorial financial website ZeroHedge.com that on POMO days the stock market exhibits statistically unlikely upward increases in the final few closing minutes. Under this scenario POMO money is shuffled out of the endless thin-air vaults of the Fed and into the banking system where it needs to find something to do. One of those things, it seems, is to goose the stock market, especially late in the day.

The goal is likely to get the stock market to move upwards, which at first glance might seem rational for an economy as dependent on rising asset prices as is the United States'. While getting people out buying and spending may seem a worthy goal to policy-makers mind, it is another example of the Fed's perpetual motion mindset where it believes the introduction of information void monetary stimulus can do anything but further misallocate resources.

Our point is twofold:

1) In a biflationary depression caused by Keynesian monetary stimulus individuals cannot trust the normal price signals of the market to be correct.
2) Given that investors likely have no choice but to be in the market, one needs to play these bubbles as bubbles and be prepared for them to burst.

Strategies For When Every Market Is Manipulated

Hint: cut the strings

If you don't know who the sucker at the card table is, it's you.

~ old gambler's saying

What do the following have in common?

Bernie Madoff, LIBOR, Peregrine Financial, MF Global, zero-percent interest rates, Social Security, Medicare, FHA, many state and municipal pension funds, quote stuffing and high frequency trading (HFT), mark-to-model asset values, and debt-based money? Every single element of that list is an example of fraud, market rigging, or both.

How are we supposed to make decisions in today's rigged and often fraudulent market environment? Where should you put your money if you don't know where the risks lie? How does an investor control risk when the market is controlled and fraud runs rampant? Unfortunately, there are no perfect answers to these questions. Instead, the task is to recognize what sort of world we happen to live in today and adjust one's actions to the realities as they happen to be. One must be hedged at all times.

21   Recognizing Ponzi Schemes

A central axiom of traders and rational market participants is that the market is always right. If the price of gasoline is $4.50/gallon or the price of gold is $1,850/ounce, then those are the correct and right prices.

However, most of the prices we see today are reflections of something at once more mundane and sinister: central planning. You simply cannot trust the prices you see as much as you used to. First prices are distorted by the pernicious effects of mispriced money, and second by selective lack of market and regulatory enforcement. The reason this is necessary is to cover up the fact that our entire economic system is now being run as a Ponzi scheme.

You Find Out Who's Been Running A Ponzi Scheme When The Pie Stops Expanding

As long as the economic pie is expanding, there is virtually zero public or political support to call out private and public Ponzi schemes for what they are. It is only once some limit to growth is reached – for example the bursting of a multi-decade credit bubble in 2008 -- that the party ends and the lack of standards and critical financial due diligence are finally revealed.

The fraud has always been there, often in plain sight, but few cared as long as the status quo was maintained. Municipal and state pension plans which are mathematically unworkable are a prime example of this dynamic. The colossal Federal deficit is another. For as long as the fiction of solvency can be maintained, few challenge the system, even though we are fast approaching a fiduciary train wreck. The recent spate of municipal bankruptcies indicates that the 'eventual' train wreck has begun and the first few cars of a very long train are off the rails.

Poorly-run companies can appear healthy during boom times but are exposed as hollow shells when the economic tide retreats. It's naturally much easier to make a profit when markets are booming, but decidedly more difficult when the economic pie is shrinking or treading water. The poster children for the stampede to failure in a falling market are the dot-com companies of the 1990s. However now entire countries are being exposed as hollow shells, the United States being one of many. The global pie is no longer expanding as shown by the relentless parade of disquieting economic and financial news.

While there are prosecutable examples of private Ponzi schemes (see Bernie Madoff), state and municipal pensions and the Social Security entitlement program also fit the definition. The most glaring Ponzi scheme is expanding public debt faster than the GDP, a nihilist economic policy many nations, states and provinces have now embraced for decades. Ponzi schemes all require exponential growth to remain 'healthy' (or more accurately, to remain *hidden*) and are mathematically doomed to fail. Now that economic prosperity is no longer growing and most likely will not grow for decades, these schemes are falling apart in full view.

Greek insolvency, now a full-bore depression, is a reflection of a multi-year Ponzi scheme now spreading throughout Europe to Spain, Italy and even France. It is impossible to perpetually borrow faster than income growth. Greece is a harbinger of the nightmare to come for all countries in similar positions of fiscal insanity. That includes all of the PIIGS, Japan, the US and even China.

Now that the economic pool has stopped expanding and is contracting, nations swimming fiscally naked are exposed. Timing will vary, as some were in more shallow water (Greece, Spain) than others (the US), but timing aside, there really isn't much of a difference between any of them.

Illegal and Condoned Fraud

To discuss the rampant financial fraud that has accumulated we need to decide whether there is suddenly a lot more fraud in the system from some new cause, or whether our lack of growth simply reveals the extent to which fraud and Ponzi schemes have been a systemic feature of our *political-financial-regulatory-banking* landscape all along. Unfortunately, our problems are systemic.

Every exponential, debt-based monetary system is, at its very core, a Ponzi scheme. It simply *has* to keep expanding so that there's enough money and credit manufactured *today* to meet *yesterday's* principal and interest loads. Without perpetual growth, the debt pile eventually collapses, causing extraordinary losses across the playing board. If our entire money system is itself a Ponzi scheme, then it follows that much of what is based on that monetary superstructure will share that fraudulent character.

Garden-variety Ponzi schemes, such as the ones run by Peregrine Financial and Bernie Madoff are easier to cover up and keep viable when the economic environment of money and credit is expanding rapidly. Their early demise just means that they were in the weakest positions and therefore unable to survive the first rounds of national credit/money stagnation.

At the next level are the banks which have borrowed at a faster rate than economic growth. That process is already well underway for Greece, Spain, Italy, and Portugal -- but just barely bailed out by the European Central Bank. Closing the enormous gap between practical levels of funding and desired spending, will be a long and exceptionally painful process.

At an even higher level are the state-sponsored schemes. Woefully underfunded pensions and entitlement programs will take longer to unravel, but that will happen too in one form or another, most likely by cutting benefits.

When credit and money expansion stops, the various schemes that relied upon the illusion of growth supplied by inflated credit are exposed as unworkable. Credit growth stalls because faith is lost that borrowers (both individual and sovereign) can repay the debt. There simply isn't enough 'juice' left in the system to cover the various 'legal' and illegal Ponzi schemes.

Officially Supported Fraud

As bad as private frauds are, and as corrosive as they are to public trust, they pale in comparison to those perpetuated at the very highest levels of the state and Federal Reserve. That this fraud is supported and encouraged by the regulatory bodies and official institutions renders it no more palatable. Financial regulatory bodies can be counted on to look the other way when certain frauds are aligned with the aims and goals of the state while punishing other frauds selectively and grudgingly.

The LIBOR scandal is a perfect example of regulators 'looking the other way when it suits us.' LIBOR is the main determinant for the rate of interest paid on tens of trillions of loans and hundreds of trillions in derivatives. Because a LIBOR rate manipulated to inappropriately low levels created the appearance of robust bank health, the Fed and other central banks and regulatory authorities were happy to look the other way for many years. The manipulation of LIBOR also padded the profits of big, well-connected banks, another prime goal of the central authorities.

If the central financial regulators are willing to ignore fraud on that scale, how far will they go to prop up other areas of malfeasance? The clear message is that lying, cheating, and stealing are all just fine, as long as they support the policy aims of the politically connected and their financial colleagues.

Gold As A Measure Of Fraud

The Fed condones any policy that boosts the apparent health of major banks (their prime clients) and the apparent health of fiat money (their only product). Despite their fixation on fiat monetary policy, they have gold squarely in their sights. The price of gold is thus neither free nor fair, at least in the short term. The US, UK and other central banks cannot risk serious questions being raised about fiat money. Gold is the only monetary barometer that exists outside of the world of fiat money and is therefore the true measure of monetary fraud.

The Fed looked the other way while banks colluded to keep LIBOR artificially low (because that sent the 'right' signal about bank health and boosted profits). It is unsurprising the Fed has also looked the other way as banks made money by manipulating the gold market into lower price bands. Even with revelations of fraud and/or price manipulation, gold should play a role as an anchor to your long term portfolio because it is the only hedge against fraud.

The grotesque mispricing of everything begins with the mispricing of money itself. Thanks to a permanent policy of pricing money at zero percent, the entire system is riddled with distorted prices, especially the price for risk. For example, virtually every pension fund is forced to lend money to the US government for ten years at 1.5% interest, a ridiculous rate given the risks of inflation and even default that a free market would price very differently.

22 Bonds

Our rule for biflationary times is to "Show Me The Money". In other words, you are better off seeing real cash flow rather than promises of appreciation which may never occur. One way to do so is by buying bonds which return a fixed rate of income, rather than speculative stocks which may pay little or zero dividend. The caveat is that because the Federal Reserve must continue its slash and burn destruction of the economy by holding interest rates at zero, bond yields have also been low. There is also a now real risk of default. We'll give you some tips on how to deal with these problems, but first some rudimentary definitions.

What Is A Bond

A bond is a debt security, in which the authorized issuer owes the holders a debt and, depending on the terms of the bond, is obliged to pay interest (the coupon) to use and/or to repay the principal amount at a later date (maturity). A bond is a formal contract to repay borrowed money with interest at fixed intervals (semiannual, annual, and sometimes monthly).

So a bond is much like a loan. The holder of the bond is the lender (or creditor). The entity issuing of the bond is the borrower (debtor), and the interest (coupon) is the rate necessary to return a profit over time to the lender. Bonds provide private borrowers with the outside funds they need to finance long-term investments. In the case of governments, bonds finance current expenditure.

The major difference between Bonds and Stocks is the difference between holding equity and holding a loan. Capital stockholders have an equity stake in the company (they are owners). In contrast, bondholders have a creditor stake in the company (they are lenders). Bonds also usually have a defined term, a maturity, after which the bond is redeemed. Stocks may be outstanding indefinitely. The exception is a consol bond, which is perpetuity (a bond with no maturity date).

Bonds are bought and traded mostly by institutions like central banks, sovereign wealth funds, pension funds, insurance companies and banks. Individuals who want to own bonds usually do so through bond funds. Still, in the U.S., nearly 10% of all bonds outstanding are held directly by households.

Sometimes, when stock markets fall, bond markets rise (while yields fall). More relevantly, the volatility of bonds (especially short and medium dated bonds) is lower than that of stocks. Thus bonds are generally viewed as safer investments than stocks and bond interest payments are often higher than the general level of dividend payments.

Bonds are liquid – it is fairly easy to sell one's bond investments, though not nearly as easy as it is to sell stocks – and the comparative certainty of a twice yearly fixed interest payment is attractive because it is financially straightforward. Under the law of most countries, bondholders also enjoy a measure of legal protection. If a company goes bankrupt, its bondholders will often receive some money back (the recovery amount), where a bankrupt company's stock may end up valueless. Some of these rules were however broken in the General Motors bankruptcy proceedings, part of what is the New Normal of financial cronyism and corruption.

Interest Rate Risk

Fixed rate bonds are not risk free and are subject to interest rate risk. This means their market price will decrease when the prevailing interest rates rise. Since bond payments are fixed, decreases in the market price of a bond means its effective yield increases to anyone purchasing the bond in the current market. When the market interest rate rises, the market price of bonds will fall, reflecting investors' ability to get a higher interest rate on their money elsewhere by purchasing newly issued bond that are based on higher prevailing interest rates. Note that this drop in the bond's market price does not affect the interest payments to the bondholder at all. Long-term bond investors who want a specific face value amount returned at the maturity date don't need to be concerned about day to day price swings and do not suffer from interest rate risk.

Of course, some people were able to lock in huge gains in bonds if they bought when interest rates were high and then saw the Federal Reserve force interest rates to the basement. This opportunity is unlikely to repeat itself for the foreseeable future as the Federal Reserve is locked into perpetual Quantitative Easing.

Bonds have a number of other risks. These include event risk, inflation risk, credit risk, call and prepayment risk, liquidity risk, exchange rate risk, sovereign risk, reinvestment risk, volatility risk, and yield curve risk.

Valuing Bonds

Factors such as current market interest rates, the length of the term and creditworthiness of the issuer all influence the interest rate the issuer of a bond must pay.

These factors change over time, so the market price of a bond varies after it is issued and this price is expressed as a percentage of nominal value. Bonds may not be issued at par (corresponding to a price of 100 or 100% of face value), but bond prices must converge to par as they approach maturity (as long as the market expects the payment at maturity to be made in full and on time). Par value is the price the issuer pays to redeem the bond and is referred to as "Pull to Par". Before maturity, prices can trade at a premium above par (bond is priced at greater than 100), or trade at a discount below par (bond is priced at less than 100).

Government bonds are generally denominated in units of $1000 in the United States, or in units of £100 in the United Kingdom. As an example, a deep discount US bond, selling at a price of 76.52, indicates a selling price of $765.20 per bond sold. In the US, bond prices may also be quoted in points and thirty-seconds of a point, rather than in decimal form. Some short-term bonds, called discount bonds as exemplified by U.S. Treasury Bills, are always issued at a discount, and rather than paying coupons pay par amount at maturity.

The market price of a bond is the present value of all expected future interest and principal payments of the bond discounted at the bond's redemption yield, or rate of return.

This relationship defines the redemption yield on the bond, which equals the current market interest rate for bonds with similar fundamentals.

Yield and price of a bond are inversely related.

When market interest rates rise, bond prices fall and vice versa. Thus the redemption yield is made of two parts: the current yield, and the expected capital gain or loss. This is roughly the current yield plus the capital gain (negative for loss) per year until redemption.

Some bond markets include accrued interest in the trading price and others add it on explicitly after trading. The market price of a bond may also include accrued interest since the last coupon date. The price including accrued interest is known as the "full" or "dirty price" while the price excluding accrued interest is known as the "flat" or "clean price".

The interest rate adjusted for (i.e. divided by) the current price of the bond is called the current yield. This is also equivalent to the nominal yield multiplied by the par value and divided by the price. Other yield measures include yield to first call, yield to worst, yield to first par call, yield to put, cash flow yield and yield to maturity.

The relationship between yield and maturity for otherwise identical bonds is called a yield curve and is essentially a measure of the term structure of bonds.

Types Of Bonds

Corporate Bonds: are debts issued by industrial, financial and service companies to finance operating cash flow and capital investment. The corporate bond market is bigger than the markets for municipal bonds, U.S. treasury securities, and government agencies securities in terms of total face value of bonds outstanding. Corporate bonds have a wide range of choices structures, coupon rates, maturity dates, credit quality and industry exposure.

U.S. Treasury securities: are debt obligations of the U.S. government and include bills, notes and bonds. Buying a U.S. Treasury security is the same as lending money to the federal government for a specified period of time.

These debt obligations are backed by the "full faith and credit" of the government, and by its ability to raise tax revenues and print currency. U.S. Treasury securities – or "Treasuries" – are often considered the safest of all investments and viewed in the market as having virtually no "credit risk," implying a high probability your interest and principal will be paid fully and on time. The caveat is that with Zero Interest Rate Policies you will be unlikely to cover the inflation rate. Also look at the course of Greek bonds as their economy crashed in 2012 to see how sovereign risk places out in the real world.

Because of this unique degree of perceived safety, interest rates are generally lower for Treasury securities than for other riskier debt securities such as corporate bonds. A good rule of thumb is that safer investments offer lower returns. Conversely, the higher the risk, the higher the return.

The problem regarding Federal Treasury Bonds is that the Federal Reserve has lowered the prime lending rate near zero which means returns on Treasuries are not enough to cover inflation risk. We may even see negative rates at some future date. In the long term, not covering the inflation rate is the same as risking complete destruction of one's principle.

Municipal Bonds: (also known as "munis") are attractive because the interest income is exempt from federal income tax, and in many cases, state and local taxes as well. Additionally, munis often represent investments in state and local government projects that have an impact on our daily lives, including schools, highways, hospitals, housing, sewer systems and other important public projects.

Purchasing a municipal bond is the same as lending money to a state or local government entity, which promises to pay you a specified amount of interest and return the principal to you on a specific maturity date. Munis are usually paid semiannually. Not all municipal bonds offer income exempt from both federal and state taxes. Municipal bonds are not as safe as they have been in the past given the economic slowdown and the unfunded liabilities of local governments.

While investing in municipal bonds often carries the advantage of their not being taxable, given the unfunded liabilities of municipal pension funds in the United States, many states and municipalities may be at risk of bankruptcy. While municipalities can go bankrupt, currently states cannot by law file for bankruptcy so their bonds would be at least somewhat protected. However given the size of the deficits in California, New York, and Illinois, it is likely that some states will be allowed to go bankrupt as well, defaulting on bondholders.

Generally, bonds rated BBB (Standard & Poor's and Fitch) or Baa better (Moody's) are considered "Investment Grade," suitable for preservation of investment capital. As always, caveat emptor.

TIPs: The United States Department of the Treasury offers a special security, called a Treasury Inflation-Protected Security (TIPS), whose principal amount is adjusted for inflation. The Treasury Department issues TIPS because it believes their issuance will reduce interest costs to the Treasury over the long term and will increase the different types of investors that buy their debt instruments. In late 2010, Treasury Inflation Protected Securities (TIPS) began trading with a negative yield – meaning that investors were paying the government for the privilege of holding its debt, rather than the other way around.

The yield on a TIPS bond is equal to the Treasury bond yield minus the rate of expected inflation, so, when standard Treasury bonds are trading at yields that are below the expected inflation rate TIPS yields will fall into negative territory.

Investors accept a negative yield is they expect the Federal Reserve's stimulative quantitative easing monetary policy will cause inflation to accelerate in the years ahead. If inflation does indeed accelerate investors could still earn a positive return on TIPS despite negative yields because TIPS' principal adjusts upwards with inflation. However, it is now clear that the inflation rate numbers are being fudged lower and interest rates are now caught in the Fed's perpetual Ponzi game. Hence betting the farm on TIPS as an inflation hedge may not be the wisest course.

Foreign Bonds: Yields on debt issued by foreign governments often beats what you can get from U.S. debt. Many investors believe this a good time to replace Treasuries with bonds from such prosperous nations as Australia, New Zealand or Canada. Once prosperous nations in Western Europe or Japan may now be considered high risk.

Bonds from most developed nations have produced positive returns, some as high as 8%. In the past, most foreign currencies have appreciated or stayed stable against the dollar, so currency translation has been either a positive or neutral in regard to returns on foreign debt. That situation will change quickly given the precarious state of not only the dollar but many other currencies in the New Normal, so make sure to spread the risk among foreign bonds.

Traditionally you needed to be a millionaire to tap the foreign government bond market; however exchange-traded funds now make foreign bond investment available to everyone. As an example, iShares JPMorgan USD Emerging Markets Bond Fund (symbol EMB) contains bonds from places such as Brazil, Russia and Turkey. Its expenses, at 0.60%, are low. But the current yield at writing, based on the latest monthly distribution, was only 5.5%, which diminishes the fund's appeal considerably.

Issuing Bonds

Bonds are issued in primary markets by public authorities, credit institutions, companies and supranational institutions. Underwriting is the most common process of issuing bonds, where one or more securities firms or banks, forming a syndicate, buy an entire issue of bonds from an issuer and re-sell them to investors. The security firm doing the underwriting risks being unable to sell the issue to end investors. Primary issuance is arranged by bookrunners who have the direct contact with investors and advise the bond issuer on timing and price of the bond issue.

Government bonds are generally issued by auctions also called a public sale, where both the public and banks may bid for bonds. The coupon is fixed, but the price is not, so the percent return is a function both the price paid as well as the coupon.

Because the cost of issuance for a publicly auctioned bond may be prohibitive for a smaller loan, smaller bonds may avoid the underwriting and auction process through the use of a private placement bond which is held by the lender and does not enter the large bond market.

Features Of Bonds

Important features of a bond investors should understand are:

nominal, principal or face amount — the amount on which the issuer pays interest, and which, has to be repaid at the end of the term. Some structured bonds have a redemption amount different from the face amount and can be linked to performance of assets such as a stock or commodity index, foreign exchange rate or a fund. This can result in an investor receiving less or more than his original investment at maturity.

issue price — the price at first issue at which investors buy a bond, typically equal to the nominal amount. The net proceeds that the issuer receives are the issue price, less issuance fees.

maturity date — the date on which the issuer must repay the nominal amount. After the maturity date the issuer has no more obligation to the bond holders As long as all payments have been made, the time until maturity is referred to as the term or tenor or maturity of a bond. Maturity can be any length of time, though debt securities with a term less than one year are usually designated money market instruments rather than bonds. Most bonds have term of thirty years or less, though bonds have been issued with maturities of one hundred years, and some do not mature at all.

In the U.S. Treasury securities market, there are three groups of bond maturities:

- short term (bills): maturities between one to five year. Instruments with maturities less than one year are called Money Market Instruments.
- medium term (notes): maturities between six to twelve years;
- long term (bonds): maturities greater than twelve years.

coupon — the interest rate t the issuer pays to bond holders. This rate is usually fixed throughout the life of the bond, but it can vary with a money market index, such as LIBOR, or can be even more exotic. The term coupon originates in that in the past, physical bonds were issued which had coupons attached to them and on coupon dates bond holders would exchange coupons with a bank in exchange for the interest payment.

quality of the issue - reflects the probability that a bondholder will receive the amount promised at the due dates.

indentures and covenants — An indenture establishes the terms of a bond issue in a formal debt agreement. Covenants are the clauses of such an agreement and specify the rights of bondholders and the duties of issuers. This includes actions that the issuer is obligated to perform or is prohibited from performing. Federal and state securities and commercial laws in the U.S. apply to the enforcement of these agreements and are construed by courts as contracts between issuers and bondholders. Terms may only be changed with great difficulty while bonds are outstanding, with amendments to the governing document generally requiring approval by a majority (or even super-majority) vote of the bondholders.

This situation has changed somewhat during the Obama administration, in which the terms of General Motors bonds were changed unilaterally by the government. In an era of corruption, one must be aware that this abrogation of contract terms may happen with more frequency as unfunded liabilities collapse.

high yield bonds - are bonds rated below investment grade by credit rating agencies, but because these bonds are more risky than investment grade bonds, investors expect to earn a higher yield. Also called junk bonds. These are not necessarily bad investments, because the risk premium often more than covers the risk.

coupon dates — the dates on which issuers pays the coupon to bond holders. In the U.S. and the U.K. and Europe, most bonds are semi-annual, paying a coupon every six months.

optionality - A bond may contain an embedded option that grants option-like features to the holder or the issuer:

callability — Some bonds give issuers the right to repay the bond before the maturity date on call dates. These bonds are referred to as callable bonds and may be termed a call option. Most callable bonds allow the issuer to repay the bond at par, while with some bonds the issuer pays a call premium (the case for many high-yield bonds). Callable bonds have strict covenants, restricting the issuer in its operations. The issuer can be free from these covenants and repay the bonds early, but only at a high cost.

putability — Some bonds give the holder the right to force the issuer to repay the bond before the maturity date on the put dates, also termed a put option. ("Putable" denotes an embedded put option; "Puttable" denotes it may be put.)

call dates and put dates—the dates on which callable and putable bonds can be redeemed early. Three main categories are in common use.

- A Bermudan callable with several call dates, often coinciding with coupon dates.
- A European callable has just one call date and is a special case of a Bermudan callable.
- An American callable can be called at any time until the maturity date.

death put - An optional redemption feature on debt instruments which allows beneficiaries of the estate of a deceased to put (sell) the bond back to the issuer due to death or legal incapacitation. Sometimes known as a "survivor's option".

sinking fund – A provision of a corporate bond indenture which requires a portion of the issue to be retired periodically. The entire bond issue may even be liquidated by the maturity date, otherwise the remainder is called balloon maturity. Issuers may either pay to trustees who call randomly selected bonds in the issue, or, purchase bonds in open market and return them to trustees.

convertible bond – This lets a bondholder exchange a bond for a number of shares of issuer common stock.

exchangeable bond - Allows for exchange to shares of a corporation other than the issuer.

Bond Structure

More than one description may apply to a particular bond.

Fixed rate bonds - The coupon remains constant throughout the life of the bond.

Floating rate notes (FRNs) - A variable coupon linked to a reference rate of interest, such as LIBOR or Euribor. FAs an example the coupon might be defined as three month USD LIBOR + 0.20%. The coupon rate is typically recalculated every one or three months.

Zero-coupon bonds - Pay no regular interest and are issued at a substantial discount to par value. The interest is rolled up to maturity and usually taxed as such when the bondholder receives the full principal amount on the redemption date. Series E savings bonds issued by the U.S. government are examples of zero coupon bonds. Zero-coupon bonds can be created from fixed rate bonds by a financial institution separating ("stripping off") the coupons from the principal and the separated coupons and the final principal payment of the bond are traded separately. Also known as IO (Interest Only) and PO (Principal Only).

Inflation linked bonds - The principal amount and interest payments are indexed to inflation. The interest rate is normally lower than for fixed rate bonds with a comparable maturity, though this can reverse for short-term situations. As the principal amount grows, payments increase with inflation. The United Kingdom was the first sovereign issuer of inflation linked Gilts in the 1980s. In the United

States, Treasury Inflation-Protected Securities (TIPS) and I-bonds are inflation linked bonds issued by the U.S. government.

The caveat with inflation linked bonds is that governments are now gaming the inflation numbers and will use this means to paper over their deficit induced inflation.

Other indexed bonds – in the category are equity-linked notes and bonds indexed on a business indicator such as income, added value or a country's GDP.

Asset-backed securities - bonds whose interest and principal payments are backed by cash flows from other underlying assets. Asset-backed securities include collateralized debt obligations (CDOs), mortgage-backed securities (MBS's) and collateralized mortgage obligations (CMOs).

Subordinated bonds - bonds that have a lower priority than other bonds of the issuer in liquidation. There is a hierarchy of creditors in bankruptcy. The liquidator is first paid, followed by government taxes, etc. So called senior bond holders are first in line to be paid. Afterwards, subordinated bond holders are paid, who therefore carry a higher risk. Subordinated bonds thus have a lower credit rating than senior bonds. Bonds issued by banks, and asset-backed securities are the main examples of subordinated bonds. Asset-backed securities are often issued in tranches in which the senior tranches get paid back first, the subordinated tranches later.

Perpetual bonds - also called perpetuities or 'Perps' have no maturity date. Best known are the UK Consols, also known as Treasury Annuities or Undated Treasuries. Some were issued in 1888 and still trade today, though the amounts are now insignificant. Ultra-long-term bonds can last centuries and are virtually perpetuities from a financial point of view, with a current value of principal near zero. West Shore Railroad issued a bond which matures in 2361 (i.e. 24th century.

Bearer bond - An official certificate issued without a named holder. The person who has the paper certificate can claim the value of the bond. Generally registered by a number to prevent counterfeiting, bearer bonds can be traded like cash, but are very risky because they can be lost or stolen. After the federal income tax began in the United States, bearer bonds were seen as an opportunity to conceal income or assets. U.S. corporations stopped issuing bearer bonds in the 1960s, the U.S. Treasury stopped in 1982, and state and local tax-exempt bearer bonds were prohibited in 1983.

Registered bond - a bond whose ownership and subsequent purchasers are recorded by the issuer, or by a transfer agent. Registered bonds became the alternative to a Bearer bond. Interest payments, and the principal upon maturity, are sent to the registered owner.

Treasury bond - or government bond, is issued by the Federal government and is theoretically not exposed to default risk. Characterized as the safest bond, with the lowest interest rate, a treasury bond is backed by the "full faith and credit" of the federal government. For while this type of bond is often referred to as risk-free, the size of sovereign debt worldwide and the size of the US debt suggests some caution is necessary on a long term horizon.

Municipal bond - a bond issued by a state, U.S. Territory, city, local government, or agencies under their governance. Holders of municipal bonds are often exempt from the federal income tax and from the income tax of the state in which they are issued ON THE Interest income received. Be aware that municipal bonds issued for certain purposes may not be tax exempt.

Build America Bonds (BABs) - authorized by the American Recovery and Reinvestment Act of 2009, this is a new form of municipal bond. Unlike traditional tax exempt municipal bonds, interest received on BABs is subject to federal taxation. However, as with municipal bonds, the bond is tax-exempt within the state it is issued. BABs often offer significantly higher yields (over 7 percent) than standard municipal bonds.

Book-entry bond - a bond that does not have a paper certificate. Physically processing paper bonds and interest coupons has become expensive, so issuers (and banks that used to collect coupon interest for depositors) have discouraged their use. Book-entry bonds may not offer the option of a paper certificate, even to investors who prefer them.

Lottery bond - a bond issued by a state, usually European. Interest is paid like traditional fixed rate bonds, but the issuer redeems randomly selected individual bonds according to a schedule. Some redemptions may be for a higher value than the face value of the bond.

War bond - a bond issued by a country to fund a war.

Serial bond - a bond that matures in installments over a period of time. For example, a $100,000, 5-year serial bond would mature in a $20,000 annuity over a 5-year interval.

Revenue bond - a type of municipal bond which guarantees repayment solely from revenues generated by a revenue-generating entity associated with the purpose of the bonds. Revenue bonds are typically "non-recourse," and in the event of default. The bond holder has no recourse to other governmental assets or revenues.

Climate bond - bonds issued by government or corporate entities to raise finance for climate change mitigation or adaptation related projects or programs. These may be subject to political manipulation an default.

Bonds Issued In Foreign Currencies

Governments, companies, banks, and other sovereign entities may issue bonds in foreign currencies that are more stable and predictable than their domestic currency. Bonds denominated in foreign currencies also gives issuers access to investment capital only available in foreign markets. Proceeds from these bond issues may be used by companies to break into foreign markets, or converted into the issuing company's local currency for use on existing operations through foreign exchange swap hedges. Foreign issuer bonds also may be used to hedge foreign exchange rate risk. Foreign issuer bonds are sometimes called by nicknames, such as the "samurai bond" and can be issued by foreign entities trying to diversify their investor base away from domestic markets. These bond issues are typically governed by the national laws of the market of issuance. A samurai bond, issued by an investor based in Europe, will be governed by Japanese law. The following is a list of foreign currency bonds, some of which may be restricted for purchase by investors in the market of issuance.

Eurodollar bond, U.S. dollar-denominated bonds issued by non-U.S. entities outside the U.S

Yankee bond, US dollar-denominated bond issued by non-US entities in the US market

Kangaroo bond, Australian dollar-denominated bonds issued by non-Australian entities in the Australian market

Maple bond, Canadian dollar-denominated bonds issued by non-Canadian entities in the Canadian market

Samurai bond, Japanese yen-denominated bonds issued by non-Japanese entities in the Japanese market

Uridashi bond, Non-yen-denominated bonds sold to Japanese retail investors.

Shibosai bond Private placement bonds in Japanese market with distribution limited to institutions and banks.

Shogun bond, Non-yen-denominated bonds issued in Japan by non-Japanese institutions or governments

Bulldog bond, Pound sterling-denominated bonds issued in London by foreign institutions or governments

Matrioshka bond, Russian ruble-denominated bonds issued in the Russian Federation by non-Russian entities. The name is derived from the famous Russian wooden dolls, Matrioshka, and are popular among foreign visitors to Russia

Arirang bond, Korean won-denominated bonds issued by non-Korean entities in the Korean market

Kimchi bond, Non-Korean won-denominated bonds issued by\ non-Korean entities in the Korean market

Formosa bond, Non-New Taiwan Dollar-denominated bonds issued by non-Taiwan entities in the Taiwan market

Panda bond, Chinese renminbi-denominated bonds issued by non-China entities in the People's Republic of China market

Dimsum bond, Chinese renminbi-denominated bonds issued by Chinese entities in Hong Kong. These bonds enables foreign investors forbidden from investing in mainland Chinese corporate debt to invest in and be exposed to Chinese currency in Hong Kong.

Huaso bond, Chilean peso-denominated bonds issued by non-Chilean entities in the Chilean market.

Trading Bonds

Unlike stock or share markets, bonds markets often lack a centralized exchange or trading system. In developed bond markets like the U.S., Japan and Western Europe, bonds are traded in decentralized, dealer-based over-the-counter markets. Market liquidity is provided by dealers and market participants who commit risk capital to trading activity. When an investor buys or sells a bond, the counterparty to the trade is usually a bank or securities firm acting as a dealer. When a dealer buys a bond from an investor, they either immediately resell the bond to another investor, or they may carry the bond "in inventory" (in which case the dealer's position is subject to price fluctuation risks).

Unlike stock markets, in some bond markets investors do not pay brokerage commissions to dealers with whom they buy or sell bonds. Instead, dealers earn revenue through the spread, or difference, between the "bid" price at which the dealer buys a bond from one investor——and the "ask" or "offer" price at which they sell a given bond to another investor. The bid/offer spread then represents the total transaction cost associated with transferring a bond from one investor to another.

Investing In Bonds

Most bonds are bought and traded by institutions like central banks, sovereign wealth funds, pension funds, insurance companies and banks. Individuals who purchase bonds normally do so through bond funds or ETFs. Nearly 10% of all bonds outstanding in the U.S. are held directly by households.

Bond markets tend to rise (while yields fall) when stock markets fall. In contrast, the volatility of short and medium dated bonds tends to be lower than that of stocks and are thus perceived to be safer investments than stocks. Bonds do suffer less day-to-day volatility than stocks, and their interest payments are often higher than the level of dividend payments. Though not as easy to sell as stocks, it is fairly easy to sell bond investments and they are considered to be liquid. The certainty of a fixed interest payment twice per year is attractive. Under the law of most countries, bondholders also enjoy a measure of legal protection. If a company goes bankrupt, its bondholders generally receive some money back (the recovery amount), while the company's stock often ends up valueless.

Perhaps the biggest drawback to bonds is that the investor does not directly participate in any upward growth in the fortunes of a company. This factor will carry different weights with investors depending on their age and the economic climate.

Bond Risk

Bonds are generally less risky than stocks, but do have risks. Bonds are subject risks including call and prepayment risk, credit risk, risk, reinvestment risk, liquidity event risk, volatility risk, exchange rate risk, inflation risk, sovereign risk and yield curve risk.

Fixed rate bonds are subject to interest rate risk, meaning market prices can decrease in value as prevailing interest rates rise. Since payments are fixed, a decrease in a bond's market price means an increase in its yield. As market interest rates rise, the market price of bonds falls, reflecting investors' ability to get a higher interest rate on their money elsewhere. Newly issued bonds will feature new higher interest rate corresponding to the current interest rate, making older bonds less desirable. This drop in a bond's market price does not affect interest payments to the bondholders, so long-term investors looking for a specific amount returned at the maturity date need not worry about price swings in their bonds and do not suffer interest rate risk.

Price changes in a bond immediately affect mutual funds holding these bonds. This can damage professional investors such as banks, insurance companies, pension funds and asset managers regardless of whether the value is immediately "marked to market" or not. Interest rate risk becomes a problem only if a holder of individual bonds needs to sell his bonds and "cash out". Conversely, bond market prices increase if the prevailing interest rate drops, as it did from 2001 through 2003. One way sometimes used to quantify the interest rate risk on a bond is in terms of its duration. Controlling for this risk is called immunization or hedging.

Bond prices may also become volatile depending on the credit rating of the issuer when credit rating agencies like Standard & Poor's and Moody's upgrade or downgrade an issuer. A downgrade causes the market price of the bond to fall. Provided the issuer does not actually default, this risk does not affect the bond's interest payments (as with interest rate risk,). It does put the market price at risk, in turn affecting mutual funds holding these bonds, and any holders of individual bonds who have to sell them.

A company's bondholders may lose all their money if a company goes bankrupt. Under the laws of the United States, Canada and many countries, bondholders are ahead of some other creditors in line to receive the proceeds of the sale of the assets of a liquidated company. Bank lenders, deposit holders (in the case of a deposit taking institution such as a bank) and trade creditors may take precedence. Many of these safeguards were over ruled by the Obama administration in regards to the General Motors bailout.

There is no guarantee money will remain to repay bondholders. In contrast to liquidation, in a bankruptcy involving reorganization or recapitalization, bondholders may have the value of their bonds reduced, often through exchange for a smaller number of newly issued bonds.

Some bonds are callable, meaning that even though the company has agreed to make payments plus interest towards the debt for a certain period of time, the company can choose to pay off the bond early. This creates reinvestment risk, meaning the investor is forced to find a new place for his money, and the investor might not be able to find as good a trade, especially since this usually occurs when interest rates are falling.

A number of bond indices exist for the purposes of managing portfolios and measuring performance, similar to the S&P 500 or Russell Indexes for stocks. The most common American benchmarks are the Barclays Capital Aggregate (ex Lehman Aggregate), Citigroup BIG and Merrill Lynch Domestic Master. Most indices are parts of families of broader indices that can be used to measure global bond portfolios, or may be further subdivided by maturity and/or sector for managing specialized portfolios.

Which Bonds To Buy

Your choice of municipal, government, corporate, mortgage-backed or asset-backed securities, or international bonds depends on your goals, your tax situation and your risk tolerance. You will find securities within each broad bond market sector with a variety of credit ratings, yields, issuers, coupon rates, maturities and other features. Each bond offers its own particular balance of risk and reward. We can't give you a cut and dry solution to picking bonds, but here are some tips to reduce the options.

- o Cover the inflation rate. Headline inflation is only 2%, but we all sense that it is running higher. Remember it is your yield to maturity that is important, not the face interest rate.
- o Shorter term bonds make sense if you believe there is the possibility of inflation returning and interest rates exploding. Bonds with maturities of one to 10 years are sufficient for most long-term investors. They yield more than shorter-term bonds, and are less volatile than longer-term issues.

- o Spread your money around. Invest in a variety of bonds with different maturities, either by buying a bond fund or buying a half-dozen or more individual bonds.

- o Build a laddered portfolio. Each rung of your ladder consists of a different maturity bond, from one year right on up to 10 years. When the one-year bond matures, you reinvest the money in a new, 10-year issue. In this way, you always have more money to reinvest every year, and you are somewhat protected from interest rate shifts because you have locked in a range of yields.

- o Municipal bonds may become worrisome as unfunded liabilities explode. Despite their tax free status, venture into municipal bonds after having done extensive due diligence.
- o Treasury Indexed Securities, or TIPS, offer some inflation protection. The real yield on TIPS is set by the market looking at break-even rates. That is the yield on nominal Treasuries vs. the yield on TIPS of the same maturity. If the investor expects inflation to exceed the break-even rate, TIPS are preferable because they will yield a higher real return (and vice versa).

23   Real Estate

In the past, real estate has been the true store of investment wealth for an individual. Land and buildings on that land are permanent, so the feeling was that real estate investments are a safe store of tangible wealth. Currently, much of the national real estate inventory is "under water", that is the equity in the home or property is not covered by the sale price. Sadly, the investment potential of real property may not recover its luster for a decade or more, despite recent uptrends. That is because with so much commercial and residential inventory being carried below its mortgage value, any increases in price will be soaked up by sellers flooding the market.

That said, there are some legitimate reasons to still own a home for yourself and to own some rental and commercial properties. Residential and commercial real estate are two very different beasts, though they do share some common characteristics in regards to valuation. We'll start first with some reasons why you might want to own residential property, given everyone needs a place to live.

Reasons For Home Ownership

- Mortgage deduction.
- Changing to a better neighborhood.
- You may simply not be able to rent what you need.
- Owning productive land. This means either buying rural property or a home with enough land for gardening.
- Living within your means. If the house you live in is above water, you might as well keep it, or trade up if a good opportunity arrives at rock bottom prices, just don't look for instant appreciation.

For those who own property that is under water, you may be forced to move at a loss. The silver lining to this is that rental homes are now available; often well below what the mortgage would cost to buy that same property.

Property Valuation

Whether you are buying residential or commercial property, there are three basic strategies to valuing a property in order to make a rational decision about whether to be in the real estate market.

- Comparable Worth – compare the property price to similar properties.
- Replacement Cost – price based on what the replacement construction, utilities and land cost would be.
- Rent Valuation – Base the price on how large a mortgage the going rent would support.

In the past, during the real estate bubble, one would look first at the comparable worth to set the price, because the feeling was "how could you go wrong" as we watched neighboring prices inflate. However, in a Depression era economy the only rational way to estimate the price of a property is through a combination of replacement cost and rent valuation. If the mortgage payments are above the rent the property could return, that is obviously a huge red flag for an economic survivalist, especially because rents can also drop further. Pricing by replacement cost is not perfect, but it should at least give you a bottom end target, which must also meet the rent valuation test.

Foreclosure

While no one wants to lose their property, in times of economic stress when your equity is "under water" (your loan is greater than the saleable value of the property), foreclosure may be the only viable option. Strategic Default: That is, walking away from mortgage debt, may be the best alternative for many people.

The process of foreclosure varies from state to state and can be rapid or lengthy. In the residential market, there are countless people who have spent years rent free as they waited for their eviction. Other options such as refinancing, a short sale, alternate financing, temporary arrangements with the lender, or even bankruptcy may present homeowners with ways to avoid foreclosure and\or being immediately forced out. In some states, especially those in which judicial foreclosure is used, due process constitutional issues of have affected the ability of lenders to foreclose.

We aren't suggesting taking advantage of the system for no purpose, but survival is a damn good purpose. The banks themselves have engaged in "strategic defaults" on properties and have run to the Feds for bailout money (that is, taxpayers bailed them out). The point is, when the whole system is corrupt from the head to the tail, you need to act accordingly. What may have been indefensible in the past may make sense when there is no room left on the lifeboat.

Short Sale

A short sale is a real estate sale in which the proceeds fall short of the mortgage balance owed on the property. It occurs when a lender decides that selling a property at a loss is better than pressing a borrower who cannot pay the mortgage loan on their property. Both parties, the bank and the owner, consent to the short sale process because it allows them to avoid foreclosure, which involves hefty fees for the bank and poorer credit report outcomes for the borrowers. This agreement, however, does not necessarily release the borrower from the obligation to pay the remaining balance of the loan, known as the *deficiency,* so one needs to make sure full forgiveness is part of the final bank documentation. Some tax obligations may also remain, depending on the vagaries of Congressional action.

Credit Forgiveness

As distasteful as it may be too many who in the past have maintained perfect credit, writing off the huge debt overhang that exists from the real estate bubble is absolutely necessary and inevitable. Assigning guilt to the banks, or realtors, or homebuyers, or mortgage bundlers, or government, etc. is at this point academic because the fault lies at each and every layer of the real estate market. Assigning blame doesn't help you, what does help is having insight into where we are headed from here.

Shadow Inventory

Shadow inventory refers to real estate properties that are either in foreclosure and have not yet been sold, or to homes that owners are delaying putting on the market until prices improve. Shadow inventory creates uncertainty about the best time to sell (for owners) and when a local market can expect full recovery. Shadow inventory causes data on market housing inventory to be understated

With the unprecedented number of foreclosures stemming from the subprime mortgage meltdown of 2007-2008 and the overall housing market collapse during that crisis, lenders were left with significant real estate holdings which are unlikely to clear until well into the future. Many lenders were slow to put their inventory up for sale for fear of flooding the market and further driving down prices, which would in turn lower their potential ROI. This has actually been detrimental to recovery because it has delayed the necessary deflationary write down corrections.

Deciding how many eggs you want to carry in your real estate investment basket depends in large part on when you believe the shadow inventory of underwater properties (both commercial and residential) might clear. That crystal ball is unfortunately clouded by Federal Reserve and regulatory intervention in the banks which has distorted the normal market clearing process. Some estimates are that it will be 2015 before the shadow inventory has been taken care of.

Investing Goals

In a Biflationary Depression, any real estate investments you might make need to be based on a hard headed cost benefit analysis of:

1) Whether rent would carry the mortgage
2) What the replacement cost to build a property from scratch would be

Because of the shadow inventory overhang, it will be a long time before basing a long term real estate investment primarily on comparable worth and short term market trends will make sense, though certainly those who are nimble will always be able to make speculative gains based on watching local conditions.

Given current federal policy and monetary uncertainties, no one can guarantee an appreciating real estate market, no matter what short term growth may promise. Therefore there are cost/benefit criteria other than price you need to keep in mind if you pursue real estate investment in a world beset by long term Biflationary Depression.

Costs:

- Given the long term shaky finances of the entire world, you need to know how much rent and/or cash you can to tie up in a property long term whose appreciation may not meet the inflation rate.
- Given the possibility that your job and livelihood might be exported to another country over the next ten years, you may want to consider the minimum residence you need rather than buying a large home hoping things will improve in ten years.
- Given that real property may not appreciate for twenty years, is the property you are looking have any resale potential in the future?
- Property taxes and fixed costs like maintenance also need to enter into your calculations.

Benefits

- If you purchase rural land or a large lot there may be some survivalist benefit in being able to have a garden (maybe even some chickens). Of course, this isn't for everyone.
- Inflation hedge. Real estate will always be worth something, especially if you are careful to buy at a price based on the properties potential rent income.
- The pleasure of having a pleasant lifestyle when everything is falling down around you may make a purchase worthwhile even if the economics aren't perfect.

Each person will no doubt be able to add to this list of cost/benefit questions. The point we are trying to make is to expand your real estate purchase decision beyond the traditional one dimensional criterion of curb appeal. Japan's lost economic decade has now evolved into its second lost decade and both America and Europe seem headed towards the same long term biflationary muddle. Consequently any lingering mindset you have that real estate is bound to appreciate should be stored in a musty attic.

We aren't trying to dissuade people from considering real estate as a hedge in biflationary times, because property is a store of real wealth. However, because real estate investments are such a large a part of people's wealth, what we are saying is that you need to take special care in balancing all your competing economic interests with the real probability of living in a biflationary environment in which real estate assets can deflate as easily as inflate.

The Perpetual Real Estate Bubble

By 2013, America had again fallen in love with real estate. But unlike the previous bubble peak which came in 2005-2006 when exotic mortgage loans known turned every ma and pa end-user homeowners into speculator, this bubble is different. This is shown dramatically by the generationally low level of purchase loan applications — despite rates being held at generational lows. Nothing is 'normal' about the post recession (if it ever ended) housing market.

Rather, controlling this market has been a small sliver of the population that "invests" in real estate using barges of cash-money which the federal Reserve has created specifically for this purpose and which is slopping around the financial system. So much cash-money has been thrown at the housing sector by various vectors of Quantitative Easing that ma and pa end users of real estate haven't stood a chance to buy by making honest offers in the open market.. This is especially if an individual needs a mortgage loan, which presents numerous risks to sellers vs the all-cash buyer.

That's why we are back in a house-price bubble right now, a bubble which may last decades given the Federal reserve's inability to cut off their addiction to QE.

Housing is a pretty simple asset class that until 2000 remained mostly in-check due to fundamentals and acted as a great inflation hedge. In a normal housing market, in which 80% of house purchases are done with "fully documented" mortgage loans, house prices are rooted in "end-user fundamentals" such as Loan To Value (LTV), appraisal, Debt To Value (DTI), etc. which together put a lid on irrational exuberance. When the majority of homes are purchased with mortgage loans it is exceedingly difficult for house prices to detach from end-user income and credit worthiness fundamentals, unless credit is artificially relaxed like from 2003 to 2007.

However, prices are no longer driven by the carrying capacity of the income being generated by residential occupants, but by cash buyers fueled with easy money pumped from the Federal Reserve through various channels, Our current bubble is driven by a herd mentality of investors fleeing other financial markets to the supposedly safe speculative real estate market. It goes without saying that individuals spending their own money should only proceed with extreme caution in such a market.

There are no financial anchors in such a situation. Making things worse is that the Federal Reserve is committed to making sure price signals will never return to the market given the threat that this would collapse the entire system. If a borrower has a downpayment, documented income, and good credit — requirements that should always be present when buying a house anyway — mortgage lending is back. However in a cash investor based market, demand for these units can dry up nearly instantaneously if investors believe the profitability of their supposed income property no longer exists.

24   Precious Metals

In a Biflationary Depression one may not know which direction asset classes will go during short periods of time; however one does know that the endgame of monetary debasement will always be inflation in the price of precious metals. Thus precious metals need to be part of your investment calculations.

We are hardly breaking new ground, the first thing that comes to mind when people are asked about preserving wealth in inflationary times is Gold. Other metals like platinum, palladium, silver and even gems can also be part of the mix. The problem is that while precious metals and gems have value as traditional stores of monetary information, they are of limited physical use, with not enough industrial use to support the astronomical valuations of a precious metal like gold. That doesn't mean precious metals and stones aren't important parts of the mix for someone trying to stabilize their wealth, but you can't eat them.

The reason gold is one of the original stores of wealth was because of its versatility and unique properties. It had a rich and warm color and was capable of being highly polished. It was the only metal that neither tarnished nor rusted. It could be extruded to the fineness of a hair or beaten to the thinness of tissue paper. Since gold concentrated considerable value in a small area, it made transportation of wealth straightforward, especially in times of war or duress. Since gold is malleable, it is easily divisible to accommodate exchanges of lesser value. Gold could be easily measured and its quality easily determined, making loans possible because repayment could be made in like kind even a continent away.

Digital money created by a keystroke at the Federal Reserve fails a number of these tests of money, most obviously in that it can be multiplied indefinitely and instantaneously, making its eventual debasement inevitable and likely catastrophic. That means loans are always at risk of not being repaid in like kind. These failings make it inevitable that gold will long exist in parallel with digital currency as a parallel money, and will likely be used to back currencies far into the future as a way of stabilizing the system.

Consequently, one way to save yourself from the ravages of inflation is to own gold and other precious metals. We don't mean gold stocks alone, which can be diluted in value by taxation, by government confiscation, or by not actually representing anything but empty paper promises for the delivery of physical gold. You should keep an amount of physical gold if you make a gold play at all.

A good example of why you need to keep physical gold is given by the collapse of the MF Global commodities brokerage run by long time Goldman Sachs executive and former New Jersey Governor John Corzine. MF Global made bad bets on Eurozone bonds and when those bets fell apart, MFG illegally dipped into its client's funds for more than $1 billion. The most disturbing part is that in bankruptcy proceedings, even those who held receipts for physical gold and silver held by MF Global were forced to take a haircut. Now imagine the potential cascading confiscatory losses should there be a worldwide banking and market breakdown and you will understand why you need to physically hold your precious metals.

Another reason to hold physical gold is because the US government has a history of trying to confiscate gold and then reset its value. More history on what happened both in 1933 and 1971 is available in another chapter on the Federal Reserve. The government can call for your gold until it is blue in the face and confiscate gold reserves, but it is doubtful it would ever actually try and confiscate gold buried in your back yard.

Because you can't eat precious metals, and they may be difficult to exchange in time of crisis, the question is how much of your portfolio to keep in precious metals. Common recommendations range from 10% to 20%, but that depends on the total size of your holdings, your age, location and whether you are merely paranoid or hyper paranoid about the direction the financial world is going. Because we have emphasized that we are in a biflationary period in which systematic theft of your wealth is occurring both through inflation and deflationary mechanisms put in place by the Federal Reserve, Foreign Central Banks and governments worldwide, we think the 10% to 20% guide is probably not a bad rule of thumb for someone who wants to survive TEOTWAWKI (The End Of The World As We Know It).

Remember, in 1933 private gold was confiscated in the United States and the price reset by federal law, so downward volatility in the value of your holdings of precious metals can be expected even in desperate times. Precious metals should therefore be considered long term plays that will hold value on average but may fluctuate widely in the interim. They are a backup for your peace of mind; they aren't meant to be your entire wealth holdings or be used as working capital.

Which Precious Metal To Hold

Regarding which precious metals to hold, gold is the easy if not always safest choice. Cost averaging (buying in small regular implements) can even out some of the risk of buying at a peak. An argument can also be made that platinum may have a potential for greater upward movement as it is usually priced above gold but recently has traded at 10% less. That is a judgment call that will not likely seriously harm your position even if you guess wrong.

Silver is another common precious metal option that has been trading quite low in comparison to its historic ratio to gold, but its volatility is higher and has been subject to various efforts to 'corner the market', so you shouldn't be panicked into buying at a peak or selling at the bottom. Silver does have the advantage of being available in smaller denominations for easier use. Another alternative in the lesser metals are stocks in copper mines; you'd have to hold a huge bulk for physical copper to be worthwhile.

Coins Vs Bars

One can buy gold and silver either as coins or bars. Either option has advantages and disadvantages.

Gold Bars: For the serious and large scale investor, gold bars are a simple and efficient way to invest in gold. The larger bars are usually available at the lowest premiums over their intrinsic gold value; smaller bars tend to cost more. There is a trade-off however, in that larger bars are not as flexible when it comes to selling. If you own a kilo bar, and you wish to sell, say 100 grams, it's not easy to slice off one end of your bar. Your choice of buyer is also more restricted as you will need to sell to a larger dealer; it is unlikely that you will find a private buyer as most people are not familiar with gold bullion bars.

Gold Coins: One ounce gold bullion coins such as the Krugerrand are essentially equivalent to one ounce circular bullion bars, but guaranteed by a government rather than a refiner. Because coins are very efficiently mass produced, they are very competitively priced compared with similar size bars. Because gold coins are almost universally recognized, they are also easy to resell.

Stocks And ETFs

Although we prefer you hold physical gold, one can participate in the gold market through securities purchases like GLD. Gold exchange-traded products include exchange-traded funds (ETFs), exchange-traded notes (ETNs) and closed-end funds (CEFs) that track the price of gold, silver and other precious metals. Gold exchange-traded investments trade on the major stock exchanges worldwide including Zurich, Mumbai, London, Paris and New York. These gold ETF, ETN, and CEF products each have a different structure outlined in their prospectus. Most do not hold physical gold and gold ETNs generally track the price of gold using derivatives.

Your goal is to diversify in order to moderate risk, but because of volatility in these prices one needs to consider your precious metal stores to be long term buy-and-hold acquisitions that you cost average with time. We know with 100% certainty that the Dollar, the Euro and many other currencies will be eventually turned into worthless paper by reckless politicians and central bankers. What we don't know is what their timeline is and whether some feeble reforms may cause temporary regressions in the market prices. Precious metals are your backup source of wealth in case everything goes to hell; they can't be your entire store of wealth, unless perhaps precious metals are your primary business.

Precious Metal Volatility Does Not Equal Risk.

Most volatility in gold and silver is deliberately manufactured by the banking cartel in fake paper derivative markets in which prices are set with little regard for the actual physical supply and demand of these two precious metals. Since banker cartel manipulation of paper gold and silver derivatives plays such a big role in price volatility, moves in gold and silver are often just as violent to the upside as they are to the downside after long periods of consolidation. Violent moves higher are often caused by short-covering of panicked hedge funds and banking cartel members that are forced to unwind shorts when the momentum to the upside becomes too great for them to suppress. After periods of very quick rises, another short-term correction triggered by day traders taking profits and/or desperate banking cartel members actions in paper markets does not mean the uptrend has reversed.

Lack of Patience is the Greatest Enemy to Buyers of Precious Metals

With physical gold and silver, volatility in paper prices often discourages the uninitiated from buying physical and goads those already invested to mistakenly sell. With precious metal mining shares, the greatest mistake investors make is also letting volatility in mining shares coerce them into selling out of all of their shares right before the next great leg higher. While it is true that the vast majority of gold and silver mining shares in the junior resource sector are junk and inflated pipe dreams, even cashed-up, solid junior mining companies will be taken down in price during bankster raids on paper gold and paper silver and thus, patience with junior mining companies is essential to coming out on top.

One of the top performing gold stocks lost more than 50% of its value a few years before the onset of the Great Depression before going on a spectacular +1,258% run higher that ended in1939. Those that were impatient because they were unable to see the big picture of the importance of gold during periods of severe economic instability sold out when this stock corrected sharply, locked in losses, and received none of the spectacular gains. Many today will repeat this same exact mistake.

Ignore Anti-Gold/Anti-Silver Campaigns of the Commercial Banking Industry.

Clients that allocate money to physical gold and physical silver purchases or PM mining share purchases translates into lost revenues for fee-based managed money commercial banking and brokerage firms because this normally translates into money that leaves these firms and never comes back. Thus, the vast majority of commercial banking/brokerage firm employees have great incentive to prevent their clients from purchasing any gold and silver assets of any nature, including even robust PM mining stocks.

Thus, when the most robust PM mining shares are at super undervalued valuations and represent a low-risk, high-reward set-up, commercial banking/brokerage firm employees are likely to tell you there is ZERO opportunity in PM mining shares. However, when great runs higher in gold and silver assets occur, uninformed commercial banking employees are likely to inform you of this situation and goad you into purchases right before the next steep correction, as was the case when silver hit $50 an ounce last year. A sharp, rapid and significant correction in the first month of buying gold and silver is a lesson likely to keep many "newbies" from ever returning to the gold and silver markets in the future.

Simple Rules For Buying Physical Gold

Buy only bullion from dealers you know (unless you're a collector that knows what they are doing.) Eagles are preferred. Keep in mind that coins like Maples and Buffalos are pure 24kt .999+ gold (unlike Eagles and Krugerrands which are **.9167**) and they will scratch very easily if handled. The Krugerrand has copper in it in addition to the 1ozt gold for some durability (22 <u>karat</u> gold 91.67%), and even though a different color shade, (the American Gold Eagle contains silver as well); they both weigh about the same (OVER 1 oz).

Diameter: Eagle 32.70 mm / Krug 32.77 Thickness: Eagle 2.87 mm / Krug 2.84 Gross weight: Eagle 33.930 g / Krug 33.930 Face value: Eagle $50 / Krug They also come in fractional amounts.

Don't buy the older coins or slabbed coins, unless the numismatics are part of an investment strategy -- in other words do NOT pay a premium for numismatics unless you're a collector, that is your hobby, or you just like wasting your fiat money. The choice of newer coins are best for safety from possible counterfeits and tampering, followed by SMALL bars (1ozt and under) perhaps in assay cases. Same for silver.

You can weigh coins you purchase with a calibrated digital scale and measure them in order to compare against published specifications -- you can't fake the size and weight combo. There is a real danger of counterfeits, mostly from China. If you have ever been to a "collectors mall" in Beijing or Shenzen then you know that it's is full of fakes. Buyer bewares.

Buy from a reputable dealer, and if you are buying in quantity (combine ordered with family and trusted friends), look for low premiums from large distributors who offer free shipping and insurance.

25 Collectibles

Another way to potentially hedge losses to your wealth in biflationary times is through the purchase of rare coins, art work (paintings, sculpture), antiques, rare books, stamps, vintages cars, niche collectibles, etc. The rich have for millennia firewalled their wealth from the effects of collapsing economic systems through the purchase of collectibles and antiques – ostentatious wealth can serve a purpose. Fortunately, this works even if you aren't particularly rich.

A combination of excessive debt, aging populations, resource scarcity and financial repression will bring on extremely poor performance in equities and bonds. Equities will suffer from potential collapse as Fed intervention weakens. Bonds, the traditional safe haven, will hugely underperform as policymakers engineer inflation and seek to trap assets as sources of government funding.

Rather than death and taxes, then, investors will come to fear money printing and financial repression, which will be used to help inflate away excessive debts and corral funds for hard-hit governments. Under this scenario, what is sure to go up is the money supply, as central banks print to fund their governments and ease the impact of high deficits by stoking inflation.

SWAG

Silver, Wine, Art and Gold – or SWAG – may be the solution for investors looking to protect their wealth. Having SWAG in your portfolio may protect investors from a grim decade of money printing and financial repression. SWAG, as in silver, wine, art and gold, are real assets that might outperform the market if official policy causes the money supply to surge.

These assets effectively act as a money supply index tracker. If the authorities are going to bail themselves out, the money supply will expand. Every single time governments have been caught in deficit traps, this is exactly what they have done. SWAG assets can act almost like alternative currencies, and, unlike fiat currencies, cannot have their supply increased at the press of a button. You can't magic up more gold or 10 new Picassos. They also, by definition, carry no debt, making their risk profile hugely different from most other assets, implying added protection.

In addition, SWAG are not denominated in any particular currency, meaning you are not hostage to a particular monetary or fiscal policy, or even to natural disasters or wars. Compared with many financial assets, SWAG tends to be simple and robust. The range of SWAG-like assets extends beyond the big four, to include in varying degrees things like palladium and stamps.

Silver A hard currency instrument like gold, but with more industrial uses. Up almost 500% over a decade. Useful as a diversifier from gold, in part because of its industrial demand. However, this makes it a less pure play on the theme of a rising money supply and inflation.

Art & Antiques: Art for art's sake may be a virtuous thing. But antiques and other forms of art are also a distinct investment class. It's an investment category that is booming – the international art and antiques market is worth around $50 billion annually while many other investment forms are under-performing.

Art appeals because it is tangible, can be traded in any currency, and comes with kudos—collectors cannot hang stocks and shares on a wall to show their friends. Art may be particularly attractive now because of the uncertainties of the stock markets, big currency fluctuations and the looming specter of inflation in some major countries, and deflation in others. Art does have large transaction costs, so it isn't in the easy-to-buy-and-sell category. However, the anti-cyclical nature of the art market could be coming into play.

As investors worldwide flood into the antiques and art market, they are undergoing an unprecedented restructuring. And with other economic developments such as rising inflation and commodity process, the market especially for Islamic and Asian antiques, offers an opportunity to hedge inflation.

The supply of antiques is fixed by definition. More cannot be produced in response to rising prices. This is not so for contemporary art, or indeed for many other classes of investment products such as stocks, real estate, commodities. Even the supply of land is not fixed – land can be cleared and reclaimed. More stock can be issued, more diamonds can be mined. The fundamental problem which the Dutch tulip bubble of the seventeenth century was that more bulbs could be grown. This is not the case with antiques.

The demand for antiques also grows constantly. Each year millions more people move into income categories for which the acquisition of antiques feasible. And the number of very wealthy individuals who can buy high-end antiques has grown exponentially. Antiques still are very much a growth story as an investment class, particularly antiques that appeal to those in newly wealthy economies: India, China, Southeast Asia and the Middle East, and even South America where large fortunes have been amassed quickly.

Art does seem to go up satisfyingly in price, with sections of the market sky-rocketing even during the tough times in recent years. While this is a market highly dependent on the 1%, and thus vulnerable to falls if their share of income falls, the growing number of the very wealthy in emerging markets should drive future price growth.

There are collective investment vehicles specializing in art, but once again charges will tend to be high and due diligence is incredibly important. Unfortunately, fraud is a real risk.

Based on the past two decades, art can be a good hedge against inflation. But for the average collector, it depends on whether one is inside the system or not. If one understands how the system works, then yes, it can be a great hedge. If not, then the answer is maybe. Those in the know can do very well if one buys during periods of low valuations of art.

There are plenty of other pitfalls for the potential investor. The art world is relatively illiquid, and prices depend on several factors—lack of supply, changes in taste, new research, when a work was bought, how often it has appeared at market, condition, provenance, and collector behavior. Small groups of collectors can easily influence "the market" (which is in reality a series of specialist mini-markets that perform very differently).

Wine The most investable fine wines have done well over the past they can perform as well as traditional assets. Finite supply of the great investment wines, portability and relatively low storage costs are an advantage. There also has been huge growth of demand from prestige-oriented drinkers in China and other emerging markets.

However, this is a double edged sword: while Chateau Lafite, the wine to serve to impress your regional party boss in China, has surged in price, so has fraud. By some estimates the amount of Lafite drunk in China in 2010 exceeded total yearly production by almost 10 times. Wine investing requires storage charges, and wine funds are often quite expensive. Due diligence and caution are key in selecting advisers and storage places, as instances of fraud and overcharging are far from unknown.

Gold This is the classic hedge against having one's pocket picked by money printing and inflation. Supply is limited and new sources take time to come on line. Gold has performed fantastically in the past decade -- up more than 400pc -- and has become far more mainstream, attracting institutional investors. Carrying costs can be low, because frankly there is, no need to pay an investment manager. We have more on precious metals in another dedicated chapter.

Beyond SWAG

Rare Coins: While not perfect, the rare coin market is probably the most structured and efficient of all the collectible, inflation-hedge markets. People can trade rare coins within a fairly narrow trading range, compared to other collectibles, and there has always been a ready market for coins at some price level, even in a down market. Rare coins have always been very liquid at the right price points.

If you're an investor who believes high inflation is just around the corner, rare coins may be a good inflation hedge, as they've been in the past. During the 1970s, when we went through our last high inflationary period, during the Jimmy Carter years, investors threw money at coin dealers. The market exploded, sending some coins that could be bought for less than $300 dollars in 1977 to nearly $3,000 in 1980.

During the mid-1980s, PCGS, the Professional Coin Grading Service, and NGC, Numismatic Guaranty Corporation, were formed. Today they are the backbones of the industry in terms of coin grading, which is one of the fundamental basics for valuing rare coins. This has led to much strengthened consumer protection and confidence in owning rare coins, unlike the days prior to this era when individual coin dealers would grade their own coins they had for sale.

Guns: If you're careful in what you buy and in getting a good price, guns tend to hold up their value. It has in the past been the case that you can sell a gun for at least as much as you bought it for. However the election of Obama caused a spike in the purchase of "black rifles" and handguns. The latter have been doing very well as more and more states got shall issue concealed carry license regimes, plus many people are buying them as they get older But be careful of historical price patterns, with CNC machining and other general advances it's gotten less expensive to make them and the barriers to entry to new firms has dropped.

Cars, Boats & RVs: The nice thing about vehicles as collectibles and inflation hedges is that if you chose wisely, they are both functional and have the potential to rise in value. As an odd example, a marina repossession that gives you five summers of fun on the water with friends/family where you return to work after each weekend fully refreshed and more productive would be a valuable purchase, especially since you may be able to sell for 100% of the purchase price.

Purchasing an immaculate 1953 Chevy Pickup is something you might be able to use regularly and still get full value from at resale. Depreciation, second hand values and rising demand matched with an initial purchase discount can put you even or in the black. But beyond cash gains, buying something that makes you smile which doesn't depreciate during a Biflationary Depression can't be beat.

For well-off investors with more than $1m in assets, as much as 20% in SWAG might be appropriate with caution and due diligence. Even those with much lesser investible amounts will also benefit, though the percentages would need to be much lower. One does have to worry about costs, fraud and the potential that the same events that are driving money printing and financial repression could have an impact on collectible values. If huge amounts of cash flow into art and wine, you can bet fraud will rise. A bit of prudence can go a long way, both in terms of protecting investors through due diligence and in the genuine hedge value of collectible assets during an all-too-believable scenario of financial repression and rampant money printing.

26   Starting A Business

One potential way out of the financial morass created by too large government, inflationary excess by the Federal Reserve, over taxation and regulation is paradoxically by creating a small business. But because of the hurdles imposed by a bureaucratic system that is now decidedly socialist, your options have been narrowed. You have to Go Galt to succeed.

That means avoiding taxes, avoiding regulation, avoiding inflationary pressures caused by the Fed. It does not mean doing anything illegal, in fact it means the opposite, being hyper aware of your legal obligations, especially regarding taxes. Building a business in the New Normal requires new goals:

- Have as few employees, zero besides yourself if possible.
- Everything is an expense for tax purposes.
- Robotize and automate everything. This goes hand in hand with keeping your employee headcount to a minimum.
- Choose a business that can't be outsourced. A plumbing business can't be outsourced. Pretty much anything clerical can be.
- Manufacturing small rubber toys that can be made in China is not a good idea. Being a call center that can be outsourced to India also not a good idea.

The Small Business Administration has a list of ten steps to starting a small business. Given the New Normal and from extensive small business experience we believe it would be the kiss of death to follow the SBA advice to the letter, so we are presenting first the buggy whip government plan for starting a business, and then a reality modified plan to give you a fighting chance.

Small Business Administration Business Startup

1) Write a Business Plan. This written guide will help you map out how you will start and run your business successfully.
2) Get Business Assistance and Training. Take advantage of free training and counseling services, from preparing a business plan and securing financing, to expanding or relocating a business.
3) Choose a Business Location. Get advice on how to select a customer-friendly location and comply with zoning laws.
4) Finance Your Business. Find government backed loans, venture capital and research grants to help you get started.
5) Determine the Legal Structure of Your Business. Decide which form of ownership is best for you: sole proprietorship, partnership, Limited Liability Company (LLC), corporation, S corporation, nonprofit or cooperative.
6) Register a Business Name ("Doing Business As"). Register your business name with your state government.
7) Get a Tax Identification Number. Learn which tax identification number you'll need to obtain from the IRS and your state revenue agency.
8) Register for State and Local Taxes. Register with your state to obtain a tax identification number, workers' compensation, unemployment and disability insurance.
9) Obtain Business Licenses and Permits. Get a list of federal, state and local licenses and permits required for your business.

10) Understand Employer Responsibilities. Learn the legal steps you need to take to hire employees.

The flaws in the SBA plan are that it presumes you have a full blown and tested business idea from the beginning. The reality is that businesses operate in fits and starts, little is obvious at the beginning and the trick is to avoid failing right out of the starting gate. Here is our alternative scenario.

New Normal Business Startup

1) Make a list of potential businesses you could enter based on :
   - Past professional or family experience. That is, your talent base.
   - Inventions or Intellectual property you own
   - Franchises
   - Available businesses for sale.
2) Guessestimate the profit margins for the potential products. A rule of thumb is that mark up must be at least 100% or the business won't be sustainable. That eliminates a lot of contenders.
3) Consider liability and regulation issues. Even a great business can be crippled by red tape.
4) Can this business be outsourced to China? Undercut by illegals? Made obsolete by robots or software?
5) See if there are viable businesses similar to what you propose and look not only at how well they are doing financially, but their talent requirements and especially their location. Can you replicate their business plan and do better?
6) Now that you've done your homework, write a minimalist business plan, maybe two pages, that you can evolve later into something formal. Any longer is a waste of effort at this point given the uncertainties of the New Normal.
7) Regarding location, if you can run a test startup out of your garage, make that your starting point rather than immediately investing in storefront/office space/mass production machinery.
8) See if you can sell small lots of your product to anyone, online if possible (E-Bay, Amazon, Craigslist). If you are a service, see if you can sell online through a variety of service markets. The online brokers can get you around some requirements for tax collection by providing inbuilt taxation or zero taxation depending on existing legal requirements.
9) Work for someone in the business for a while if possible.
10) Get Business Assistance and Training. Take advantage of free training and counseling services, from preparing a business plan and securing financing, to expanding or relocating a business. Take advantage of free online tutorials on YouTube, trade associations, etc.
11) Once you have a minimalist business operating, now expand your Business Plan. This written guide can help you map out how you will expand and run your business successfully. But it's most important use will be for investors who may be needed to fund you to the next level. Note that by writing the full plan in this later stage rather than as the first act you now have an idea what your business is actually about, rather than having wasted time writing a novel built on illusion.
12) Determine the Legal Structure of Your Business. Decide which form of ownership is best for you: sole proprietorship, partnership, Limited Liability Company (LLC), corporation, S corporation, nonprofit or cooperative. Earlier in the process, you were operating as a sole proprietor, now you can get serious.

13) Choose a permanent Business Location. Get advice on how to select a customer-friendly location and comply with zoning laws. Hopefully you are already operating a mini business and now know what will be needed.
14) Register a Business Name ("Doing Business As"). Register the business name with your state government secretary of state.
15) Get a Tax Identification Number. Learn which tax identification number you'll need to obtain from the IRS and your state revenue agency.
16) Register for State and Local Taxes. Obtain a tax identification number, workers' compensation account, unemployment and disability insurance.
17) Obtain Business Licenses and Permits. Get a list of federal, state and local licenses and permits required for your business.
18) Understand Employer Responsibilities. Learn the legal steps you need to take to hire employees.

Notice the huge difference between our approach and that of the SBA. Our goal is to get you up and running with baby steps before you even think of involving government regulators through licenses, employee requirements, entity structure. This isn't so you can avoid taxes, but so you can get a handle on your cash flow and expenses before doing a costly ramp up that doesn't result in an income stream. This is the difference between financial survival in the new normal, and dying a painful and expensive financial death at the hands of bureaucrats.

Taxation

27   Taxes

Middle Class Tax Rates 75%

The "official" income tax rate understates the amount most middle income citizens are mandated to pay by the state. For Americans earning between $34,500 and $106,000, the middle class tax burden in high-tax locales is closer to 75% than 25%. This is because any fee mandated by law or legal necessity is the equivalent of a tax.

Fee taxes vary from nation to nation and state to state. For example, France and England have what amounts to a "television tax" because virtually every household has a TV that has a non optional fee. Universal healthcare in Europe, Canada and elsewhere is typically paid by tax revenues. In the U.S., healthcare insurance is "optional" but in the real world, private healthcare insurance is mandatory because the alternative--having zero insurance--places your entire net worth and income at risk of catastrophic loss. To calculate a real world tax burden these effective mandates have to be equalized.

Going without healthcare insurance only makes sense if you have no real assets and a low income. At that point, your care will be provided by the taxpayer-funded Medicaid program, which is the default universal-care program in the U.S. The super-wealthy can absorb a $150,000 hospital bill, but the 99.9% cannot. For this reason the cost of private healthcare insurance in the U.S. is the equivalent of a tax. Americans pay over $12,000 annually for barebones healthcare insurance, which amounts to about 15% of gross income. Some countries pay for healthcare with a 15% tax, here we pay the 15% directly.

Property tax is mandatory. Some countries have no property tax, others do. Once again, only counting social-insurance and income taxes as the "official tax rate" is horrendously misleading. For countries without property taxes, the revenues are collected as value-added taxes (VAT) or higher income taxes. One way or another, the services paid by property taxes in the U.S. are paid by other tax schemes in countries without property taxes. So property taxes must be included in any accounting of total taxes paid.

Many residents in states such as Illinois, New York, New Jersey and California pay $12,000 or more annually in property taxes. - about 15% of household income. Renters pay property taxes indirectly, but to the degree that rents would be lower if property taxes were eliminated and the tax burden shifted to a VAT, then renters "pay" the tax just like property owners.

Health Benefits As Tax. Employees looking at their paycheck stubs do not see the entire tax paid on their labor. Employees wondering why their net pay has stagnated for decades need to understand that the total compensation costs of employees has risen substantially.

Social Security taxes were once modest, 3% paid by the employee and 3% paid by the employer for a total of 6% of the wage. Now the total for Social Security (12.4%) and Medicare (2.9%) is 15.3%. Self-employed people pay the total 15.3% as "self-employment tax." This is the real-world tax burden of Social Security and Medicare. The 15.3% Social Security/Medicare tax starts with dollar one of net income. The Social Security tax goes away above around $106,000 in income, the Medicare tax does not.

Most employees do not know how much healthcare insurance "tax" is paid by their employer. To the degree that wages would rise if the healthcare "tax" was not paid by employers, then employees pay for this "tax" indirectly.

The only transparent way to calculate the total tax burden is to count all taxes (or equivalent) paid by self-employed property owners. Not counting the indirect taxes of healthcare and property taxes is misleading misrepresentation. The basic Federal income tax gives each individual earner $9,500 in standard deductions and exemptions. The tax rate for all income above that is:

Tax Rates			
Rate	Single Filers	Married Joint Filers	Head of Household Filers
10%	$0 to $8,925	$0 to $17,850	$0 to $12,750
15%	$8,925 to $36,250	$17,850 to $72,500	$12,750 to $48,600
25%	$36,250 to $87,850	$72,500 to $146,400	$48,600 to $125,450
28%	$87,850 to $183,250	$146,400 to $223,050	$125,450 to $203,150
33%	$183,250 to $398,350	$223,050 to $398,350	$203,150 to $398,350
35%	$398,350 to $400,000	$398,350 to $450,000	$398,350 to $425,000
39.6%	$400,000 and up	$450,000 and up	$425,000 and up

Tax rates listed in the above table are marginal rates. That means you don't owe that rate on all of your income. For example, if you are single, you earn $100,000 per year, **you would not owe 28% on all of your income** — you would not owe $28,000 to the federal government.

Some households have gigantic interest deductions stemming from gigantic mortgages, but let's set aside outsized debt-based tax deductions as far from universal. Above a rather modest $34,600 in taxable income and up to around $106,000, the real-world middle class tax burden in high-tax American locales is 75%:

Social Security and Medicare: 15.3%
Federal income tax: 25% (28% above $83,600)
State income tax: 5% (mid-range)
Healthcare insurance: 15%
Property tax: 15%

15% + 25% + 5% + 15% + 15% = 75%

Clearly, the percentage of income devoted to healthcare insurance and property taxes declines as income rises. Someone earning $200,000 has not only dropped the 12.4% Social Security tax for income above $106,000, healthcare insurance and property taxes as a percentage of their income drops from about 30% for those earning around $86,000 to 15%. But the basic fact is that the effective real-world tax rate for the "middle class" earning more than $34,500 in taxable income in high-tax locales is a confiscatory 75%.

Lowering Your Tax Burden

This is book isn't about avoiding your share of taxes, whether fair or not. Others can and have made many arguments on both sides of that debate. However, legally minimizing your taxes is the entire reason for the tax code, for tax lawyers and accountants, and for the IRS itself. If there weren't legal ways to reduce your tax signature, tax law would be trivial and you would just receive a bill and that would be it. Given these legislated means of lowering your taxes, there are certain general rules categories of expenses that you should consider as possible sources of tax reduction:

Do It Yourself: You aren't taxed on what you do for yourself. Home improvements, gardening, working on your car and other self help crafts are not (as yet) taxed. That isn't to suggest that dropping out of the system completely is wise because being self sustainable requires a huge amount of work – there are cost advantages that markets bring that allow them to produce vast quantities of goods cheaply. Still, anything you can do on your own will not be subject to a tax bite.

Business Expenses: Most of the minimization strategies you will see are for people with small businesses. You open up a world of deductions by starting a business; however this whole area of deductions doesn't apply to most of us. Consider starting a business if you have one in mind. Find side business to generate a schedule C to write off meals and autos.

Tax-Deferred Accounts: Make sure you put any money into your IRA, 401(k), HAS or any other tax advantaged accounts you have. Not having to pay taxes can be a huge savings by itself. When you throw in the capacity of some of the accounts to grow tax-free, they may seem a no brainer. However, be aware that the government may be forced to nationalize pension holdings if things really get bad, as has recently happened to some extent in Ireland during its crash.

Unemployment: If you lost your job, many of the expenses that you incur in your job search are tax deductable. Phone calls, agency fees, travel to potential employers as well as costs for printing resumes may all be deductible. Be sure to take advantage of any opportunities to lessen your tax burden in this climate.

Medical: If you had serious medical expenses, you may be able to deduct some of them. Most people will not qualify, but if you spent more than 7.5% of your adjusted gross income on medical expenses, you may be able to deduct the excess. Once again, this can be beneficial to those who are experiencing medical hardship.

Charitable Donations: Be sure to keep these in mind as well. You may have been glad to get rid of that bundle of clothes, but it also had some value and you may be able to deduct that amount. Did you donate some money to Haiti? You may have just wanted to help your fellow man, but why forget to take the tax deduction?

House Expenses: Do you still have receipts for any home improvements you did? People often forget that these are deductible. You also of course can deduct mortgage interest as well as property taxes (at least for now).

Investments: Sell your losses - look at your portfolio and see which are losers and sell to offset gains. Capital Gains are taxed at a lower rate than income - learn what property qualifies for these reductions in taxes. Find out about Tax Exempt Bonds and Mutual Funds. You may need a tax professional to sort it all out.

Preparing For The Future

Currently the federal Government is only collecting 60% of what it spends. To cover the difference, the Federal Reserve has been plugging the difference by buying Treasuries, which is to say they have been printing money. However, your real taxes are what the government spends, not just what citizens and corporations send to the IRS. We can't help you solve this problem; all we can do is point out what is in the future and why our economic problems and this Biflationary Depression aren't going away any time soon.

Hiking taxes to pay for entitlements would require doubling tax rates. The cost of Medicare, Medicaid, and Social Security is rising substantially. Paying for this spending solely through federal income tax increases would require more than a twofold increase of current tax rates, even for the lowest tax bracket. The following chart from Congressional Budget Office figures shows what would be needed and what you need to prepare for.

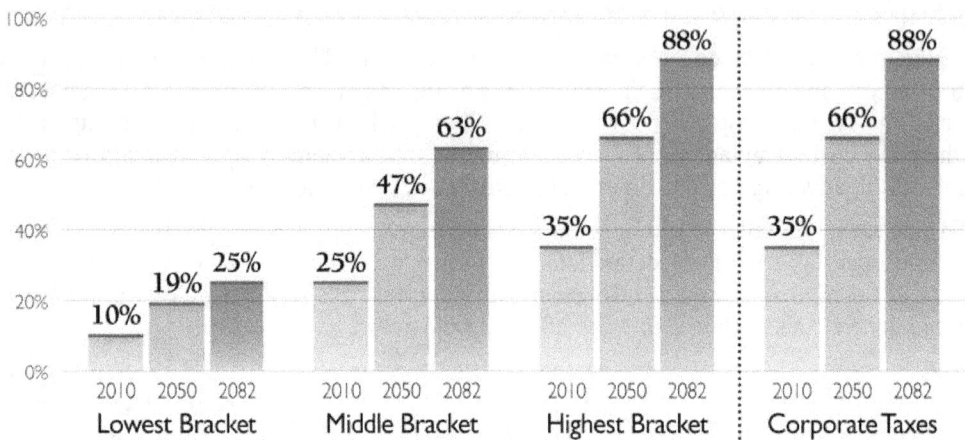

28   Tax The Rich

Presidents and Congress have continually fooled the American people into believing they are sincere about reducing the deficit and reining in spending. While increased numbers of Republicans in Congress, buoyed by the Tea Party, provide some hope of spending cuts, increasing taxes on the wealthy and corporations is still seen by progressives as a magic bullet solving the debt and deficit problem. Unfortunately, we have no history of increasing taxes AND cutting spending.

The wealth of Americans is an obsession with the left. Populist class warfare plays well among economic illiterates of the left-wing base by enflaming passions and potential violence while keeping Democrats and their allies in power. This is class envy right out of the Marxist playbook. However, as shown by IRS statistics, raising taxes and demonizing the wealthy solves nothing and exacerbates the current economic predicament.

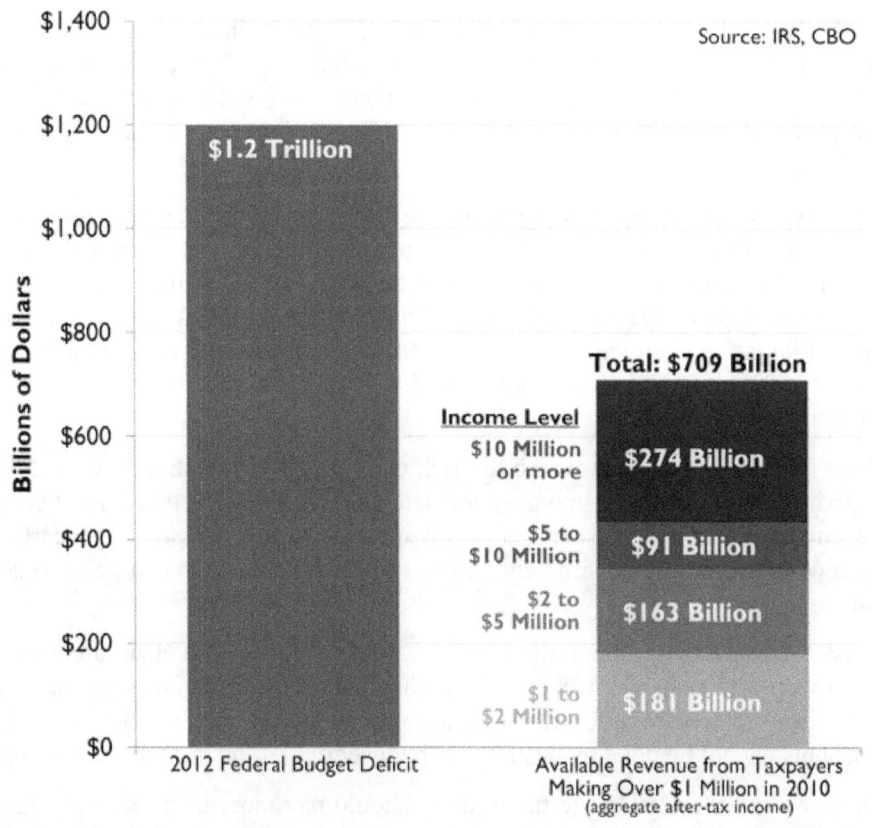

Taxing the Incomes of Those Earning Over $1 Million at 100% Won't Erase the Deficit

Source: IRS, CBO

According to IRS statistics published in 2004, there were 2.7 million adults in the United States with a net worth (total value of all assets less debts and liabilities) in excess of $1.5 million for a total net worth of $10.2 Trillion. If the government confiscated all wealth above a net worth of $1.5 million, there would be a one-time windfall of $6.1 Trillion to the Treasury. As the total national debt is nearly $14.5 Trillion, this would only reduce the debt to $8.4 Trillion.

But how is the government to realize the value of seized assets? Confiscated assets would include $2+ Trillion in real estate, but without leverage or cash (held by previously rich people) who would buy those properties at market value? There are nearly $3 Trillion in publicly traded and closely held stocks, but who would buy them without collapsing the markets entirely? The same is true of state and local bond issues or corporate bonds, U.S. Treasury Bonds, mutual funds etc. etc. Without rich entrepreneurs, the government might realize a quarter of the value of the seized assets.

No one creates jobs and wealth if they know their assets will be seized above a low threshold. The left knows their tactics are counterproductive, but then argues the wealthy should pay more income taxes as a moral issue to reduce the annual deficit and minimize the spending cuts necessary to balance the budget. From 1958 to 2008 Federal Government tax revenues have averaged between 16% and 20% of GDP. The highest level in history was in 1944 when it hit 20.9 %. This is despite the fact that the top marginal rate have varied between 90% and 35% over that period. The historical lesson is that because humans adapt to negative stimuli (avoiding taxes in this case) the government cannot increase its revenue above approximately 20% of income short of outright confiscation with permanent damage inflicted on the economy.

The budget deficit has been running about $1.5 Trillion. In tax year 2008, the last date the IRS has done this kind of analysis, the highest marginal tax rate of 35% was applied to all income above $357,700.00. In that year the total amount subject to the highest rate was $662.8 Billion. The government collected in taxes $218.0 Billion (35%) at that rate, not the largest portion of its revenue.

If progressives convince Congress to raise taxes on the rich, and assuming no change in behavior (or even an eagerness to pay more), the potential increase in revenue is be trivial. If the highest rate of 35% were raised by a factor of 29% to 42%, the additional revenue would be $43.5 Billion, a small fraction of the $1.5 Trillion deficit. If the rate was raised by a factor of 50% to 52.5%, the additional revenue would be $108.9 Billion, still nowhere near enough. Even raising the tax rate to 100%, bringing in an additional $404.8 Billion still leaves the country $1,086.0 Billion in the hole for the year.

There is a tax threshold at which the rich cease to have incentive to earn. Moreover, our thought experiment does not take into account state and local income taxes, Medicare, as well as myriad "revenue enhancers." The top 1% of all income earners already pay nearly 40% of all income taxes collected by the government and it is unlikely this turnip can be squeezed for much more blood.

Democrats, unions and the radical left berate the wealthy and chant a continuous mantra of the need to tax the rich. However, history has shown the only way to increase Treasury revenue is to grow the economy by dramatically reducing spending, regulations and the size of government. This cannot be done by destroying the incentive of the producer class to pay taxes.

So, why would the left argue the wealthy should pay more even if it only makes a slight impact on the deficit, other than spite? It isn't because they believe this is a viable solution to the country's fiscal woes or thy genuinely care about the citizenry, but because it divides the people against each other and maintains the state power base. Reckless spending buys votes and entitlement constituencies.

Wealth Disparity Implies Crony Socialism

The liberal argument for tax increases is that all the profits in the economy have been captured over the past decades by a small number of capitalists as reflected in growing income inequality in America. Supposedly, middle class wages have stagnated because the rich haven't shared the wealth. The deficit, according to this narrative, is primarily caused by a refusal of the capitalists to pay higher taxes. If only taxes were raised the fiscal problems of the country would be over and much of the entitlement crisis would go away.

Progressives further argue that over the past decade, we squandered trillions of dollars on rampant speculation rather than on making investments — in technology, infrastructure, clean energy and education — that theoretically would have increased productivity and our economic strength. The financial sector's share of corporate profits climbed from 15 percent in 1980 to 33 percent by the early 2000s, while financial-sector debt soared from $3 trillion in 1978 to $36 trillion by 2007. With tens of millions still unemployed, all that is needed is to magically shift from an economy based on money-making-money to an economy based on money-creating-jobs and genuine prosperity.

However, if capitalists made all so much money and it has remained untaxed being only subject to low capital gains rates, it would have been reinvested in the economy. The rich do not consume as great a proportion of their income as the rest of us (that's why they are 'rich'), so that money should have already been 'put to work' and jobs and the economy should be rising.

What broke the economy to make it change its behavior so drastically? Did it occur due to some political development, such as Republicans issuing a secret order for the rich to pillage the poor, which the Democrats now intend to rectify? In fact we all know this social justice and fairness posturing is political kabuki and that the "we" who are supposedly going to fix the economy are the same unions and crony bankers and privileged corporatists who got us into this mess. If it is the people in the administration who are going to take the money from the rich and 'put it to work', their history of economic ineptitude makes this claim ludicrous.

An alternative explanation is that if markets worked well we would not observe the wealth disparities posited by progressives. Money would be reinvested according to its highest marginal return and the economy would grow — and incomes with it — as fast as possible. Nor would we see the sudden emergence of a class of super-rich. The class warfare by the rich against the masses described by progressives is more consistent with a crony capitalist scenario. If what we have is crony capitalism, rent seeking beyond market rates would be the norm and resources would be driven to uses that were economically unproductive but monetarily lucrative. Of course, that's just what we are experiencing, and the financial services industry and housing come immediately to mind as in bed with the government.

The rise in the super rich is thus not due to capitalism, but to government picking and choosing winners, a form of corporate socialism. Warren Buffet's success is due as much to picking companies that were due for bailouts and government largesse as to genius. America, in short, has begun to look like a Latin American economy because a crony class had emerged. Even if voters were to grant the President the power to tax away all that money and 'put it to work' it would only serve to increase, not decrease, the trend towards crony socialism. Cronyism arises when the government becomes so powerful that it becomes imperative for industry to capture the regulator in order to prosper. That tendency will be exacerbated, not diminished, by giving government ever more power.

If the government were much less able to influence the market, there would be little point to lobbying government. Any rich person who made a profit would face the choice between consuming the profit or reinvesting it. If he decides to reinvest it, he would have little choice but to choose the alternative with the highest margin return, which in a well functioning economy, corresponds to actual productivity.

How The Rich Have And Will Avoid Higher Taxes

While refusal to pay income tax is illegal, it has always been legal to minimize ones tax exposure within the laws. The rich, with armies of lawyers and accountants are of course adept at this, which is why trying to raise tax rates to punitive levels doesn't work. However, in a widespread economic depression brought on by bloated entitlement policy, the state will no longer be as picky about following normal procedures. Indeed, the IRS has been vastly expanding its army of auditors in a search for missed income streams. This isn't because of a rise of tax cheats as much as because the Government is strapped for cash.

Tax minimization thus becomes an act of civil disobedience when the government tax revenues are insufficient to cover their expenditures and the state is forced to confiscate wealth. The actions of Robert Mugabe in Zimbabwe might act as a model in this case, who crushed the wealthy white farm class even though this was counterproductive to the wealth of his economy, in turn causing a mass exodus of capital. So not only will the rich minimize their tax profile legally, but at some point they will begin to shelter their wealth as a matter of self preservation. This too will be criminalized. The ways to minimize ones wealth profile have classically been:

- Capital flight to other countries
- The purchase of collectibles (art and cars) to store wealth
- Gold, silver and other cash substitutes
- Emigration

Because of the global economy and e-commerce, money is more fungible than ever, but the fragile reserve currency position of a weakening Dollar means that capital flight might become risky to those who wait. Expect a rushing sound as money flows to Canada, Australia, New Zealand, Singapore, the Scandinavian countries and Chile. This flight will be more debilitating than any civil disobedience the Tea Party could imagine. Tax the rich, and watch them disappear. That's about as revolutionary as it gets.

29 IRS Audit Army

The Internal Revenue Service is a bureaucracy at war with the population. The number of agents is swelling rapidly, both in response to the needs of Obamacare and also as a vendetta against "the Rich". If government were not at war with its people, there would be no need for a surge in audits since the only thing that has changed over the last decade is that the populace is decidedly poorer. To protect your financial health, you will need to know how the IRS is evolving from a collection agency to an enforcement arm of the welfare state.

Obamacare Gulag

The Internal Revenue Service requested an additional 1054 staffers and additional office space to implement the initial tax implications of the Healthcare Reform Bill of 2010. The IRS estimates that the additional auditors, and office space to house them, will cost the American taxpayers over $359 million in fiscal 2012, to ensure that that taxpayers comply with the tax codes embedded within the Affordable Care Act (ACA) also known as Obamacare. Some estimates put the number of new agents eventually needed as high as 16,000 to administer Obamacare.

The IRS breaks down some of the categories that will require additional enforcement officers such as:

81 auditors assigned to enforce the new 10% excise tax on tanning salons.

76 auditors to make sure that drug manufacturers and importers pay a new fee.

Taxing 'The Rich'

In 2009, the Internal Revenue Service announced plans to unleash a new enforcement unit called the Global High Wealth Industry, the goal being to better investigate the complex finances of America's wealthiest taxpayers. Recently released IRS statistics indicate that the federal government increased their audits of America's richest taxpayers -- those with incomes above $10 million -- by 75 percent through 2010. Nearly one in five -- 18.5 percent -- of America's richest households dealt with an audit. In 2009, the Global High Wealth Industry's first year of operation, the IRS audited only one in ten of America's richest taxpayers.

Audit rates also increased among some lower income brackets. The second highest audit increase was among the second highest income bracket: those reporting incomes of $5M-$10M, who saw a 55 percent increase in their audit rate, totaling 11.6 percent. High, but much smaller than the increase experienced by the $10M-plus bracket. Audits rate for those with incomes between $1-$75K remained largely the same.

Overall, the IRS increased the percentage of audits by about 11 percent from the year prior. That means 1.58 million tax returns -- about 1.11 percent of all returns filed -- were audited, costing the IRS about 53 cents per $100 collected -- a 3 cent increase from 2009.

Foreign Reach

The claim is that complex tax evasion has become an increasing problem in recent years, with popular strategies including conversion of income into capital gains and stashing cash in Swiss banks. However such actions are more indicative of people who believe their tax rates are overly high than of a suddenly corrupt populace. Another trend not even yet attacked by the IRS is the incorporation of business outside the United States in order to evade the high corporate tax rate of 35%, now the highest in the developed world (above Japan). When the IRS begins to shut down the escape route for Americans to form businesses outside the U.S., you will know the national prison doors are closing.

The IRS has been wildly successful capturing income and capital gains from offshore or foreign investments that US residents have utilized. Taxes are either applied as gains are made, or they are applied when an investment is realized, with taxes being calculated back over the period of the investment and compounded forward to the time of payment.

Tax collection mechanisms have been targeted at Controlled Foreign Corporations, Foreign Investment Companies, Foreign Personal Holding Companies, Grantor Trust Provisions, Passive Foreign Investment Companies, and Foreign Trust Reporting Requirements.

Although US citizens may still choose to set up offshore trusts, the rationale will be asset protection rather than tax minimization. The legislation catches trusts as frequently as other investment structures, and should be viewed as tax-neutral at best.

Regarding 'passive' income, international tax planning for US citizens is targets creating fiscally transparent investment structures, so gains on high-yielding international and/or offshore investments are taxed the same as domestic investments. This can mean creating limited partnership or limited liability business structures, as provided in many untaxed offshore jurisdictions, and which are treated as fiscally transparent by the IRS.

Investments in public offshore investment funds, many of which offer superior returns compared to domestic funds, are captured by the Passive Foreign Investment Company laws. Making a "QEF election" may be in order to pay tax year-by-year on a fund's increased asset value.

Offshore corporate tax shelters may be available to those who have significant 'active' business income, although the foreign sales corporation has now been outlawed by the WTO and abolished.

Foreign Bank Account Reporting (FBAR)

United States individuals must file a Foreign Bank and Financial Accounts (FBAR) report Under the Bank Secrecy Act, if they have a financial interest or signature authority over any accounts in a foreign country, and the value of those accounts exceeds $10,000 during the calendar year.

FATCA

The Qualified Intermediary (QI) program has been a key element of the IRS's regime for overseas investments by US citizens, but proposed changes to the program were put out to consultation by the IRS in October, 2008. The IRS requires Qualified Intermediaries to report all accounts held by are US individuals. The existence of offshore accounts, and transfers to them, must be reported on tax returns (as well as on Foreign Bank and Financial Accounts forms). US financial intermediaries are also required to report any transfer of $10,000 or more to or from foreign banks, brokerages or other financial accounts for US persons.

US source interest, dividends, and other forms of income paid to a non-qualified intermediary would be subject to 30% reporting, although eligible holders would be entitled to refunds. Also, a refundable 20% withholding tax would be imposed on gross proceeds paid to non-qualified intermediaries located in jurisdictions that do not have a comprehensive income tax treaty with satisfactory exchange of information provisions.

The United States Treasury and the Internal Revenue Service (IRS) will issue guidance on the reporting requirements imposed on foreign financial institutions (FFIs) by FATCA.

FFIs are required to deduct and withhold a tax equal to 30% of the amount of any payment to an FFI unless the FFI agrees to disclose the identity of the US resident and to report their bank transactions. The name, address and taxpayer identification number (TIN) is required of each US account holder; and, in the case of any account holder which is a US-owned foreign entity, the name, address, and TIN of each US owner of that entity. Also required are the account number, the account balance, and the gross receipts and withdrawals from the account.

Obamacare Tax Audits

In 2012, the IRS finalized a regulatory regarding issuing tax credits through the Affordable Care Act (PPACA) and federal insurance exchanges. The IRS was not granted any legal authority by Congress to issue such credits. In fact, PPACA only authorizes premium-assistance tax credits for individuals purchasing plans on state-run Exchanges.

Even if the federal government sets up an exchange in a state that declines to do so, the IRS wouldn't be authorized to issue tax credits. Currently, 27 states have refused to set up exchanges, and without the ability to issue tax credits and subsidies in half of the states, Obamacare will be hamstrung.

The IRS is attempting to save Obamacare by issuing tax credits through all exchanges, federal and state alike. A number of health care law experts have pointed out this is illegal and effectively creates two new entitlements not authorized by Congress. The IRS has arrogated "the power of the purse" by seizing the authority to spend $800 billion over 10 years on benefits not authorized by Congress.

This IRS rule is an unprecedented power grab and allows it to tax employers Congress did not authorize the agency to tax. PPACA stipulates tax credits can only be issued through state-run exchanges and employer mandates can only originate from these entities. Theoretically, the IRS isn't authorized to fine noncompliant businesses in states which refused to set up exchanges.

As with the tax-exempt applications of conservative groups and their seizure of millions of confidential medical records, the IRS simply disregards the law. Because of the harm these rulings will inflict on many businesses, they have generated several lawsuits. Nevertheless, one can no longer count on our courts to rule in favor of Constitutional principles and one should be aware that Obamacare will generate ample opportunities for the IRS to engage in the audit of American citizens.

Avoiding those audits should be one of your primary financial objectives as this byzantine law is fleshed out. Unfortunately, it is impossible to clearly predict where the dice will fall at this stage.

30　Tax Reform

One of the means by which the federal government enslaves its population is through a byzantine tax code meant to obfuscate the massive cost of the entitlement state. While the lower half of the population officially pays zero to negligible tax, in reality we are all taxed for government largesse either directly or through the Fed's monetization of the debt and the resulting inflation.

Key components of an insurgent rebellion will thus be tax reform. Everyone who earns an income must have skin in the game; otherwise the vital feedback between the size of the juggernaut state and the size of your taxes is lost. If you cannot see the amount deducted from your paycheck for profligate government waste, you are unlikely to clamor for reform.

Creating a nation of people who can vote for their entitlements will destroy the nation as that percentage reaches a plurality. This appears to have been the case in the 2012 elections. In a rational world, if you receive benefits from the government and have income you must in some form pay for that government so your voting and political involvement reflects self-interest. This concept has been known at least since Aristotle, it is not rocket science.

Hauser's Law

What is called Hauser's law is the proposition that, in the United States, federal tax revenues since World War II have always been approximately equal to 19.5% of GDP, regardless of wide fluctuations in the marginal tax rate. This has been true in times of peace, war, Democrats, or Republicans. It was true when top marginal tax rates were 90% all the way down to today's rates. The reasons are varied, but the primary one is that people don't have to work, and there is a pain threshold beyond which they simply work and get paid less, or at least "paid less" in terms that can be taxed.

Tax rates as a percentage of GDP reached nearly 26% in 2010 before drifting down slightly to 24%. This would not be sustainable, except for the intervention of the Federal Reserve which has been funding revenue shortfalls in perpetuity with Treasury sales. Thus tax reform, while driven by a return to the 19.5% natural rate, is superfluous unless major reform is also taken at the Federal Reserve to stop the monetization of debt.

Taxation must be a transparent means of raising revenue, rather than a form of social policy. Social policy should be done with legislation. Using the tax code as a means of directing social policy is evil, especially when hidden benefits and costs in federal law and administrative code books take up linear feet at the IRS. Two proposed models of taxation have a popular constituency: the Fair Tax and the Flat Tax.

Fair Tax

The Fair Tax, also known as HR-25, has been filed in several Congressional sessions. It replaces all federal income taxes (including FICA, Medicare, Unemployment, personal and corporate Income tax and similar) with one consumption tax on the first retail sale of any new product or service. Transactions in used goods are exempt. The 16th Amendment is effectively repealed on an interim basis by de-funding the IRS and deleting the entire Internal Revenue Code (the authorizing law for all those other taxes) and a formal repeal of the 16th Amendment is part of the process. There are no exemptions of any sort from taxation in consumption of new products and services. The "tax inclusive" rate is set at 23% (tax "inclusive" is how federal income taxes are set now.)

A "prebate" is sent by Treasury to all households in the United States of US Citizens. This "prebate" contains the amount of tax that is due on poverty-level spending for that household size, in advance, on a monthly basis. This results in a household that lives at the poverty line paying no federal tax at all. Those who live at two times the Federal Poverty Line would pay an effective tax rate of 1/2 the Fair Tax rate (or about 11.5%), tapering off until at approximately 10x the Federal Poverty Line (roughly $108,000 for a single person and $223,000 for a family of four) you would be exposed to the full level of taxation (that is, 23% inclusive.) As an example a family of four that spends $44,700 a year would pay an effective tax rate of 11.5%.

Flat Tax

The second option would be to replace the entire existing tax code with a simple bracketed flat tax, getting rid of the fiction of FICA and Medicare taxes as separate items. FICA and Medicare are highly regressive with the poor paying about 15% of their incomes in this tax from the first dollar. An acceptable replacement might be something similar to the following for single people (add 50% for a married couple filing jointly):

- $0 - $10,000: 10% (much lower than is paid now via Social Security and Medicare)
- 10,000 - $50,000: 15% (note this and beyond is a marginal rate)
- $50,000 - $100,000: 25%
- $100,000 - $250,000 : 35%
- $250,000+: 45%

Flattening the code is not a tax increase. For those simple tax returns and deductions it is moderate tax decrease as FICA and Medicare, along with unemployment (FUTA), are bundled in. These hidden taxes are currently deducted from your pay either directly or by reduction in the wages your employer is willing to offer.

With a flat tax, dividends, interest (including carried interest) and short-term capital gains are taxable at the same rate for individuals. There are no deductions or credits and EITC, mortgage interest and similar deductions all go away. The 1040 tax form fits on one piece of paper.

Corporations are taxed at a flat 20% of net income. Any corporation doing business in the United States is taxed on their worldwide income subject to a set-aside for taxes paid in other jurisdictions up to the US rate. This stops the "tax shifting" game that GE and others play. There are no deductions permitted for interest expense but dividends are deductible dollar-for-dollar against net income (since they will be taxed at the individual level.) The current tax code creates an unfair competitive advantage for large multi-national corporations against small, home-grown entrepreneurs which create jobs. With the flat tax, the corporate 1120 tax form fits on one piece of paper.

Long-term capital gains (defined as investments held for more than one year) are taxed at 20% or your base bracket, whichever is lower. Very long-term capital gains held by individuals only (defined as held for more than five years) are taxed at 10% or your base bracket, whichever is lower. This change in corporate tax policy would provide incentives for corporations to pay their net income to the owners, which is taxed when the owner gets the money. Retained earnings spent on development are business expenses and do not get taxed; allowing investment in R&D without penalty.

Debt has no offset in the flat tax code, so there is no incentive to take debt. Interest is not deductible for either people or corporations. There is no reason for the government to provide an incentive for people take on additional leverage.

Problems With Tax Reform

The problem with going to either a Fair Tax or Flat Tax is we can't trust politicians any longer to do the right thing. What we are likely to get with any major overhaul is a mishmash of the current system combined with whatever new system to create the worst of all worlds. In the end you are likely to end up with multiple new forms of taxation AND higher levels of taxation AND a more complicated system.

Given the current shallowness of our political class, we may well be better off revising the current rickety IRS system and waiting until there are such large majorities in Congress for reform that it will be possible to do the whole restructuring in one swoop. It doesn't sound likely that this will happen anytime soon, so concentrating on the spending and debt side of the fiscal problem may be a better use of activists' time.

Healthcare

31 Obamacare Revolt

Anyone who believes the government is acting on their behalf and is not at war with them need only look at Obamacare (see organizational chart) to see that revolt is coming. The whole structure is so monstrous and unsustainable, that its inevitable collapse will render many healthcare providers bankrupt, patients uncared for and the elderly bereft of services.

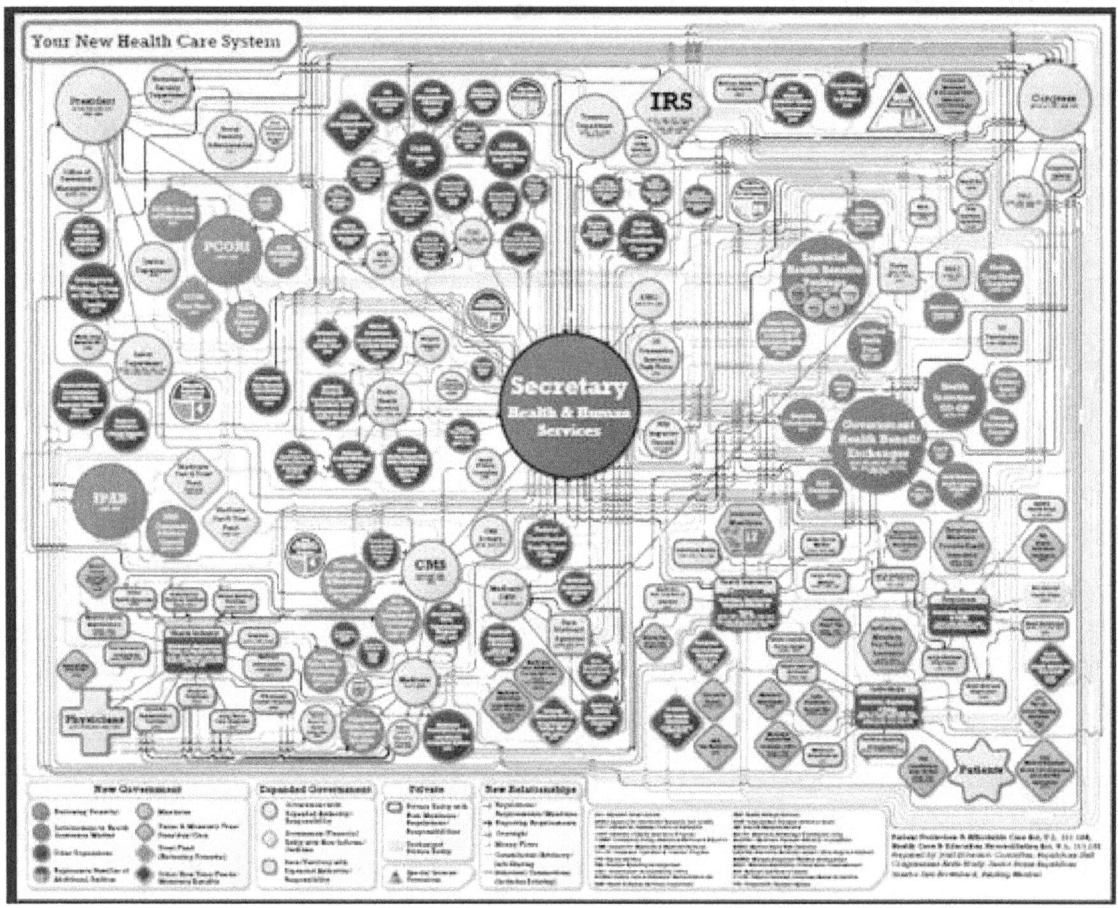

There's no question the Patient Protection and Affordable Care Act (PPACA), Obamacare, will collapse. It has 10 structural flaws so damaging, Congress will have to resort to major surgery just to avoid chaos. Unfortunately, there is no mechanism for filling the legislative hole Obamacare's demise will leave, assuring future chaos.

- *Impossible mandate.* The new health care law requires all Americans to buy a health insurance plan with a cost that is expected to grow at twice the rate of their incomes. Not only will health care claim more of every family's disposable income, Obamacare prevents families from using many of the tools like less expensive limited-benefit plans and higher cost sharing that private sector insurance plans now use to control costs.

- *Irrational subsidies.* PPACA offers radically different subsidies to people at the same income level, predicated on where they obtain their health insurance: whether at work, through an exchange, or through Medicaid for example. These subsidies and the accompanying mandates will encourage more than 30% of employers to drop insurance coverage altogether for millions of workers, also cause them to lose jobs.
- *Perverse incentives for insurers.* Obamacare creates perverse incentives for insurers and employers—worse than under the current system—to attract the healthy and avoid the sick. There is a bias towards over-providing benefits to healthy individuals to keep them enrolled and under-provide sicker customers in the hope they move to state subsidized plans.
- *Perverse incentives for patients.* PPAC allows Americans to remain uninsured while they are healthy—paying a small fine (tax) or perhaps none at all—only enrolling in a health plan after they get sick and paying the same premiums as healthier individuals. No sound insurance pool will be able to survive this gaming of the system.
- *Large benefit cuts for seniors.* A separate, inferior health-care system will be pushed onto the elderly and disabled. PPAC's Medicare cuts are draconian and seniors in many states will lose one-third of their benefits by 2017. Medicare will pay doctors and hospitals nationwide less than what Medicaid pays by 2020. Seniors will be queued behind Medicaid patients at community health centers.
- *Impossible state burdens.* Even as Obamacare requires people to buy insurance and fines noncompliance, states will receive no additional help if they enroll an estimated 10 million uninsured people who are eligible for Medicaid. Although there are federal funds for the newly eligible enrollees, states will still face a multibillion-dollar unfunded liability they cannot afford. States need the flexibility to manage health programs without federal micromanagement.
- *Unachievable expectations/a shredded safety net.* PPACA attempts to insure 34 million plus currently uninsured Americans. Early results from Obamacare implementation and economic studies suggest the medical care consumption of the newly insured will double. Yet PPAC doesn't fund any new doctors, nurses, or paramedics. Up to 900,000 additional emergency room visits can be expected each year—mostly new Medicaid enrollees — even while 23 million remain uninsured. As in Massachusetts, funding for health care facilities that take up this greater workload is not provided and "disproportionate share" funds will evaporate.
- *Lack of portability.* The biggest problem Americans have with their current health insurance plans is a lack of portability. Of 78 million Baby Boomers, 80 percent will retire before becoming eligible for Medicare. Two-thirds lack employer funded retirement health care. When those with above-average incomes try to buy insurance in the newly created health insurance exchanges, they will receive minimal tax relief. PPACA encourage employers to drop retirement health plans now in place.
- *Overregulated doctors.* America's 800,000 doctors are the best positioned to reduce costs and increase quality of care. However, Medicare now dictates their payment system. Obamacare magnifies the problem by encouraging even more unhealthy government intervention in the practice of medicine.

- *Overregulated patients.* Instead of dictating deductibles and copayments, we should allow patients greater opportunity to take advantage of health savings accounts. Patients who own and control these accounts have a huge incentive to make the best health care decisions.

The PPACA sections described below are certainly not all the problems with Obamacare, that would require another volume, but they do provide a sense of how bad the bill is.

1. (Section 1501) If you are young and don't want health insurance, or are starting up a small business and need to minimize expenses, it will no longer be possible to forego health insurance without paying $750 annually for the "privilege".

2. Young and healthy citizens who want to pay for insurance reflecting that status will pay for premiums that cover not only themselves, but also a three pack a day smoker/alcoholic who lives on lard burgers. Insurance companies will no longer be able to underwrite on the basis of a person's health status. (Section 2701).

3. Health insurers will no longer be able to offer policies which charge less in premiums by offering insurance with lifetime or annual limits on coverage, even when customers prefer these policies. (Section 2711).

4. Health insurers will no longer be able to offer policies that do not cover preventive services or offer them with cost-sharing, even if that's what the customer wants. (Section 2712).

5. Employers must now offer coverage for their employees' children to stay on their policy until age 26, despite the cost. (see Section 2714).

6. Your mandated policy must cover emergency services, ambulatory patient services, maternity and newborn care, hospitalization, prescription drugs; mental health, substance abuse, including behavioral health treatment; habilitative and rehabilitative services; laboratory services; wellness and preventive services; chronic disease management; and pediatric services, including oral and vision care. Policies for single males without children must cover pediatric services. Policies for woman who can't have children must cover maternity services. Policies for teetotalers have to cover substance abuse treatment. (Section 1302).

7. If you want a plan with lots of cost-sharing and low premiums the best you can do is a "Bronze plan," which has benefits that are actuarially equivalent to 60% of the full actuarial value of the benefits provided under the plan. (see Section 1302 (d) (1) (A))

8. Employers in the small-group insurance market can't offer policies with deductibles higher than $2,000 for individuals and $4,000 for families. (see Section 1302 (c) (2) (A).

9. Large employers (those with at least 50 employees) who don't want to provide health insurance to employees must pay a $750 fine per employee. (Section 1513).

10. Employers are no longer allowed to offer health flexible spending arrangements if your employees deduct more than $2,500 from their salaries for it. (see Section 9005 (i)).

11. If you are a physician the Secretary of Health and Human Services is authorized to use your claims data to issue you reports that measure the resources you use, provide information on the quality of care you provide, and compare the resources you use to those used by other physicians. Potentially the government will use the information to intervene in your practice and patients' care. (Section 3003 (i))

12. Physician who want to own their own hospital must be an owner and have a "Medicare provider agreement" by Dec. 31, 2010 as set forth in reconciliation. (see Section 6001 (i) (1) (A))

13. If you are a physician owner and want to expand your hospital, you can't (Section 6001 (i) (1) (B). Unless, it is located in a county where, over the last five years, population growth has been 150% of what it has been in the state (Section 6601 (i) (3) (E)). And then you can't increase capacity by more than 200% (Section 6001 (i) (3) (C)).

14. Health insurers who want to raise premiums to meet costs will be subject to review and can be denied if that increase is deemed "unreasonable" by the Secretary of Health and Human Services it. (Section 1003)

15. The government will extract a fee of $2.3 billion annually from the pharmaceutical industry depending on the ratio of the number of brand-name drugs sold to the total number of brand-name drugs sold in the U.S. So, if you sell 10% of the brand-name drugs in the U.S., what you pay will be 10% multiplied by $2.3 billion, or $230,000,000. (Section 9008 (b)).

16. Section 1405(a) of the Health Care and Education Reconciliation Act (HCERA), which amended the Patient Protection and Affordable Care Act (PPACA), provides that any "manufacturer, producer, or importer" of taxable medical devices must pay a tax equal to 2.3 percent of the sales price of the device.

17. The government will tax insurance companies $6.7 billion annually. Insurers will pay based on their share of net premiums plus 200% of administrative costs. If your net premiums and administrative costs are 10% of the total, they will pay 10% of $6.7 billion, or $670,000,000. Amended in the reconciliation bill, in 2014 fees will start at $8 billion, rise to $11.3 billion in 2015, then $1.9 billion in 2017, and peaking at $14.3 billion in 2018 (see Section 1406).(Section 9010 (b) (1) (A and B).)

18. Limits on compensation to insurance company CEOs also kick in if the board or think he's worth $500,000 or more in deferred compensation. Section 9014).

20. The bill even taxes tanning salons (section 10907).

ObamaCare raises taxes on employers and investors but doesn't spare middle-income families either. It imposes taxes on people without health insurance, with too little insurance and even those with too much. **Prosthetics, pacemakers, and other vital medical equipment are also taxed.** Pacemakers, prosthetics, and other vital medical equipment are not fashionable trinkets rich people buy and stuff into vaults, along with the dusty piles of gold coins and rubies. Those are items vital to the quality of life for a great many poor and middle-income people. ObamaCare is dropping many $billions of new taxes, waste and regulation on all of us, costs which will be passed along to the patients.

The following chart WAS the timetable for the imposition of Obamacare taxes. President Obama has since modified the timetable 30 times as of this writing n 2014 and will no doubt do so many times more. So we provide this more as an outline of what taxes may strike in the future as it is impossible to plan definitively in this environment.

Timetable of Taxes from Obamacare

Several taxes from Obamacare have already taken effect, though the largest—an increase in the hospital insurance (HI) portion of the payroll tax—begins in 2013. Combined, the taxes will cost Americans $836.3 billion through 2022.

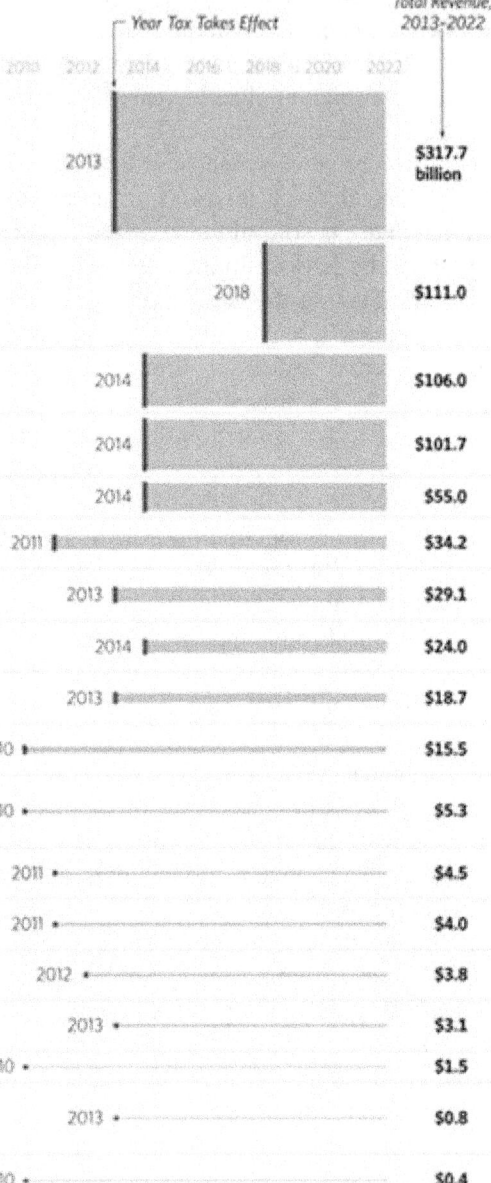

Year Tax Takes Effect

2010 2012 2014 2016 2018 2020 2022

Total Revenue, 2013-2022

#	Description	Year Tax Takes Effect	Total Revenue, 2013-2022
1.	Increased HI portion of the payroll tax from 2.9% to 3.8% for couples earning more than $250,000 a year ($200,000 for single filers); increased HI tax applied to investment income for the first time	2013	$317.7 billion
2.	40% excise tax on "Cadillac" health insurance plans costing more than $10,200 for individuals and $27,500 for families	2018	$111.0
3.	Penalty paid by employers that do not offer health coverage to their employees	2014	$106.0
4.	Annual fee on health insurance providers based on each company's share of the total market	2014	$101.7
5.	Tax on individuals who do not purchase health insurance	2014	$55.0
6.	Fee on manufacturers and importers of branded drugs based on each individual company's share of the total market	2011	$34.2
7.	2.3% excise tax on manufacturers and importers of certain medical devices	2013	$29.1
8.	Limit on the amount taxpayers can deposit in flexible spending accounts (FSAs) to $2,500 a year	2014	$24.0
9.	7.5% adjusted gross income floor on medical expenses deduction raised to 10%	2013	$18.7
10.	Exclusion of unprocessed fuels from the existing cellulosic biofuel producer credit	2010	$15.5
11.	Increase in corporate taxes by making it more difficult for businesses to engage in business activities that reduce their tax liability	2010	$5.3
12.	Increased penalty for purchasing disallowed products with HSAs to 20%	2011	$4.5
13.	Reduction in the number of medical products taxpayers can purchase using funds they put aside in HSAs and FSAs	2011	$4.0
14.	Fee on insured and self-insured health plans to fund PCORI	2012	$3.8
15.	Elimination of the corporate deduction for prescription expenses for retirees	2013	$3.1
16.	10% excise tax on indoor tanning services	2010	$1.5
17.	Increase in taxes on health insurance companies by limiting the amount of compensation paid to certain employees they can deduct from their taxes	2013	$0.8
18.	End of special deduction for Blue Cross/Blue Shield organizations	2010	$0.4

Sources: Joint Committee on Taxation and Congressional Budget Office.

32   Unfunded Healthcare

Medical costs are doubling every ten years or less, maybe much less with Obamacare. We can provide excellent medical care in this country, but we cannot subsidize the world's medical development, nor can we allow one group to forcibly bill another for their treatment. This is a crisis driven by financial mathematics, not a lack of compassion.

Unless individuals fund the diagnosis and treatment of their own conditions, the vital feedback loop between cost and benefit is lost. Instead, those unable to pay now demand that others pay their medical bills. If you cannot afford healthcare, or cannot find charitable means of help, you do not have the right to extort treatment from others through the power of the state. While it is politically correct to say we are a rich nation and should be able to afford universal healthcare, in reality we have already been bankrupted by healthcare costs. The potential demand for free healthcare is infinite and unsustainable, as shown below by the trajectory of Medicare costs.

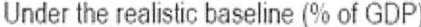

Under the realistic baseline (% of GDP)

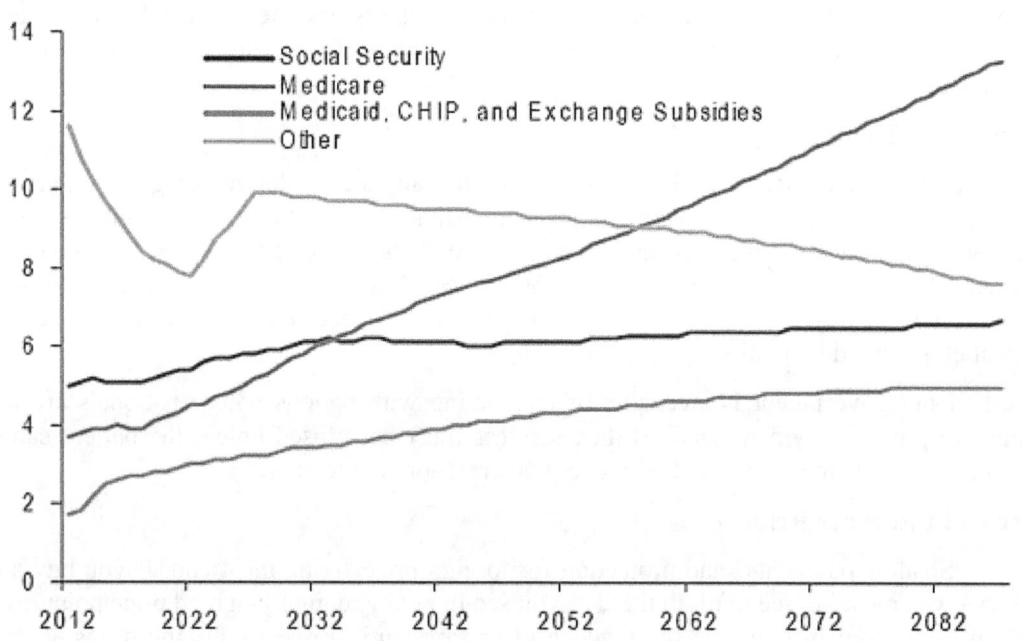

The Federal Budget cannot fund medical care as currently constituted. Government involvement in the current medical system has distorted price discovery and the normal market mechanisms that allocate scarce resources. The medical industry either has to get rid of the elements that cause this distortion, or be crushed by government mandated spending (Obamacare, Medicaid and Medicare). You in turn must plan for the financial reality that these programs may collapse long before you have expired.

No cosmetic adjustment to these programs will work. We can write checks with our medical technology that we simply cannot cash as a society. Dialysis, for example, is extremely expensive (thousands a month) but is not sustainable permanently and invariably leads to a transplant which costs tens of thousands of dollars. The patient then requires thousands a month indefinitely in anti-rejection drugs. We cannot fund, as a matter of public policy, dialysis and transplants for everyone who might need one, much less treatments like Provenge or heart bypass operations.

Before the advent of EMTALA (the 1980s law that required treatment irrespective of ability of pay), churches and other similar institutions funded a network of private charity hospitals and clinics that provided medical care. They did not meet everyone's needs, but they served those who had no resources. Few of these charitable medical operations remain but we will be forced to return to that model because we cannot provide the infinite care being demanded by our citizens. The problem is that in the interim, as Obamacare, Medicare and Medicaid collapse, charitable organizations will not reappear instantaneously. We have built a medical disaster into our future.

While we are scientifically capable of extending life, paying the cost is another matter. It isn't possible for society to provide a heart bypass to everyone who needs it. Nor can we give every man with metastatic prostate cancer another four months of life for $100,000 a month. Nobody has the right, as many argue, to demand that others pay their medical bill as a human right because the amount of health care one might demand is infinite. Enforced charity is no charity at all.

Subsidizing Illegals

Our medical system is distorted by allowing anyone, including illegal immigrants, to show up at a hospital with everything from labor pains to high maintenance ailments and bill "someone else" (the taxpayer) for their medical care. This will end because it is unsustainable, especially for those who are not citizens of the United States. This will be considered cruel, but there are literally billions of humans worldwide who are in need of medical care and the size of our wallet is limited by reality.

If our government is incapable of negotiating with nations whose nationals are in our country to provide payment services then services must be refused unless the patient can fund themselves. This is the case in virtually every other nation on the planet.

Price and Insurance Reform

"Shadow payments" and protection for foreign price-fixing must end. If you buy a drug or device you must be free to resell them as you see fit at any mutually-agreed price point. Ending medical protectionism will stop the practice of pharmaceutical makers pricing drugs at or near reproduction cost in other countries, forcing the United States to effectively bear the entire development cost of these drugs and devices. This sort of restraint of trade is supposed to be unlawful, yet is protected in the medical field by current "re-importation bans."

Providers must bill and accept payment in identical amounts for identical services; it must become unlawful to cross-subsidize treatment. Medical providers claim that Medicare and

Medicaid (in particular) pay below their costs. This is an admission that they are shifting part of the expense of that service to the privately insured or uninsured private customer.

"Prepaid, no bill seen" insurance claims must be eliminated. Every person must be presented the actual bill for their medical services and products. If you have an insurance policy that will pay that bill, that's fine - but the exact amount must be shown to you and you must accept it with a signature. That amount must match that billed and paid by any other party, irrespective of how the party pays.

Tort Reform

The tort system must be completely overhauled, if not rationally then by collapse of the system. . Litigation is built into the system because a person who presents a doctor with symptoms that could be caused by four different conditions plays litigation Powerball. For example, one condition might have an 80% probability and require a short-term medication (e.g. a course of antibiotics) for treatment. The second might have a 10% probability and require a $500 test to rule out, but if it is present is dangerous to the person's long-term health. The third might have a 7% probability but require a $3,000 MRI to rule out, and the fourth might have a 3% probability and require a $5,000 CAT scan with contrast to rule out. The latter two, if either is the condition involved, could be fatal if not caught in time.

Today's medical tort system leads patients to demand expensive tests because they don't see the cost of those tests. If the tests aren't done and a disease occurs, a winning lawsuit with potentially windfall penalties ensues. This is unsustainable, especially when the government is providing the care through Medicare and Medicaid. Instead, providers of medical care must present you with the possibilities and the cost of the procedures, and you as a patient must rule on each of those possibilities. You decide, after consulting with your insurance carrier what you wish to do and the risks associated with each choice are yours, eliminating the tort lottery.

Solutions

Reformed tax policy, coupled with a monetary policy that results in zero inflation, would mean you could save enough to have a shot at providing medical care, whether through private insurance or private savings. Every person in our nation should have the right to pay for as much life extension as they have the funds to cover the cost. Given the infinite potential demand for healthcare and the limited public checkbook, the only remedy to the health care dilemma is to allow a medical free market to be reestablished. While many will contend this is cold hearted, the alternative we face is a collapsed system where no one receives adequate health care.

33   Federal Drug Administration

Unfortunately, we are living too long (pushing towards an average lifespan of 90 years). It is unfortunate in the sense that each year of extra lifespan come with a geometrically rising healthcare cost. To cut your healthcare expenditures, which can be a sizeable proportion of one's lifelong financial budget, one way is to cut the cost of your pharmaceuticals. Unfortunately, The Food And Drug Administration stands squarely in the way of reducing costs because it introduces huge market inefficiencies and inertia.

How The FDA Affects Your Pocketbook

To obtain permission to market a drug in the United States, manufacturers must satisfy the FDA that the drug is both safe and effective. The 1962 Kefauver-Harris Amendments to the Food, Drug, and Cosmetics Act of 1938, significantly enhanced FDA powers. The amendments added a proof-of-efficacy requirement to the existing proof-of-safety requirement, removed time constraints on the FDA disposition of New Drug Applications (NDAs), and gave the FDA extensive powers over the clinical testing procedures drug companies used to support their applications.

Additional testing may enhance safety and effectiveness, but requiring excessive testing has negative consequences. First, it delays the arrival of superior drugs and some people who would have lived end up dying. Second, additional testing requirements raise the costs of bringing new drugs to market; hence, many drugs that would have been developed are not, and all the people who would have been helped, even saved, are not. The FDA is another example of how your government is at war with you.

Because FDA approval is mandatory, industry and medicine must heed FDA standards regardless of their relevance, efficiency, and appropriateness. Not all testing is equally beneficial. The FDA apparatus mandates testing that is often not useful or not appropriately designed. The case against the FDA is not that premarket testing is unnecessary, but that the costs and benefits of premarket testing would be better evaluated and the trade-offs better navigated in a voluntary, competitive system of drug development.

Three lines of evidence show that the costs of FDA requirements exceed the benefits and on net the FDA kills and causes great harm.

- First, comparing pre-1962 drug approval times and rates of drug introduction with post-1962 approval times and rates shows a quantum decline in drug introduction.
- Second, drug availability and safety in the United States when compared with other countries is no better and actually lags their progress.
- Third, comparing the relatively unregulated market of off-label drug uses in the United States with the on-label market shows no advantage to FDA regulation.

The delay and large reduction in the total number of new drugs has had terrible consequences. It is difficult to estimate how many lives the post-1962 FDA controls have cost, but the number is substantial; estimates of the loss of life from delay alone are in the hundreds of thousands and perhaps millions who endured unnecessary morbidity. When we look back to the pre-1962 period, do we find anything like this tragedy? The historical record—decades of a relatively free market up to 1962—shows that voluntary institutions, the tort system, and the pre-

1962 FDA succeeded in keeping unsafe drugs to a low level. The Elixir Sulfanilamide tragedy, in which 107 people died, was the worst of those decades. The number of victims of Elixir Sulfanilamide tragedy and of all other drug tragedies prior to 1962 is very small compared to the death toll of the post-1962 FDA.

If the U.S. system resulted in appreciably safer drugs, we would expect to see far fewer post market safety withdrawals in the United States than in other countries. Comparing safety withdrawals in the United States with those in Great Britain and Spain, each of which approved more drugs than the United States during the same time period, should showed marked differences if the FDA were effective. Yet, approximately 3 percent of all drug approvals were withdrawn for safety reasons in the United States, approximately 3 percent in Spain, and approximately 4 percent in Great Britain. There is no evidence that U.S. drug laws brings greater safety and in view of the clear benefits from some drugs introduced into Britain, it appears that the United States has lost more than it has gained from adopting a more conservative approach.

Finally, the off-label evidence indicates that the network of doctors, patients, pharmaceutical firms, hospitals, universities and rating organizations is really in charge of defining and judging efficacy and functions smoothly in the realm of uses not approved by the FDA. The mortality and morbidity that result from proof-of-efficacy requirements aren't compensated by safety improvements from a coercive FDA apparatus. The off-label market is regulated by thousands of doctors and patients acting in a decentralized manner. Compared to the FDA, this market adjusts quickly to new information, shows less sign of biased incentives, and allows a more precise adjusting of treatment decisions to preferences and the conditions of time and place. The off-label market operates with much less government intervention than the on-label market and provides a good idea of the benefits to be had from reducing FDA control over approval decisions.

Health Supplements

The FDA is also trying to use their regulatory control to gain the power to label almost everything used in complementary and alternative medicine as "drugs". This would include labeling as "drugs" nutritional supplements such as vitamins, minerals, essential fatty acids, amino acids, probiotics, prebiotics, digestive enzymes, etc. It would also include labeling as "drugs" "functional foods", herbs, and even raw vegetable juices! (as well as much more). Senator John McCain introduced legislation in 2010 to formalize what the FDA was attempting through regulatory overreach but has so far been unsuccessful in moving the legislation forward.

The drug approval process commonly costs hundreds of millions of dollars for a single drug. If nutritional supplements are labeled as drugs, as the FDA is trying to do, this will mean the end of the free public access to nutritional supplements. No nutritional supplement manufacturer makes enough money on what they sell to be able to afford the drug approval process for ANY supplement that they make, much less all of them.

Avoiding The FDA

Obviously your financial health is seriously compromised by our FDA, so the question is how to get around the bottleneck. Not only is the nanny state costly, but it is ineffective and costs lives in a war against its own citizens. The alternatives include not only medical tourism, but also grey and black market healthcare. The real crime is that the FDA makes criminals out of those who are merely seeking life sustaining healthcare.

34   Healthcare Alternatives

If you are going to survive the financial assaults posed by the collapse of Obamacare, the aging of the population, the insolvency of Medicare and a Depression economy, you will have to try as best you can to get off the rollercoaster. There are six main ways to do this:

1. Maintain Your Health
2. Play the System – pay only the Obama penalty
3. Move to self insuring and cash based medical care
4. Go out of country for surgery
5. Online Pharmaceuticals
6. Natural Supplements

Repeal of the Affordable Care Act, ObamaCare, is no longer realistic. Some states continue to resist, especially the creation of exchanges and there are some pending legal challenges, but prudent Americans should prepare for the law being eventually implemented in full. However, Obamacare will be so poorly implemented that whole sectors of healthcare will collapse.

ObamaCare will worsen the current physician shortage. Physicians will be driven to become hospital employees or to join large Accountable Care Organizations (ACOs), where their treatment decisions will be monitored with mandatory electronic medical records. Government and private insurers will increasingly link payments to adherence to "comparative effectiveness" practice guidelines. Physician will risk nonpayment (or losing his ACO contract) and significant conflicts-of-interest when their patients might benefit from treatments outside the guidelines.

How To Protect Yourself Against Obamacare

Obamacare is going to implode in a painful death of over reach, complexity, cost and unintended consequences over the next five tears. Ordinary Americans need to protect themselves from ObamaCare?, and here are some tips:

1) Get a good primary care doctor, if you haven't already done so.

The Association of American Medical Colleges projects a shortage of 60,000 physicians by 2015 and 90,000 physicians by 2020, roughly a 10-15% shortfall. Although the shortage preceded The Affordable Care Act, the new law will make matters much worse. The Physicians Foundation predicts a "silent exodus" of physicians retiring early or reducing work hours in response to ObamaCare.

If you don't have a doctor yet, get one before it's too late. Many primary care physicians are overworked and will be closing their practices to new patients.

If you're approaching Medicare age (65), check to see if your current doctor will retire in a few years; if so consider switching to a younger doctor now. Many doctors no longer accept new Medicare patients, and this problem will worsen with anticipated Medicare payment cuts. However, most doctors will continue seeing their current patients even after they turn 65. But if you wait until after age 65 to look for a new doctor, you may have a hard time finding one.

2) Use a Health Savings Account (HSA).

HSAs are tax-free savings accounts where patients can deposit their own money to be spent later for medical needs. Most patients use HSAs for routine predictable expenses (e.g., flu shots, well-baby checks), coupled with a high-deductible insurance plan to cover unlikely-but-expensive serious accidents and illnesses.

Because patients with HSAs control their own medical spending, they and their doctors have greater control over treatment choices without requiring approval from government or private insurers. Patients with HSAs enjoy comparably good outcomes as patients with traditional insurance, while spending significantly less. Doctors' offices may offer HSA patients significant discounts, because it avoids having to deal with insurance paperwork.

In the new Obamacare world of health-care-choices-managed-by-bureaucrats, the Health Savings Account may take on the role of the lowest cost plan. Since Americans will be forced to purchase health insurance, at least for now, HSAs will be chosen by tens of millions of Americans. The real question is whether the new regulations and the HHS Secretary's ability to issue damaging edicts to HSAs (or any other type of health insurance) with the flick of a pen is a world any market can live under.

3) Consider a concierge or "direct pay" physician.

Many primary care doctors are establishing "concierge" practices. An annual fee is paid in exchange for 24-hour telephone access and personalized consultation time for complex medical problems. Compared to the rushed 15 minute appointments common in many overcrowded primary care practices, this can be well worth the money. Concierge physicians may also act as your advocate if you have a serious illness and require hospitalization, coordinating your care with specialists based on their detailed knowledge of your full medical history. "Direct pay" practices operate in a similar way, but without annual retainers.

Because you pay your physician directly, he is not beholden to the government or other third parties. Concierge practices are usually a win-win proposition for both patients and physicians. Physicians spend more time with their patients and can practice according to their best medical conscience, for reasonable reimbursement. Patients normally receive higher quality care for a fair price.

Concierge practices are not necessarily expensive. Some services are surprisingly affordable, costing approximately $150 per month — i.e., the cost of a daily latte at Starbucks.

4) Medical tourism.

Non-emergency medical conditions are often amenable to "medical tourism." A hip replacement costing $30,000 in the United States might cost only $10,000 in India. Many overseas medical tourism facilities are modern high-tech clinics catering specifically to Western patients, staffed by American and European-trained physicians, with success rates comparable to good US hospitals.

Entrepreneurial doctors have also started offering "medical tourism" services within the US, for patients willing to pay cash for certain elective procedures. Provided you properly investigate a facility's quality and success rates, medical tourism can be an excellent option for many patients.

5) Help your doctor work on your behalf.

Ask your doctor if he will be joining an Accountable Care Organizations (ACO). Not all doctors will.

Right now, the average Medicare patient has two primary care physicians and five specialists; the average is 13 for those with chronic illnesses. Typically, these physicians aren't coordinating with each other. Better-coordinated care can save costs but ends up leading to reduced Medicare payments, thus creating a disincentive for reform.

ACOs, in theory, are supposed to change all that, by better coordinating care, and by reorganizing the way in which providers are paid, to focus more on health outcomes instead of simply performing tests and procedures. Obamacare's advocates point to its support for ACOs as one of the important cost-control initiatives in the law. Except that, like nearly everything about Obamacare, the government's idea of an accountable care organization is completely unworkable, to the point where nearly all leading health providers have declared it dead on arrival.

Ask if your personal medical records can be excluded from your doctor's ACO practice statistics. If ACO rules allow it, this will help him practice outside the guidelines when medically appropriate (e.g., ordering an MRI scan sooner than usual or prescribing a stronger but more expensive antibiotic) without fear of hurting his overall statistics.

Of course, don't ask in a hostile or accusatory manner. Rather, ask in a way that demonstrates your desire to help him better work on your behalf without conflict-of-interest. Most doctors want to do the best their patients, but they will be much more willing to make an extra effort (or challenge the ACA administrators) on your behalf if you demonstrate an active concern in your own health. Conversely, doctors will be less likely to stick out their own necks for you if you don't appear to value your health.

35   Cash Medical Care

As Obamacare collapses under the weight of over promising 'free' healthcare, two things will occur:

- The ratcheting up of prices
- Rationing of health services

One possible way to skirt the coming disaster of Obamacare, which will create shortages of healthcare of massive proportions, is to contract for medical procedures directly. One such example is The Surgery Center of Oklahoma, a 32,535 square foot, state-of-the-art multispecialty facility in Oklahoma City. Owned and operated by approximately 40 of the top surgeons and anesthesiologists in central Oklahoma, the facility has been accredited since 1998 without interruption and annually provides care to thousands of patients.

As a matter of financial self preservation, you or your business should consider this type of cash based facility as an alternative to what will be an ill fated Obamacare experiment. Especially if you have no insurance at all, this facility can provide quality without bloated pricing.

We have listed Surgery Center pricing at the end of this chapter as a reference for comparison with typical hospitals which are burdened subsidizing the care of indigents, illegals, and capped Medicare payments. The alternative is to consider a trip to a foreign country to have your surgery, but foreign medical care entails hidden costs.

The pricing of surgical services tops the list of problems confronting our dysfunctional healthcare system. Cost shifting, bureaucratic waste at the insurance and hospital levels, and an absence of free market principles are some of the culprits causing surgical care to become cost prohibitive. As more and more patients find themselves paying more and more out of pocket, a different approach is necessary involving transparent and direct pricing.

Patients need transparent, direct, package pricing so they know exactly what the cost of medical service will be upfront. Fees for the surgeon, anesthesiologist and facility are all included in one price without hidden costs, charges or surprises. Such facilities can offer low prices if they are physician-owned and managed. Controlling every aspect from real estate costs, to the most efficient use of staff, to the elimination of wasteful operating room practices that non-profit hospitals have no incentive to curb, they can provide quality care at lower prices.

Comparison Pricing

The prices shown below are not provided to promote The Surgery Center, but to give you a basis for cost comparison with other insurance funded facilities. Procedure prices include the facility fee, the surgeon's fee and the anesthesiologist's fee. The initial consultation with the surgeon is also included, as well as uncomplicated follow-up care. Postoperative care duration is different for each surgical procedure. Therefore, at the initial consultation the surgeon also estimates the amount of postoperative care covered by the price. The $200 initial consultation fee is applied to the total cost of the procedure should surgery be indicated, otherwise the $200 is retained. The goal is for the price to be as transparent as possible. What the Surgery Center does NOT **include in its fee** are:

- Any diagnostic studies necessary prior to the surgery such as lab, MRI, X-rays, consultations with specialists to determine medical risk/management, physical therapy and rehabilitation.

- Any hardware or implants necessary for completion of the procedure (plates and screws, e.g. for orthopedic procedures). This price information is provided prior to surgery but after the surgical consultation. The surgical staff knows with near certainty what will be needed to complete surgery and needed hardware or implants are provided at invoice cost without markup. Copies of the invoices are provided.

- Any overnight stay at the facility. Housing can be arranged on a case-by-case basis for an additional fee.

- Lodging or travel expenses.

- Expenses or fees resulting from complications subsequent to the completion of the surgery and discharge from the facility.

The whole point of the Surgery Center is that prices listed are non negotiable and available only to those paying the entire amount in advance. The Surgery Center can offer these prices due to the lower expense in processing claims and the absence of risk for non-payment.

Major price differentials will exist at other similar cash only facilities around the country and can be invaluable options when the full destructive weight of Obamacare hits.

The Surgery Center of Oklahoma

PROCEDURES	TOTAL
Arthroscopy	
Knee	$3,740.00
Knee with lateral release or microfracture	$4,510.00
Shoulder	$5,720.00
Elbow	$3,740.00
Wrist	$4,300.00
Hip	$5,575.00
Ankle	$3,740.00
OPEN PROCEDURES	
Knee	
Anterior cruciate ligament repair	$6,990.00
Posterior cruciate ligament repair	$6,990.00
Medial Collateral Ligament	$6,160.00
Tibial Tubercle Osteotomy	$6,270.00
Shoulder	
Open Rotator Cuff Repair	$6,160.00
Bankhart Stabilization	$6,160.00
Distal Clavicle Excision	$4,730.00
Elbow	
Ulnar Nerve Trasposition / Epicondylectomy	$4,510.00
Wrist/Hand	
Carpal Tunnel Release	$2,750.00
Dupuytrens Contracture	$2,950.00
Trigger Finger	$2,750.00
Ganglion Excision	$2,750.00
Ankle	
Achilles Repair	$5,730.00

Foot	
Bunion	$4,125.00
Hammertoe (1)	$2,475.00
Hammertoe (2)	$2,860.00
Hammertoe (3)	$3,355.00
Gastrocnemius Recession	$4,180.00
Plantar Fasciotomy	$3,080.00
Neuroma Excision	$2,750.00
Fractures	
Closed Reduction and Casting	$1,925.00
Percutaneous Pinning - finger 1-2 pins	$2,805.00
Open Reduction Internal Fixation	
Simple	$4,455.00
Complex (includes rodding Humerus/Tibia/Femur)	$6,375.00
Hardware Removal	
Simple	$2,530.00
Complex	$4,510.00
Miscellaneous	
Manipulation under anesthesia with block	$2,000.00
GENERAL SURGERY	
Hernia - Includes Mesh	
Inguinal	$3,060.00
Bilateral	$4,325.00
Umbilical	$3,190.00
Incisional	$4,500.00
Cholecystectomy	$5,865.00
Breast	
Mass - Excision / Biospy	$2,365.00
Mastectomy with or without Node Dissection	$5,005.00
1st stage: reconstruction w/expanders, single	$5,280.00
1st stage: reconstruction w/expanders, bilateral	$7,480.00
2nd stage: w/ implant placement, single	$4,235.00

2nd stage: w/implant placement, bilateral	$5,555.00
Hemorrhoidectomy	$3,300.00
Vein Stripping - single	$3,520.00
Vein Stripping - right and left	$4,995.00
Central Venous Catheter	$3,190.00
Spine	
Microdiscectomy	$8,855.00
Lumbar Laminectomy	$9,900.00
Anterior Cervical Disc Fusion, One Level	$16,500.00
Anterior Cervical Disc Fusion, Two Levels	$21,500.00
Pain	
Lumbar Epidural Steroid	$1,100.00
Cervical Epidural	$1,400.00
Lumbar Sympathetic	$1,580.00
Stellate Ganglion Block	$1,100.00
Reblock for Acute Postop Pain	$1,200.00
Epidural Blood Patch	$1,100.00
Eye	
Nasolacrimal Duct Probe - Single	$1,870.00
Nasolacrimal Duct Probe - Right and Left	$2,420.00
Strabismus, 1 muscle	$3,300.00
Strabismus, 2 muscles	$4,000.00
Strabismus - More than 2 muscles	$4,840.00
Chalazion	$1,870.00
Neck	
Thyroidectomy	$6,160.00
Lymph Node Excision / Biopsy	$2,255.00
Ear	
Myringoplasty	$2,400.00
Bilateral Myringotomy with tubes	$1,700.00

Tympanoplasty	$5,060.00
Tympanoplasty - Mastoidectomy	$7,050.00
Mastoidectomy	$6,640.00
Inner Ear - Stapedectomy	$5,390.00
Ossiculoplasty	$5,060.00
Cochlear Implant	$8,800.00
Foreign Body Removal	$1,500.00
Nose	
Bilateral SMR Turb	$2,700.00
Sinus / Turbinates 1 side	$3,795.00
complex	$4,950.00
Sinus / Turbinates both sides	$4,510.00
complex	$5,885.00
Septoplasty	$3,550.00
Septoplasty and Sinus/Turbinates	$5,060.00
Nasal Fracture Simple Closed	$1,900.00
Nasal Frature Complex Open	$4,015.00
Throat	
Tonsillectomy	$3,050.00
Adenoidectomy	$2,695.00
Tonsillectomy and Adenoidectomy	$3,695.00
Adenoidectomy and BMT	$3,300.00
Tonsillectomy and Adenoidectomy and BMT	$4,400.00
Frenulectomy	$1,600.00
Uvulopalatopharyngoplasty	$5,445.00
Diagnostic Laryngoscopy with biopsy	$2,970.00
Oral Surgery	
Mandibular Osteotomy	$12,000.00
Urology	
Bladder Suspension	
Mini-Arc Mid-Urethral Suspension	$4,480.00
Anterior Repair	$6,495.00
Posterior Repair	$6,180.00
Hydrocelectomy	$3,600.00

Epididymectomy – Partial	$3,600.00
Epididymectomy – Total	$4,100.00
Testicular Biopsy	$1,900.00
Vasovasostomy	$5,300.00
Circumcision	$2,000.00
Penile Prosthesis	$15,425.00
Ultrasound and biopsy of prostate	$1,900.00
Cystoscopy	
With bilateral retrograde pyelogram	$2,150.00
Stone extraction/stint	$3,600.00
Transurethral Resection of Prostate	$3,600.00
Transurethral Resection of Bladder Tumor	$2,800.00
Gynecology	
Hysterectomy (includes overnight stay)	$8,000.00
Tubal Reversal (includes overnight stay)	$9,100.00

Education & Self Retooling

36   Saving For College

America is increasingly aware that the student loan bubble is a major problem for millions of students, families, and our nation as a whole. While far too many politicians from both sides talk in platitudes about the need for education, few if any are willing to pull back the cover and expose the ugly reality embedded in current data on the student loan bubble.

Total student debt now exceeds all other forms of consumer debt and is now approaching $1 trillion dollars. The cost of education at public and private colleges and universities has to adjust downward but that is unlikely to happen soon because of the politics of vested teacher interests.

In 2012, the amount of outstanding debt reached the highest level ever recorded. A report from the New York Fed suggests that even while the rest of household debt improves, driven by decreasing credit card and housing debt, student loans have worsened. Their report finds that, while overall household indebtedness declined $53 billion from the first quarter of 2012, student loan debt rose $10 billion to reach its $914 billion peak.

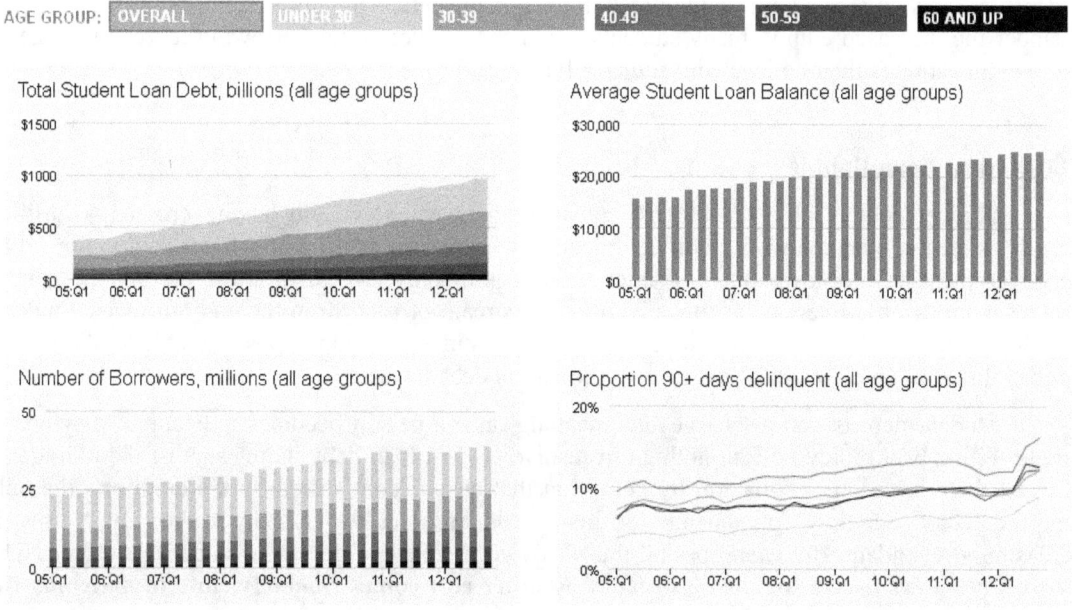

The Future Is Bleaker Than It Appears

The delinquency rates for student loans have risen above 9%, but as bad as that is that number is understated. It doesn't account for people who are currently in a deferral period from their loans or for students currently enrolled in college, who've taken on more student loan debt than any preceding generation.

Excluding students currently in college, and who are therefore exempt from becoming delinquent, the delinquency rate rises from 9 to 21%, double the amount of credit card delinquencies (10.9%). A delinquency rate of 21% spells a near certain crash for both borrowers and lenders alike and will also serve as a serious drag on our economy. This bubble has been fueled by the federal government's lavish subsidization of the student loan program (which was nationalized in 2008), in a way similar to how the housing bubble was fueled by government agencies unwisely pushing subprime mortgages.

This extensive government largess has produced a number of unintended -- though not necessarily unforeseeable -- negative consequences. First, it has dramatically driven up the tuition and fees charged by colleges, which in turn has forced more students to take out loans. This should have been easy to foresee, since the agents running the colleges would know that their clients had access to government-backed loans and so would jack up tuition quickly to extract that money.

Second, this flood of money has only encouraged administrative bloat, which in turn has increased college costs with no increase in the quality of education. Again, this should have been foreseeable. Self-interested administrators are the ones who decide where to spend the money, so you don't need to guess where they will (and did) spend the new honey-pot of taxpayer-backed loans.

Third, the rising price of college tends to erase the potential returns of a college education for students of only average ability. In effect, like homeowners who refinance their homes only to squander the increased equity, many students are spending more (and borrowing more) of whatever future extra earnings their college educations will bring.

The Student Loan Bubble

Student debt is now the biggest consumer debt category, and having crossed $1 trillion recently is greater even than US credit card debt. An increasing portion of student debt is funded by the government at ever lower rates of interest: it is politically critical to allow the bubble to keep growing with as little interest expense diverting the stream of cash from the end borrower. Students increasingly realize they are stuck with tens of thousands in loans and no jobs available to allow them to repay this debt, in effect making an entire generation debt slaves.

Student debt is non-dischargeable, meaning once a person becomes indentured, they are so for life. Filing bankruptcy will do nothing to resolve student loan debt claims against the individual. After all there is no other collateral by definition that can be confiscated by the creditor - the only thing the debtor "acquires" in exchange for this debt is a skillset, which sadly in the New Normal is increasingly redundant. But what does all this easily accessible and pervasive student debt fund? The chart below shows that **in the past 3 decades no other cost comes remotely close to matching the hyperinflationary surge in college tuition costs.**

Since 1979, college fees and tuition have risen 1120% compared to the Consumer Price Index rise of 300% (which is also outrageous). Where do all these dollars funded with cheap debt go? Why to pay the salaries, and lifetime guaranteed pensions of tenured neo-Marxist/Keynesian professors in "established" universities, who are delighted to keep peddling cheap debt if it means their compensation rises at a rate of 5-10% each year, every year, no matter how the economy performs.

After all they and their *"ZIRP is the answer to all"* academic brethren are the immediate beneficiaries of this 1120% cost explosion since 1978.

As to who foots the bill? It is all those young men and women who are indoctrinated day in and day out by every possible legacy media that the only way to succeed in this world is through untenable debt. Of course, it is packaged differently: study, get a loan, get a job and pay off the loan. Sadly, this is no longer always possible in the New Normal where one is lucky to get a part-time job paying minimum wage, let alone one which allows the repayment of debt principal. And the situation just outlined is rosy; it ignores the possibility of interest rates rising at some point in the future).

Did the cheap credit allow this explosion in tuition costs, or did soaring costs require the latest debt bubble? The answer may be irrelevant: one thing is certain - a 1,100%+ increase in prices in just over 30 years for any "asset class" is way beyond the ordinary course of inflationary business, and may as well be classified with the -hyper- prefix on a long-enough timeline.

This kind of price surge in unsustainable, as is the associated exponential increase in student debt. Both bubbles will pop sooner rather than later and you need to avoid both of them. The status quo professors, who have been benefiting from this phenomenon for years, are likely to be out on the streets themselves when the bubble bursts, having to take out a loan as they themselves become indentured servants.

37   **Your Educational Goals**

Because technology is changing so quickly, you need to resign yourself to perpetual re-education to continuously update your skillset. However, given the dire state of the educational system, you need to look at your educational goals and those of your family from a financial perspective. Some education is clearly a major advantage to ones financial health, so being illiterate and therefore barefoot isn't an option. Yet, neither will it be an advantage to be caught in a collapsing educational superstructure of bloat funded ivory towers which you subsidize with massive student loan debt. So here are some refined goals you can pursue given the New Normal.

- Procure as much education as you can to enhance your productivity
- Pay as little as possible for that education
- Pay as little as possible for credentials
- Incur limited debt

Education Financing

Obviously to avoid financial catastrophe, you are going to have to approach the financing of you and your children's higher education with caution. Some non-intuitive tips follow:

1. A large college fund can lower financial aid.

This is mostly due to how financial aid offices calculate need. Most public schools use the Free Application for Federal Student Aid or FAFSA, and many private schools use a combination of FAFSA, CSS/Financial Aid PROFILE, and their own formula. Regardless of the method used, generally parents and students have to list their assets, and more savings means less need.

So it is not unusual for two families with equal incomes to receive different amounts of financial aid, and the family with fewer saving would receive more. Retirement accounts are usually excluded from these calculations, so it is to the parents' advantage to sock away more for retirement rather than a child's college fund. The calculations also usually count a student's assets fully, so if you put a college fund under your child's name, that would hurt your financial aid numbers as well.

2. Working during college can be beneficial for students.

Research from the U.S. Department of Labor showed that young adults who had to work and pay for at least part of their college actually did better in school than those who didn't have to work. This is not that surprising because the kids who have to work and study at the same time are more invested in their education and are generally more disciplined to be able to manage school and work.

Those who have to work probably value their education more than those who don't. Additionally, students who have work experience usually fare better after they graduate in their job searches because any job experience is better than none in the eyes of employers.

3. College isn't the right choice for everyone.

There are many college graduates with no marketable skills who are not doing better than those who pursued an apprenticeship in a trade. If parents put away a lot of money in a college fund like a 529 plan and later find that their children no longer want to go to college, then they would have to pay a tax penalty to take the money out for other uses. Wait and see what a child's pursuits and talents are before deciding that college is the best path.

4. Maximizing Education vs. Maximizing Degree Value

People go to college for two fundamental reasons:
1) To get an education
2) For social interaction, business connections and the cachet of a university name

Getting an education is now increasingly inexpensive because of the Internet; you can even learn Russian on YouTube for free. Obtaining the social connections of a college education are what have become especially expensive.

Consequently, obtaining an inexpensive associates degree might make sense, as well as relatively inexpensive tutoring or online experiences to fulfill your real needs for education. In other words, you might be able to significantly reduce your higher education costs by separating the educational from the social aspects and considering the university more as a finishing school than as the primary source of education.

Ways To Maximize Education Inexpensively Or For Free

Junior College

For many students, the most obvious way to minimize educational expenses is to take Junior College/Community College courses four two years. Not only are prices cheaper than state or private universities, but you will have access to vocational training that might actually be useful in the real world. A course in welding might just be worth more to you than a high level course in women's gender bias.

Private Tutoring/ Homeschooling

From kings and queens to nobility much less our founding forefathers, private tutoring and homeschooling produced leaders of great intellect. While providing a full time tutor would be expensive, homeschooling supplemented by tutors for specific subjects (math, piano, fine arts, etc) is now being carried out by families on an industrial level. That is, there are vast sources for educational materials and support networks.

There is so much support for homeschoolers that we won't single out any organization in particular. A simple Google search for 'homeschooling' will bring up hundreds of hits.

Kahn Academy

An excellent example of how free education is revolutionizing learning is Kahn Academy. Their courses can be found at found at www.kahnacademy.org.

Kahn Academy is a not-for-profit with the goal of changing education for the better by providing a free world-class education for anyone anywhere. All of the site's resources are available to anyone. Whether you are a student, teacher, home-schooler, principal or adult returning to the classroom, Khan Academy's materials and resources are available to you completely free of charge.

YouTube And Internet

Youtube.com now hosts thousands of tutorials on everything from TIG welding, to sewing, to growing a garden, to making beer. You can learn the ins and outs of just about any trade if you are diligent enough in searching these tutorials. Many companies also have instructional videos at their websites, many of which are co-hosted at Youtube.com

Free Online University Courses

Carnegie Mellon University (CMU Open Learning Initiative)

Free online courses are offered in the social sciences, languages, engineering and sciences. Required software and other materials are specified in the course details. Courses are formatted in text and audio, also allowing targeted feedback so students can check their understanding as they progress. Users can configure and test their systems before beginning a course.

Johns Hopkins University (JHSPHOPEN Courseware)

Students can choose from courses in health and the sciences that are from face-to-face courses. Users read lectures from PDF files or listen in MP3 format. Reading lists cover textbooks and other necessary sources.

Massachusetts Institute of Technology (MITOPENCOURSEWARE)

Students can choose from architecture, engineering, health, humanities, management and science. Courses have icons denoting what's available in each subject area, such as lecture notes, assignments, online textbooks, projects, exams, images, study groups or multimedia content.

Open University (OU LearningSpace)

Course material presented through text, image, audio or video. Areas of study include the arts, business, youth, computing, education, engineering, health, languages, sciences, law, math and social sciences. Students access courses online where they can download them or print them out.

Stanford University (Stanford on iTunes U)

Multi-media courses and lectures available in teaching/learning, science, religion, social science, math, literature, history, health/medicine, business, art/architecture and engineering. Supplementary materials, such as exams and assignments also sometimes available.

University of California at Berkeley (Webcast.Berkeley)

Students have access to courses in art, science, business, computer science, engineering, health and math. Students view YouTube and iTunes webcasts of lectures. iTunes also offers additional audio recordings.

University of Notre Dame (Notre Dame OpenCourseWare)

Students may scroll down the list of offered courses, immediately seeing icons depicting which ones include syllabi, lectures, assignments, additional resources, audio or video. Students can choose areas of study including engineering, computer applications, English, history, Africana studies, physics, math, literature and theology.

Utah State University (USU OpenCourseWare)

These courses may implement text, image, audio or video. While some sources have available links, students may need to locate some sources noted on reading lists. A large number of departments offer courses, from anthropology to wild land resources. A variety of landscaping courses are also available through the university cooperative extension department.

Yale University (Open Yale)

Courses were recorded in Yale classrooms and are available as text transcripts, with video and audio from YouTube and iTunes. A full set of lectures are included for each course. Classes include courses astronomy, literature, chemistry, economics, history, geology, music and philosophy.

Political Reform

38   Starve the Beast

For forty years Republicans and conservatives have argued that the most effective way to control federal government spending is to "starve the beast" by reducing federal tax revenues. Two Nobel laureate economists, Milton Friedman and Gary Becker, endorsed this argument. Friedman (2003) summarized this perspective as follows:

"How can we ever cut government down to size? I believe there is one and only one way: the way parents control spendthrift children, cutting their allowance. For governments, this means cutting taxes. Resulting deficits will be an effective-I would go so far as to say, the only effective-restraint on the spending propensities of the executive branch and the legislature. The public reaction will make that restraint effective."

This has been described as "the double benefit of tax cuts". This argument has unified the Republican Party in favor of reducing federal taxes, but at the cost of undermining traditional Republican concern about fiscal responsibility, drawing attention away from the political reforms needed to limit government growth.

Perversely, reducing the tax burden of federal spending does not reduce the amount of federal services that voters demand or that politicians are willing to provide to buy votes. Price theory is unambiguous; reducing the price of a good or service increases the amount demanded. Reducing the tax burden of federal spending has the same effect as a price control, it increases the amount demanded relative to that supplied from revenues, an effect economists correctly oppose in private markets. We have delinked the consumption of federal entitlements from the pain of paying for them.

The starve-the-beast hypothesis is also inconsistent with history. Since the Reagan administration, changes in the relative level of federal spending have been inversely proportional to changes in the relative federal tax burden. In other words, politicians learned that as long as the tax burden kept going down, they could spend and borrow without political consequence.

The starve-the-beast perspective has thus led conservatives and libertarians to be casual about the sustained political discipline necessary to control federal spending directly, succumbing to the fantasy that tax cuts would solve this problem. President George W. Bush won the approval of most congressional Republicans for large increases in federal spending for agriculture, defense, education, energy, homeland security, medical care, and transportation, all without vetoing a single spending bill. As a consequence, real per capita federal spending during the younger Bush administration increased at the highest rate since the Johnson administration. It mushroomed even further under Obama, to over 25% of GDP.

The Federal Reserve As Deficit Enabler

There is no evidence that high deficits ever had an effect similar to that of reducing a child's allowance; the difference is that the federal government has a credit card with no effective debt limit. Federal spending is economically described as buying government services at a discount equal to the deficit, the costs of which will be borne by someone sometime in the future.

There is no positive relation between increases in federal spending as a percent of GDP and federal receipts as a percent of GDP necessary for the starve-the-beast hypothesis to work. Starve the beast just does not work because the more politicians spend, the less the population pays and the more federal benefits they receive. The difference in revenues versus expenditures (about 40%) is simply printed by the Federal Reserve.

Consequently, the ONLY way to save our country from a suicidal debt spiral is to take control of the monetary levers away from the Federal Reserve.

Turning The Tables

Clearly taxes need to be at a point where they cover expenditures to complete the negative feedback loop necessary for a stable economic system. Unfortunately, raising taxes is used as an excuse to spend even more. One solution is to tax those who are the biggest tax advocates. Tort lawyers would be one group (heavy funders of the Democrat Party). Another would be to tax predominantly liberal Hollywood stars, who it could be argued are benefiting from a windfall of interest in entertainment. Removing the tax exemptions of Media Matters, Planned Parenthood and the Nader consumer groups would also help. Other examples will quickly come to mind.

One will never have budget sanity unless outlays equal tax revenue and those who are the advocates for largesse of the public treasury feel the pain of their advocacy.

Until this feedback loop is established between beneficiaries and the taxes they pay AND the Federal Reserve is cut off as an infinite piggy bank, your only recourse will be to preserve your hard earned wealth by playing the system for what it is, a rigged carnival game.

39   Constitution Restoration

To the extent that both political parties have been complicit in the massive growth and rise in power of the federal government at the expense of States and individual rights, both parties are responsible for undermining the Constitution and laying down hard pavement on the road to economic serfdom. Your financial future depends on our government being constrained by our Constitution.

The steady expansion of the federal government since the early 20th century has allowed them to push further and further into areas of traditional state governance while intruding deeper into our lives. This threat to liberty—one that James Madison thought the several States would be strong enough to resist—is now apparent to millions of Americans. Though the Federalists were advocates of a strong national government, they expected the States would retain sufficient power to enforce the constitutional limitations on the federal government.

Steady erosion of Constitutional constraints meant to both limit federal power and prevent relentless expansion of the federal bureaucracy pose dangers to self-government and individual liberty that the Framers feared might lead to tyranny. The rise of the Tea Party movement is far more a response to these constitutional dangers than due to any dubious latent racism (a charge often parroted but never demonstrated by critics). Your financial future depends on our country restoring Constitutional principles.

The Tenth Amendment

State based self-government and individual liberty went hand in hand in the Framers' conception of democracy. Therefore they insisted on a federal government of strictly limited powers enshrined in the Tenth Amendment of the Constitution: "The powers not delegated to the United States by the Constitution, nor prohibited by it to the States, are reserved to the States respectively, or to the people."

The last decades has witnessed an unprecedented expansion of federal power in parallel with trillions of dollars in federal debt; the greatest explosion in federal spending and borrowing in history. An inevitable federal takeover of health care along with environmental regulation of historic sweep, further infringe on areas of traditional state jurisdiction while smothering less-favored industries in uncertainty. These policies not only endanger our economic future—they erode the constitutional constraints that were meant to shield local self-government and individual liberty from the dangerous accumulation of power in Washington. That is why the balance between state and federal powers matters and why the Tenth Amendment matters.

The Tenth Amendment, is far more than an academic legal construct, it is the embodiment of the American tradition of self-governance. As observed by Alexis de Tocqueville, the ability to spontaneously self-organize at the local level to solve problems is essential to American democracy. The Constitution was designed to protect this self organizing attribute. While respect and deference to state authority is implied in the Constitution itself, the Tenth Amendment was deemed necessary to assure that self-governance would never give way to tyranny. Coming at the end of the Bill of Rights, the Tenth Amendment was a summation of the Framers' notion of American democratic republicanism. It is also a warning that those powers granted to the federal government needed to be kept strictly limited within the Constitution's constraints, or else the States and individuals who formed the Union, along with the Union itself, would be in peril. However, threats by states to take back power and constrain the Federal government is not credible if there is no chance that power will be exercised.

In short, that means your financial future will require you to stay involved in your state's politics.

Balanced Budget Amendment

America obviously cannot continue generating multi-trillion dollar deficits indefinitely. The Achilles Heel of our Constitution is that there is no brake on the propensity of democratically elected representatives to vote their constituents not only the national treasury, but the treasure of fellow citizens to boot. A balanced budget amendment has been proposed as a solution, but the devil is in the details.

The Articles of Confederation and Perpetual Union originally granted to the Continental Congress the power

"to borrow money, or emit bills on the credit of the United States, transmitting every half-year to the respective States an account of the sums of money so borrowed or emitted"

And, with this as a model Article I, Section 8, Clause 2 of the Constitution grants to the United States Congress the power

"To borrow money on the credit of the United States; "

At the time that the Constitution came into effect, the United States had a significant debt, primarily associated with the Revolutionary War. There were differences within and between the major political coalitions over the possible liquidation or increase of this debt. As early as 1798, Thomas Jefferson wrote

"I wish it were possible to obtain a single amendment to our Constitution. I would be willing to depend on that alone for the reduction of the administration of our government; I mean an additional article taking from the Federal Government the power of borrowing. I now deny their power of making paper money or anything else a legal tender. I know that to pay all proper expenses within the year would, in case of war, be hard on us. But not so hard as ten wars instead of one. For wars could be reduced in that proportion; besides that the State governments would be free to lend their credit in borrowing quotas."

While Jefferson sought a balanced budget during his early years of administration, he later reversed his aversion to borrowing in purchasing the Louisiana Territory. Note that he made no exception for war and saw the requirement of maintaining a balanced budget as a deterrent to adventurism. Getting our modern Congress and State Legislatures to enact this necessary amendment may require the total collapse of our economy to focus attention on this glaring defect. Freedom hangs in the balance if the government's ability to deficit spend its subjects into oblivion is not addressed.

Enforcing The Existing Constitution

We could certainly debate further ways to enhance our constitution, but the purpose of such a sovereign document is not to be perfect, but to provide a contract which levels the playing field for all citizens. The "penumbra" theories of progressive Supreme Court justices destroy the certainty that citizens should have that they can read the plain meaning of their own laws. Freedom of speech, freedom to bear arms, and the many other guarantees of our Constitution are a solid framework on which to build our future without endless tinkering and interpretation by the elites.

To secure your financial freedom, you are going to have to devote some of your energy (along with the energy of like minded compatriots) to restoring the Constitutional guarantees that keep us free. Consider it an investment in your future, and the future of your children.

40   Avoiding Federal Overreach

The EPA, FDA, TSA, IRS and a dozen other agencies will put your financial future at risk as our welfare state implodes. We could fill volumes with examples of the overreach of dozens of agencies, but establishing the pattern is what is most useful to understanding how to avoid being caught in the vise.

- Federal bureaucracies are now operating outside the mandate of legislators through delegated rule making. This gives them an incentive to expand exponentially and an inherent conflict of interest.
- The bureaucracies are filled with agents who have political agendas – the EPA to fulfill the Green apocalyptic agenda, the BATFE to forward abrogation of the Second Amendment, the FDA to control all health and foodstuffs in a Naderite paroxysm, etc. Federal agencies attract acolytes of the progressive agendas that they regulate.
- The bureaucracies are defined by their need to expand taxation to support their intrusions and regulation to further grow exponentially.

In short, the agencies of government are at war with free men. The solution would require a massive restructuring of the political environment that goes far beyond our crystal ball. This restructuring is inevitable because we can no longer pay our bills or compete globally to support our indulgences. However, being in the vanguard of such a restructuring is a sure way to be crushed by the federal juggernaut. Hence we relate the cautionary tale of Irwin Schiff, father of well known financial advisor Peter Schiff.

Irwin Schiff Tax Protest

Irwin Allan Schiff is a prominent figure in the United States tax protester movement and is known for writing and promoting literature that claims the United States income tax is applied incorrectly. He has lost several civil cases against the federal government and has a record of multiple convictions for various federal tax crimes. Schiff is serving a 13-plus year sentence for tax crimes (with his location listed as the Federal Correctional Institution at Fort Worth, Texas. His projected release date is October 7, 2016. Irwin Schiff is the father of the well known stockbroker and former United States Senate candidate Peter Schiff who was one of the most prominent to predict the 2008 subprime collapse.

Among the arguments raised over the years by Irwin Schiff are:

- That no statutory deficiency in Federal income tax can exist until an assessment has been made;
- That no tax assessment can be made unless a tax return has been voluntarily filed;
- That the Internal Revenue Service, in enforcing the income tax, seeks to impose a tax not authorized by the taxing clauses of the United States Constitution;
- That the United States Tax Court has no jurisdiction over Schiff; and
- That the United States Tax Court is not a court.

These arguments were ruled invalid in Schiff v. Commissioner. It really doesn't matter for our purposes whether any of Schiff's arguments are valid or not (some sound right on the money). What we would argue from his personal history is that the way to protect your financial future is to follow every dot and tittle of the law. The real protest against deficits and taxation will come when the entitlement society crashes of its own weight. Your revenge will be having survived that collapse with your finances intact.

The Federal Mafia is a book written in prison by Schiff. In the book, Schiff contended that the income tax system and Internal Revenue Service were illegal. On August 9, 2004, the Ninth Circuit Court of Appeals upheld an injunction issued by a U.S. District Court in Nevada under 26 U.S.C. § 7408 against Irwin Schiff and associates Cynthia Neun and Lawrence Cohen, against the sale of this book by those persons. This prohibition does not extend to other sellers of the book. The court rejected Schiff's contention on appeal that the First Amendment protects sales of the book, as the court found that the information it contains is fraudulent.

Schiff, Neun and Cohen are currently barred under the preliminary injunction from selling or advertising material advocating nonpayment of tax, preparing a tax return for others, and from otherwise providing assistance or encouragement to others in violating tax law. Schiff and his associates were additionally required to provide copies of the injunctions to each of their customers. They were also required to post it on their website, and provide the government with a customer list.

The extent to which the Federal government has gone to silence Schiff suggests both that the Federal government will become desperate in its attempts to confiscate wealth as deficits become exponential and that standing in the way of this juggernaut does not make sense for individuals intent on surviving the collapse of the welfare state.

Macro Economic Theory

41   Austrian Economics

There are two broadly competing economic lines of thought in the world. The best known is Keynesianism, which is the current favorite but also a known failure. The counterweight is what is broadly known as the Austrian School of economics. You need a passing understanding of these two schools to be able to predict which ways the global economy will evolve under government policy and the effects on your assets. We deal with the Austrian School in this chapter.

The Austrian School of economics focuses on individual decision-making in economic issues, holding that the way in which money is produced and distributed has real economic effects, argues that interest rates should be determined by the market, asserts that the capital structure of economies consists of heterogeneous goods which must be aligned and emphasizes the organizing power of the price mechanism.

Mainstream economists are generally critical of Austrian methodology – though recent economic history has shown great failures in consensus economic wisdom. Mainstream economists rely on models and statistical methods to describe economic behavior, but Austrian School economists argue these methods are flawed, unreliable, and insufficient means of evaluating economic theories. Instead, they advocate deriving economic theory logically from basic principles of human action, a study called praxeology. While experimental research and natural experiments are often used in mainstream economics, Austrians generally hold that testability in economics and precise mathematical modeling of a market are virtually impossible. They argue that modeling a market relies on human actors who cannot be placed in a lab setting without altering their actions. Supporters of using models of market behavior to analyze and test economic theory argue that economists have developed numerous experiments that elicit useful information about individual preferences

The story of the Austrian School begins in the fifteenth century with St. Thomas Aquinas, then writing and teaching at the University of Salamanca in Spain. Aquinas' Late Scholastics followers attempted to explain the full panorama of human action and social organization and posited the existence of economic laws of cause and effect that operate very much as other inexorable natural laws. Over several generations, they outlined the laws of supply and demand, the root causes of inflation, how foreign exchange rates operated, and perhaps most importantly, the subjective nature of economic value.

The Late Scholastics advocated property rights, freedom to contract and free trade. They applauded the contribution of business to society, while strongly the inhibition of enterprise through taxes, price controls, and regulations. They urged governments to fight theft and murder as moral theologians but also as academicians. They lived by Ludwig von Mises's rule: "the first job of an economist is to tell governments *what they cannot do.*"

Richard Cantillon is accredited with writing the first general treatise on economics in 1730, *Essay on the Nature of Commerce*. Schooled in the scholastic tradition, Cantillon was born in Ireland but emigrated to France. He saw economics as an independent area of investigation, and explained the formation of prices using "thought experiments." He described the market as an entrepreneurial process, and held to an Austrian theory of money creation: that it enters the economy in a step-by-step fashion, disrupting prices.

Anne Robert Jacques Turgot, a French aristocrat and finance minister under the *ancien regime* followed Cantillon. His pro-market paper "Value and Money" mapped the origins of money, and nature of economic choice: showing that it reflects an individual's subjective rankings preferences. Turgot was first to solve the diamond-water paradox that so baffled later classical economists. He also criticized usury laws and explained the law of diminishing returns. He developed a classical liberal economic policy, which repealed the special privileges granted government-connected industries. Turgot spawned a long line of French economists of the eighteenth and nineteenth century including Jean Baptiste Say and Claude-Frederic Bastiat.

Jean Baptiste Say was the first economist to think deeply about economic method. He realized that economics is not about the amassing of data, but rather about the verbal elucidation of universal facts (for example, wants are unlimited, means are scarce) and their logical implications. Say discovered the productivity theory of resource pricing, the role of capital in the division of labor, and "Say's Law": there can never be sustained "overproduction" or "underconsumption" on the free market if prices are allowed to adjust. He was a defender of laissez-faire and the industrial revolution, as was Bastiat. As a free-market journalist, Bastiat also argued that nonmaterial services are subject to the same economic laws as material goods. In one of his many economic allegories, Bastiat spelled out the "broken-window fallacy" later popularized by Henry Hazlitt.

Despite the theoretical sophistication of this developing pre-Austrian tradition, the British school of the late eighteenth and early nineteenth centuries won the day, mostly for political reasons. This British tradition (based on the objective-cost and labor-productivity theory of value) ultimately led to the rise of the Marxist doctrine of capitalist exploitation.

The dominant British tradition received its first serious challenge when Carl Menger's *Principles of Economics* was published in 1871. Menger, the founder of the Austrian School proper, resurrected the Scholastic-French approach to economics, and put it on firmer ground.

Together with the contemporaneous writings of Leon Walras and Stanley Jevons, Menger spelled out the subjective basis of economic value, and fully explained, for the first time, the theory of marginal utility (the greater the number of units of a good that an individual possesses, the less he will value any given unit). In addition, Menger showed how money originates in a free market when the most marketable commodity is desired, not for consumption, but for use in trading for other goods.

Menger's book was a pillar of the "marginalist revolution" in the history of economic science. When Mises said it "made an economist" out of him, he was not only referring to Menger's theory of money and prices, but also his approach to the discipline itself. Like his predecessors, Menger was a classical liberal and methodological individualist, viewing economics as the science of individual choice. His *Investigations*, which came out twelve years later, battled the German Historical School, which rejected theory and saw economics as the accumulation of data in service of the state.

As professor of economics at the University of Vienna, and then tutor to the young but ill-fated Crown Prince Rudolf of the House of Habsburg, Menger restored economics as the science of human action based on deductive logic, and prepared the way for later theorists to counter the influence of socialist thought. Indeed, his student Friederich von Wieser strongly influenced Friedrich von Hayek's later writings. Menger's work remains an excellent introduction to the economic way of thinking. At some level, every Austrian since has seen himself as a student of Menger.

Menger's admirer and follower at the University of Innsbruck, Eugen von Boehm-Bawerk, took Menger's exposition, reformulated it, and applied it to a host of new problems involving value, price, capital, and interest. His *History and Critique of Interest Theories*, appearing in 1884, is a sweeping account of fallacies in the history of thought and a firm defense of the idea that the interest rate is not an artificial construct but an inherent part of the market. It reflects the universal fact of "time preference," the tendency of people to prefer satisfaction of wants sooner rather than later (a theory later expanded and defended by Frank Fetter).

Boehm-Bawerk's *Positive Theory of Capital* demonstrated that the normal rate of business profit is the interest rate. Capitalists save money, pay laborers, and wait until the final product is sold to receive profit. In addition, he demonstrated that capital is not homogeneous but an intricate and diverse structure that has a time dimension. A growing economy is not just a consequence of increased capital investment, but also of longer processes of production.

Boehm-Bawerk engaged in a prolonged battle with the Marxists over the exploitation theory of capital, and refuted the socialist doctrine of capital and wages long before the communists came to power in Russia. Boehm-Bawerk also conducted a seminar that would later become the model for Mises's own Vienna seminar.

Boehm-Bawerk regarded interventionism as an attack on market economic forces that cannot succeed in the long run. In the last years of the Habsburg monarchy, he served as finance minister three times, fighting for balanced budgets, sound money, the gold standard, free trade, and the repeal of export subsidies and other monopoly privileges.

It was his research and writing that solidified the status of the Austrian School as a unified way of looking at economic problems, and set the stage for the School to make huge inroads in the English-speaking world. But one area where Boehm-Bawerk had not elaborated on the analysis of Menger was money, the institutional intersection of the "micro" and "macro" approach. A young Mises, economic advisor to the Austrian Chamber of Commerce, took on the challenge.

The result of Mises's research was *The Theory of Money and Credit,* published in 1912. He spelled out how the theory of marginal utility applies to money, and laid out his "regression theorem," showing that money not only originates in the market, but must always do so. Mises presented the broad outline of the Austrian theory of business cycle drawing on Knut Wicksell's theory of interest rates, on the British Currency Schook and on Boehm-Bawerk's theory of the structure of production,. Mises was appointed a year later to the faculty of the University of Vienna. Boehm-Bawerk's seminar spent two semesters debating Mises's book.

Mises's career was interrupted for four years by World War I. He spent three of those years as an artillery officer, and one as a staff officer in economic intelligence. At war's end, he published *Nation, State, and Economy* (1919), arguing on behalf of the economic and cultural freedoms of minorities in the now-shattered empire, and spelling out a theory of the economics of war. Meanwhile, Mises's monetary theory received attention in the U.S. through the work of Benjamin M. Anderson, Jr., an economist at Chase National Bank. (Mises's book was panned by John Maynard Keynes, who later admitted he could not read German.)

In the political chaos after the war, the main theoretician of the now-socialist Austrian government was Marxist Otto Bauer. Mises knew Bauer from the Boehm-Bawerk seminar and explained economics to him nightly, convincing him to back away from Bolshevik-style policies. The Austrian socialists never forgave Mises for this, waging war against him in academic politics and successfully preventing him from getting a paid professorship at the university.

Undeterred, Mises turned to the problem of socialism itself, writing a blockbuster essay in 1921, which he turned into the book *Socialism* over the next two years. Socialism permits no private property or exchange in capital goods, and thus no way for resources to find their most highly valued use. Socialism, Mises predicted, would result in utter chaos and the end of civilization.

Mises challenged the socialists to explain, in economic terms, precisely how their system would work, a task which the socialists had avoided. The debate between the Austrians and the socialists continued for the next decade and beyond, and, until the collapse of world socialism in 1989, academics had long thought that the debate was resolved in favor of the socialists.

Meanwhile, Mises's arguments on behalf of the free market attracted a group of converts from the socialist cause, including Hayek, Wilhelm Roepke, and Lionel Robbins. Mises began holding a private seminar in his offices at the Chamber of Commerce that was attended by Fritz Machlup, Oskar Morgenstern, Gottfried von Haberler, Alfred Schutz, Richard von Strigl, Eric Voegelin, Paul Rosenstein-Rodan, and many other intellectuals from all over Europe.

Also during the 1920s and 30s, Mises was battling on two other academic fronts. He delivered the decisive blow to the German Historical School with a series of essays in defense of the deductive method in economics, which he would later call praxeology or the logic of action. He also founded the Austrian Institute for Business Cycle Research, and put his student Hayek in charge of it.

During these years, Hayek and Mises authored many studies on the business cycle, warned of the danger of credit expansion, and predicted the coming currency crisis. This work was cited by the Nobel Prize committee in 1974 when Hayek received the award for economics. Working in England and America, Hayek later became a prime opponent of Keynesian economics with books on exchange rates, capital theory, and monetary reform. His popular book *Road to Serfdom* helped revive the classical liberal movement in America after the New Deal and World War II. And his series *Law, Legislation, and Liberty* elaborated on the Late Scholastic approach to law, and applied it to criticize egalitarianism and nostrums like social justice.

Suffering from the worldwide depression, Austria was threatened in the late 1930s by a Nazi takeover. Hayek had already left for London in 1931 at Mises's urging, and in 1934, Mises himself moved to Geneva to teach and write at the International Institute for Graduate Studies, later emigrating to the United States. Knowing Mises as the sworn enemy of national socialism, the Nazis confiscated Mises's papers from his apartment and hid them for the duration of the war. Ironically, it was Mises's ideas, filtered through the work of Roepke and the statesmanship of Ludwig Erhard, that led to Germany's postwar economic reforms and rebuilt the country. Then, in 1992, Austrian archivists discovered Mises's stolen Vienna papers in a reopened archive in Moscow.

While in Geneva, Mises's wrote his masterwork, *Nationalokonomie*, and, after coming to the United States, revised and expanded it into *Human Action*, which appeared in 1949. His student Murray N. Rothbard called it "Mises's greatest achievement and one of the finest products of the human mind in our century. It is economics made whole." The appearance of this work was the hinge of the whole history of the Austrian School, and it remains the economic treatise that defines the School. Even so, it was not well received in the economics profession, which had already made a decisive turn towards Keynesian.

Just as he had in Vienna, Mises gathered students around him at New York University, despite never being given the paid academic post he deserved. Even before Mises emigrated, journalist Henry Hazlitt had become his most prominent champion, reviewing his books in the *New York Times* and *Newsweek*, and popularizing his ideas in such classics as *Economics in One Lesson*. Yet Hazlitt made his own contributions to the Austrian School. He wrote a line-by-line critique of Keynes's *General Theory*, defended the writings of Say, and restored him to a central place in Austrian macroeconomic theory. Hazlitt followed Mises's example of intransigent adherence to principle, and as a result was pushed out of four high-profile positions in the journalistic world.

Mises's New York seminar continued until two years before his death in 1973. During those years, Rothbard was his student. In fact, Rothbard's *Man, Economy, and State* (1963) paralleled Mises' *Human Action*, and strengthened Mises's own views in monopoly theory, utility and welfare, and the theory of the state. Rothbard's approach to the Austrian School followed directly in the line of Late Scholastic thought by applying economic science within a framework of a natural-rights theory of property. What resulted was a full-fledged defense of a capitalistic and stateless social order, based on property and freedom of association and contract.

Rothbard followed his economic treatise with an investigation of the great depression, which applied Austrian business cycle theory to show that the stock market crash and economic downturn was attributable to a prior bank credit expansion. Then in a series of studies on government policy, he established the theoretical framework for examining the effects of all types of intervention in the market.

In his later years, Mises saw the beginnings of the revival of the Austrian School that dates from the appearance of *Man, Economy, and State* and continues to this day. It was Rothbard who firmly established the Austrian School and classical liberal doctrine in the U.S., especially with *Conceived in Liberty*, his four-volume history of colonial America and the secession from Britain. In his philosophical work, *The Ethics of Liberty*, Rothbard reunited natural-rights theory and the Austrian School. He also wrote a series of scholarly economic pieces later compiled in the two-volume *Logic of Action*, as part of Edward Elgar's "Economists of the Century" series.

These seminal works serve as the crucial link between the Mises-Hayek generation and the Austrians now working to expand the tradition. Indeed, without Rothbard's willingness to defy the intellectual trends of his time, progress in the Austrian School tradition might have come to a halt. As it was, his wide and deep scholarship, cheerful personality, encyclopedic knowledge, and optimistic outlook inspired countless students to turn their attention to the cause of liberty.

Though Austrians are now in a more prominent position than at any point since the 1930s, Rothbard, like Mises before him, was not well treated by academia. In his later years he did hold a chair at the University of Nevada, Las Vegas, but never taught in a capacity that permitted him to direct dissertations. Nevertheless, he managed to recruit a large, active, and interdisciplinary following for the Austrian School. The founding of the Ludwig von Mises Institute in 1982, with the aid of Margit von Mises as well as Hayek and Hazlitt, provided a range of new opportunities for both Rothbard and the Austrian School.

42　Keynesian Epic Fail

As the recession and financial debacle has deepened, we have been deluged by an enormous outpouring of diagnosis, prognosis, and prescription by pundits, journalists, public officials and academics. Most of this analysis is worthless because those who claim expertise about the economy rely on a common set of defective presuppositions. This pseudo-intellectual theory loosely fits under the umbrella of Keynesianism and has masqueraded as economic wisdom for more than 50 years. Keynesianism is the counter economic theory to the Austrian School.

Paul Samuelson's *Economics* (1948), the best-selling economics textbook of all time, introduced Keynesianism to generations of college students and economic analysis established itself as orthodoxy amongst academia, the news media, and politicians. Unfortunately, Keynesian analysis of the economy's operation and fluctuations causes errors of commission and omission in policy. The notion that the government can and should use fiscal and monetary policies to control the macroeconomy and stabilize its fluctuations has consistently failed over generations since 1949.

In order to survive financially, you have to know why the Keynesian policy favored by our bureaucrat and academic overlords has always been doomed to failure. The Keynesian approach does not ameliorate, but in fact creates economic booms and busts – a self fulfilling prophecy of destruction. It relies on six tenets:

Aggregation

John Maynard Keynes persuaded fellow economists and then the public that it makes sense to think of the economy in terms of a handful of economy-wide aggregates: total income or output (Y), total consumption spending (C), total investment spending (I), government spending (G) and total net exports (exports (X) minus imports (I)). This is embodied in the equation $Y = C + I + G + (X - M)$.

Sometimes physical output (Q) times the price level (P) is equated to the variables on the right-hand side of the equation, or $Q * P$. So the idea is that aggregate supply equals aggregate demand, equals the sum of four types of money expenditure for newly produced final goods and services.

This simplistic way of compressing diverse, economy-wide transactions into single variables suppresses recognition of the complex relationships and differences within each of the aggregates. The effect of adding a million dollars of investment spending for teddy-bear inventories becomes the same as adding a million dollars of investment to dig a new copper mine. Likewise, a million dollars of consumption spending for movie tickets equates to a million dollars of consumption spending for gasoline, a million dollars of government spending for children's inoculations, or a million dollars of government spending for UAV drones.

Suppressing the differences within each aggregate obviously causes economic analysis to go seriously awry, but that is the heart of the Keynesian model. In fact, "the economy" does not produce undifferentiated "output." Instead, the millions of producers who create "aggregate supply" provide an infinite variety of goods and services that differ in countless ways. An immense amount of what goes on in a modern market-oriented economy also consists of dealings among producers who supply no "final" goods and services, but instead trade raw materials, components, and intermediate services to one another.

In other words, you can't just hope to add money to the Government term of the economic equation and miraculously get increases in Consumption and Investment. But that doesn't stop politicians and academics from trying to convince you that they can create wealth out of thin air by increasing taxes and spending that money on worthless government boondoggles that fritter away wealth.

Extraordinarily complex micro relationships make up "the economy", not a single, formulaic process that produces uniform aggregate widgets. Free market price discovery is indispensible in such a system, where the price of a parachute can change instantaneously from near zero to infinity when a jet engine falls off. "Economic action," is composed of millions of such choices by diverse participants. Without free choice, constrained by market scarcity, true economic action cannot take place. Keynesianism, rather than providing a coherent economic analysis, actually excludes the possibility of genuine economic action, substituting for it a simplistic, aggregate conception.

Relative Prices

Keynesianism ignores relative prices and changes in such prices. There is only one price, "the price level" which represents a weighted average of all the money prices at which the economy's countless actual goods and services are sold. The rate of interest is also treated as a price in a limited and misleading way. If relative prices change — as they do even in the most stable periods — these changes are "averaged out" and affect change only at the aggregate price level.

So if the economy expands along certain lines, but not along others, and the configuration of relative prices changes, Keynesians know that "aggregate demand" and "aggregate supply" have risen, but they have no idea why or how they have risen. They view the economy's aggregate output as driven by aggregate demand, to which aggregate supply responds more or less automatically. It doesn't matter whether only the demand for oranges has risen, or as Keynes himself posited, only the demand for pyramids has risen. Aggregate demand is always a broad brush average of all demand no matter what its composition. Of course this is the type of mindless number crunching used by the Federal Reserve to justify its endless twiddling of the economic knobs.

Because Keynesians ignore the economy's output microstructure, they cannot conceive how expansion of demand along some lines but not others might be problematic. In their view, one cannot have too many houses and apartments. They believe increasing spending for houses and apartments is always good whenever the economy has unemployed resources, regardless of how many houses and apartments stand vacant and regardless of what kinds of resources are unemployed or located.

This smacks of the old Soviet Union and its shoe quotas. Although unemployed laborers may be skilled silver miners in Idaho, it is supposedly still a good thing if somehow the demand for condos is increased in Palm Beach. For the Keynesian there are no individual classes of laborers or separate labor markets: labor is labor is labor. If someone — whatever his skills, preferences, or location — is unemployed, then they expect to put him back to work by increasing aggregate demand, regardless of what we spend the money for, whether it be ham or computers.

This naive simplicity exists because mathematically they write aggregate output is a simple increasing function of aggregate labor employed: $Q = f(L)$, where $dQ/dL > 0$.

In words, output is a function of labor and the naïve claim is that the change in output per change in labor is always greater than zero. This "aggregate-production function" has only one input, aggregate labor and workers seemingly produce without the aid of capital! Keynesians may admit that workers use capital, but they insist capital stock may be taken as "given" and fixed in the short run. In the long run, they may insist, we are "all dead," as Keynes put it, or they may deny that the long run is what we get when we place a series of short runs end to end. The Keynesian in effect treats living for the moment as a major virtue and the future may safely be left to take care of itself.

The Rate of Interest

Keynesians only care about the rate of interest as the "price of money" — or rental rate paid on borrowed money. They suppose such borrowing is always good, and more of it is always better because individuals use borrowed money to purchase consumer goods, thereby "creating jobs", which is the end goal of their theory no matter the consequences. While the lower the interest rate, the more people will borrow and spend, the economy does not inherently function better because savings are depressed and "make-work" employment becomes an inevitable drag.

Unemployment always exists, so Keynesians always want the rate of interest to be forced lower. If it can be lowered artificially by central-bank action, they strongly favor such action. The Federal Reserve System has pushed its target for the interest rate on "federal funds" — overnight balances the banks borrow from one another — to near zero, and crackpot economists have even toyed with a negative rate of interest. Yet unemployment has barely budged through the Great Recession, making this theory moot.

In a free market, the prevailing market rate of interest would be that at which the amount demanders want to borrow equals the amount suppliers want to lend. However, borrowers and lenders both make their choices based on their "time preference," that is the rate at which they're willing to trade present goods for goods in the future. Those with a "high rate of time preference" will consume goods now rather than later, so to induce them to forgo present consumption, borrowers must compensate lenders by paying a high enough rate of interest for the use of the lenders funds.

Keynesians recognize that a lower rate of interest will spur business firms to borrow money and invest, but that business investment plans are naturally volatile and essentially irrational — driven, as Keynes is famously quoted (1936), by the entrepreneurs' "animal spirits". Consequently, investment responds to a change in the rate of interest only in small degree and may be disregarded. This runs counter to the experience of most practical businessmen, who watch both interest and tax rates closely.

For Keynesians, the importance of the rate of interest is that it regulates the amount that individuals will borrow to finance their purchases of consumer goods. This they believe is the essential element determining how much firms want to produce and invest in expand their capacity. This falsely implies it doesn't matter what kind of investment takes place: investment is investment is investment. Any businessman knows differently.

Capital Structure

Modern Keynesians views the capital stock as a "given", a sort of massive inheritance from the past, with little thought to its structure. In their naive analysis, it doesn't matter whether firms invest in new telephones or new hydroelectric dams: capital is capital is capital. The patterns of specialization and interrelation among countless forms of capital goods encapsulating past saving and investment decisions are simply ignored.

Modern Keynesians disregard how changes in the rate of interest bring about changes in the structure of the capital stock, insisting it is an undifferentiated glob of monetary value which may be substituted for any other part of equal monetary value. This willful blindness causes economists like Nobel laureate, Paul Krugman, to misinterpret the Austrian theory of the business cycle as a theory of "overinvestment" versus malinvestment.

In the first half of the 20th century the theory of mal-investment pioneered by Ludwig von Mises and F.A. Hayek posited that artificially reduced rates of interest lead business firms to invest in the wrong kinds of capital. In this Austrian view, the longest-lived capital goods, such as residential and industrial buildings are overinvested as opposed to inventories, equipment, and software with a relatively short life. Fed-induced low rates of interest, like those between 2002 and 2005, led firms to overvalue longer-term capital projects and shift investment spending in that direction — producing booms in building construction, among other things. Even worse is the current Zero Interest Policy.

Keynesians believe the government should "try something," and if that fails, try something else. But if people are artificially led to prefer present consumption, then businesses will mal-invest in projects which anticipate demands that will never happen. When these projects ultimately fail, the boom that artificially lowered interest rates set in motion collapses into a bust with bankruptcies and unemployed labor, as unsustainable projects are liquidated and resources are painfully converted to viable uses.

Because the Keynesian is blind to these microdistortions and the need for their correction after an artificially induced boom, he fails to see the need for the bankruptcies and unemployment that are necessary during a substantial economic restructuring. He supposes: the government can always use deficit spending to make up for reduced private investment and consumption spending and business will be restored to profitability and workers reemployed without economic restructuring.

Subsidized lending to homeowners who cannot meet normal commercial qualifications for receiving such loans is still being forwarded to restart a policy that perversely contributed to producing the unsustainable boom of 2002–2006. However, too many resources have been directed into house and condo construction. Lending to homeowners who cannot afford to purchase homes unless subsidized, signals an uneconomic use of resources (malinvestment) at the expense of the taxpayers who finance these subsidies.

Malinvestments and Money Pumping

Keynesians' simple faith in government spending as a macroeconomic balance wheel disregards malinvestment. Government spending in excess of revenues requires the difference to be covered by borrowing. Central-bank actions make such borrowing cheaper for the government, which chronically prefers "easy money" to more restrictive central-bank policies. They prefer inflationary easy money because it both lowers the cost of financing the government's deficit spending and induces individuals to borrow more money and spend it on consumption goods. Increased consumption spending is always viewed as a good thing, despite the near-zero rate of saving it induces and the fact it induces people to buy thing they don't need.

Keynesians don't worrying about potential inflation; on the contrary, they are obsessed with an irrational fear of even the slightest hint of deflation, though deflation helps those on fixed incomes and savers. If inflation should become an undeniable problem, they will support price controls instead of monetary austerity, which they are convinced will work based on sketchy knowledge of such controls during World War II.

Regime Uncertainty

Keynesians are policy activists. Like Franklin D. Roosevelt, they naively believe that the government should "try something," and if that doesn't work, try something else. The eras they most esteem in US politico-economic history are Roosevelt's first term as president and Lyndon B. Johnson's first spendthrift years in the presidency. These periods witnessed an outpouring of new government measures to spend, tax, regulate, subsidize, and create economic mischief on an extraordinary scale. The Obama administration's government action on many fronts are a Keynesian third Great Leap Forward.

But policy activism works against economic prosperity by creating "regime uncertainty," a pervasive uncertainty about the impending economic order and how the government will treat private-property rights in the future. This uncertainty discourages investors from putting money into long-term projects. Such investment almost disappeared after 1929 and did not recover fully until after World War II.

Regime uncertainty has resulted from the government's frenetic series of bailouts, capital infusions, emergency loans, takeovers, stimulus packages, and other extraordinary measures crammed into periods of a few years. A continuation of this kind of frantic policy activism cannot help seems inevitable and threatens your financial survival.

43 Spending

A debt spiral is a black hole of ever-compounding obligations which swallows your ability to pay and demands ever-larger capital injections until the entire wealth of the nation is consumed. At that point, the only alternative will be to tell the bankers to take their losses and default. Our banking system, federal government and many state and local entities are so overextended. The only question is when the house of cards collapses.

Federal Spending

Those who oppose balancing the budget today must justify exactly when they will support spending reductions because there will always be excuses to "stimulate the economy" through higher spending. They must provide evidence that between now and that point they will be able to continue the present course of inaction without economic collapse. Otherwise we must take our medicine and slash the budget, telling those who claim to be "too big to fail" that they are not too big to go to jail.

We currently have five entitlement programs that alone consume the entire Federal revenue stream. Those are Social Security, Medicare, Medicaid, Unemployment and Welfare. These social welfare experiments are expanding geometrically and will crowd out both the legitimate activities of government as well as the private sector.

Over a trillion dollars a year in savings is needed on the spending side to keep us from insolvency, requiring a complete halt to the escalation of social programs. Tax revenues would stabilize with these cuts and economic growth could begin again. We have no real choice but to:

- Stabilize Social Security and stop its growth.
- Cut Medicare and Medicaid spending in half and stop their growth.
- Cut Defense spending.
- Eliminate the Departments of Education, Homeland Security etc.
- Stabilize tax revenues while we rationalize the tax code.

Many of these cuts will seem draconian, even to limited government penny pinchers. However, such a course is the only option other than forced spending cuts when our Federal Government credit card gets cut up. If we refuse to take these steps (as seems likely) either the Federal Reserve will continue monetizing debt causing energy, food and other commodities skyrocket in price (effectively stealing the money you think the government is giving you) or we will be forced into a much worse set of austerity programs when bond buyers cut off our credit line.

General Welfare payments, whether in the form of Section 8, SNAP (Food Stamps) or similar programs must be time-limited and conditioned on job training, educational enrollment and progress. The libertarian view is that these programs should not exist at all, but unfortunately the nation's population disagrees. Civil unrest comes when humanitarian good intentions meet the brick wall reality that we are bankrupt.

When one looks not only at public marketable debt but also the forward promises for Medicare, Medicaid and Social Security, we have over $100 trillion in actual liabilities in the Federal Government. This exceeds the net worth of households and corporations by some 40%. This amount is impossible to pay and even if our government was to confiscate all privately-held wealth, we would still be in the hole by nearly half.

Social Security is not sustainable as currently operated no matter what Washington claims. While the existing step-functions which cap at modest benefits are fine, the inflation escalator must be redefined to use headline CPI, not wages, as well as allowing negative adjustments. In addition the CPI calculation must be made for two points; the highest Social Security payment (approximately the existing CPI number) and the base payment. This prevents the penalty that lower-income retirees suffer from food and energy price escalations in Social Security. The retirement age must also be indexed to longevity based.

Unemployment payments for the first 26 weeks are an insurance program and should be maintained. All other unemployment provided by the government must be dropped. Persons should be free to contract privately for unemployment insurance beyond 26 weeks, but they should also pay for it. If a company wishes to offer this as a benefit and deduct from paychecks for it or absorb it, that's up to them.

We currently spend about 3/4 of a trillion dollars a year on military "adventures." Roughly half of this is spent protecting our access to foreign energy sources. The only way to end this is to decrease our need for foreign oil sources. The current cost of a barrel of imported oil, including the back-door subsidy of our military protection, exceeds $200/bbl. This cannot be sustained - our economy simply cannot afford it, especially since we can replace that oil for far less than $200.

Many Federal programs are worthless and are properly the function of the States, not the Federal Government. The Department of Education is one of these. Homeland Security is properly a function of the FBI, not a separate agency. Programs ranging from HUD to the FDA to the EPA can be slashed without causing a ripple.

The Hard Road Ahead

"Liquidate labor, liquidate stocks, liquidate farmers, liquidate real estate… it will purge the rottenness out of the system. High costs of living and high living will come down. People will work harder, live a more moral life. Values will be adjusted, and enterprising people will pick up from less competent people."

According to Herbert Hoover, that was the advice he was given by Andrew Mellon, then Treasury secretary, as America plunged into the Great Depression. However: Hoover refused the advice. Hoover, serving at the time as Commerce Secretary to Warren Harding following his election in 1920 during the worst of the deflationary depression which began under Wilson, counseled substantial intervention by the Federal Government to prevent business failures, prop up local governments through public works projects and similar "management" of the economic cycle.

Hoover also believed in "too big to fail" and "federal intervention" to bail out the bankrupt. President Harding refused his advice. A decade later Hoover was in position to actually act on his own counsel. Again Mellon advised the liquidation of bad debts - no matter where they were found, but Hoover refused to listen. Hoover and FDR engaged in what was (until 2007) unprecedented interference in the clearance of bad debts.

Mellon had good reason to give his advice as it had worked a decade earlier under Warren Harding; the sharp deflationary depression of 1920/21 was over in less than 18 months, and the economy again came roaring back. Mellonism wasn't undertaken in 1930. In fact, the Keynesian/Krugman position was employed in 1930 forward, leading to the expansion of the Depression and failed recovery for more than a decade.

The Mellon view was also ignored in 2000 when we decided to try to kick the can instead of face the fact that we had built infrastructure and false demand for which we could not pay. Forwarded by Greenspan, Bush and Congress, we enacted policy to "stimulate" through debt. No part of this was sustainable then and none of it is today. In order to sustain our current debt growth path we would need a compound GDP growth rate of more than 7% each and every year. But we haven't seen a nominal GDP growth rate for a single year over 7% since 1989.

The actual compound level of growth since 1990 forward is 4.86%, or more than two full percentage points short of what is necessary to make these debt levels sustainable. From 2000 forward, that growth rate has been 4.16%. As the 'new normal' kicks in, we may be lucky to see 3% GDP growth. At 4.16% GDP grows just 50.3% over a decade. At 7% it grows 97% over the same time period. That less-than-three-percent difference turns into a monstrous 50% deficit against debt growth over ten years.

This apparently doesn't matter to mainstream economic philosophers though their theories have proven bankrupt after decades of experiment. Dissimulation with claims that Clinton ran a "surplus" and thus his Keynesian proclivities were a viable option is intentionally false (he used the Social Security surplus to make his deficits "disappear") and masks the exponential growth in debt that occurred in the 1990s in business, financial and mortgage credit, which led to market bubbles.

After the meltdown of the Internet Bubble, government "stimulated" via borrow-and-spend from 2001 onward to try to pull the economy out of its nosedive. They failed and we never recovered in real terms or saw a 2% adjusted growth rate again. The debt bubble will hit the wall because we failed not only to put up actual 7% GDP increase numbers that were necessary, but we faked the numbers we did put up with government borrowing un-supported by actual output.

Our Banking Problem

Many argue the repeal of Glass-Steagall (allowing investment banks and commercial banks to merge), along with the Commodity Futures Modernization Act of 2000 (which deregulated OTC derivatives) lay at the foundation of the financial crisis. But in no case did a bank go bankrupt because they were using depositor money to speculate in the market. Some argue that the only solution is more regulation, but this crisis was caused by too much debt.

In fact, much of the blame for the ongoing crisis lies with Fannie Mae and Freddie Mac, two of the most regulated entities in the United States. Instead of protecting the average

American, institutions like the Federal Deposit Insurance Corporation and the Federal Reserve that have supported "Too Big to Fail" policies at banks have enriched the banking elite to the detriment of taxpayers, redistributing wealth from middle class and low class Americans to the CEOs of these banks.

We choose only how long we would like to pretend, and while doing so the balance shifts ever-more-unfavorably against us, as we watch the debt grow. In 2000 the total contraction in GDP necessary to clear the system was approximately 10%. Today, it is in excess of 30%. If we continue on the path we are now on through "one more cycle" we will reach the point that Ireland reached, where our banks will be proportionately demanding bailouts of over two and a half trillion dollars. Tellingly, the Irish demand for more bailouts as a result of their "stress tests" came just one year after the banks there were all declared "healthy" through the previous round of stress testing. We are in a similar situation.

Ireland has been told it must implement a property tax and must bail its banks to avert ruinous consequences. The "ruinous" consequences if the government refused to act would be to force private lenders to default on huge risks they made in pursuit of profit. Cease lending means the government and private industry would have to live within its means. Ireland's fate is that of Greece, and Spain, etc. and may soon be ours as well.

Iceland took the default route in 2010 and began to recover soon after its banks were forced to take huge losses. It appears that Iceland did the right thing in forcing default on private banks who couldn't repay bad debts, while we ballooned our debt with the TARP bailout. Iceland didn't rescue its banks. It couldn't afford to do it, so, they went bust. Iceland looked like it was on a path of permanent financial Armageddon. However, Iceland is in better financial shape than the rest of Europe today.

The price was severe, Icelandic income levels halved in real terms before resuming growth. But better to do that and grow again with lower unemployment than have your income levels halved through steadily increasing taxation with high unemployment and no light at the end of the tunnel for a decade or more. If we had been smart, we would have followed the Icelandic model. Three years after their banking sector collapsed, the Icelandic Government returned to the bond markets. They made bondholders accept their losses, and began economic growth in 2011. Meanwhile, the Irish are still slaves to the European Union, bleeding their taxpayers dry for the benefit of foreign bondholders.

We are now more than five years into our new Second Great Depression. When one removes artificial government stimulus, our real GDP growth rate has been negative since 2007. In 2008, the contraction was about 8%. The contraction in 2009 and 2010 was over 10% and about 7.5%, respectively. That is a 28% contraction top-to-bottom, which dramatically exceeds the economist definition of "Depression" as a 10% cumulative decline.

Excising our debt means refusing to pay the banking cartel. It means governments ceasing borrowing and running a primary surplus. It means government refusing to backstop bad debts and allowing those who are bankrupt to be recognized as bankrupt, forcing their bad debts into the open and liquidating them. It means spending less than you make personally and spending less than you tax as a government and actually paying down debts.

That which cannot be paid will not be paid. This is not a matter of opinion or politics, it is mathematics. Mathematics does not care about the political landscape or whether you are Democrat, Republican. If you have debt which exceeds assets, and production cannot possibly pay the debt, then some part of that debt will default.

44   Economic Propaganda

Perhaps the best way to know that your government is at war with its own people is that it is forced to lie about the economic numbers. Most of the major media outlets like AP, Reuters, etc are lying, spinning and propagandizing constantly to try to misrepresent the state of the economy. These lies are meant to reduce panic and keep the wheels from flying off the economic bus. The harm this misinformation causes you is in misdirecting your efforts to prepare your finances for the decade long economic tsunami about to hit us.

Biased, lying, propaganda laced reporting quickly reveals itself when you see one or more of the following happening:

1) Language to the effect of economic data coming in "better than expected".....
2) Comparing horrible numbers from one month with a little less horrible numbers the next Month and making it sound tremendously positive, when in reality both numbers are horrible (see unemployment figures).
3) Talk about "the recovery" in the past tense, when there is obviously no sign anywhere of a recovery in the economy, except when you use fuzzy math government numbers
4) Using meaningless and anecdotal evidence of things getting better for a small individual or company and extrapolating to say it is representative of the whole economy (green shoots).
5) Cherry picking data to make things look better than they really are.
6) Deliberately confusing cause with effect, for example, saying that higher gas prices are due a stronger global economy, rather than from Federal Reserve policies and QEn.
7) Using adjectives and verbs like "surging", "strong" "improving", etc, when there no evidence of any such occurrences.
8) Calling a small increase in something a large increase.
9) Falsely claiming an improving trend is occurring with data that is either false or of short duration and without meaning or predictive value. A favorite is the "three out of four" trick, where news that unemployment claims have fallen in "three out of the last four weeks" is followed by a claim that this is the start of a new trend.
10) Ignoring news or data that sounds bad, while overemphasizing any news or data that looks even a little good or encouraging.
11) Talk about how a problem is "stabilizing", when in reality it is getting worse.
12) Incessantly referring to global warming or the weather as the cause of bad economic numbers.

The lies in the media today are everywhere, about everything from immigration impact to social upheaval to financial reporting. A great check on economic reality is to follow the readjusted statistics published by economist John Williams on **www.shadowstats.com**.

The Shadowstats record for inflation for example (see below) is much more in line with citizens everyday experience than the supposedly near zero inflation numbers being touted by the government. When gold prices skyrocket from $1000 an ounce to $1500 an ounce at this writing and head for the moon, you know in your heart that inflation isn't running at 2% or less. It is closer to 10%, which halves the value of your money in seven years.

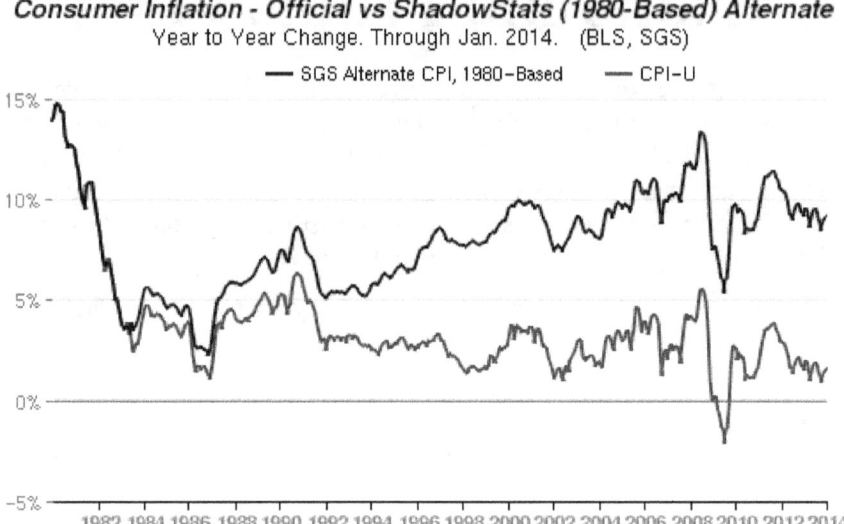

Consumer Inflation - Official vs ShadowStats (1980-Based) Alternate
Year to Year Change. Through Jan. 2014.   (BLS, SGS)

— SGS Alternate CPI, 1980-Based   — CPI-U

Published: Feb. 20, 2014   *shadowstats.com*

The Shadowstats unemployment figures also show just how bad our Great Recession has been, as shown below. Official unemployment figures have been designed to keep the number under 10% for psychological reasons, but using traditional means of calculation show that we are well into or above Great depression era numbers.

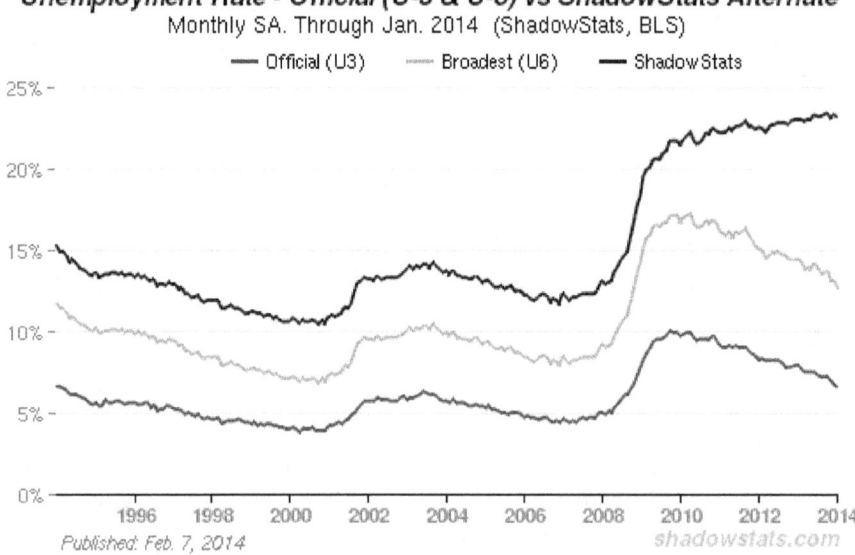

Unemployment Rate - Official (U-3 & U-6) vs ShadowStats Alternate
Monthly SA. Through Jan. 2014 (ShadowStats, BLS)

— Official (U3)   ····· Broadest (U6)   — ShadowStats

Published: Feb. 7, 2014   *shadowstats.com*

Another number to track that isn't as subject to distortion that confirms the Shadowstats trends is the total percentage of Americans employed, the participation rate, which is at its lowest since 1984. See following chapter.

With numbers skewed this far, it is clear you can't believe any economic numbers coming out of the bureaucracy. This matters greatly to individuals who are trying to plan their investment strategies for a better future for themselves and their families. If the dollar is sound, employment is rebounding and inflation is low, you should invest in American companies. If we are falling apart, as suggested by the Shadowstats numbers, you should be buying gold and converting your money to real assets or moving it out of the country.

Who are you going to believe?

45   Reliable Economic Statistics

It is clear the U.S. government is now in the game of fudging primary inflation, unemployment and GDP statistics as shown by the statistics from Shadowstats.com. This allows bureaucrats to perpetually present arguments that "green shoots" are growing when in fact the economic situation has remained quite dismal and will continue to do so given our structural deficit problems, adverse demographic trends, and the Eurosocialist policies of our leadership.

To get around this problem, we have created a permanent web page of non-fudged economic statistics to supplement and extend those from Shadowstats.com. These charts are proxies for where the nation's economy is headed, but without manipulation by politicians. If you are tired of hearing Orwellian double speak from the Ministry of Disinformation, bookmark this page: http://ww.futurnamics.com/slfed.php

We start with the historical percentage of Government Outlays to GDP. Other than the war time peak of WWII, we are at historic highs.

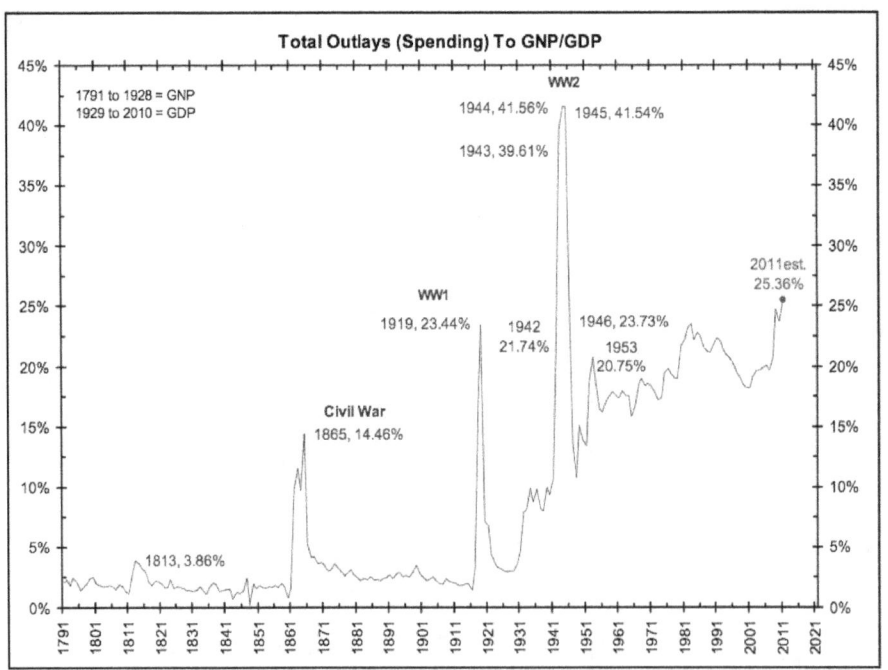

The government is like a steam engine without a governor, a freight train headed off the rails at high speed.

Next, the Labor Participation rate, the cold hard number of how many people are working as a percentage of the population. Until this number inflects in a positive direction, there is no way the employment situation is improving no matter what you hear. As I write this, it looks pretty grim, we are still in free fall to levels not seen since the Carter malaise years in the late 70s. This shows the complete collapse of Keynesian economic theory - continuous pump priming should mean we are swimming in jobs.

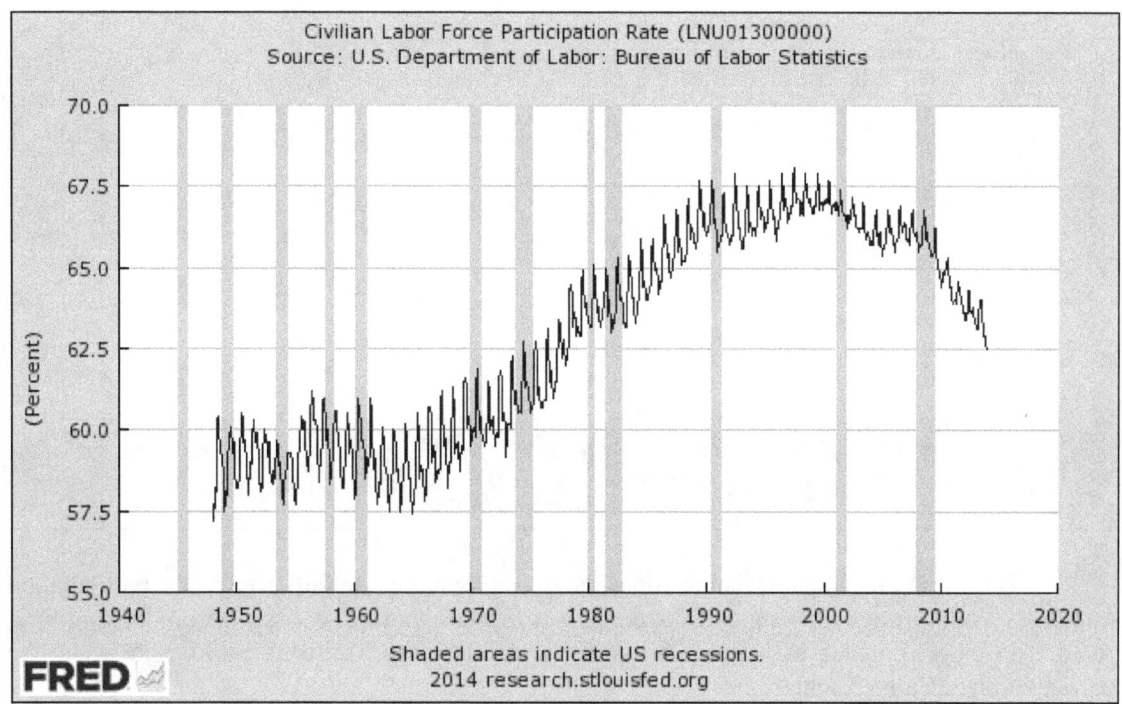

A better gauge of unemployment than what is the traditionally reported U3 number is the U6 number (Total unemployed, plus all marginally attached workers plus total employed part time for economic reasons) shown following. We aren't even going to show a graph of U3 because it is distorted propaganda of the political class. While improving somewhat from the crash of 2008, U6 is still in nosebleed territory. Moreover, it appears much of any positive change is due to engineers becoming burger flippers and displaced elderly being forced back into the work force. There are also questions raised by John Williams of ShadowStats.com whether the tailoff after 2008 actually exists or is more disinformation.

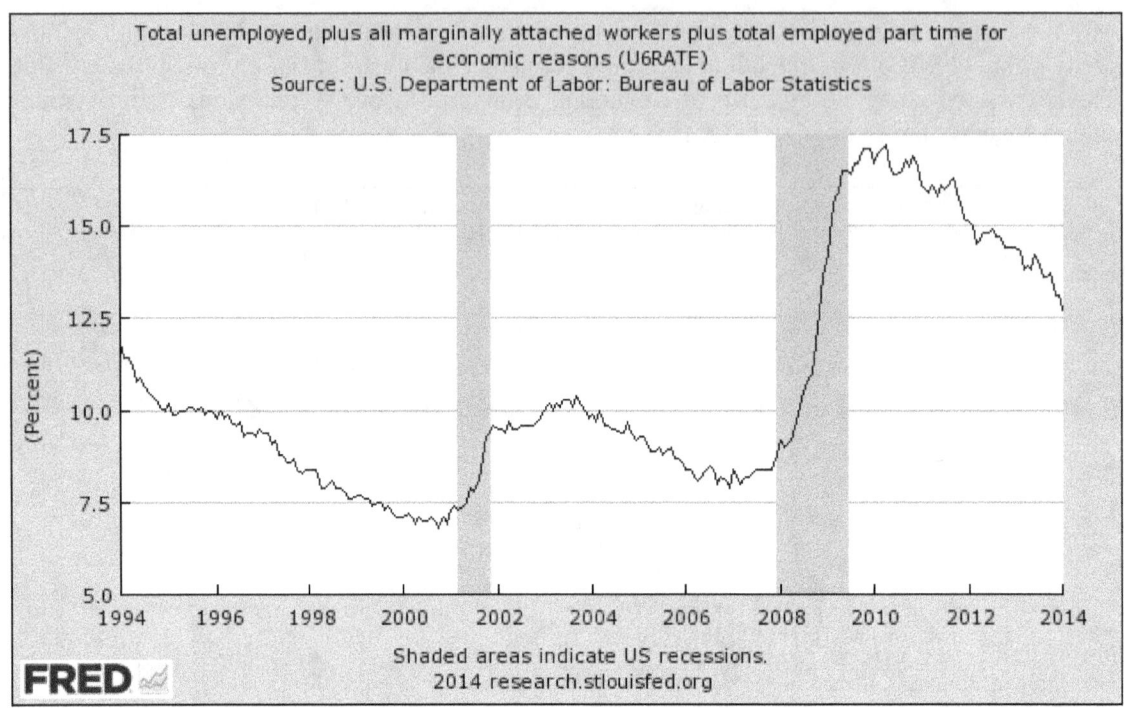

Total unemployed, plus all marginally attached workers plus total employed part time for economic reasons (U6RATE)
Source: U.S. Department of Labor: Bureau of Labor Statistics

Shaded areas indicate US recessions.
2014 research.stlouisfed.org

    The glaring discrepancy is how does the unemployment rate fall, even as the participation rate falls? Well through the magic of govthink, it is because those discouraged from looking for a job are no longer counted as jobless. We would apparently reach zero unemployment when the participation rate also reached zero.

    Another scary chart is the following Labor Force Participation Rate of men. They obviously have been dropping out of the labor force for quite a while. They are "Going Galt" [also see my book *Going Galt: Surviving Economic Armageddon*]. While some of these men have decided to take over home duties or simply go on the dole, one suspects a sizeable number have also found their way into underground employment. Obviously men have clued in that either 1) it is easier to take welfare, or 2) the economic game is stacked against them. It may be an even broader combination of factors as the socialist state tends to sap the will of honest men at many levels.

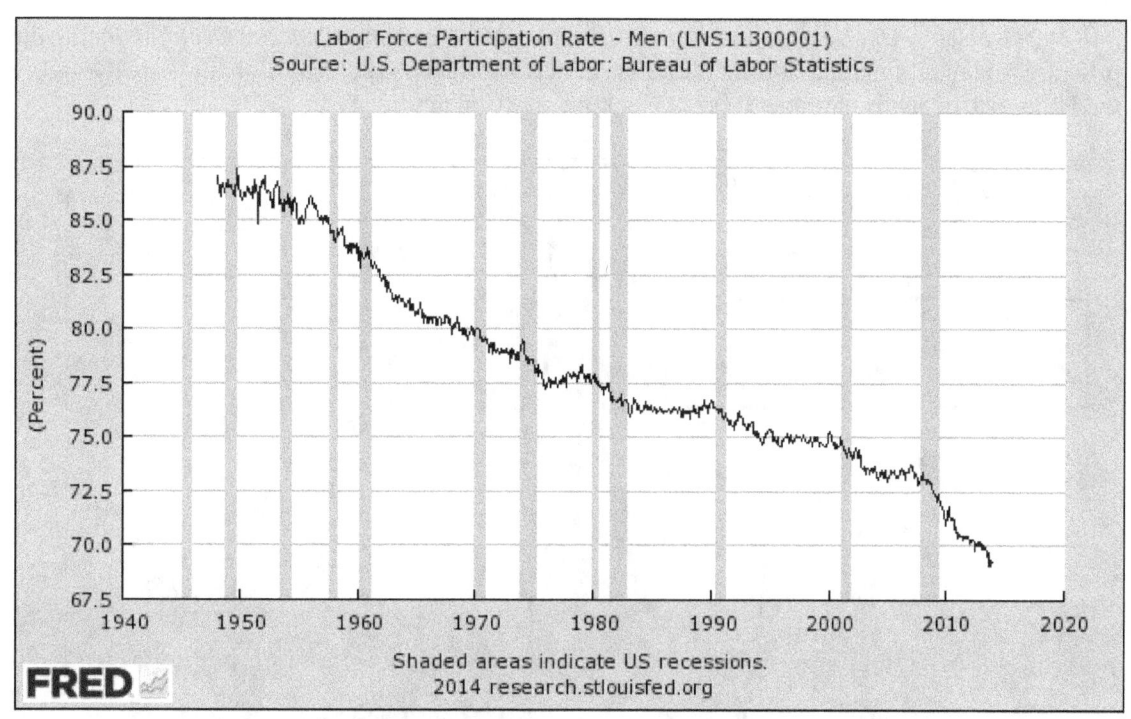

But surely, the GDP is growing smartly. Apparently it is doing so using a new form of perpetual motion free energy, since our gasoline consumption is in a nosedive (not explained by increased fuel efficiency). This portends another recession, not a recovery.

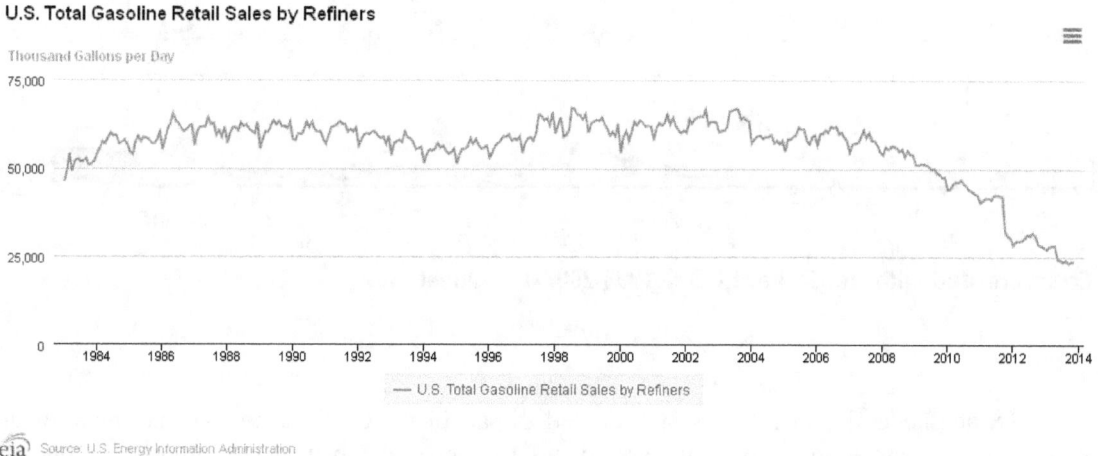

The Baltic Dry Index is another well known proxy for global economic activity, being the price of container shipping and therefore an indicator of economic activity both globally and in the US which depends on trade. It is also looking pretty anemic.

Chart created with NeoTicker EOD © 1998-2007 TickQuest Inc.

Since Federal Expenditures are counted as part of the GDP, it is clear that much of the green shoots we are supposedly seeing are due not to improved private sector production, but to a ramp up of government debt – i.e. bread and circuses. Total Public debt continues to grow exponentially, meaning absolutely nothing has been done to repair past problems much less look forward to future liabilities.

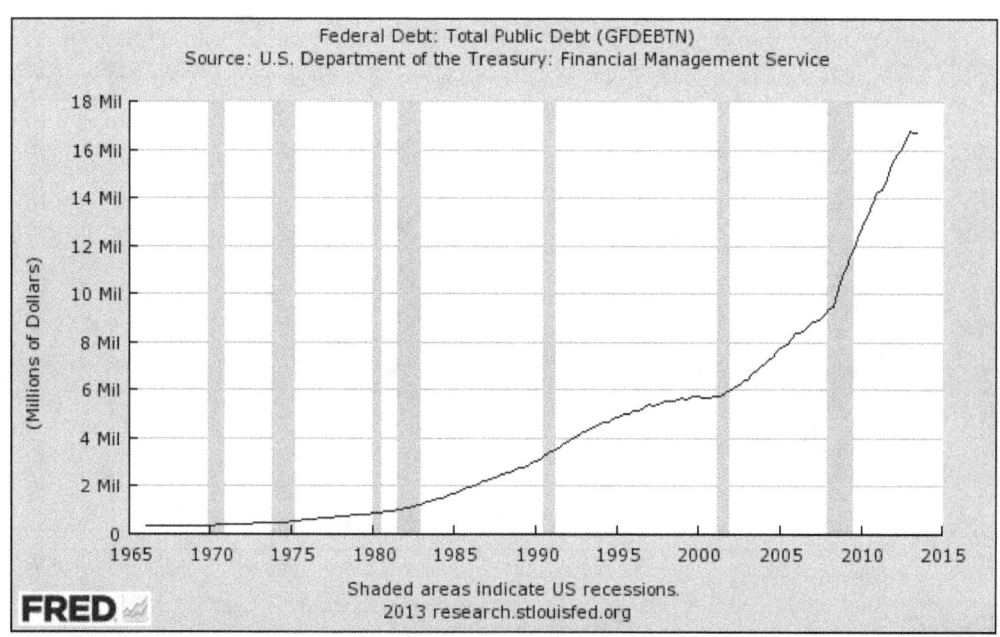

When anyone tells you we are not at risk of inflation, show them the following two charts on the money stock and money velocity.

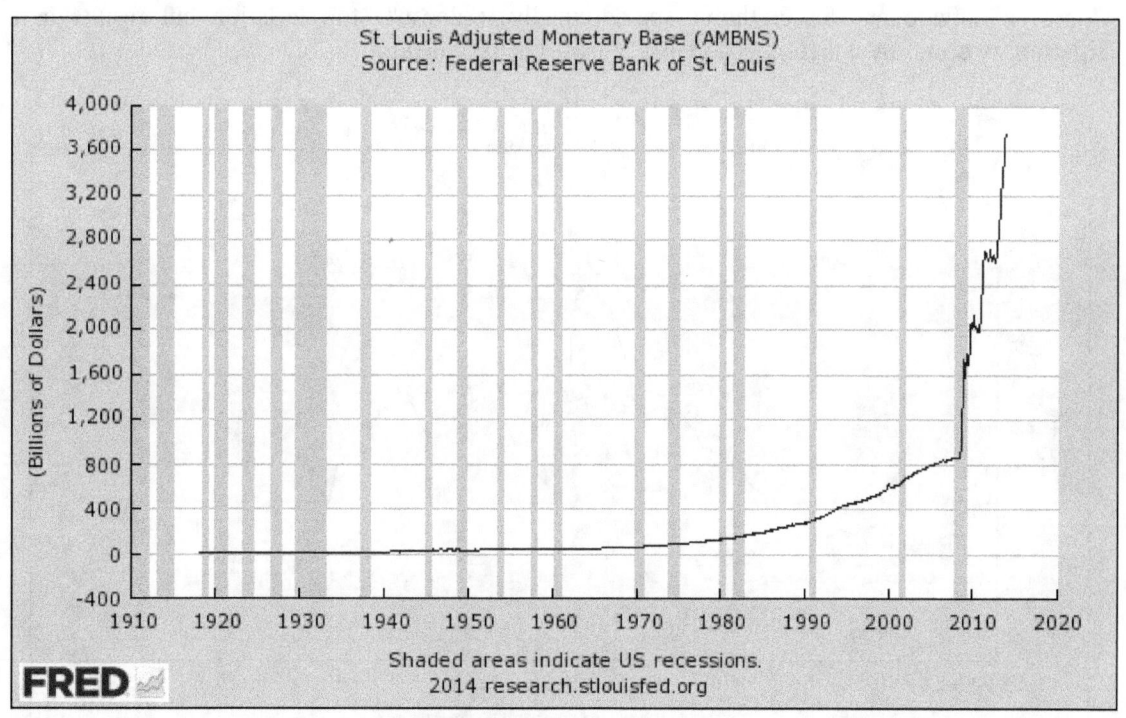

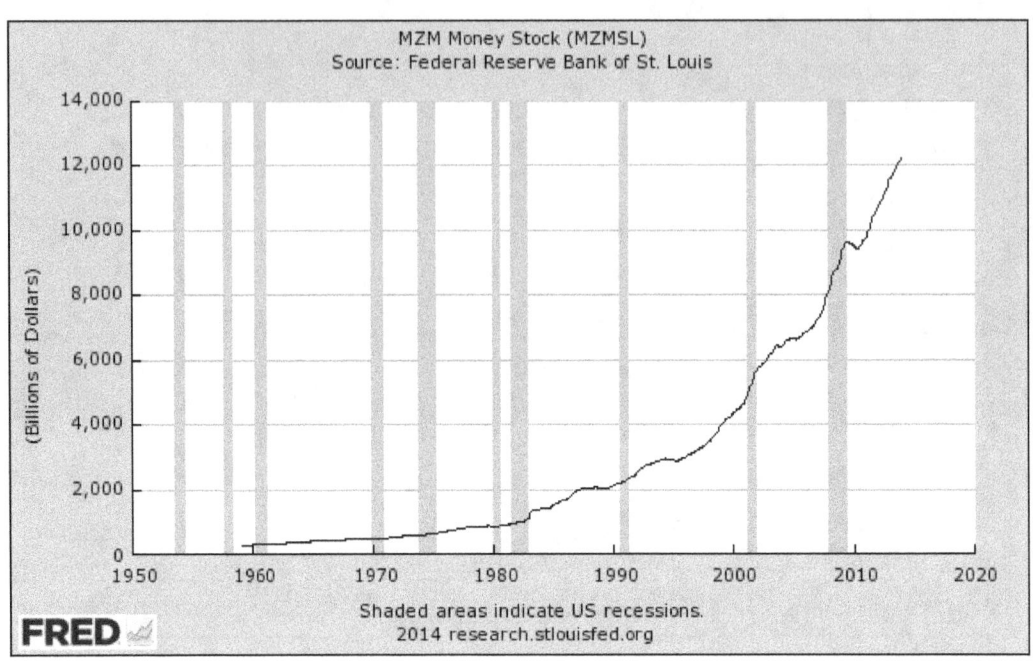

The real kick though is the velocity of money (the number of times a dollar has turned over during a year), has taken a dive. It means people are afraid to make economic transactions. This is a deflationary force, though paradoxically it doesn't stop inflation but results in a Biflationary economy which is in collapse. Keynes is truly dead.

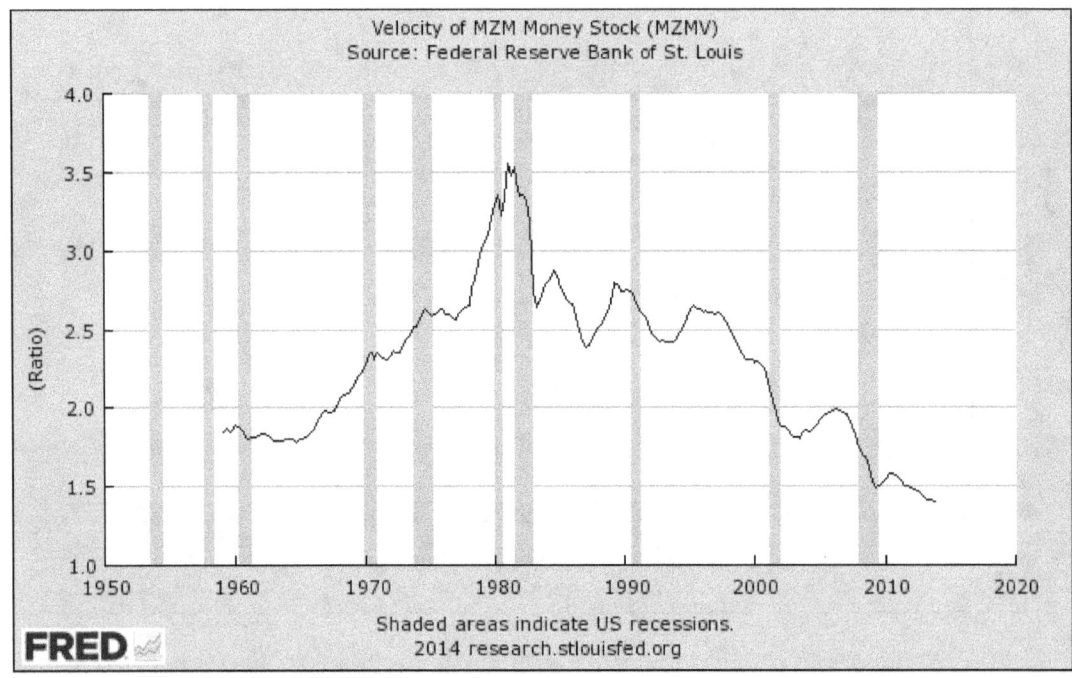

Next we add the Real Disposable Income, which after a brief recovery from the shocks of 2008 have now flatlined. Maybe it feels like we are in a claustrophobic Depression, because we are. The little guy really can't get ahead.

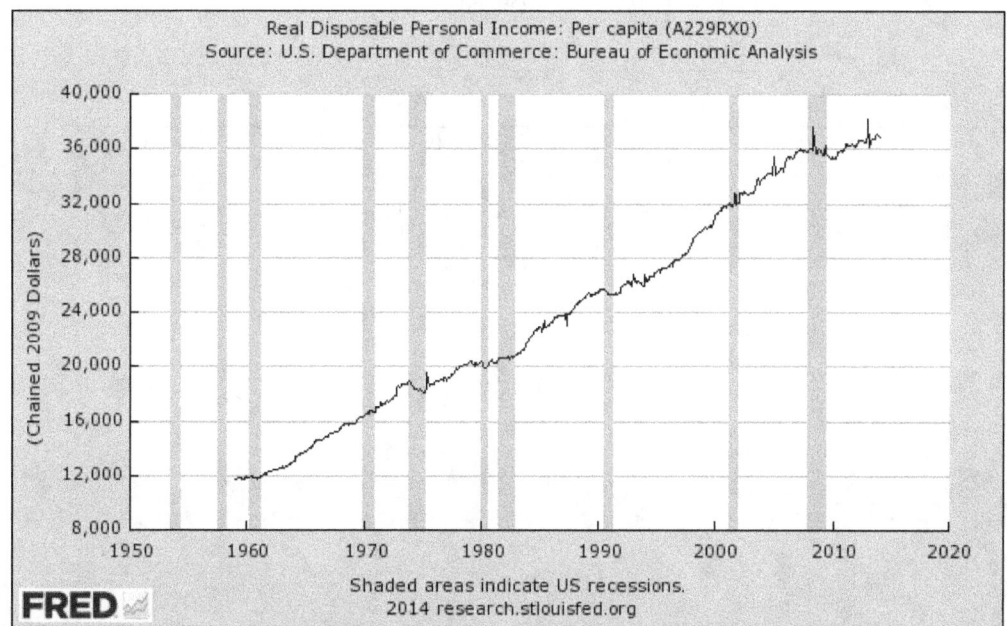

Owners' Equity in Household Real Estate - Net Worth - Balance Sheet of Households and Nonprofit Organizations (OEHRENWBSHNO): While this has rebounded some, another dip is already in progress. The middle class continues to be crushed by the drop in home prices.

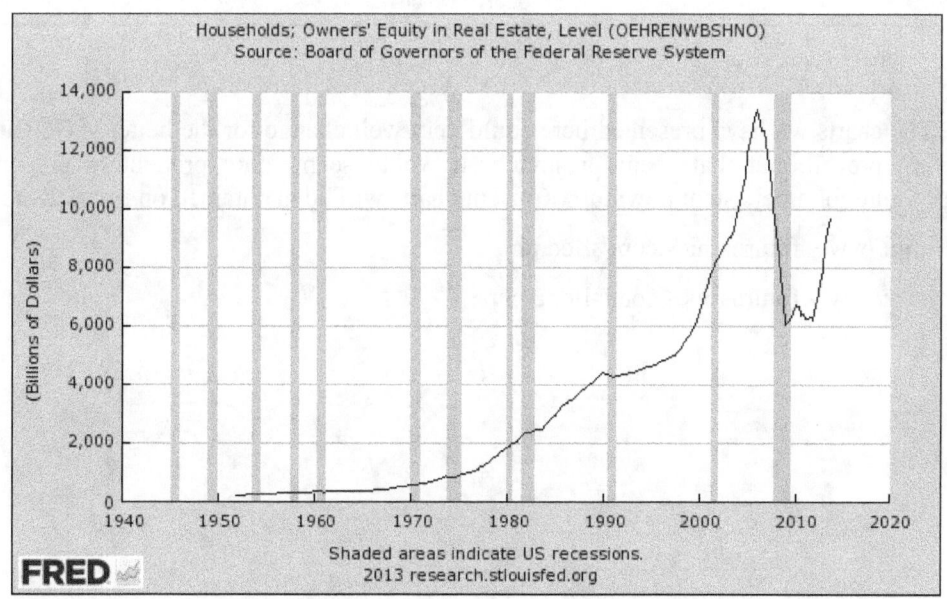

Finally we present: Compensation of Employees: Wages & Salary Accruals (WASCUR)/Gross Domestic Product, 1 Decimal (GDP). Wages and salaries as a percentage of GDP are being crushed. No more middle class. No more middle class. How do you have a recovery when per capita income hasn't increased?

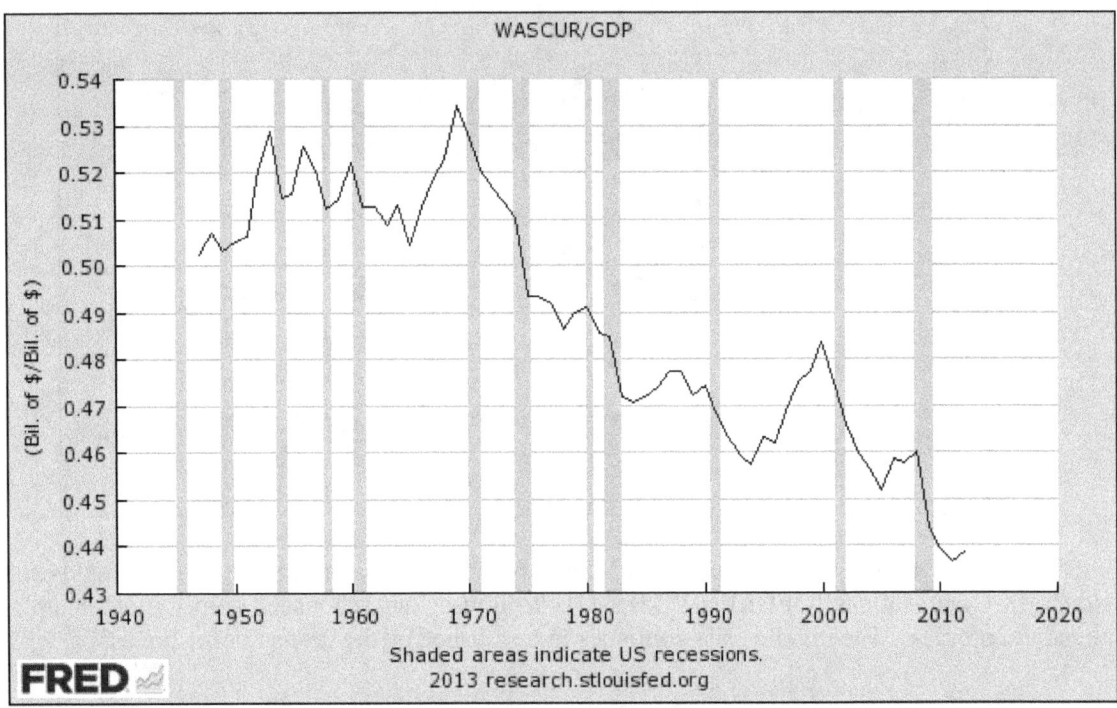

The charts we have presented here could very well change for the better if Hopeium and Changeium prevail, but that seems a stretch. It would seem more prudent to prepare your financial future for a persistent downturn. Current charts will be maintained on my website at:

http://www.futurnamics.com/slfed.php

http://www.futurnamics.com/slfed2.php

Employment

46   Outsourcing Our Future

Most of the Twentieth Century, America ruled not only its own destiny, but the destiny of the world. We really were better than everyone else; harder working with great natural resources and a free populace. We have squandered much of that inheritance over the last decades, becoming an entitlement state little different than the petty European powers we once ridiculed. Even worse, we have outsourced our jobs and industry to foreign workers and become a debtor nation groveling at the knees of the Chinese. Given this environment, you will need to adapt your personal financial position to avoid the possibility of being outsourced, if your job hasn't already left.

For the last century America used its balance sheet to affect its policies around the world. American hegemony began during World War I under Woodrow Wilson when New York banks, guided by the House of Morgan, financed allied powers against the Kaiser's Germany.

The Bretton Woods monetary system in 1945 created the International Monetary Fund dominated by the United States, which became the financial powerhouse of the world. The IMF became an extension of the U. S. financial system. In 1971 the United States defaulted on its obligations to the IMF and the world by unilaterally removing the dollar from gold convertibility, but established the paper dollar as the world reserve currency.

Ironically, by establishing ourselves as the reserve world fiat currency, America's dominance is now on the brink of collapse. A weak dollar destroys our reserve status, putting us at the mercy of stronger currencies. Financing the war with Iraq and Afghanistan didn't help, but those expenses will wind down. Unremedied is the huge domestic debt, much of which was financed by foreign purchases of treasuries. This debt imbalance has effectively outsourced jobs and productive wealth to nations willing to work as slave labor. The bubble creating policies of the Federal Reserve and Congress set the stage for the 2008 financial collapse and future financial strife as Americans are forced to retreat from their spending binge.

Outsourcing Our Wealth

China is well on its way to replacing the U. S. as the leading financial power in the world. China's $2.7 trillion International Investment Fund, dwarfs the IMF balance sheet which 240 billion Special Drawing Rights (SDRs), is only equivalent to about $370 billion. China even stepped into the EU crisis with an offer of aid.

The United States is on its way to looking like a third world country financially. Total debt stood at over $18 trillion in 2014 versus a $15.5 trillion GDP with operating deficits in the U. S near $1 trillion for half a decade. None of this recognizes a $30 trillion unfunded liability for the Social Security Trust Fund, similar unfunded liabilities for Medicare, nor the cost of the new health care bill known as Obamacare.

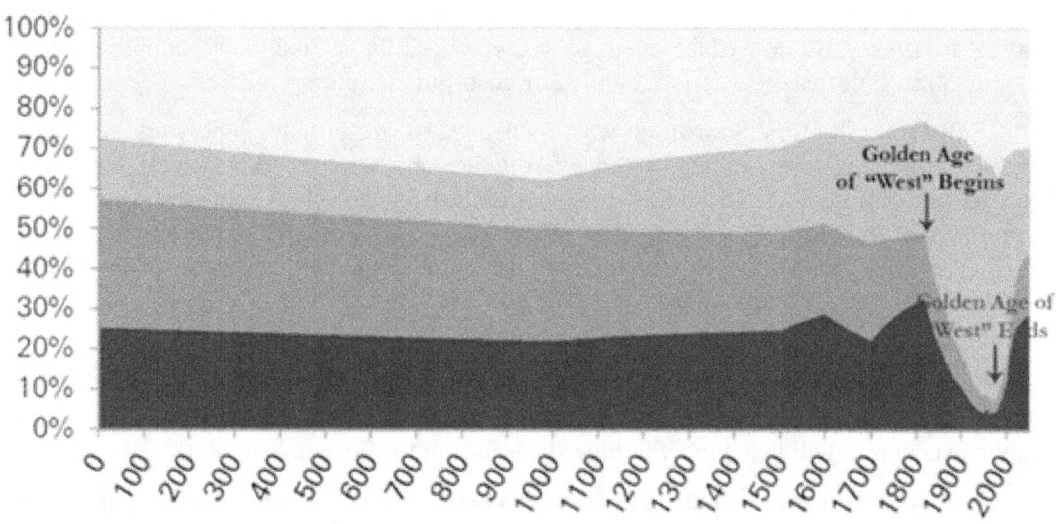

Share of total global GDP (1 – 2050E)

% Rest of World   % North America, Europe, Japan   % India   % China

Over the years each time U. S. banks and the IMF provided funding for a failing government they extracted promises. Those promises without exception included tax increases, reduction of public expenditures on operating budgets and entitlements, open markets requirements and currency stabilization, usually linked to some currency peg. For lenders, being repaid in worthless fiat currency is as big a risk as not being repaid at all.

While China teases bailouts for the Eurozone, the EU is extracting those same commitments from its own client states. This implicitly sets China up as the lender of last resort. It also puts the United States in line for the same types of social upheaval as basket cases like Greece and Spain. We have outsourced our financial freedom to China and the International Monetary Fund.

Outsourcing Our Jobs

The job market is changing, and not just manufacturing jobs are disappearing. Even highly-paid workers will need to re-tool their skills. Employment growth has stopped, or even declined, among many middle- class jobs that are high wage and don't require a college degree. The movement of jobs to countries where labor is cheap, plus development of new technologies, will mean fewer jobs and social strife at all levels.

Traditional middle-class and upper-middle-class jobs like general managers and middle-management jobs have been in decline and will decline further. Workers making $40,000 to $80,000 a year constitute the bulk of labor costs for many companies, and these middle class workers are on the chopping block. Companies are finding ways to reduce the number of people in those areas, and change the jobs to make them simpler, to reduce the skill that is required.

Radiologists are an example of a well-paid worker that could be hit by technology and cheap global labor. There will be fewer radiologists in the U.S. because there is little reason for a radiologist to be in the same place as a patient. A radiologist can read an X-ray as easily in India as she can in Indiana. A lot of medical diagnostic work will be done overseas. You can have the initial diagnostic done elsewhere, and have a domestic supervising physician. There is enormous incentive to find ways to reduce medical costs especially as the baby boomers age. The internationalization of medical services will slow costs but also export jobs.

Software will also cut down on workers needed to sort through paperwork, such as legal documents, which can be digitized, read by software and catalogued. A lot of legal work is subject to automation, and that will affect opportunities for lawyers. Computer programming is also on the road to becoming a commodity. What used to be good programming jobs, or routine legal work, are things that are easily broken into parts, and done in other places. In short, much of the workforce is ripe for elimination.

State governments within the United States are also approaching default. California is potentially the largest but New York might be first. Illinois, Michigan and New Jersey are also on the verge. The Federal Government's balance sheet is in no shape for bailouts and it is unlikely a Republican congress will take kindly to blue states asking for financial support.

The irony is that the same banks that launched a century of ever expanding leverage and were complicit with government in bringing on the 2008 collapse are now the biggest beneficiaries of government policies to ameliorate their pain. In parallel, the accelerating unraveling of the European debt crisis looks like a replay of Argentina after 2000 and a prelude of what will occur here in the United States over the next ten years. Progressive politicians have long held up European socialism as our model and now they will get what they wish for, America transformed into an economic basket case.

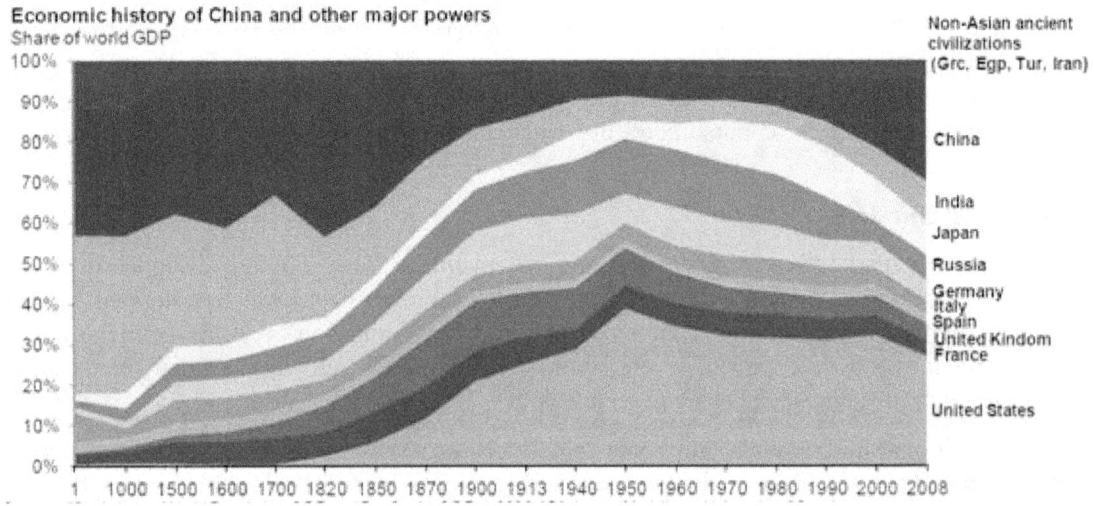

As the Federal Reserve continues to leverage its balance sheet, it will only take a singular moment of fear to lead to panic sending interest rates higher, or a push of the button on a computer keyboard for capital, now leaving the United States at a modest pace, to flee. When the currency raiders come over the ramparts there will be no defense but to raise interest rates. And as interest rates rise massive default is close at hand. Then the question becomes what concessions do we make and how much will we have to pay for China's International Investment Fund to buy our debt.

47 Structural Lost Jobs

There's been continuing debate about the "hollowing out" of America's middle class. A study by the National Employment Law Project (NELP) which breaks down jobs into lower/ middle/and high-wage groups utilizing median incomes confirms the disturbing trend. The study found that from early 2008 through first quarter 2012:

- "High-wage" occupations accounted for 19% of the jobs lost during the Great Recession and 20% of the jobs gained during the recovery.
- "Mid-wage" occupations suffered 60% of job losses during the recession, but only 22% of the growth during the recovery.
- "Low-wage" occupations accounted for 21% of the losses and a whopping 58% of the growth.

In short, NELP found what American wage earners already know: Middle class jobs have shrunk in quantity and quality and a majority of the jobs created during the recession a cluster in low-income trades like retail and food services. Going forward beyond the 2012 study, the situation will not improve; it is a structural jobs problem.

America's deficit in good jobs continues and will likely get worse. Policymakers have been focused on getting U.S. employment back to where it was before the recession, but job quality is emerging as a second front in the struggling economy. These trends are not just the result of the immediate recession, several long term factors also contribute to the hollowing of the middle class:

- Globalization, which has sent manufacturing jobs overseas.
- Robotization of even skilled jobs (such as the legal profession).
- The bursting of the housing market, which crushed the construction industry.
- Deep cuts in state and local governments, which accounts for 485,000 mainly mid-wage jobs lost since February 2011.

Labor-intensive manufacturing is never going to return to the US. Labor intensive work never returned to the cottage after it left for the factories due to the rise of the city state. It never returned to Europe after it left for the UK due to the industrial revolution. It never returned to the UK after manufacturing left for the US due to mass production and Ford's assembly line. The following chart shows the Civilian employment-population ratio, % (left), and the number of US citizens employed in manufacturing, in thousands (right), both since 1975.

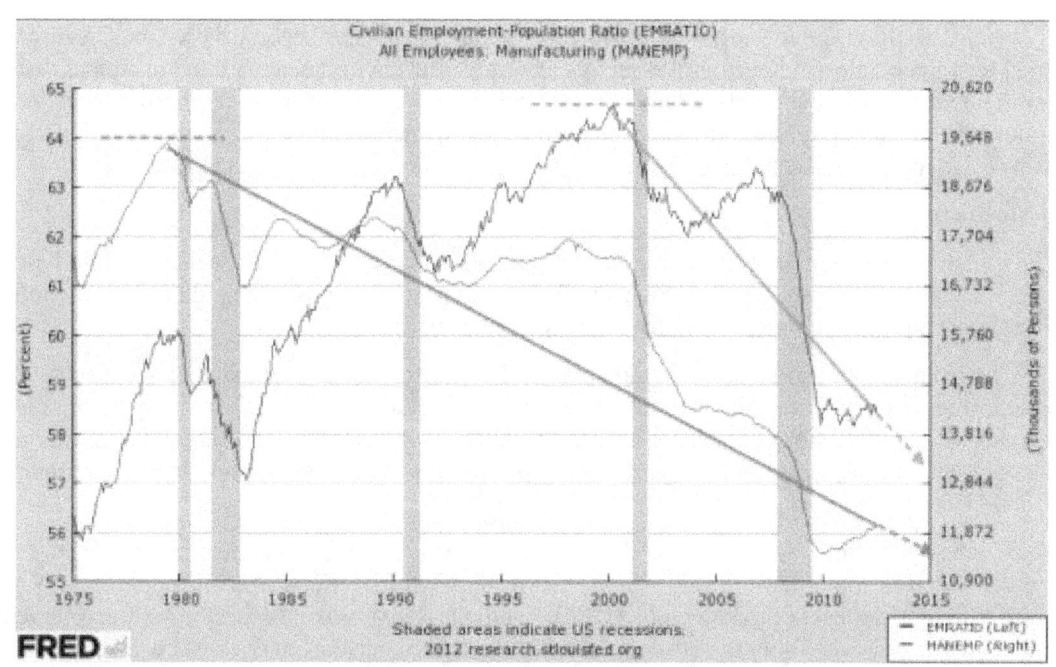

The trends are obvious: the United States has been shedding manufacturing jobs since 1979, and in 1999 this began to have a strong effect on the employment-population ratio. It is only logical to adapt expectations for lower employment. As shown following, the decline in labor's share of the GDP (gross domestic product) is sobering:

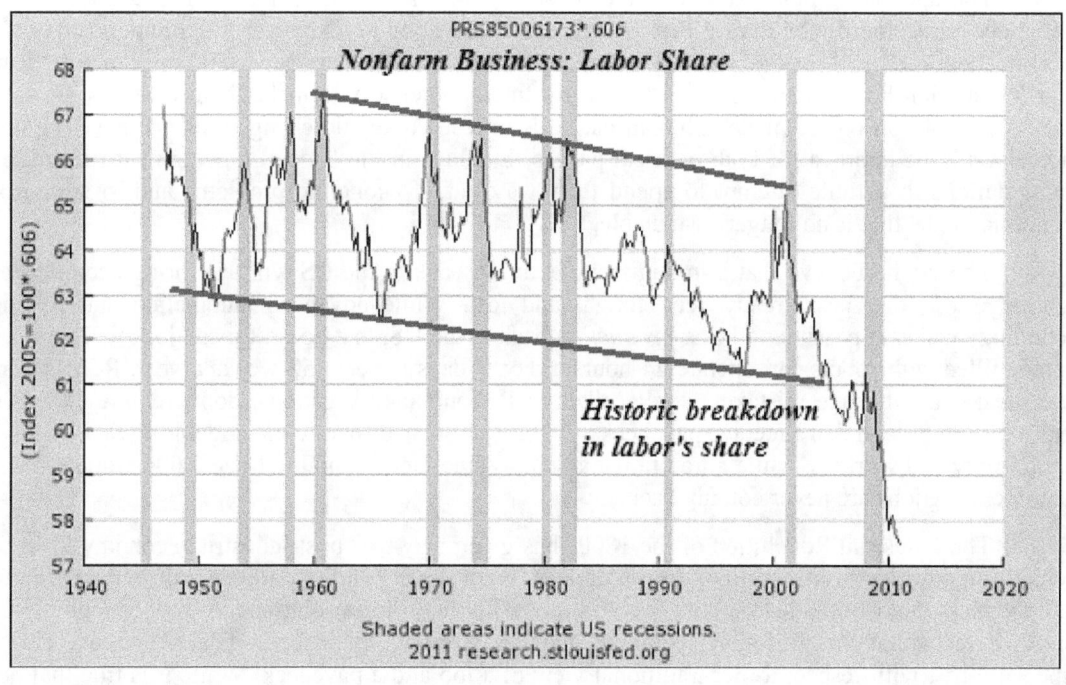

This atypical Great Recession has forced business owners to become savvy: businesses have learned how to operate--and even thrive--in this dry economic environment, and the main tool that has allowed them to do so is cost-cutting. Unfortunately for the labor market, these cost-reduction techniques are sticking, and for the time being business owners (particularly manufacturers) see no reason to add more human employees when they can purchase robots at a cheaper rate.

Job Mechanization

Just as troubling as outsourcing is for both the US economy and specifically middle-class laborers: Robotics. In coming years, robots will not only usurp the jobs of manufacturers, but jobs of any automated, repetitive process (burger flippers, even construction).

As old line manufacturers re-tool plants (Kroger) and new manufacturers conceive fresh production processes (Tesla), the marked characteristic of today's US manufacturing paradigm is the preference for robotic labor over manual labor. The benefits are obvious: 24/7 production, lower costs of "labor," and more precise assembly. Robots can produce faster, better, and cleaner than humans can, and US employment data is indicative of this trend.

Many jobs lost over the past decades have been due to out-sourcing, but as US-based companies such as Intuitive Surgical ($ISRG), Mako Surgical ($MAKO), AeroVironment ($AVAV), iRobot ($IRBT), Adept Technology ($ADEP), and the likes make strides in surgery, defense, manufacturing, and everything in between, jobs that were once outsourced overseas will come back to the US. The bad news is those jobs will be completed robotically because the US labor force has been regulated out of competitiveness. For dislocated US employees, jobs will not be returning even if we see more "Made in America" stickers on products because few Americans will be involved in the production of those goods. It is simply too expensive and risky to hire American. The concept of the Western economy within the world economy needs to be re-thought.

The underlying political and financial assumption of the Status Quo is that technology will ultimately create more jobs than it destroys. There are reasons to dispute that assumption. At *some* point in the future, most manufacturing and most services *will* be automated. 300 million Americans (and 300 million Europeans) are going to have to find another way to make themselves useful to the other 6,000 million on the planet. Human nature is to resist dramatic change until we have no other choice. With the approval of both political parties, Luddites in the Federal Government run trillion-dollar deficits in a futile attempt to spend their way out of economic problems and to sustain an economic model that is no longer sustainable.

Those who believe that bringing manufacturing back to the US will also bring back jobs are fighting a war that has already been fought and lost. While advanced automation and robotics technology makes it possible to bring *production* back to the US, that doesn't mean jobs will return. A factory filled with robots can operate 24 hours a day, 7 days a week, 52 weeks a year. Robots don't take breaks, don't make mistakes, don't call in sick, don't take vacations, don't require expensive health insurance, and don't receive paychecks. A fully automated robotic manufacturing facility might require only 100 workers, while a traditional assembly line facility might utilize 3,000 workers. Most manufacturing jobs are never coming back.

The Industrial Revolution of the 1800s has given way to a post-industrial economy in which technology now destroys more jobs than it creates. Even if we find the political will to deal with the mathematics of our unfunded deficits, we will never find long-term solutions to our economic issues until we recognize the profound economic changes wrought by technological advances. This is especially true with respect to our traditional view of a job and a paycheck. While it is true that new opportunities will always exist, these opportunities may not be as plentiful as the jobs of the past once were. And these opportunities will generally require more advanced skills than many of the jobs of the past.

Where Will The Losses Come?

Technology has fundamentally changed the nature of paying work, and it is also one of the major economic issues of our time. The low-hanging fruit of technology may have already been plucked. Take healthcare as an example: antibiotics and vaccines virtually eliminated many diseases at a very low cost per dose (though some diseases are coming back due to unvaccinated host populations and bacterial adaptation).

The Internet is destroying vast income streams that once supported tens of thousands of jobs in industries from finance to music. Craigslist has gutted the once-immense income stream from newspapers, and web-based marketing has shredded print-media advert page counts. Global competition and pressure to maintain profits and margins relentlessly drive enterprises to slash payrolls.

Software is leading the next-generation industrial revolution, automating many tasks that were considered "safe" from automation. This includes securities trading, accounting and tax preparation for the majority of tax situations. The law, academia and government are also not immune.

Many marketing, administrative, accounting, and IT jobs can be outsourced or automated. Retail enterprises already tailor special offers directly to individual customers by automated data mining from reward programs without an expensive ad budget or a huge marketing department. Most of the advertising you see while you surf the Web is tailored to things you might be interested in buying by algorithms. Huge numbers of marketing professionals are just not needed.

'Lean accounting' streamlines processes and eliminates inefficiencies through greater use of technology, but results in significant reduction in the number of accountants and accounting clerks. In Information Technology, computers have become a plug and play commodity not needing specialists. That reduces job opportunities for programmers and IT support. The net result of all these examples is not job creation. It's job destruction.

Many government jobs are also technologically obsolete. We don't really need daily postal mail service in an electronic world. We do not need as many tanks and fighter jets as we used to, now that we have remote-controlled drones to do many of the jobs required. And with the availability of these drones, we might not need as many aircraft carriers, ships, or military personnel either.

Technology As Job Destroyer

The build-out of a new technology inevitably creates a large but temporary number of jobs. The construction of the railroads created a jobs boom that soon disappeared in a financial bust as rail was over-built and profits plunged for extraneous or duplicate lines. Telephony and telecom followed similar arcs, as did the build-out of the Internet infrastructure.

Technology maturation then leads to diminishing return on labor as incremental advances in productivity are capital-intensive. Semiconductor manufacturing is a good example; fabrication facilities (fabs) cost upwards of $2 billion each even as the number of workers need to operate the fab declines. Profit margins on many high-technology products are razor-thin, flat-screen displays being a prime example, and diminishing margins further pressure labor costs.

The rising costs of taxes, benefits and regulations have squeezed small businesses. In response, many small companies rely on automation and software to perform tasks that until recently required a human worker. Those small businesses that cannot prosper via technology or outsourcing are going under, and the risks posed by ever-higher costs have raised entry barriers to starting a small business. Many of the Blue collar jobs that do exist have been shipped overseas where hourly rates are low and working conditions akin to those at the beginning of the industrial revolution. Lack of worker safety, pollution controls, benefits and any number of other issues will persist and perhaps migrate to our shores. These trends are visible in this chart:

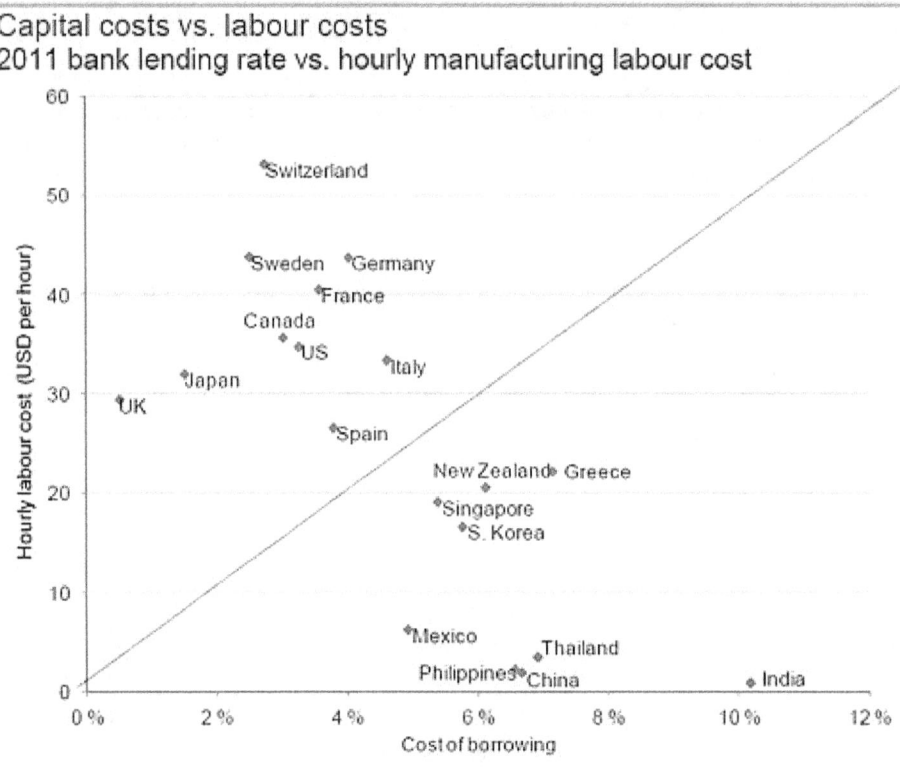

Capital costs vs. labour costs
2011 bank lending rate vs. hourly manufacturing labour cost

American workers are competing against countries where borrowing costs are relatively high, but workers wages are substantially lower. Our government and Federal reserve have spent a great amount of effort trying to convince us that low interest rates are the path to success, but once you are effectively at zero interest rate, and businesses still don't want to hire, then you have to recognize there is a real structural problem of over regulation and taxation that is choking businesses' willingness to create jobs.

As a financial survivalist, you can look at this as devastating news, or as a signpost telling you which way you need to go to survive. If employers are not hiring, then you, your family members and your children have three options in the future:

- Go on welfare
- Upgrade your skills to those that fit a diminished job market
- Create your own job by starting a business that relies on mechanization

Preservation of one's dignity suggests a clear preference towards self employment, with diversification. The next chart shows the decline of businesses with employees. You can cry over it, or use it to see where the future is.

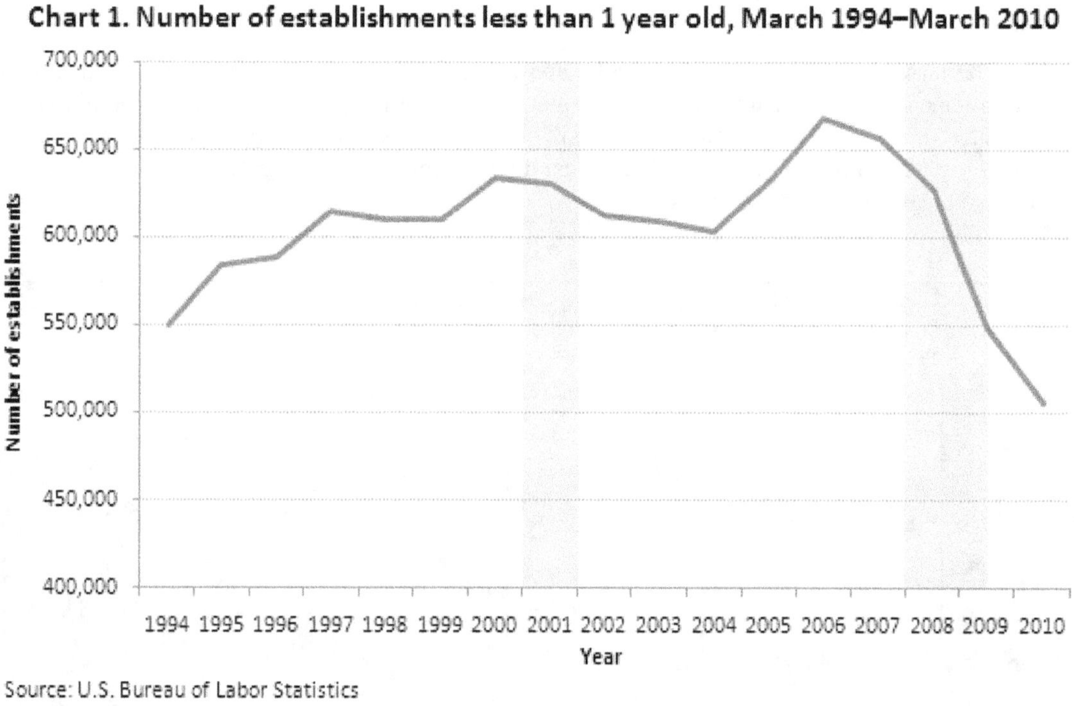

Chart 1. Number of establishments less than 1 year old, March 1994–March 2010

Source: U.S. Bureau of Labor Statistics

The array of web-based tools available to entrepreneurs now is astonishing. Why take on the risks of hiring people when you can do the work yourself with low-cost web tools and software? For many small enterprises, that is the only way to survive.

Advanced societies face a dilemma that cannot be solved by more debt or more technology: how to distribute not just the output of the economy, but the work and responsibility so that everyone has an opportunity to contribute and earn their keep.

As we let go of old methodologies, whether in the private sector or government, huge numbers of jobs will disappear. Free-market capitalism is not going to bring back these lost jobs, in fact coupled with high taxes and regulations that discourage job creation, capitalism hastens the adoption of job killing robotization and outsourcing. Thanks to technology, society is capable of meeting basic human needs (food, clothing, shelter, transportation) with far fewer workers percentage-wise than were needed in the past. You need to aggressively position yourself and your family so your job skills are flexible, diversified and not at the whim of global financial tides.

You can reduce human labor to a minimum - throughout the world. But then what do you do with all the unemployed? Do you somehow 'support' their basic existence, or even kill them (that was one purpose of war in the past)? They are still there - employed or not. Technology and the Web are destroying far more jobs than they create. A "Third Way" to adapt to this reality will prove difficult.

Don't confuse the inevitable job downsizing that comes with capitalism with disapproval of free markets. Socialistic solutions that distribute work are much worse and will be subject to epic failure. It is human nature for bureaucrats to take care of themselves and their families first, not you. Individuals simply have to adapt to fundamental changes in the structure of our economic universe and create their own employment.

The massive overhang of debt (public and private) cannot possibly be repaid. Demands for future entitlement payments cannot possibly be met. We cannot borrow our way to prosperity. Unless interest rates are zero forever and creditors are willing to forego scheduled repayments forever, borrowing our way to prosperity is a mathematical impossibility. In this climate, jobs will not grow on trees and you may have to create your own.

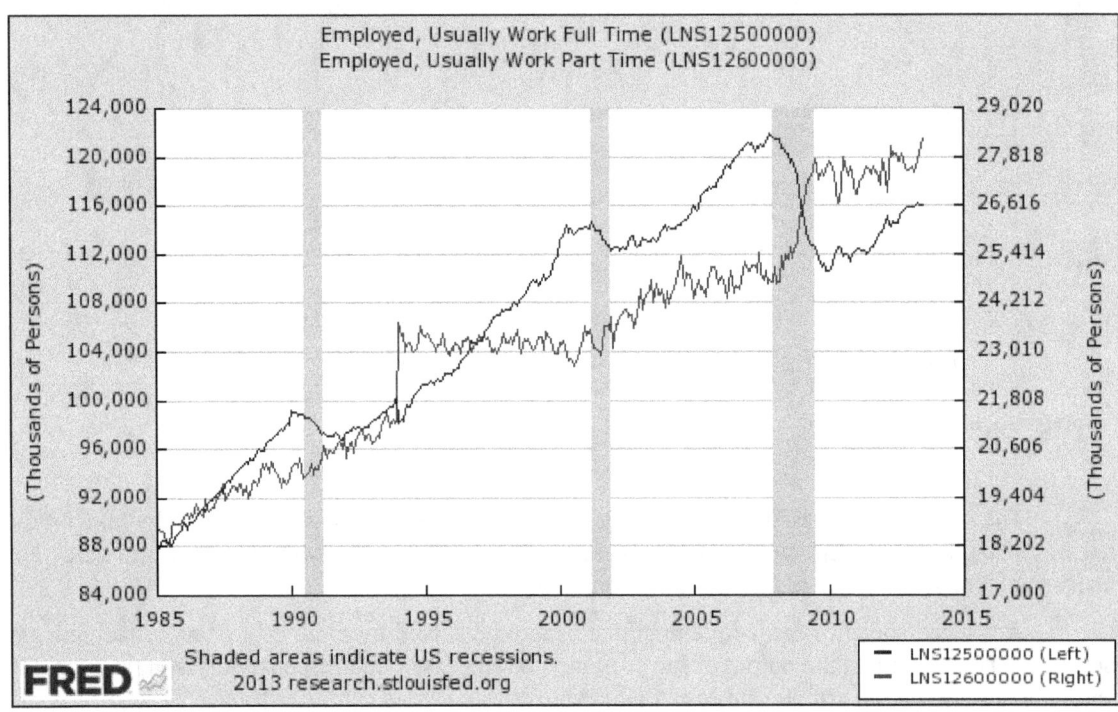

48   Staying Employed

The last two chapters were the employment bad news. Not only are jobs being outsourced to slave labor worldwide, but American companies are hell bent on robotizing their factories and eliminating as many jobs as possible. In order to be financially stable, you must make choices:

- Be more productive/proficient in declining labor markets. Educate yourself to the max and hope you are the last employee to survive all downsizing.
- Start your own business and create a market niche.
- Downsize your expectations and resign yourself to periods of underemployment, unemployment and welfare.

Here are the 10 fastest growing occupations from 2008 to 2018, and their median wages, according to the Labor Department:

- Biomedical engineers, median wages of $77,400
- Network systems and data communications analysts, $71,100
- Home health aides, $20,460
- Personal and home care aides, $19,180
- Financial examiners, $70,930
- Medical scientists, except epidemiologists, $72,590
- Physician assistants, $81,230
- Skin care specialists, $28,730
- Biochemists and biophysicists, $82,840
- Athletic trainers, $39,640

More than half of the 20 occupations with the fastest projected decline — sewing machine operators, photographic processing machine operators and file clerks — were below the national median wage. Here are the 10 fastest declining occupations:

- Textile bleaching and dyeing machine operators and tenders, $23,680
- Textile winding, twisting, and drawing out machine setters, operators, and tenders, $23,970
- Textile knitting and weaving machine setters, operators, and tenders, $25,400
- Shoe machine operators and tenders, $25,090
- Extruding and forming machine setters, operators, and tenders, synthetic and glass fibers, $31,160
- Sewing machine operators, $19,870
- Semiconductor processors, $32,230
- Textile cutting machine setters, operators, and tenders, $22,620
- Postal Service mail sorters, processors, and processing machine operators, $50,020
- Fabric menders, except garment, $28,470

Adaptation As Act Of Rebellion

To survive the outsourcing of wealth and jobs, adaptation is critical. Workers with diminishing prospects will need to evolve. People with a good set of flexible skills will be able to adapt, those who are inflexible will gravitate towards unemployment and welfare. Creativity and flexibility will be greatly valued. People with a certain specific set of vocational skills are going to have a tough time without new training.

While technology may replace some workers, it also creates opportunities to use new skills. Some types of engineers won't be doing the type of engineering they are doing now if someone comes up with a technology that makes what they do obsolete. But they are likely to do something related.

To succeed, a worker should be an active learner, taking on responsibility for invention and innovation gives you a better chance of remaining in a position than others. As long as Keynesian policies are employed at the national level, expect your job could either be made obsolete or outsourced. Those who act according to that pessimistic job model will survive and even prosper no matter how difficult times become.

49   Federal Reserve Performance

The Federal Reserve has a dual mandate to pursue price stability and maximum employment. While annual inflation in prices is trending closely to the Fed's 2% target, the headline unemployment rate is still well above the pre-recession level of 5%. The chart below from the CFR (Council on Foreign Relations) plots actual inflation and unemployment performance relative to the two targets (CFR uses 5.6% as Fed's target for unemployment) since 2002.

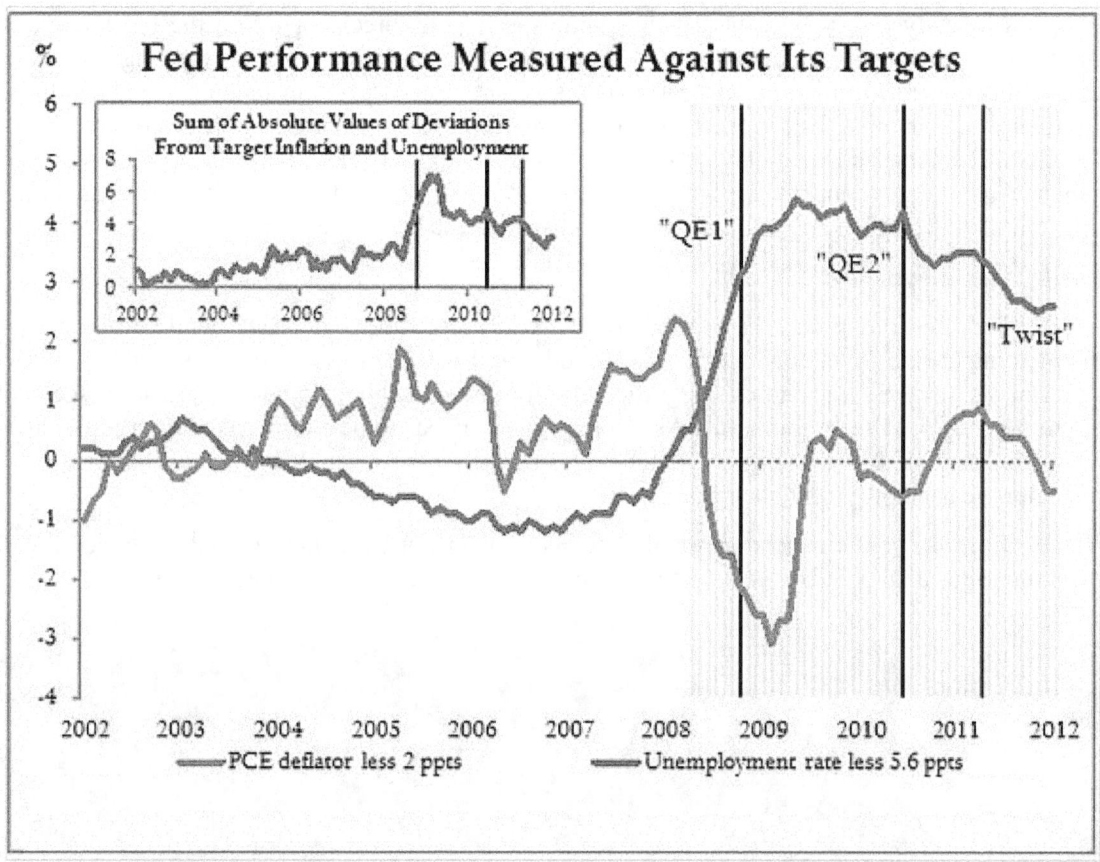

As the chart shows, the sum of the deviations has declined since the peak in July 2009, but it is still well above zero. Zero would be the benchmark for fulfilling the dual mandate, and the continuing gap signifies the Fed has failed in its dual mission. In fact, the Fed sees its failure as a mandate to continue to be accommodative.

Given the debt crisis, Japan's lost decades, the recession in the Euro Zone, and the significant slow-down in China, traders' expectation of multiple rounds of Quantitative Easing (QEn) from the Fed seemed more designed to support the equity and commodities markets than to affect the unemployment rate. Indeed, QE4 seemed most designed to bail out bankers through the open ended purchase of mortgage backed securities. This would indicate the Fed has run out of bullets to positively affect labor markets.

Fed Policy & The Labor Market

The Fed seems to draw a straight theoretical line between the increase in stock market performance/GDP growth and improved employment. That assumption might have been valid pre 2008 financial crisis. However, corporations are now running scared of an unending Great Recession and have streamlined operations at an unprecedented pace. While this increases corporate profits and stock prices, this does not translate into more investment and hiring in the real economy.

Monetary policy by central banks simply has little direct impact on the labor markets, which is why their primary directive now is price/inflation stability, while only giving lip service to unemployment. QEn by the central banks is meant to loosen credit lending, theoretically to stimulate the economy. But as the Fed's previous QE's have demonstrated, due to the structure of the global banking and financial system, QE mostly benefits banks. Banks have hoarded cheap capital from the government to speculate in commodities and stocks to get better returns, rather than circulating and lending to business and consumers like banks are supposed to.

Futile Unemployment-QE Cycle

Fed Reserve policy has failed to increase employment or GDP while inflation are manifesting in the "non-core" items (i.e. Food and Energy) not on Fed's "watch list." This situation is unlikely to improve significantly for quite awhile, so taking risks in such an environment would seem foolhardy. Asset preservation needs to be a primary goal for individuals as Fed induced bubbles no longer are able to spike, much less sustain, long term economic growth nor improve unemployment statistics.

In short, your financial survival depends on your not believing the Federal Reserve will meet any of its dual mandate goals, and has little track record to suggest it ever hoped too.

Dysfunctional Economics

50   Confiscation of Wealth

Average Americans are experiencing a declining standard of living and it is not by accident. Everything you own is slowly being taken away from you. Americans have been taught to think of themselves as "well off", but we don't "own" nearly as much as we think we do. We must frantically accumulate wealth as rapidly as we can just to stay ahead of the wealth being taken away.

The entire system is designed to take what you have - through taxation, inflation, debt, interest, fines, fees, tickets, government seizures and corporate greed. If you do nothing but hold on to the wealth that you already have, it will quickly disappear. The system is designed to funnel everything you think you own to corporatists and the government. Hopefully this book has provided you with some positive ways to protect your wealth by Going Galt. However you should be clear headed about the challenges we face. Some of the ways that your wealth is being taken from you:

#1 Most Americans who "own a home" are paying a mortgage and are actually enslaved to 20 or 30 year debt contracts. If you stop paying that mortgage you lose that home. Over a million American families were foreclosed on in 2010 with millions more to come. Families booted onto the street don't get their down payments back nor the mortgage payments already made. The banks get to keep all of the money and all of the houses.

Even if you have paid off your home and don't have a mortgage you don't really "own your home". Refuse to pay your property taxes and your home will have a lien attached and the house eventually sold to satisfy that lien. At best you can say that you have the right to rent your home from the government.

The banks now own more of "our homes" than we do. During the most recent recession, the total amount of U.S. home equity owned by the banks surpassed the total amount of U.S. home equity owned by the rest of us for the first time ever. In past times American families owned most of the houses and land in this nation, but now ownership has passed to the banks.

#2 Do you think you own your car? You don't own it if you still have a loan on it and you will rapidly lose that car if you stop making payments.

Even if your car is paid off, you can only operate that car if you pay:

- the license fee
- car registration
- emissions inspection fee
- the property taxes on that car (if that applies in your area)
- tire taxes
- gasoline taxes

If you have paid all of those taxes, then you are permitted to drive only where the government allows you to drive and only under the rules that the government sets for you.

#3 You probably own some possessions, but that doesn't mean they aren't enslaving you. If you used a credit card to pay for them, you will pay much more for your possessions than the original cost. If you only make the minimum payment on your credit card each month, a $6,000 credit card bill will cost you over $30,000.

#4 Do you own your education? No one can take your education away from you, but if you took out student loans that debt may end up enslaving you for decades. The borrower is the servant of the lender and student loan debt is more of a financial drain on Americans than ever before. Americans now owe more on student loans than they do on credit cards. Americans owe more than $900 billion on student loans, an all-time record.

#5 Putting your money in the bank will not protect it; in fact your wealth will be systematically destroyed in the bank. Inflation is a hidden tax on every single dollar that you own. It destroys the value of all dollars in existence. There are some Americans that have been saving money for decades, but those savings are being taxed into oblivion by inflation. As the average price of a gallon of gasoline approaches $5 think about how your wealth is being drained away by inflation the next time you go to the gas pump.

#6 Insurance costs continue to soar, health insurance premiums in particular. Blue Shield of California raised rates 30% to 35%, and this is before all the ramifications of Obamacare are tallied. Mandated insurance that subsidizes others must always be considered a tax.

#7 Many state and local governments have turned to ticket writing as a primary revenue source. The good of citizens has been replaced by the need for revenue.

#8 Some states simply confiscate wealth even if nothing wrong has been done. For example, the state of California is aggressively seizing "unclaimed" safe deposit boxes. If you have a safe deposit box that you have not checked on in a while you might want to make sure that it is still there.

#9 If you don't pay your property taxes, you will lose your house and it will likely be a big Wall Street bank that will be taking it from you.

#10 The biggest way your wealth is drained is through federal income taxes. The reason that the Federal Reserve and the IRS were established back in 1913 was to redistribute wealth. Wealth is transferred from the American people to the U.S. government and then ultimately to the elite and to the entitlement causes that the elite favor.

Federal taxes are only one of many taxes that we pay. A few examples of the other taxes that drain your wealth are:

- Accounts Receivable Taxes
- Building Permit Taxes
- Capital Gains Taxes
- CDL License Taxes
- Cigarette Taxes
- Corporate Income Taxes
- Court Fines (indirect taxes)
- Dog License Taxes

- Federal Unemployment Taxes (FUTA)
- Fishing License Taxes
- Food License Taxes
- Gasoline Taxes
- Gift Taxes
- Hunting License Taxes
- Inheritance Taxes
- Inventory Taxes
- IRS Interest Charges (tax on top of tax)
- IRS Penalties (tax on top of tax)
- Liquor Taxes
- Local Income Taxes
- Luxury Taxes
- Marriage License Taxes
- Medicare Taxes
- Payroll Taxes
- Property Taxes
- Real Estate Taxes
- Recreational Vehicle Taxes
- Road Toll Booth Taxes
- Road Usage Taxes (Truckers)
- Sales Taxes
- Self-Employment Taxes
- School Taxes
- Septic Permit Taxes
- Service Charge Taxes
- Social Security Taxes
- State Income Taxes
- State Unemployment Taxes (SUTA)
- Telephone federal excise taxes
- Telephone federal universal service fee taxes
- Telephone federal, state and local surcharge taxes
- Telephone minimum usage surcharge taxes
- Telephone recurring and non-recurring taxes
- Telephone state and local taxes
- Telephone usage charge taxes
- Toll Bridge Taxes
- Toll Tunnel Taxes
- Traffic Fines (indirect taxation)

- Trailer Registration Taxes
- Utility Taxes
- Vehicle License Registration Taxes
- Vehicle Sales Taxes
- Watercraft Registration Taxes
- Well Permit Taxes
- Workers Compensation Taxes

The future is being stolen from our children and our grandchildren. They will be inheriting 20 trillion dollar (and rising) national debt and a hundred trillion of unfunded liabilities. What we have done to future generations is to push our current debts on to them. They will own nothing and have a negative net worth – unless they are smart enough to disown this confiscatory inheritance.

When you base an entire economy on debt, you end up with never ending money problems that enslave us all, destroying everything our forefathers worked so hard to build.

51   Crony Capitalism/Socialism

The Federal Reserve, the large banks and a horde of politically connected crony capitalists (a form of socialism for the elite) really are out to steal everything you have. The financial collapse we suffered beginning in 2007 should have led to the decimation of bankers and jail terms of their CEOs, yet not a single person has been perp walked for selling worthless Mortgage Backed Securities. While it's politically expedient to say that the whole system would have collapsed and we would have suffered a depression if the banks weren't bailed out, in fact Main Street and the common man has suffered immensely while bank CEOs have received their bonuses. The banks are not your friends; you just bailed them out and owe them nothing.

The bailout of General Motors on exceedingly favorable terms to the unions and to the detriment of bond holders is another example of political intrusion into the market. If GM had been forced into bankruptcy, its pieces would have been picked up and reconstituted as a lean and mean profit making center. Instead, we are served up the Chevy Volt as an example of an unprofitable and technologically inappropriate product designed by politically correct committee.

There are at least a dozen other companies that should also have been allowed to die or their subsidies cut. There is a reason GE pays no taxes but was also a large contributor to the Obama campaign and it isn't for the good of American citizens. When industry prospers not through innovation but through where it sits at the lobbying table, you know your government is fighting against you.

Our government is on a collision course with the health and well being of its population through a Ponzi scheme of unsustainable social welfare spending. Our energy resources are under attack, we are propagandized with fake economic numbers and our currency is being shredded. These problems are not being resolved, in part because it is possible for leftwing bureaucrats to make huge amounts of money cashing in on their expertise after having authored abysmal legislation.

Former senator Chris Dodd is President of the Motion Picture Assoc for a cool $1.5m PER YEAR. Liz Fowler, one of the key authors of Obamacare, now works for Johnson and Johnson. Democrats who controlled Congress and the White House used the $700 billion TARP program and the $860 billion stimulus as a giant ATM to pay back favored constituencies, at the expense of the rest of us. Members of Obama's campaign finance committee, his campaign bundlers and major Democratic donors received $16.4 billion of the $20.5 billion in loans and grants doled out under "green stimulus" programs run by Obama's Energy Department. The revolving door between Goldman Sachs, the Federal Reserve and regulatory bodies ensures a corruptocratic business environment.

We could add to the list continuously from both political parties; however you already sense these problems and the question becomes how to adapt to them rather than just cry in our beer.

Options For Investors

In an era where crony socialists are the beneficiaries of large government contracts and regulatory relief, it is hard to not be tempted by the dark side. It would be soooo easy to become a lobbyist, or get on the government gravy train. We are not immune from such thoughts, except that we come back to a central problem. What kind a future will we be leaving our children?

There is however an ethical way to profit from crony socialism. That is by judiciously betting against these boondoggles. For example, here is a list of just alternative energy companies that have failed:

Evergreen Solar ($25 million)
SpectraWatt ($500,000)
Solyndra ($535 million)
Beacon Power ($43 million)
Nevada Geothermal ($98.5 million)
SunPower ($1.2 billion)
First Solar ($1.46 billion)
Babcock and Brown ($178 million)
EnerDel's subsidiary Ener1 ($118.5 million)
Amonix ($5.9 million)
Fisker Automotive ($529 million)
Abound Solar ($400 million)
A123 Systems ($279 million)
Willard and Kelsey Solar Group ($700,981)
Johnson Controls ($299 million)
Brightsource ($1.6 billion)
Mountain Plaza, Inc. ($2 million)
ECOtality ($126.2 million)
Raser Technologies ($33 million)
Energy Conversion Devices ($13.3 million)
Olsen's Crop Service and Olsen's Mills Acquisition Company ($10 million)
Stirling Energy Systems ($7 million)
Range Fuels ($80 million)
Thompson River Power ($6.5 million)
Azure Dynamics ($5.4 million)
GreenVolts ($500,000)
Vestas ($50 million)
LG Chem's subsidiary Compact Power ($151 million)
Nordic Windpower ($16 million)
Navistar ($39 million)
Satcon ($3 million)
Konarka Technologies Inc. ($20 million)
Mascoma Corp. ($100 million)

So while it may be unwise to bet against businesses who have Uncle Sam's infinite wallet at their disposal, it is also clearly unwise to get caught up in the Tulip Bulb like fever that says they will all be successes. With some judicious timing, one could make a killing by shorting the obvious trend of these companies to crater. All those solar companies were considered "sure bets", but the smart money will be those who know how to short the sure bets our government and Federal Reserve have doomed with their reverse Midas touch.

52 Black and Gray Markets

During any economic collapse, Black and Gray markets will arise. While by definition these are illegal or quasi legal markets the state has outlawed (ostensibly for your own good), when your family's very survival depends on making money or acquiring goods on the side it is hard to see where many would not consider this option. Indeed, nations like Italy have long made a habit out of using black markets to evade onerous economic laws.

- **Gray Market** Also known as a parallel market, is the trade of a commodity through distribution channels which, while legal, are unofficial, unauthorized, or unintended by the original manufacturer. The term gray *economy*, however, refers to workers being paid under the table, without paying income taxes or contributing to such public services as Social Security and Medicare. It is sometimes referred to as the underground economy or "hidden economy." The two main types of gray market are imported manufactured goods that would normally be unavailable or more expensive in a certain country and unissued securities that are not yet traded in official markets.
- **Black Market** Is the trade of goods and services that are illegal in themselves and/or distributed through illegal channels, such as the selling of stolen goods, certain drugs or unregistered handguns. Sometimes the term dark market is used to describe secretive, unregulated (though often technically legal) trading in commodity futures, notably crude oil. This can be considered a third type of "gray market" since it is legal, yet unregulated, and probably not intended or explicitly authorized by oil producers.

Black markets currently exist in cigarettes, narcotics, drugs and a lesser extent liquor (Internet wine sales). While sales of heavy narcotics like cocaine and heroin really have no place for consideration by those intent on survival because of the backwash of criminal ill effects they cause, ethics become less clear in the other instances. High taxation of cigarettes in states like New York drives an underground interstate trade in a product that would otherwise be legal except for the loss of tax receipts. The marijuana trade seems headed towards a degree of legalization (or at least lessening of penalties) which has spawned a huge growing spree.

What interests us more here than 'recreational' products is possible trade in items that affect survival, which include food, drugs, housing, energy and jobs. Ironically, your model may be that of illegal aliens who already thrive in this type of economy.

Food & Drug Production

The most basic necessity is food, but even here congress has moved to make illegal the production of food. Growing your own Victory garden may not at some point be allowed, especially for resale, because it does not meet FDA requirements. That said, relatively significant amounts of food can be potentially grown on small plots and even be commercial on as little as 10,000 square feet. Selling your produce may constitute a gray market, but certainly consuming what you grow could make your family more resilient to the economic tide approaching.

Drugs are now imported by many from Canada, India and elsewhere. This might be a profitable business for some as the Obamacare system will of necessity choke off non-prescription access to American pharmaceuticals. An even broader category is natural foods and supplements, also being considered for inclusion in the FDA regulatory maw and therefore candidates for under the counter sales. Both natural foods and supplements and foreign pharmaceuticals will be areas ripe for black and gray markets as scarcity drives profits like during prohibition.

Barter & Internet Trade

It is also obvious that many transactions will move out of normal brick and mortar commerce channels to avoid being subject to taxation. Large Internet presences like Amazon.com and EBay have long been fighting a battle to avoid becoming the tax collectors for the states. This will likely be a losing battle as government becomes more desperate for funds.

However, direct buyer to seller trading has now long been supported by portals like Craigslist.com, often bypassing the entire tax system. Off channel business is also being conducted through social media like Facebook and Twitter. The irony is that the harder government entities attack online sales in search of revenue, the more incentive there will be to take these activities underground.

Inevitable Future

Once an economic collapse begins, black/gray markets will take no time to appear, the question is whether you can capitalize on them. Gray markets will be accepted parts of the economy in the end, as they have been in places like Italy and Argentina. It may begin as the innocent trading of skills and/or craft products for food as already takes place daily on www.craigslist.com. Localities may also form their own barter markets, and create their own tickets/script, another money really, to trade. However, since script is easy to make on a home computer, eventually barter markets return to paper money.

These markets end up in warehouses or on empty land, and might be managed by some wise guy and a few thugs or hired security. Anyone can rent a kiosk inside and sell their goods and services. Uniformed cops may manage security at these markets as a second job, but you have to be careful. The bad economy hits everyone and once you leave the building, you are on your own. These markets generally run peacefully, free markets at their best, because the managers want to make money and may not wait for the police to solve problems.

We do not advocate defying any enacted laws, regulations or taxes. If you are trying to survive the coming economic fall intact without knocks on the door by regulators and enforcers, you will try to follow the law no matter how absurd. However, the system is failing quickly of its own weight. As the system fails, people will skirt legalities as a matter of economic survival. To be unaware of the technologies that make this possible would be to expose yourself to risks should these avenues become the only ways to conduct business.

53   NIRP/ZIRP: Financial System Death Knell?

On July 18th, 2012, US$5.13 billion worth of 2-year bonds were sold by the German government at an average yield of -0.06%. Please note the negative symbol in front of that yield number. What this means is that the German government was able to borrow money for less than nothing. When those specific bonds expire in two years' time, the German government will pay back the original $5.13 billion minus 0.06%. Expressed another way, investors knowingly and willingly bid the German government $5.13 billion in exchange for bonds that will pay no interest and are guaranteed to lose them money on expiration.[1] Welcome to the new status quo.

Germany is not alone. The countries of Netherlands, Switzerland and France have also issued short-term government debt at negative yields. Like Germany, they've been able to do this because European bond investors are so shell shocked that they'd rather park money in a bond that's guaranteed to only lose a miniscule amount rather than risk losing more in a PIIGS bond that theoretically pays some interest. In addition, many investors view German, French and Dutch bonds to be cheap options on the break-up of the Eurozone. If the EU currency union collapses, euro-denominated bonds issued by those specific countries may be paid back in re-issued deutschmarks, francs or guilders, which will be far more valuable than the Euros that were spent to buy the bonds in the first place. As a result of this thinking, bond market auctions for these select countries have seen overwhelming demand, making NIRP (Negative Interest Rate Policy) the new ZIRP (Zero Interest Rate Policy).

The NIRP acronym is misleading, however, because unlike ZIRP, NIRP isn't actually an official "policy" per se, but rather a symptom of a broken financial system increasingly starved for good 'collateral'. Aside from those speculating on a Eurozone currency collapse, a large portion of the bond investors participating in NIRP bond auctions are the banks. As the euro crisis has dragged on, banks in perceived "strong" countries like Germany and Switzerland have seen record inflows of deposits from banks in peripheral EU countries, like Spain. As most of these "strong country" banks have been hesitant to lend those deposits out (for obvious reasons), they are forced to park them in short-term government bonds.

Moreover, new rules imposed by various regulators such as Basel III force banks to hold a larger percentage of their balance sheet in government bonds, regardless of their country of domicile. The result has been a mad dash into the bond auctions of select "safe" countries just as the pool of available AAA-bonds has been drastically reduced. Banks pile into NIRP bond auctions today because they have nowhere else to go. This is why nobody seems to be alarmed by the recent ubiquity of NIRP bond auctions – they are merely thought to be a short term phenomenon that will pass in time… just like zero-percent interest rates were supposed to pass when they were widely introduced in 2008.

NIRP is different than ZIRP, however. NIRP causes outright financial destruction. Economies can hardly survive extended periods of ZIRP rates, let alone survive a long-term NIRP environment. Institutional investors like pension plans and life insurance companies cannot earn enough "spread" to function properly. And many aren't allowed to buy different asset classes that might produce a better "spread", even if they wanted to. They are stuck holding the AAA government debt issuers – positive-yield, or not.

Negative rates also punish the individual investor. Try going online and using one of the banks' retirement savings simulators and plugging in a negative expected return – you'll break the program. The same also goes for the investment advisory business. When so-called safe-haven bonds start to consistently produce a negative return, try charging advisory fees to clients while recommending a 50% allocation to negative-yielding government debt. Advisors can try it for a while, but investors won't put up with it for long.

The emergence of NIRP auctions are a signal that the relationship between governments, banks and investors has broken down. While the market still presumes that NIRP is a short-term phenomenon confined to Europe, the lack of AAA-assets coupled with banks' captive bond purchasing suggests it may be structurally enforced for a long time to come, with the potential for NIRP to emerge in the US bond market. The gap between US bank deposits and loans hit a record $1.77 trillion at the end of July 2012, representing an expansion of 15% since May. With 2-year US Treasury bills yielding a paltry 0.29%, it doesn't take much to upset the applecart. If something exciting happens in Europe, what's to stop the bond market's typical knee-jerk move into US Treasuries from pushing that yield down past zero? Not much, especially if the banks continue to gorge on ongoing US Treasury auctions in the meantime.

How well can the financial system (much less your own financial health) cope in a relentless low-to-no yield environment for bonds? Years of low rates have already damaged 'spread'-dependent industries. Insurers are one group whose earnings have deteriorated given current interest rates, driving up premiums. The pension plans are also deteriorating; the funded status of US corporate pension plans hit a record low in July 2012. In the pension business, lower yields on long-term AAA bonds results in higher plan liabilities.

It's even worse for the public pensions. New pension accounting rules imposed by bond-rating firm Moody's are expected to triple the gap between what states and municipalities report they have in their funds and what they have promised to pay out retirees. If implemented, that new public pension gap will balloon to $2.2 trillion. New accounting rules from Moody's and the Governmental Accounting Standards Board (GASB) limit the rate of return on future investments that pension funds can assume for accounting purposes. Most government pension funds assume a 7 percent to 8 percent return, which overstates future investment income. With the US 10-year bond now paying less than 2% a year, assuming a 7-8% return is fantasy.

Banks also suffer from NIRP and ZIRP, as evidenced by the performance of Wall Street's five biggest banks. JPMorgan Chase & Co. (JPM), the Bank of America Corp., Citigroup Inc., Morgan Stanley and Goldman Sachs Group Inc. had declining revenues in 2012, the lowest since 2008. The firms blamed the decline in large part on low interest rates. Banks make money on the spread between the interest they charge on loans and the interest they pay on deposits. called the net-interest margin).

From a government perspective – especially governments like Germany who currently issue short-term debt for less than nothing, the current abundance of NIRP and ZIRP bond auctions represent a sweet irony. Here we are, on the interminable verge of collapse in Europe, and at a time when Western governments have never been more indebted, and bond investors are lining up to pay for the pleasure of owning their bond paper! But no matter how much pain the current low-to-no yield environment causes the rest of the financial industry, governments will not do anything to change their current set-up.

The following chart shows the impact low rates have had on the net-interest margin for the Big 6 Canadian banks, and how tightly correlated their profits are to bond yields themselves. Similar correlations exist for banks internationally. Like the insurers, low bond yields hurt profit margins. The more deposits the banks take on, the more they are inadvertently forced to participate in short-term bond auctions –supporting the very market causing the margin compression in the first place.

Canadian Banks' Net-Interest Margins Trending Down Correlation: 87%

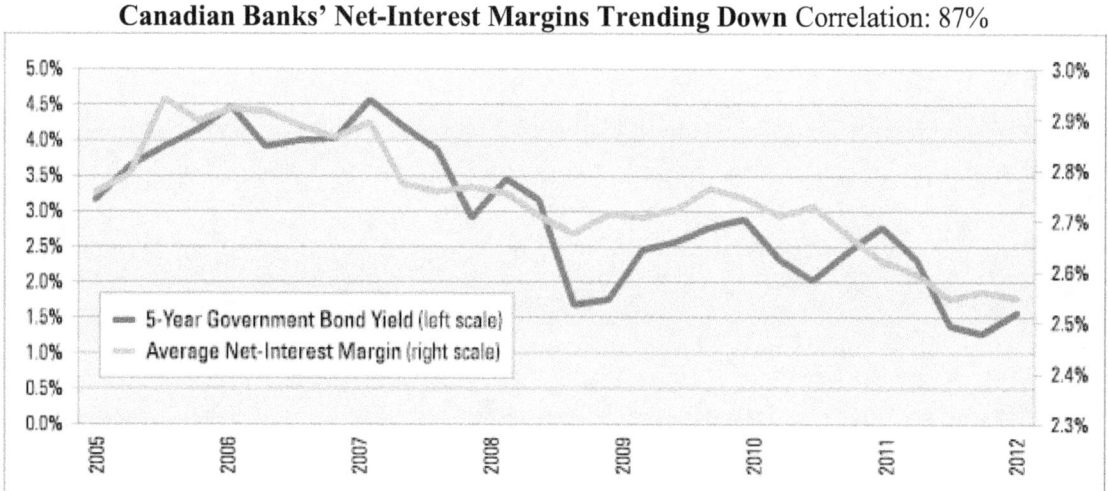

No government has an incentive to proactively raise their bond auction yields for the sake of savers, and barring the surprise emergence of major inflation, no central bank would ever raise interest rates and risk curtailing their expensive efforts to foster growth through money-printing. The banks' continuing need for safe "collateral" means they'll buy government bonds at virtually any price, leaving the governments with a "captive" buyer for their bonds. Unless the banking system diversifies into different forms of AAA-collateral (like gold), or until we experience a default or major inflation, investors will be forced to survive with a AAA-bond market that pays absolutely nothing, just like Japanese investors have suffered through for the past twenty years.

Under widespread NIRP, pensions, annuities, insurers, banks and ultimately all savers will suffer a slow but steady decline in real wealth over time. Just as ZIRP has stuck around since the early 2000's, NIRP may be here to stay for many years to come. Given the widespread damage ZIRP has caused since its introduction in 2002, negative interest rates will cause even more harm, and at a faster clip. NIRP represents the death knell for the financial system as we know it today. There are simply too many working parts of the financial industry that are directly impacted by negative rates.

In this low-to-no rate environment hard assets like gold and silver should be hedges, along with select commodities and real estate. Investors should continue to expect an attempted inflationary solution in almost all developed economies over the next years and even decades. NIRP and ZIRP are critical components of that solution, and are here to stay until something unpredictable disrupts the current relationship between the banks and government bond auctions.

54   Collapsing Education/Healthcare

Two employment sectors that have expanded without interruption for decades are healthcare and education, which together have functioned as gigantic make-work projects. Both healthcare and education, have costs that are out of control and point to where we are headed as a nation when we subsidize bubbles for social good. *We can no longer afford the expansion of or their out-of-control costs.*

The outsized gains can be seen by comparing total population growth and the number of full-time jobs generated, versus the number of jobs generated in education/healthcare since 1990. Total population: has increased 27% increase since 1990:

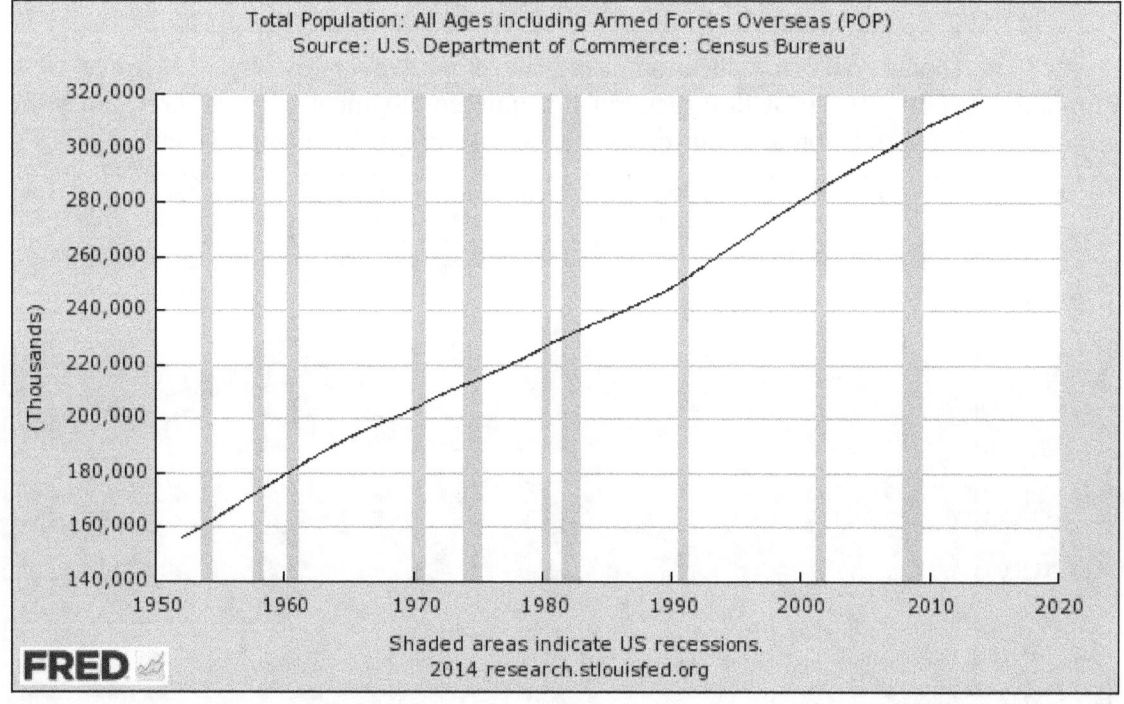

To make a fair comparison, one needs to separate out jobs that support households from part-time work. In official statistics, even a one hour a week job is counted as a part time job, so we need to use full-time employment as a baseline. Full-time employment only rose 20% since 1990, less than the population.

The shocker is that Education/healthcare employment rose by 81% since 1990 compared to only 20% growth in general full time employment. This is three times the 27% growth in population and four times the increase in full-time employment.

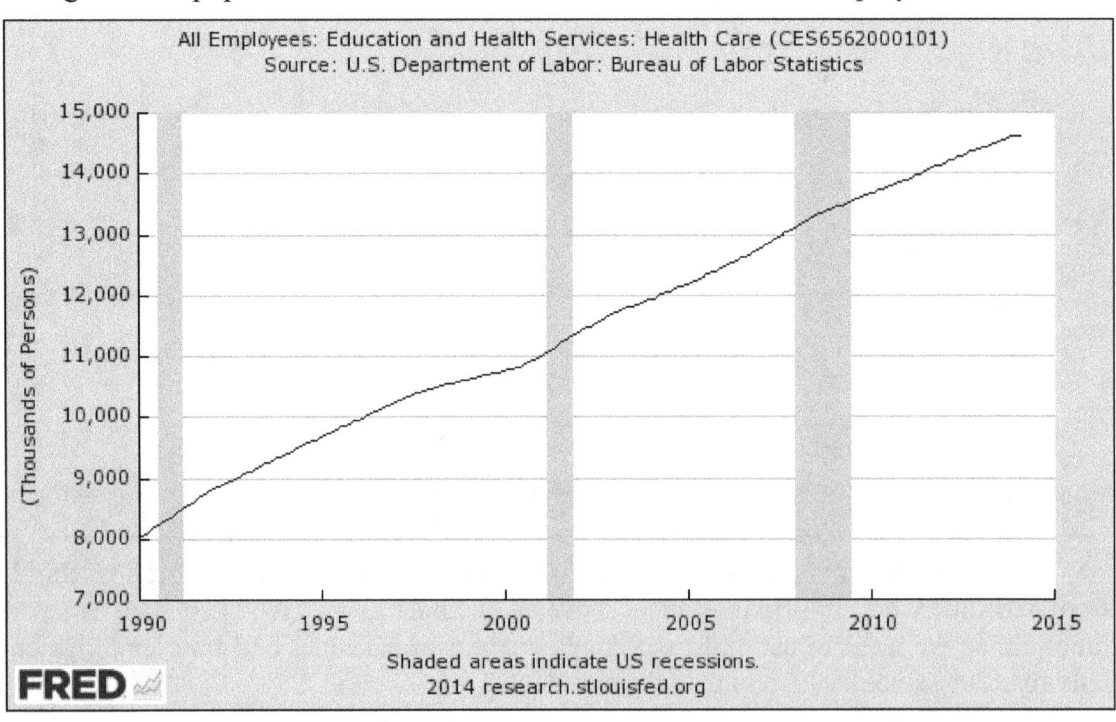

Education and healthcare employment should only have expanded approximately 30% since 1990 to meet the needs of a larger population, not 81%. This would especially be the case if there had been technological advances in those areas, which there certainly have given the rise of the Internet and advances in biology. Clearly 50% of these sectors' expansion is above population growth.

Instead of education and medical services having improved and expanded by 50% through demand since 1990, the yield on our investments in these sectors has declined even with soaring employment.

Education Overreach

For a large proportion of American students higher education offers limited or no learning. In the last decade student loans have ballooned to over $1 trillion and direct Federal loans from $115 billion to over $700 billion. Only 37% of freshmen graduate in four years while 58% finally graduate in six years. Yet despite these expenditures 53% of college graduates under age of 25 are unemployed or doing work that doesn't require a college degree.

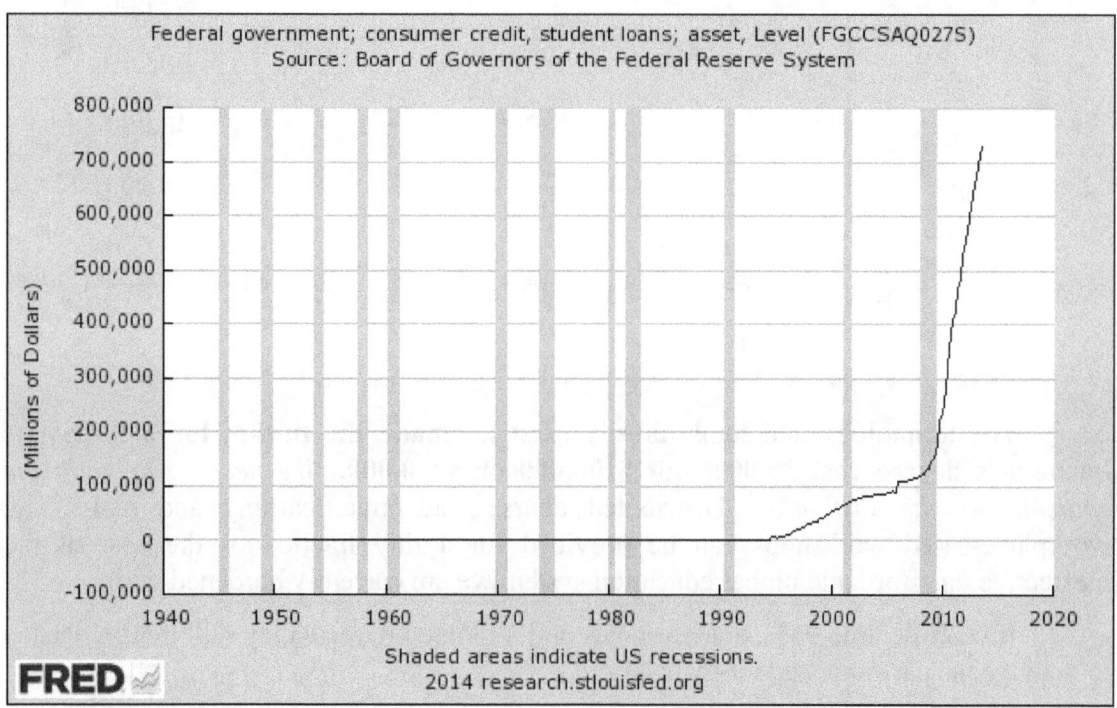

Employment in higher education has soared mainly in bloated administration and non-teaching staff. From 1987 until 2011-12 universities and colleges added 517,636 administrators and professional employees. The huge amount of money per student being spent on administration raises a question of priorities. Since 1987, employees in central system offices has increased six-fold, and the number of administrators in them by a factor of more than 34. The ratio of nonacademic employees to faculty has doubled. For every full-time, tenure-track member of faculty there are now two nonacademic employees at public and two and a half at private universities and colleges

Perversely, tens of millions of students now need student loans to pay sky-high tuition and fees, which in turn subsidizes huge administrative staffs to manage the student loan process. The yield in earnings on the increasingly unaffordable college degree is declining sharply:

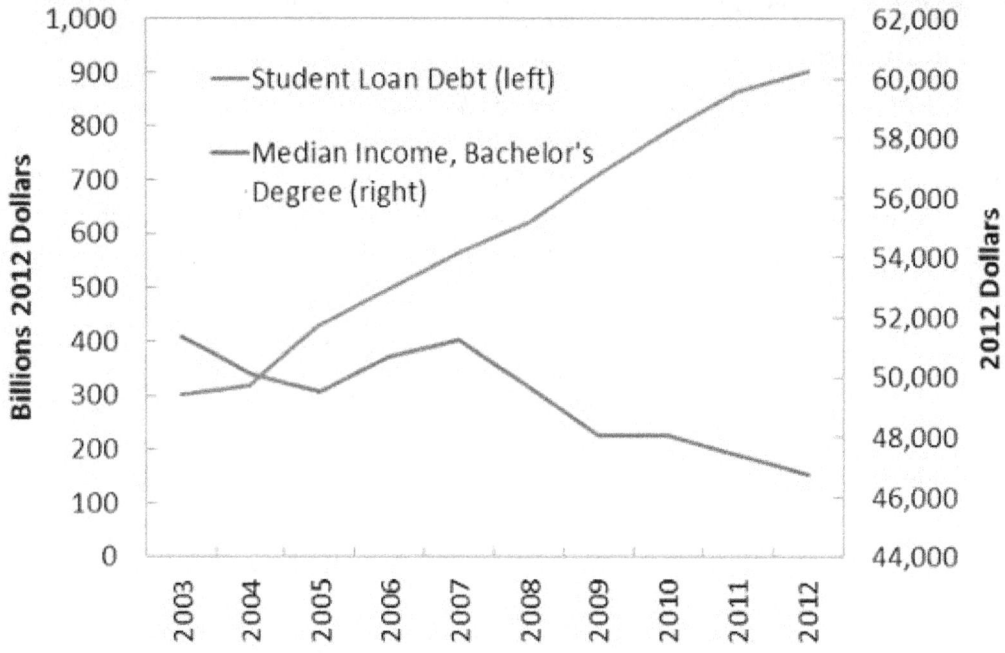

Sources: FRBNY Consumer Credit Panel, US Census Bureau Current Population Survey, BLS Consumer Price Index

The technology and tools already exist to **make the tuition for a four-year bachelor's degree cost $5,000, not $100,000 or $200,000.** *We need to accredit the student, not the institution.* Distributed courses, adaptive learning and real-world, workplace-based workshops can be provided for a tiny fraction of the cost of the ineffective, unaffordable higher education system we are currently burdened with.

If costs decline 95%, student loans and a bloated bureaucracy will not be needed to manage the parasitic student-loan system.

Healthcare Bloat

While there are many metrics of overall health, the U.S. has not experienced a 50% improvement in any of them since 1990. In U.S. healthcare, life expectancy since

1990 has fallen well below that of the United Kingdom (U.K.), a nation whose healthcare system is justifiably criticized in the U.S. despite soaring employment and expenditures.

Even as the nation pours nearly 20% of its gross domestic product (GDP) into healthcare the health of the populace has arguably declined.

This isn't the fault of healthcare workers; it is simply that healthcare has been made a "make-work" sources of jobs. The enormous sums of money needed to pay for these make-work sectors is coming out of household incomes which for 90% of households have been stagnating.

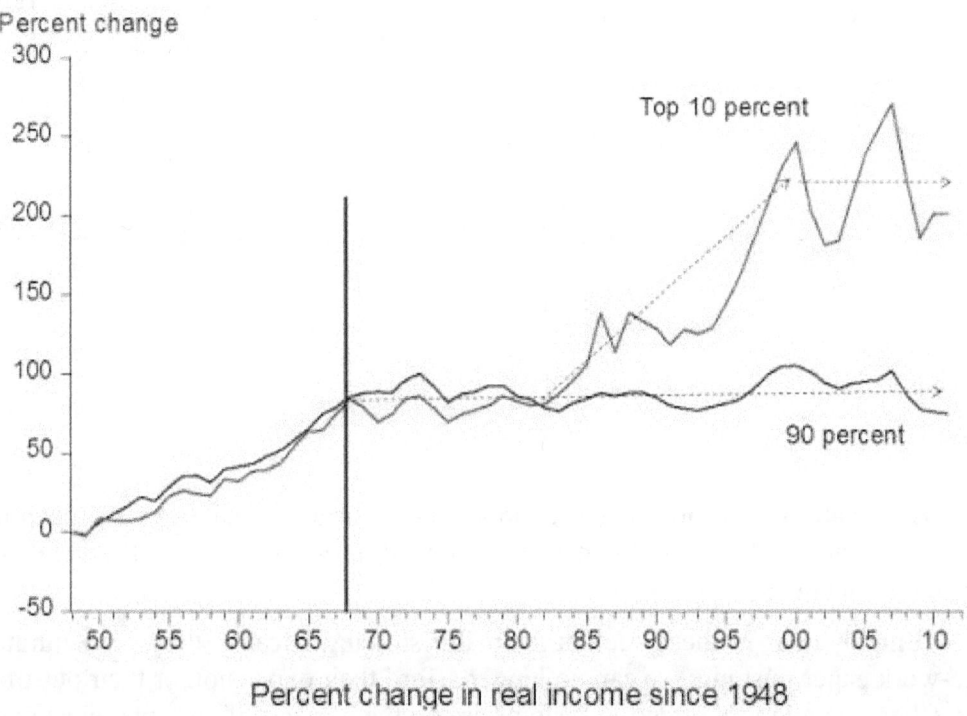

Percent change in real income since 1948

America's dysfunctional potpourri of private cartels and Federal programs has created paper-shuffling healthcare employment which some estimate sucks up 30% of the healthcare bill. This neglects staggering sums lost to over-charging, duplicate or needless tests, fraud, embezzlement, useless or even harmful procedures which will be exacerbated by the Obamacare Hindenburg.

Comparing our per-person expenses for healthcare with other advanced democracies such as Australia and Japan, we find those nations spend roughly 50% of what the U.S. spends per-person, with better and more evenly distributed results. This strongly suggests that healthcare should cost half of what it currently costs, if the U.S. system wasn't so wasteful, ineffective and dysfunctional.

Subtracting healthcare and debt service from household earnings, we find that wages/salaries are in recession territory:

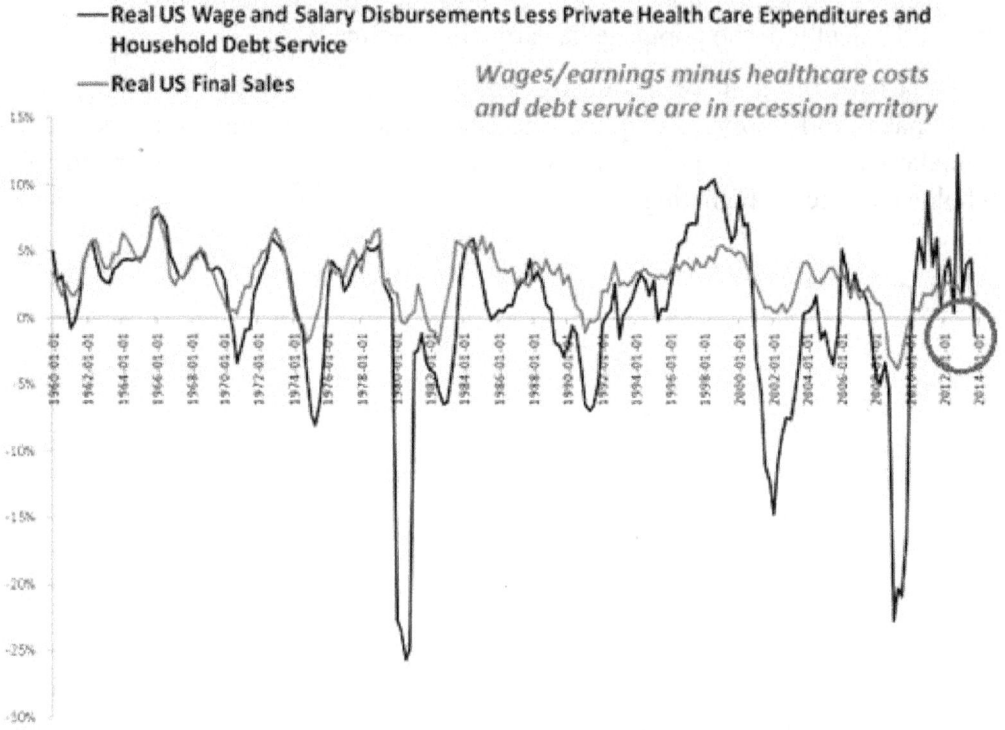

The nation can no longer support the enormous make-work education and healthcare sectors, where employment and expenditures rise even as the yield on those investments declines.

Employment in these sectors is finally slowing because they are saturated with make-work paper pushing: we can no longer afford their expansion or their out-of-control costs. Cheaper and more effective systems are on the horizon, if only we reject past failed models and the politically powerful cartels.

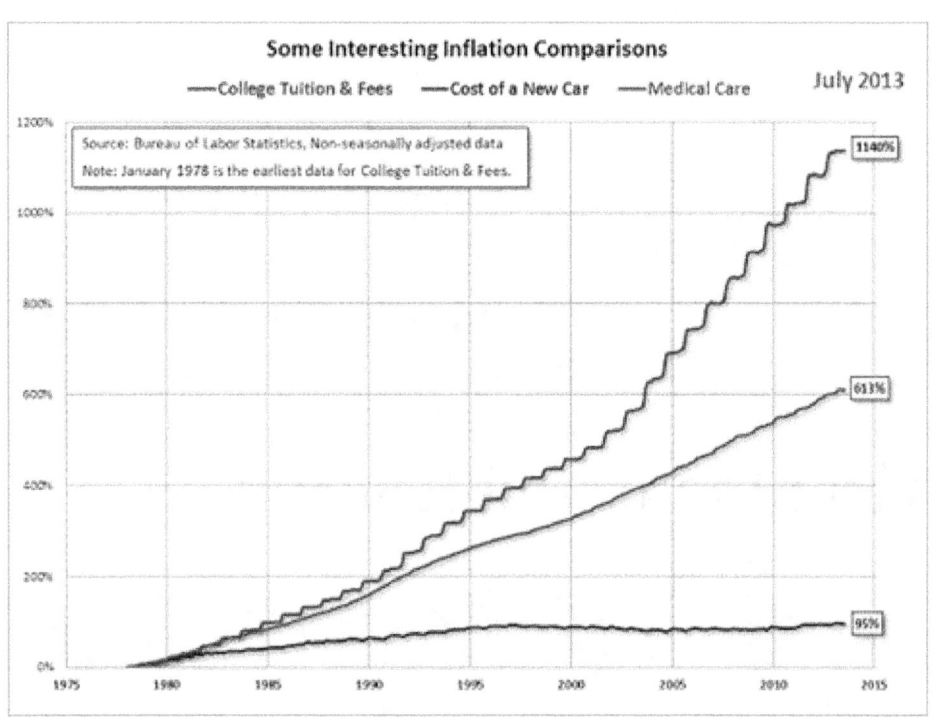

Environment and Energy

55 Green Dystopia

The environmental gravy train is too big, with too many jobs, industries, trading profits and political careers to stop its advance before it precipitates immense economic damage. Governments, and their climate scientists, maintain the fiction that carbon dioxide is an incredibly dangerous pollutant and that energy resource starvation is the only way to save Mother Earth. Not only their paychecks depend on this claim; they also know raw political power and possibility of world government also rides on the outcome.

Green Dystopia would all be an amusing parlor game if it also didn't seriously affect your financial well being. You need to know both how you are being forced to pay the bill for impractical green technology, and how to avoid the negative consequences of profligate eco spending and even profit from it. First, the ways you pay for green technologies and global warmism are many:

- Higher oil, gas and heating prices from restricted drilling
- Increased electrical bills from mandated alternative energy
- Increased food costs from mandated corn based ethanol production
- Infrastructure costs for upgrading the national grid to meet impractical electric car needs

Despite the claims of environmentalists about the rosy future of solar power, fundamental technical hurdles will keep solar from being the major source of energy in the foreseeable future. Among the problems are solar power's intermittency and low energy density, and the fact that it is resource intensive, requiring large amounts of infrastructure. Other alternative energies have problems too. Hydroelectric power generation will not grow from its present level because the U.S. river system has already been dammed to near capacity. Geothermal is geographically limited. Wind power is capital intensive, plagued by structural failures, and suffers from the same intermittency problems as other solar alternatives.

Clearly, the national energy equation will have to be reformulated to take into account the failure of alternative energy sources to come close to meeting demand.

Limits Of Alternative technology

Ironically, many of the technologies greens believe will save the world are counterproductive because they have failed to do a full cost/benefit analysis.

Electric Cars:

A study has found, produce higher emissions over their lifetimes than hydrocarbon equivalents because of the energy consumed in making their batteries. An electric car owner would have to drive at least 90,000 miles before producing a net saving in CO_2. Many electric cars will not travel that far in their lifetime because they typically have a range of less than 100 mile on a single charge and are unsuitable for long trips. Even those driven 105,000 miles would save only about a ton of CO2 over their lifetimes.

The Committee on Climate Change, a British government watchdog, has called for the number of electric cars on Britain's roads to increase from a few hundred now to 1.7 million by 2020. However, a study commissioned by the Low Carbon Vehicle Partnership, jointly funded by the British government and the car industry, found that a mid-size electric car would produce 23.1 tons of CO2 over its lifetime, compared with 24 tons for a similar petrol car. Emissions from electric car manufacture are at 50 per cent higher than conventional cars because batteries made from materials including lithium, copper and refined silicon require substantial energy for processing.

Electric cars also may also need a replacement battery after only a few years. Once the emissions from producing the second battery are added in, the total CO2 from producing an electric car rises to 12.6 tons, compared with 5.6 tons for a gasoline car. Energy consumed recovering and recycling metals during battery disposal can also double emissions.

Wind Power:

It was reported that 20 per cent of the European Union's trillion-euro budget may soon be spent on "fighting climate change", the direction America has also been heading. But British energy companies have raised problems with the Department of Energy and Climate Change DECC) and it's Government's obsession with wind power. Centrica and other energy companies told DECC that, if Britain is to spend £100 billion on building thousands of wind turbines, it will require the building of 17 new gas-fired power stations to provide sufficient back-up for times when the wind falls below threshold levels and windmills produce even less power than usual (or zero). These physics obviously apply in the United States and worldwide as well.

The Brits will be in the ludicrous position of spending an additional £10 billion on those 17 dedicated power stations, which will be kept running on "spinning reserve", 24 hours a day, just to compensate for the inherent fluctuations and mismatched output of wind turbines. That intrinsic problem is that wind power continually fluctuates anywhere between full capacity to zero, where it often stood during the exceptionally cold winter of 2010, when UK national electricity demand was at a peak. Lights will go out unless back-up power is available instantaneously to match any shortfall. We Americans aren't far behind in this march to madness.

As the energy companies pointed out to DECC, wind power is costly and wildly uneconomical, since the dedicated power plants will often have to run at a low rate of efficiency, burning gas but not producing electricity. This will add billions more to fuel bills for no practical purpose. Gas-fired power stations running on "spinning reserve" throw off much more CO2 than when they are running at full efficiency – thus negating any savings in CO2 emissions supposedly achieved by the windmills themselves.

Photo-Voltaics

The installed cost of a grid tied photovoltaic system of solar panels and inverter is in the range of $10,000 at the low end to run a decent sized home. A grid tie system takes advantage of the local power company to act as a 'battery' during off peak low daylight and night time hours rather than adding the expense of maintaining a battery array. Given current national electrical rates of around \$.12 per kilowatt hour, the payback time for such a system is around 10 years with a service life of around 20 to 25 years.

While this represents about half the price of a photovoltaic system from 2005, the payback time is still sufficiently long that solar electrical systems are not likely to make sense for most homeowners. That doesn't mean there is no reason to consider a solar electrical system, especially if prices were to drop again by half again. PV systems can in fact make a lot of sense for those who want to be completely firewalled from a potentially collapsing economic system, so we don't want to discourage readers from investigating the possibilities.

However, our main point is that solar panels are at best a wash economically versus hydrocarbon and nuclear powered energy and will continue to only marginally add to the energy independence of our nation as a whole.

Similar stories of increased costs and unintended negative consequences can be found for most of the alternative energy technologies now being touted as magic bullets. Engineers are taught to do not just benefit analyses on their projects (the only analysis which seems to be applied to Green technology), but also to consider the costs. That's why our energy system looks the way it does, not because engineers have conspired against solar.

56　Energy Starvation

Another area where our government is at war with us is through the Environmental Protection Agency, the Department of Energy and their strangulation of our energy sources. America is by necessity an energy intensive country – energy is by definition the ability to do work. We cannot compete globally based on labor rates; else we would all be working at $3 per day like some do in China. So to maintain our standard of living we must compete on the basis of mechanized production and computerized services (e.g. high tech Google is an energy hog), driven by cheap energy.

If a foreign nation destroyed major sectors of our energy production through a premeditated act of demolition, we would consider that an act of war. Progressives have spent decades not only shutting down nuclear power and nuclear waste disposal (Yucca Mountain), but now through CO_2 regulation are in the process of shutting down our coal fired electrical production. Moreover, they have shut down oil exploration in ANWR, derailed oil exploration along our coasts and delayed critical technologies like fracking. Our transportation system is also under assault with attempts to move toward 65 mpg efficiency standards, which would mandate the production of expensive crackerbox vehicles that are underpowered death traps.

Ironically, the energy we save through various Green schemes will do not one iota of good for the environment, since the energy we forgo will simply be consumed offshore in India, China, or other developing countries. In fact, the entire argument for global warming also stands on shaky legs. Why would progressives pursue such policies except in pursuit of political power? At least that is a logical explanation; the alternative is that they are suicidal nihilists.

Either way, your financial future and stability depends on understanding the future of the energy production and consumption in the United States. The following charts from the Energy Institute of America will give you an idea of what is on our energy horizon. Note that their predictions, taken to 2040, do not foresee a total collapse of oil usage, nor an alternative energy nirvana at the other extreme. The crystal ball shows something in between, an energy milieu in which we are saved from some of our mistakes by the windfall of natural gas production, but at risk especially from political intervention for boondoggle alternative energy schemes.

A substantial portion of your future expenses will be taken up by energy costs. In part, this is the predictable effect of the Federal Reserve enabling federal deficits with loose monetary policy. Free money is not free, and as we have shown the negative effects of profligate spending can appear in many shapes in a biflationary collapse. One major way Biflation is occurring is in the inflation of energy prices, even as wages and savings interest are deflated. Continued money printing makes oil the de facto world currency in parallel with gold as a standard of value.

The following charts from the Energy Institute of America shed some light on your energy future, starting with the current sources of energy production.

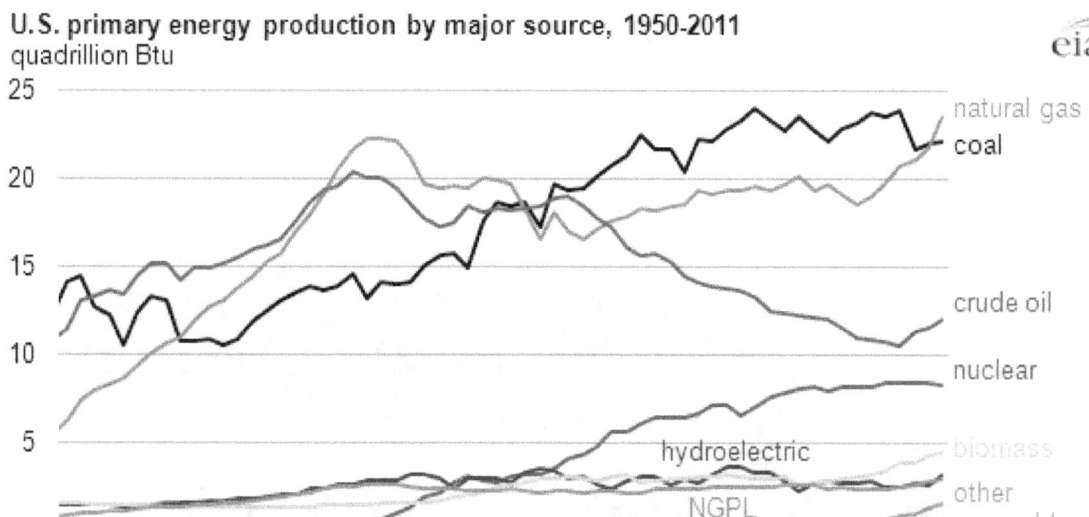

U.S. primary energy production by major source, 1950-2011
quadrillion Btu

The above chart is notable in that it shows the rise of natural gas as an energy source, eclipsing even coal. Most interesting is that renewables, other than biomass and hydroelectric, still contribute only a small fraction of our energy needs, despite massive investments and political intervention.

For an investor, the siren song of investing in non-hydro renewable beckons because they presumably have the most room to gain market share given renewable are the suckling favorite of politicians. The physics problem of course is that the low energy density of renewables, and their inability to provide continuous power without massive storage buffers, will limit their practical implementation. That doesn't mean their political implementation won't continue to proceed with legislative mandates, but the risk is investors will be left high and dry within a shifting political environment. Solyndra should be a warning sign to investors to steer clear of can't lose governmentally backed energy projects

More interesting are the projections for fuel usage through 2040 presented in the next charts. Notable is the rise of natural gas as the premier energy source, while coal and nuclear stagnate, liquid hydrocarbons drop and non-hydro renewable supposedly skyrocket. However, as seen unfolding in Spain, Germany, and England the hype for renewable is much greater than its real potential, where they have been forced to retrench on green energy initiatives. We expect there to be a substantial shortfall in the production of real non-hydro renewable as physics and relative economics play their hand. Natural gas and fracking technology have on the other hand produced measurable positive profits

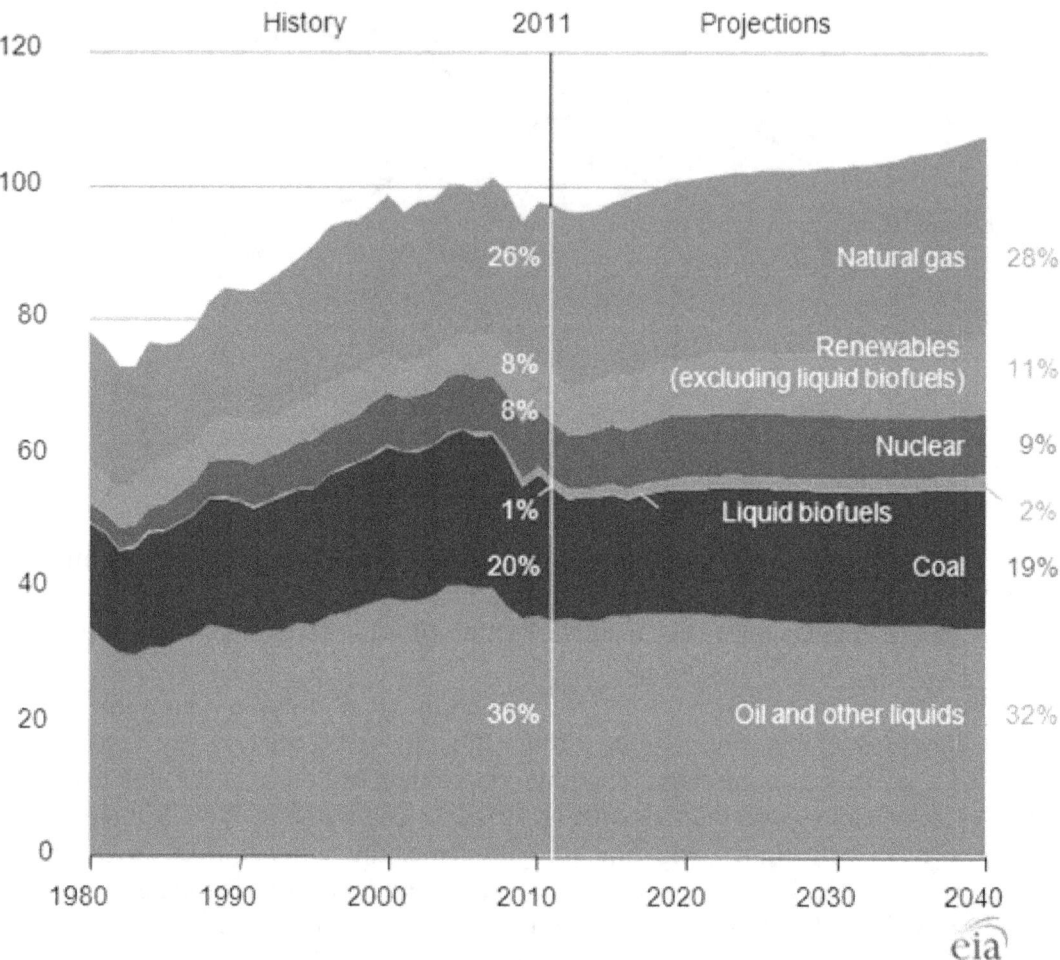

U.S. primary energy consumption by fuel, 1980-2040
quadrillion Btu per year

History   2011   Projections

- Natural gas — 26% / 28%
- Renewables (excluding liquid biofuels) — 8% / 11%
- Nuclear — 8% / 9%
- Liquid biofuels — 1% / 2%
- Coal — 20% / 19%
- Oil and other liquids — 36% / 32%

eia

    Since natural gas seems to be the low cost solution for the foreseeable future, conversion of everything from household appliances to vehicles to run on natural gas seems to be a good financial bet. The EIA predictions must of necessity carry a large political component in their crystal ball, so counting on the inexorable rise of renewable and demise of coal and nuclear seems premature.

    As the global energy situation deteriorates because of collapsing welfare states, people around the world will eventually realize that the energy spigots will need to be turned back on if they want to not only keep their jobs, but literally keep their lights on. Both Germany and Spain have begun to retrench from their dreams of a subsidized solar utopia as the costs have escalated. America will also eventually return to its senses when it realizes cutting off vast untapped coal reserves and limiting nuclear powerplants to fifty year old technology is no longer tenable.

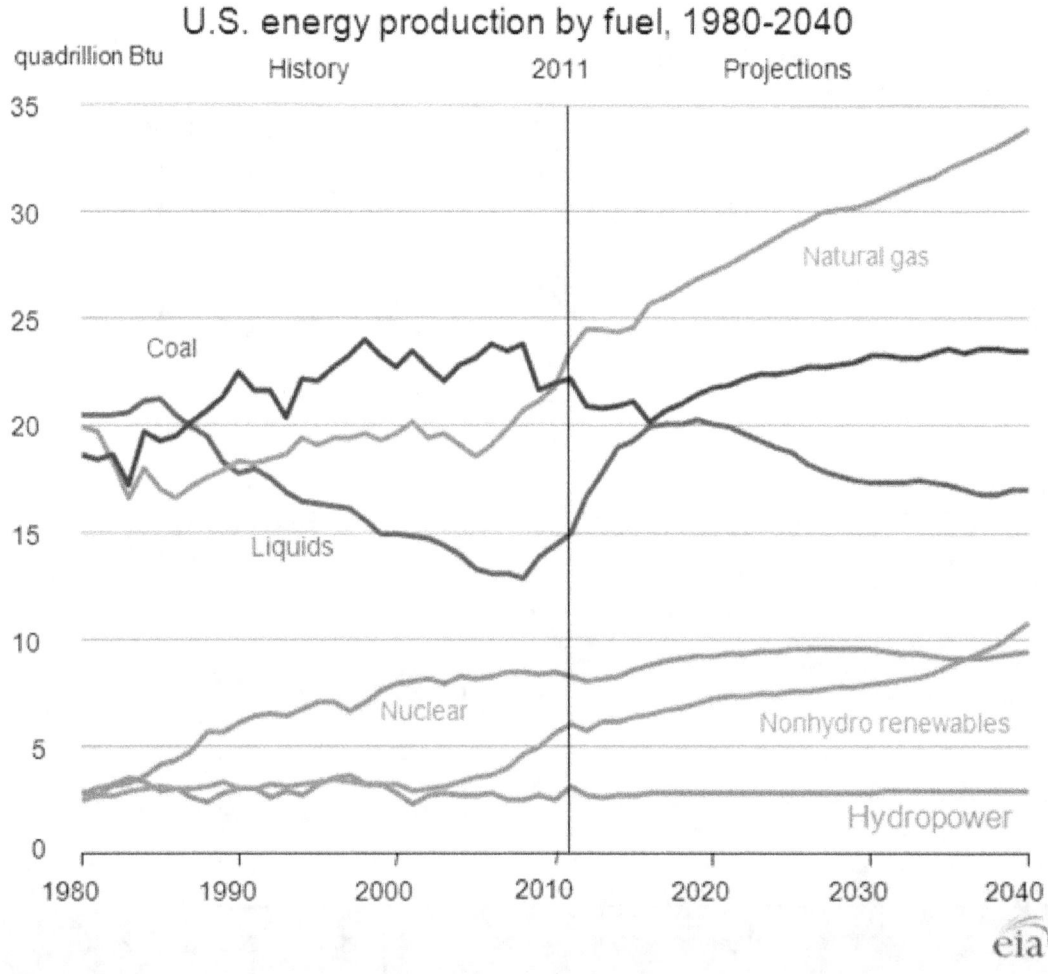

U.S. energy production by fuel, 1980-2040

quadrillion Btu   History   2011   Projections

Natural gas

Coal

Liquids

Nuclear   Nonhydro renewables

Hydropower

eia

The next chart shows the shortfall between exports and imports of liquid hydrocarbon fuels will remain relatively fixed well beyond 2040, despite claims that we are entering a new age of liquid fuel production. This indicates we will continue to be dependent on foreign oil sources for the foreseeable future, long centers of instability and wars. It is possible some of this shortfall will be countered by the ingenuity of American oil producers; however the regulatory hurdles imposed by the EPA are severe.

The failure of government mandates to create a utopian society transported by electric vehicles means your location options will be restricted by your ability to pay for fuel. Some of that cost may be offset my investing in oil companies as a hedge against energy inflation. Despite some progress, the gap between liquid fuel consumption and production will persist, as shown in the following graph.

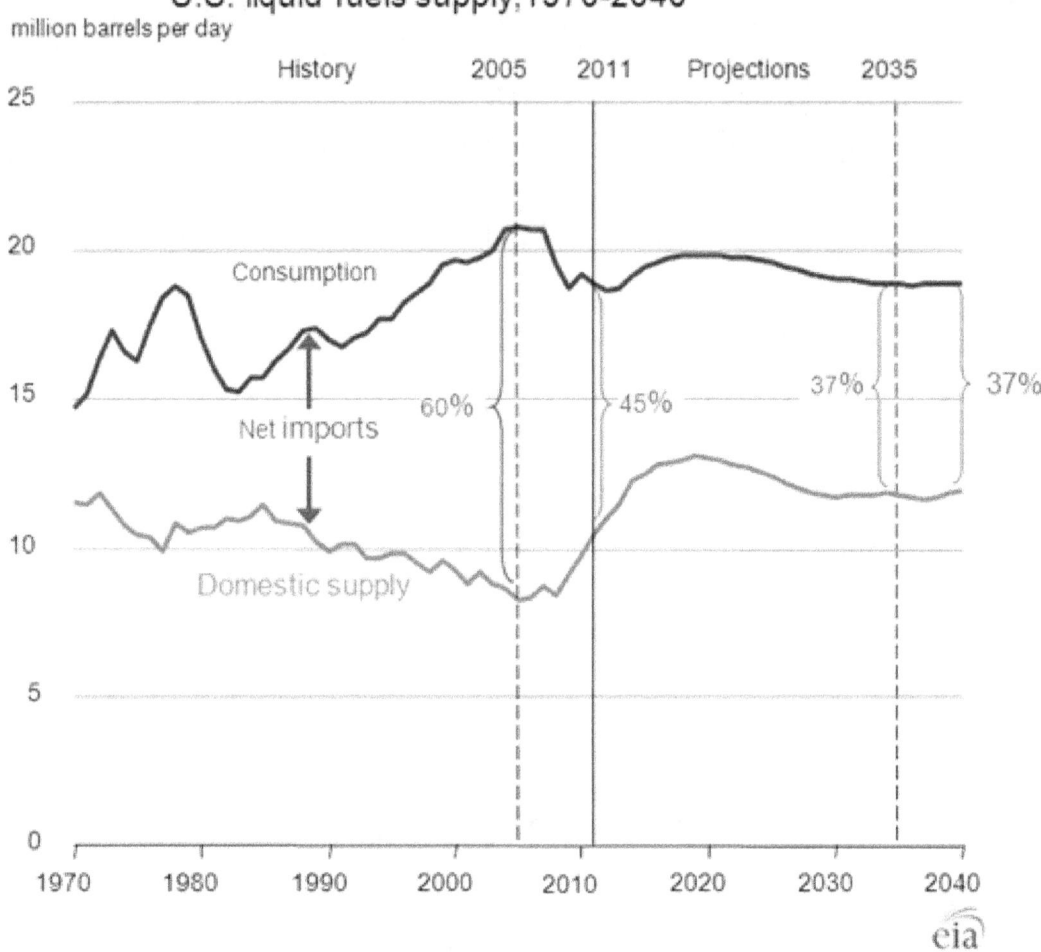

The supposed solution being forced down our throats by the political establishment is renewable energy. Costs for photovoltaics have come down in recent years, to the point where they are viable solutions in niche locations, but won't power the nation. The following chart shows the breakdown of where renewable energy is coming from.

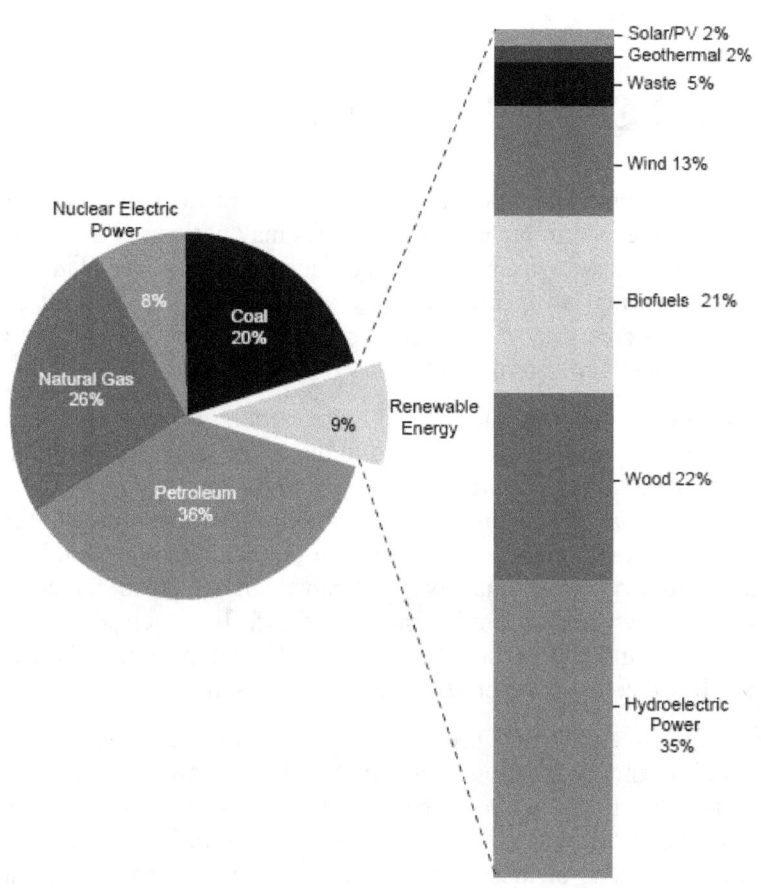

57   Nuclear Power

It is difficult to imagine air-conditioners and microwave ovens in our future unless nuclear energy plays some role in the energy mix. This may not sound like a viable choice until one compares the form of wastes from hydrocarbon and nuclear power plants. The Second Law of Thermodynamics says that all processes create waste, so no matter what energy generation system we choose it will create some form of waste problem. The only choice is which type of waste poses the least potential disposal problems.

The big difference between nuclear and hydrocarbon wastes is that nuclear residues are concentrated and eventually end up as solids while the waste from coal and petroleum powered plants is gaseous carbon dioxide, nitrous oxides, carbon monoxide, sulfur oxides, ash and multiple other chemicals that end up dispersed worldwide. True environmentalists might endorse nuclear power plants whose waste is compact and can be buried in one spot, like at the proposed Yucca Mountain repository, rather than being dumped on the wind for all to suffer. Future generations may well view the most environmentally destructive agents of our age as those who opposed nuclear energy and the construction of a geologic repository, thereby promoting the dispersal of carbon based combustion products into the atmosphere.

Unfortunately, Green activists seem to prefer global pollution to the thought of burying the waste from nuclear energy creation in a drift 800 feet below the surface in Nevada. They would rather risk the threat of massive global warming from fossil fuel combustion gases than admit the possibility that nuclear waste can be safely disposed of in a geological repository. This traces to the political agendas of these groups which trump their environmental concerns over radiation. Restructuring society is a higher priority than promoting technologies that actually solve environmental problems.

Particularly disturbing is the possibility that by opposing nuclear power, environmentalists are ensuring we all will be subject to more radiation than before. Coal fired plants are in themselves a source of radiation, releasing more radioactive elements into the air than nuclear plants. In the real world, the record of nuclear energy in preserving the environment stands on its own.

- Today, 438 nuclear power plants produce about one-sixth of the world's electricity. This is more than the electricity generated from all fuel sources as recently as 1958. As well as enhancing international energy security, nuclear power has reduced greenhouse gases and air pollution in the 26 countries that use the atom to generate electricity. Since the first oil embargo in 1973, nuclear power plants worldwide have:
- reduced carbon dioxide emissions by 30 billion tons
- cut sulfur dioxide emissions by 200 million tons
- eliminated 100 million tons of nitrogen oxides

Environmentalists seem driven by an apocalyptic vision in which nuclear technology eventually pollutes the world through dispersal of radioactive substances, possibly through nuclear war. However, an alternative scenario is that the anti-nuclear solar utopianism of the Greens becomes a nightmare because of its internal contradictions. Some elements of this nightmare are easy to envision:

1) For lack of American nuclear expertise (both in reactor construction and waste disposal), China fails to clean up its ever widening nuclear contamination.

2) Iran constructs a missile system for its burgeoning nuclear bombmaking abilities. Middle Eastern oil export is halted by Iran as it seeks retribution and power.

3) America loses 22% of its electrical energy producing capacity as aging reactors are retired. To compete in global markets, it is forced to import ever increasing amounts of petroleum products.

4) For lack of sophisticated U.S. nuclear reactor designs, the Third World turns to increasingly "dirty" reactors that are environmental time bombs.

5) Mixed oxide reactors which include plutonium in their reaction mix proliferate as America's involvement in world nuclear matters diminishes. Weapons proliferation is the end result.

The above factors ironically hint at war scenarios induced by green environmental pacifism, a counterintuitive Armageddon. The anti-nuclear movement portrays itself as both a pacifist and environmental movement, opposed to destruction of Mother Earth through pollution of any form. However, a war over hydrocarbon energy, fought with tactical nuclear warheads, would certainly be the most environmentally destructive event imaginable. Unless we were to coercively limit third World populations, or industrial nations return to subsistence societies, there is little hope of preventing frictional global competition for hydrocarbon fuels. Consequently, nuclear energy is a critical element in the effort to save the environment, and perhaps save a significant portion of the human race from energy wars.

58   Global Food Crisis

Most Americans are so accustomed to supermarkets that are packed to the gills with massive amounts of inexpensive food that they cannot imagine life could be any other way. However, financial survival means preparing for a time when there may be food shortages worldwide.

The world is being pushed towards a chronic global food crisis because our government policies create artificial scarcity. This affects not just beggars in Bangladesh, but you and your family. Food shortages will be an increasing source of friction as the government can't hide inflation when it shows up in the price of hamburger for every housewife to see.

The End Of Cheap Food

The entire global economy is predicated on the ability to use massive amounts of inexpensive oil to cheaply produce food and other goods and transport them over vast distances. Should oil again spike in price, the whole game changes. Add to this the massive subsidies to ethanol fuel production, which steal corn production from the food chain. Crazy weather and horrifying natural disasters always play havoc with global agricultural production introducing yet another layer of uncertainty. Topsoil and aquifer depletion is also occurring at an alarming pace. Added all up you have the potential for a food crisis.

Global food prices are already at all-time highs and will continue to move up because of the inflationary policies of global central banks. So what happens if hundreds of millions more people cannot afford to feed themselves? As competition for food supplies increases, food prices may go way up. Some key reasons why a food crisis can occur overnight:

1) According to the World Bank, 44 million people around the globe have been pushed into extreme poverty because of rising food prices.
2) The world is losing topsoil. One third of the world's cropland is losing topsoil faster than new soil is forming through natural processes.
3) Due to U.S. ethanol subsidies, almost a third of all corn grown in the United States is now used for fuel, putting substantial stress on the price of corn.
4) Lacking adequate water resources, some Middle Eastern countries almost totally rely on other nations for basic food staples. Water tables all over the globe are being depleted due to "overpumping". According to the World Bank, there are 130 million people in China and 175 million people in India that are being fed with grain grown with water that is being pumped out of aquifers faster than it can be replaced. In the United States, the systematic depletion of the Ogallala Aquifer could eventually turn "America's Breadbasket" back into the "Dust Bowl".
5) Diseases such as UG99 wheat rust are wiping out increasingly large segments of the world food supply.

6) The tsunami and subsequent nuclear crisis in Japan rendered vast agricultural areas in that nation unusable. The Japanese economy, the third largest economy in the world, will likely be stressed long term because of lowered food production.

7) The price of oil may be the biggest factor on this list. The way we produce and transport our food is very heavily dependent on oil. If oil prices skyrocket, our entire food production system becomes much more expensive. With rising oil prices come higher food prices.

8) At some point the world could experience a very serious fertilizer shortage. According to scientists with the Global Phosphorus Research Initiative, the world is not going to have enough phosphorous to meet agricultural demand in just 30 to 40 years.

9) Food inflation is already devastating many economies around the globe. India has been dealing with a food inflation rate of 18 percent.

10) According to the United Nations, the global price of food reached a new all-time high in 2011.

11) There are about 3 billion people around the globe that live on the equivalent of 2 dollars a day or less and the world was already on the verge of economic disaster before this year even began.

12) Revolutions have swept across the Middle East, in part driven by food scarcity. Europe is on in a financial meltdown and the U.S. dollar is dying. None of this is good news for global food production.

"Preppers" have been warning that a food crisis is possible for years. Food prices have already risen by substantial percentages, though our stores are still well supplied with food. But in Japan after the tsunami and nuclear meltdown in March of 2011, store shelves were cleared out almost instantly. If any catalyst could set off an economic tsunami, it would be the realization that consumers were no longer able to afford to feed themselves, or more ominously that they had been cut off from critical food supplies. Those who are forewarned will prepare accordingly.

Two strategies will come to mind:

1) Becoming self sufficient by growing your own food. This might mean taking up a more rural existence, or at least having a large suburban garden.
2) Stockpiling food and water.

Neither of these strategies is without drawbacks in a modern society devoted to just-on-time consumerism. However your financial survival is of little use if you cannot purchase a can of beans in a collapsing economic Black Swan event (see Venezuela). While you may not be able to devote full time energy to becoming food self sufficient, certainly stockpiling even small amounts and growing a few tomato plants won't disrupt your lifestyle.

Food self sufficiency and stockpiling are beyond the scope of this book devoted to financial survival. However, food security and financial security are inextricably linked. We have written two companion works, *Going Galt: Survival Gardening*, and *Going Galt: Surviving Economic Armageddon* that fully address food growing and stockpile prepping. More information of food survival strategies is available at: http://www.futurnamics.com

Survival Strategies

59   Financial Resistance

We don't advocate breaking laws, even nonsensical ones, given the potentially severe repercussions. However, let us suppose for the sake of argument that some people might resist the central forces of leviathan government out of self preservation given a collapsing economy, political paralysis, social upheaval and breadlines. What form would that resistance take? Protestors certainly wouldn't want to stick their head up too high because the technology the government can bring to bear against dissenters is now extraordinary, ranging from low tech harassment by IRS goons to high tech UAV surveillance leading to SWAT teams at your door.

Be aware that no matter how logical your political opposition might be, you will be outed and scapegoated by the mainstream media as part of a "dangerous right wing conspiracy", even if your objective is to be left alone and everything you do is of a defensive nature. For example, a CBS 60 Minutes episode took special pains to marginalize the Sovereign Citizen movement, and while fringe elements are open to criticism, the point of the reporting was to criminalize the entire movement. Elements of Sovereign Citizen philosophy do border on nutty, however this used to be a free country of limited government where such movements survived un-noticed and un-harassed.

Tax Revolt

We aren't advocating tax resistance or tax avoidance. The exact opposite, pay all your taxes. We don't advocate breaking any laws, whether those laws trash the Constitution or not. However, minimal (but legal) compliance, and opting out wherever possible is a legal option. Not paying taxes (illegal) is entirely different than not having taxable income, or having deductions that reduce your tax burden to zero (legal minimization).

Having a top notch tax accountant who reduces your payments is fighting the system legally. When someone consumes the produce of their garden, that is not taxable (not yet). When one works on one's car, or sews their own clothes, or improves their home, those are also (normally) not taxable events. Buying and holding gold and silver avoids the inflation tax and is not taxable until sold (expect attempts to confiscate precious metals as happened under Roosevelt). There are numerous ways citizens will find to choke the system of the revenue it so desperately requires to maintain the Ponzi scheme. The smart resistors will do so in legal ways.

Taking Advantage Of Entitlements

Some might take a contrarian path - resistance through acquiescence. Take for example onerous laws like Obamacare, which are doomed to failure by their centrally planned ravenous need for funds. Some patriots will realize that overburdening the system with real claims (for healthcare previously foregone) is likely to crush the system much faster than NOT taking advantage of the benefits and acting a martyr. The same applies for Medicare, Medicaid, Foodstamps and a host of other government services. How long will it be before independents and conservatives figure out that the system is about to crash, and the faster it does so the sooner we can begin to rebuild?

By nature, American conservatives have believed that the right thing to do was to act responsibly, shoulder one's own burdens and pay their own bills. However, when the banks unwisely spend themselves into oblivion, they are rescued with bailouts. When GM produces worthless cars (see the Volt), its unions get bailed out. If the entire system is rigged, it doesn't take long to decide to join the gravy train; otherwise you will be at a disadvantage. This includes small businesses as well as individuals, when presented with the option to accept outrageous grants and subsidies for boondoggle green jobs. Resistance may mean being first in line at the pig trough.

Legitimate Inability To Pay Taxes

A bigger question is at what point does it become impossible to pay your taxes? When does it become impossible to submit to Obamacare because it actually threatens your health or livelihood; impossible to follow EPA rules if your farm or factory will go bust? What if you can't afford to buy a $50,000 electric car, and pay mandatory healthcare and the BATFE wants to confiscate your guns, all while there are food riots in the streets? At that point, you are not the cause of upheaval; you are the victim of civil war. So while we don't condone resistance that falls outside the law, we all already know people who have been crushed in the government's maw and cannot afford to comply. At that point you have reached debt slavery and a slave revolt is not far behind.

And that's the point where your actions might look like resistance, but would really be a matter of survival. *Defensive response* versus *active resistance* will look to progressives and many in the state apparatus as exactly the same thing. The Ayn Rand option, Going Galt as it is termed, is when the productive class goes on strike. Your personal goal is not to become a martyr for any cause, but to realize there will come a time to rebuild after the inevitable financial collapse if you are smart enough to avoid being sucked into the whirlpool. Who knows, perhaps you will even get reparations.

60 Economic Civil War

The purpose of this book has been to expose the reader to harsh new realities of a New Normal economic world brought about by collapsing global welfare states enabled by the loose money policies of central banks, most notable the Federal Reserve. These constraints are so onerous that we would be remiss if we did not warn the reader that their finances are threatened by a civil war brought about by the debt slavery of citizens in failed states.

The idea that we might end up in an economic Civil War is sensed by thinking people, even if at a subliminal level – we all know the system is broken. Fortunately, the possibility of hundreds of thousands of casualties this time around seems remote because there are certain flywheels on the social and economic system opposing open warfare which would likely keep casualties minimal. However the long term economic, political and social challenges are just as profound today as during our first Civil War.

Ironically, a modern war would again be fought over slavery, but of a more hidden sort. This time it will be the enslavement of the productive classes of society by an entitlement class – in other words debt bondage. This class warfare already exists, the only questions remaining being on which side one is on.

The inevitability of a modern economic civil war is brought on by a number of common observations:

1) The governments of the United States and most of the Western World are bankrupt, meaning they will have to confiscate wealth, either through egregious taxation or inflation. This is a matter of self survival of the ruling class, to remain viable they must provide dispensations to their entitled bureaucrat and welfare drones (spending reduction seems improbable).

2) Racial demographics of the western nations are preordained to create severe political conflict as minority populations grow geometrically faster than the white populations. This is not a racial problem per se, if the minority populations acculturate to the political and social norms of their host countries. However, especially in the case of Hispanic and Muslim immigration, these populations remain cultural islands heavily dependent on entitlement income and with mixed national allegiance. The resident black community has also become monolithically left wing and thereby also consigns itself to being part of the entitlement problem as a victim class.

3) The unfunded future liabilities of western governments makes an Generation-War inevitable unless younger generations are willing to become the financial slaves of their elders in support of their retirements and age defying medical struggles to defeat mortality.

4) The environmental movement's war on energy production will cripple western civilization's ability to compete against cheap foreign labor. Technology is based on the substitution of energy dependent mechanical work for human labor and therefore a deficient solar strategy dooms 'advanced' nations to poverty.

5) Remnants of Marxist Socialism and other progressive philosophies like Rawlsianism, in both academia and the political sphere, are revolutionary philosophies whose root purpose is to create the conditions for an economic civil war.

6) The Federal Reserve and Banking system have become corrupt with the notion that they are 'too big to fail'. The financial system is a Ponzi scheme built on the printing of money by the Fed which will impoverish those with assets.

7) The Green evolution is in truth as much about enforcing a socialist control agenda as in environmental protection. Gaia worship makes this a religious civil war.

8) Enforced healthcare is an attempt to dispossess certain classes of their assets. However, the demand for healthcare is as infinite as the desire to avoid death and will therefore bankrupt any economic system that attempts to placate it.

In short, we are headed towards upheaval if not collapse. The federal debt will be $20 Trillion by 2016 and rising, which sum is dwarfed by what are considered the unfunded liabilities of local, state and Federal governments to the tune of $100 trillion plus. This leads to the conclusion that each citizen of the United States is on the hook for amounts above $500,000 of debt. Since only 63% of adults are currently working (the lowest participation rate since 1980), what this means is that there is no way to raise such funds unless one of the five following things happens:

1) The debt is monetized through extreme inflation
2) Wealth is confiscated by the Federal government.
3) Taxes are raised to stratospheric levels.
4) The debt is defaulted.
5) The Federal budget is severely slashed.

Inflation, wealth confiscation and punitive tax levels are all forms of debt bondage for the average worker. However, default on the debt would cause severe grief to the political and banker classes, as would slashing the Federal budget, so while these last two remedies are the ones called for to solve the problem at its root, they are perhaps the least likely to happen. Monetization of the debt, abusive taxation and outright confiscation of wealth are by far the most likely courses, however they are by definition acts of economic warfare against the populace. Consequently, the battle lines are drawn.

Political Parties Are Patronage Parties

The rise of the Tea Party movement (it is not really a party) is a direct response to the realization that the two major political parties are co-enablers of the decline into catastrophic socialism. However, as seen after the Tea Party electoral successes of 2010, even electing a substantial cohort of politicians who pledge fiscal sanity is little guarantee of restraint. Just how bad is our situation?

The U.S. is bankrupt. Spending more will certainly not help the country pay its bills (even given the bizarre theory that government spending leads to productivity), but paradoxically neither will taxing more help as additional funds will simply be swept into the vortex. What is necessary is to radically simplify our tax, health-care, retirement and financial systems while brutally slashing spending, but it is clear this isn't going to happen. The economy will not be revitalized, at least not soon and perhaps not for a generation.

The problem with taxes is they never go down. The problem with politicians is they never fade away. The problem with government is it always spends more and more. The problem with paper money is it always decreases in value. The problem with the USA is we have too much taxes, politicians, government, and dollar bills.

Something that can't go on, will stop. When you run a massive Ponzi scheme for six decades straight, taking ever larger resources from the young and giving them to the old while promising the young their eventual turn at passing the generational buck, bad things are bound to happen. Uncle Sam's Ponzi scheme will stop, but this time it will stop too late. and will end in one of three very nasty ways:

- Through massive benefit cuts visited on the baby boomers in retirement.
- Through astronomical tax increases that leave the young with little incentive to work and save.
- Through the government simply printing vast quantities of money to cover its bills.

We will likely see a combination of all three responses with quantum increases in poverty, tax, interest rates and consumer prices. Unfortunately, bond traders will eventually wake up and realize the U.S. is in the same fiscal shape as Greece or Japan. This is an awful, downhill road to follow, but it's the one we are on. At least you can craft a financial response if your eyes are open.

Political And Banking Class Has Too Much To Lose

The reason these egregious financial problems will not be adequately addressed in time to avert disaster is because the political and banking class stand to be decimated by the cure – a return to small government and a return to allowing large enterprises to fail. Keynesian economists favored by the ruling class and bankers continue to claim new rounds of stimulus won't affect our ability to deal with deficits in the long run. This is self serving for the political and banking classes which reap power and money from each new round of bailouts.

As the U.S. economy fitfully limps in and out of the Great Recession, naïve analysts assume that the Federal Reserve will join other central banks and end the era of unprecedented monetary expansion. Markets expected the Fed would withdraw liquidity by the end of 2010, then 2011 and on and on, after the latest rounds of quantitative easing come to an end. But this is a delusion.

For political and economic reasons the Fed will find it impossible to absorb the liquidity it has relentlessly pumped into the economy since the beginning of the financial crisis. Even worse, the ammunition it carries on its balance sheet is insufficient to the task. To withdraw liquidity the Fed must sell most of the assets on its balance sheet, leading to four critical questions:

- What types of assets will the Fed sell?
- How fast will they sell them?
- Who will buy?
- What price will the market bear?

Before the Great Recession began in 2008 the Fed had an equity ratio of 6% on a balance sheet that totaled approximately $900 billion. For the majority of Fed history, the assets it held were almost exclusively short term Treasury debt. The value of such a portfolio was considered virtually bulletproof, given the gargantuan size of the Treasury market and the bankability of its short term debt.

In contrast, after the bailouts, the Fed now holds more mortgage instruments than their entire balance sheet before the crash. The Fed lending facilities (TAF, TSLF, PDCF and the CPFF, etc.) bought all kinds of assets the Fed never held before in late 2008, even as financial institutions careened towards insolvency. Ben Bernanke added $1.8 trillion of longer term GSE debt and Mortgage Backed Securities (MBS) through quantitative easing efforts, drastically changing the complexion of the assets it must now sell.

If financial institutions were forced to pay par value for the Fed's mortgage assets, the Fed would destroy a great deal of their capital and a new breed of zombie banks would re-emerge. There is no political will in the United States to force the financial industry further into the public sector. If the assets are sold at the fair market price far below what the Fed paid, they will burn through their balance sheet before all of the prior Fed liquidity injections were neutralized.

Our government, abetted by the Federal Reserve, is at war with its productive citizens, confiscating their wealth through monetary manipulation, to support an army of the entitled. Politically, the two halves of the nation have diverged and polarized between essentially a socialist state and its dependents and a free market oriented Tea Party Nation.

Burgeoning Social State

At some point the US will be forced to confront the fact that it has borrowed way too much in the past few decades and must severely cut back spending, prompted either through a market crash or default on our debt. There is no IMF or European Union sugar daddy to bail us out. We point this out not to be a doomsayer, but to make clear how important it is for you to solidify your financial health

For ordinary Americans, forced austerity will mean crushing taxes, significantly reduced Medicare and Medicaid spending along with cuts to almost everything else in the federal budget, including the military and education. More immediate will be the impact to personal budgets. Stunning facts highlight the struggles average Americans already have getting a decent-paying job and keeping up with rising cost of living:

- There are 8.5 million people receiving unemployment insurance and 47 million receiving food stamps.
- At the current pace of job creation, the economy won't return to full employment until 2018 – if not later.
- Middle-income jobs are disappearing from the economy. The share of middle-income jobs in the United States has fallen from 52% in 1980 to 42% in 2010.
- Middle-income jobs have been replaced by low-income jobs, which now make up 41% of total employment.
- 17 million Americans with college degrees are doing jobs that require less than the skill levels associated with a bachelor's degree.
- Nominal wages have only been growing by 1.7% while all consumer prices, including food and energy, increased by 2.7%.

- Wages and salaries have fallen from 60% of personal income in 1980 to 51% in 2010. Government transfers have risen from 11.7% of personal income in 1980 to 18.4% in 2010, a post-war high.

The middle class is shrinking and this threatens the stability of the world's biggest economy. We've become a barbell society - money wealth and power at the top with increasing hollowness at the center. We are crumbling from within.

Given these dismal facts, amply shown by economic statistics if not admitted by elected officials and bureaucrats, you have no choice but to adapt. Hopefully rather than just being purveyors of doom, this book has provided you with both a sense of urgency to get your economic affairs in order, and at least some means of making that financial security come true.

In a nutshell, you must:

- Ruthlessly slash debt
- Forget about retirement
- Be prepared to create your own job
- Expand your skill set regularly
- Understand the rigged nature of stock and bond markets
- Understand the physical nature of money and the doomed trajectory of Keynesianism

Optimism is born of knowledge of the true nature of one's situation, allowing one to react rationally. We wish you all the best in your financial endeavors, buckle up for a wild ride.

www.ingramcontent.com/pod-product-compliance
Lightning Source LLC
Chambersburg PA
CBHW080236180526
45167CB00006B/2295